丛书主编 周江

海洋·极地·自然资源法研究丛书 国别海洋法系列

孟加拉国、斯里兰卡海洋法律体系研究

周江 著

知识产权出版社

全国百佳图书出版单位

—北京—

图书在版编目（CIP）数据

孟加拉国、斯里兰卡海洋法律体系研究/周江著. —北京：知识产权出版社，
2022.04

（海洋·极地·自然资源法研究丛书/周江主编. 国别海洋法系列）
ISBN 978 - 7 - 5130 - 7916 - 7

Ⅰ.①孟…　Ⅱ.①周…　Ⅲ.①海洋法—研究　Ⅳ.①D993.5

中国版本图书馆 CIP 数据核字（2021）第 243398 号

责任编辑：薛迎春　　　　　　　　　　　责任校对：王　岩
执行编辑：张琪惠　　　　　　　　　　　责任印制：刘译文
封面设计：黄慧君

孟加拉国、斯里兰卡海洋法律体系研究

周　江 ◎ 著

出版发行：知识产权出版社 有限责任公司　　网　　址：http://www.ipph.cn
社　　址：北京市海淀区气象路 50 号院　　　邮　　编：100081
责编电话：010 - 82000860 转 8724　　　　　责编邮箱：471451342@qq.com
发行电话：010 - 82000860 转 8101/8102　　 发行传真：010 - 82000893/82005070/82000270
印　　刷：三河市国英印务有限公司　　　　 经　　销：新华书店、各大网上书店及相关专业书店
开　　本：710mm×1000mm　1/16　　　　 印　　张：16.75
版　　次：2022 年 4 月第 1 版　　　　　　　印　　次：2022 年 4 月第 1 次印刷
字　　数：320 千字　　　　　　　　　　　 定　　价：88.00 元
ISBN 978 - 7 - 5130 - 7916 - 7

重庆市高校哲学社会科学协同创新团队
"海洋与自然资源法研究团队"阶段性成果

总　序

中国是陆海兼备的海洋大国，海洋开发历史悠久，曾创造了举世瞩目的海洋文明。"鱼盐之利，舟楫之便"是先人认识和利用海洋之精炼概括，仍不悖于当今海洋之时势。然数百年前，泰西诸国携坚船利炮由海而至，先祖眼中的天然屏障竟成列强鱼肉九州之通道。海洋强国兴衰，殷鉴不远。

吾辈身处百年未有之变局，加快建设海洋强国已成为中华民族伟大复兴的重要组成。扎实的海洋工业、尖端的海洋科技及强大的海军战力，无疑为海洋强国之必需。此外，完备的海洋治理体系和卓越的海洋治理能力等软实力亦不可或缺。海洋治理体系之完备，海洋治理能力之卓越，皆与海洋法治息息相关。经由法律的治理以造福生民，为古今中外人类实践之最佳路径。

海洋法治之达致，需赖全体国人之努力，应无沿海内陆之别。西南政法大学虽处内陆，一向以"心系天下"为精神导引。作为中国法学教育研究的重镇，西南政法大学独具光荣的历史传承、深厚的学术底蕴和完备的人才积累。她以党的基本理论、基本路线、基本方略和国家的重大战略需求为学术研究之出发点和归宿。

西南政法大学海洋与自然资源法研究所之成立，正是虑及吾辈应为建设海洋强国贡献绵薄。国际法学院、经济法学院（生态法学院）、国家安全学院相关研究团队，合众为一，同心勠力，与中国海洋法学会合作共建而成。我所将持续系统地研究涉海法律问题，现以"海洋·极地·自然资源法研究丛书"之名，推出首批公开出版成果。

本丛书拟设四大系列：国别海洋法系列、海洋治理系列、极地治理系列及自然资源法系列。系列之间既各有侧重又相互呼应，其共同的目标在于助力中国海洋治理体系与治理能力的现代化。

本丛书推崇创作之包容性，对当下及今后各作者的学术观点，都将予以最大程度的尊重；本丛书亦秉持研究之开放性，诚挚欢迎同人惠赐契合丛书主题及各系列议题的佳作；本丛书更倡导学术的批判性，愿广纳学友对同一问题的补正、商榷甚或质疑。若经由上述努力与坚持，可将本丛书打造为学界交流与争鸣的平台，则是我们莫大的荣幸。

本丛书能由构想变为现实，离不开诸多前辈、领导及同人的关心、指导与支持，我相信，丛书的付梓是对他们玉成此事最好的感谢！

是为序！

2020 年 3 月 31 日

目　录

第Ⅱ部分　斯里兰卡海洋法律体系研究

第 I 部分

孟加拉国海洋法律体系研究

一、孟加拉国海洋基本情况

孟加拉人民共和国（The People's Republic of Bangladesh，以下简称"孟加拉国"），是南亚地区的重要国家之一。历史上孟加拉地区曾数次建立独立国家，版图一度包括现印度西孟加拉邦、比哈尔邦等区划。16 世纪，孟加拉已发展成南亚次大陆上人口稠密、经济发达、文化繁荣的地区。18 世纪中叶，该地区成为英国对印度进行殖民统治的中心，并于 19 世纪后半叶成为英属印度的一个省。1947 年印巴分治之初，孟加拉国被分为东、西两部分，其东部归属巴基斯坦，西部归属印度。1971 年 3 月，东巴基斯坦宣布独立。1972 年 1 月，孟加拉人民共和国正式成立。[1]

（一）地理位置

孟加拉国位于南亚次大陆东北部的恒河与布拉马普特拉河冲积而成的三角洲上，跨越北回归线，为南亚与东南亚的衔接地带。其东、西、北三面与印度毗邻，两国共同边界线绵延 4053 公里；东南与缅甸接壤，共同拥有较短的陆地边界与 193 公里的水上边界；南临孟加拉湾，有 580 公里极不规则的向内凹进呈三角状的海岸线。[2] 孟加拉国领土面积为 147570 平方公里，大部分地区属亚热带季风气候，湿热多雨。[3] 在季风季节，不但其发达的国内水系（全国约有 700 条河流）常常洪水泛滥，海水涨潮所引起的热带旋风、飓风、潮水激浪等自然灾害也几乎每年都对孟加拉国的港口、农田、道路交通及其他设施造成严重破坏。[4]

（二）政治概况

孟加拉国党派众多，20 世纪 90 年代以来，主要由孟加拉国民族主义党

---

〔1〕《对外投资合作国别（地区）指南——孟加拉国（2021 年版）》，载中华人民共和国商务部网站，http：//www.mofcom.gov.cn/dl/gbdqzn/upload/mengjiala.pdf，最后访问日期：2021 年3 月 20 日。

〔2〕"Know Bangladesh"，Ministry of Foreign Affairs，https：//mofa.gov.bd/site/page/6dde350b-1ca6-4c69-becd-a3f12cf14ac1/Bangladesh--An-Introduction，February 27，2020.

〔3〕《孟加拉国概况》，载中华人民共和国外交部网站，https：//www.fmprc.gov.cn/web/gjhdq_676201/gj_676203/yz_676205/1206_676764/1206x0_676766/，最后访问日期：2020 年 2月 27 日。

〔4〕张汝德主编：《当代孟加拉国》，四川人民出版社 1999 年版，第 7—10 页。

（Bangladesh Nationalist Party）和人民联盟（Awami League）轮流执政。2018
年12月30日，孟加拉国举行第11届议会选举，哈西娜（Hasina）领导的人
民联盟以压倒性优势赢得大选。2019年1月7日，哈西娜连续第三次就任总
理。孟加拉国实行一院议会制，即国民议会。现任议长为希琳·沙尔敏·乔
杜里（Shirin Sharmin Chowdhury），2014年1月29日就任，2019年连任。[1]

行政区划上，孟加拉国全国划分为达卡（Dhaka）、吉大港（Chit-
tagong）、库尔纳（Khulna）、拉杰沙希（Rajshahi）、巴里萨尔（Barisal）、锡
莱特（Sylhet）和朗故尔（Rangpur）7个行政区，下设64个县，472个分
县，4490个乡，约6万个村。其城市人口占比已经逐渐升至37.4%。

宗教信仰方面，孟加拉国约1.6亿人口中有86.6%为穆斯林，另有
12.1%为印度教信徒。同时，尽管以孟加拉语为其国语，但英语仍在该国被
广泛使用，为该国官方语言。[2]

（三）经济概况

孟加拉国是世界最不发达国家之一，经济发展水平较低，国民经济主要
依靠农业。孟加拉国近两届政府均主张实行市场经济，推行私有化政策，改
善投资环境，大力吸引外国投资，积极创建出口加工区，优先发展农业。人
民联盟政府上台以来，制定了庞大的经济发展计划，包括建设"数字孟加
拉"、提高发电容量、实现粮食自给等，但面临资金、技术、能源短缺等挑
战。总体而言，孟加拉国的国内经济建设在近十年来有了长足的发展，其国
内生产总值从2011年的1286.38亿美元上升至2019年的3025.71亿
美元。[3]

孟加拉国与130多个国家和地区有贸易关系。2017—2018财年，孟加拉
国的出口额为362亿美元，进口额为544.6亿美元，主要出口市场有美国、
德国、英国、法国、荷兰、意大利、比利时、西班牙、加拿大和中国香港；
主要出口产品包括：黄麻及其制品、皮革、茶叶、水产、服装等。同时，其
主要进口市场有印度、中国、新加坡、日本、中国香港、韩国、美国、英
国、澳大利亚和泰国；主要进口商品为生产资料、纺织品、石油及石油相关

---

〔1〕《孟加拉国概况》，载中华人民共和国外交部网站，https：//www. fmprc. gov. cn/web/gjhdq_
676201/gj_ 676203/yz_ 676205/1206_ 676764/1206x0_ 676766/，最后访问日期：2020年2
月27日。

〔2〕 Bangladesh, "Know Bangladesh", https：//mofa. gov. bd/site/page/6dde350b-1ca6-4c69-becd-a3
f12cf14ac1/Bangladesh--An-Introduction, February 27, 2020.

〔3〕 The World Bank, "Bangladesh", https：//data. worldbank. org/country/bangladesh, February 27, 2020.

产品、钢铁等基础金属、食用油、棉花等。[1]

（四）外交关系

1. 外交概况

根据《孟加拉国宪法》第 25 条，孟加拉国的外交关系应基于尊重国家主权和平等原则、不干涉他国内政原则、和平解决国际争端原则，并遵守国际法和《联合国宪章》基本原则。[2]

孟加拉国奉行独立自主和不结盟政策，在平衡发展同大国关系的同时，注重维护与伊斯兰国家的传统关系，努力改善与印度的关系，并致力于加强同西方国家的友好往来。孟加拉国积极参加联合国、不结盟运动、伊斯兰会议组织、英联邦等国际或地区性组织的活动，主张全面、彻底裁军，反对西方国家利用人权问题干涉他国内政。同时，孟加拉国注重经济外交，强调建立公正的国际经济新秩序，致力于推动南亚区域合作进程，积极参与次区域和跨区域经济合作。

2. 与印度的关系

孟加拉国重视改善和发展与印度的关系。2010 年 1 月，孟加拉国总理哈西娜访问印度，孟印在基础设施建设、贸易、电力等领域达成具体成果，印度允诺向孟加拉国提供 10 亿美元贷款，孟加拉国允许印度使用吉大港和蒙格拉港。2011 年 9 月，印度总理辛格访问孟加拉国，两国在贸易、教育、交通等领域签署多项合作文件，但在孟方关心的跨境河流分水和印方关心的跨境交通等方面未能取得进展。自 2014 年 6 月印度莫迪政府执政以来，印度愈加重视同孟加拉国的关系。2015 年 6 月，印度总理莫迪访问孟加拉国，双方签署 22 项合作文件，涉及经贸、交通、科技、安全和人文等众多领域。2017 年 4 月，孟加拉国总理哈西娜访问印度，双方签署了关于防务合作、贸易投资、能源电子等 34 项合作文本。2018 年 5 月，孟加拉国总理哈西娜访问印度西孟加拉邦，并同莫迪总理会面。2019 年 5 月 30 日，孟加拉国总统哈米德出席印度总理莫迪的宣誓就职仪式。2019 年 10 月，孟加拉国总理哈西娜访问印度，并同印度总理莫迪签署 7 项双边合作文件。

---

[1] 《孟加拉国概况》，载中华人民共和国外交部网站，https：//www. fmprc. gov. cn/web/gjhdq_676201/gj_676203/yz_676205/1206_676764/1206x0_676766/，最后访问日期：2020 年 2 月 27 日。

[2] Bangladesh Ministry of Foreign Affairs, "Know Bangladesh", https：//mofa. gov. bd/site/page/0498 e3d1-9bb7-45f0-988c-cb360e9949e2, February 27, 2020.

3. 与中国的关系

孟中两国于 1975 年 10 月 4 日建交，此后关系发展迅速，双方领导人互访频繁。1989 年，孟中友好协会团结中心（Bangladesh China Friendship Association Unity Center）成立，并于 1995 年更名为孟中友好中心（Bangladesh China Friendship Center），致力于促进孟中两国人民间的友谊和理解。[1] 2010 年，孟中建交 35 周年之际，孟加拉国总理哈西娜访问中国，宣布建立和发展孟中更加紧密的全面合作伙伴关系。2016 年 10 月，习近平主席对孟加拉国进行国事访问，宣布将中孟关系提升为战略合作伙伴关系。2019 年 7 月，孟加拉国总理哈西娜正式访华并出席第 13 届夏季达沃斯论坛。[2]

（五）海洋资源利用情况

在海洋生物资源方面，在孟加拉国专属经济区已发现大约 475 种鱼类，一直为孟加拉国人民获取蛋白质类食物的主要来源。孟加拉国全国约有 7 万艘手工机械化和非机械化的木船（artisanal mechanized and non-mechanized wooden boats）和约 250 艘工业钢制拖网渔船（industrial steel body trawlers）在距其海岸线 60 公里（40 米深）以内的沿海水域捕鱼。云鲥（hilsa shad）是孟加拉国海洋渔获中最大且最具价值的鱼类，占全球云鲥捕获总量的 50% —60%，年捕捞量超过 496417 吨，为 250 万人创造就业和收入，年产值达 13 亿美元。此外，虾、巨泥蟹（giant mud crab）和河口鳗鱼（estuarine eel）等也是重要的捕捞和出口对象。然而，孟加拉国的深海捕鱼能力十分落后。2017 年，其他国家在孟加拉湾深海区域的鱼类捕捞量达 800 万吨，而孟加拉国仅捕捞了 9.3 万吨。在引进先进科技、增强长线捕鱼能力和提高在海岸线 60 公里以外海域捕鱼能力等方面，孟加拉国还有巨大的提升空间。近年来，为保护海洋生物多样性，孟加拉国建立了若干海洋保护区，在海洋保护区内全面禁止使用破坏性捕鱼方法和渔具（如拖网等）。

在非生物资源方面，孟加拉国尚未完全探明其海上石油和天然气的储量。到目前为止，孟加拉国已经发现了大约 7362 亿立方米的天然气储量，其中只有大约 283 亿立方米位于近海区域。截至 2014 年，孟加拉湾共钻探了 19 口探井，仅发现两处有储量较少的天然气。除了海洋油气资源，孟加拉国

---

[1] Bangladesh China Friendship Center, "About BCFC", https：//bangladeshchina. org/about/, March 15, 2020.

[2] 《孟加拉国概况》，载中华人民共和国外交部网站，https：//www. fmprc. gov. cn/web/gjhdq_ 676201/gj_ 676203/yz_ 676205/1206_ 676764/1206x0_ 676766/，最后访问日期：2020 年 2 月 27 日。

的考克斯巴扎（Cox's Bazar）海岸是传统的海盐生产地区，大多数盐场规模较小，通过手工操作设备进行生产。在较长的旱季，盐农可获得约每公顷 20 吨的海盐产量。[1]

在海洋运输和港口建设方面，孟加拉国全国有超过 300 家造船厂，几乎所有的内河船舶、快速巡逻艇、疏浚驳船和水道测量船等船舶都由这些造船厂生产制造。目前，部分造船厂正在建造 10000 吨级的远洋船舶用于出口，并计划建造 25000 吨级的船舶。此外，船舶回收产业（ship recycling industries）是孟加拉国的重要产业之一，它提供大约 70%—75% 的废钢作为轧钢厂的原材料，为孟加拉国节省了大量外汇。该行业不仅满足了孟加拉国家具、各类家用配件、锅炉、救生船、发电机等制造业对钢材日益增长的需求，也提供了大量就业机会。孟加拉国现有约 125 个船舶拆解场（ship breaking yards），年营业额约 24 亿美元。当前，孟加拉国正致力于将船舶回收产业转变为符合生态友好标准的现代产业。

孟加拉国的经济严重依赖国际贸易，而其对外贸易的 94% 都通过海运完成。孟加拉国现有港口主要为吉大港和勐拉港（Mongla），并计划在马塔巴里（Matarbari）和培拉（Payra）建造吞吐量更大和装卸设备更为现代化的深海港口，以满足日益增长的贸易和商业需求。[2]

---

〔1〕　Bangladesh Ministry of Foreign Affairs, "Blue Economy – Development of Sea Resources for Bangladesh", https：//mofa. gov. bd/site/page/8c5b2a3f-9873-4f27-8761-2737db83c2ec/OCEAN/BLUE-ECONOMY--FOR-BANGLADESH, March 15, 2020.

〔2〕　Bangladesh Ministry of Foreign Affairs, "Blue Economy – Development of Sea Resources for Bangladesh", https：//mofa. gov. bd/site/page/8c5b2a3f-9873-4f27-8761-2737db83c2ec/OCEAN/BLUE-ECONOMY--FOR-BANGLADESH, March 15, 2020.

二、海洋事务主管部门及其职能

（一）基本政治结构

1. 立法机关

国民议会（The House of the Nation，孟加拉语称 *Jatiya Sangsad*）是孟加拉国的最高立法机关。国民议会实行"一院制"，原有 300 个席位，每五年由公民普选产生；后据 2011 年宪法修正案，专为女性增添 50 个席位，并分配至各政党以保证国民议会中的女性比例。[1]

国民议会设议长和副议长各 1 人，由议员选举产生。议长担任议会会议主席，领导议会工作，主持议会活动，在总统辞职、患病或外出时履行国家元首职责。

国民议会的立法程序分提案、评议和表决三个阶段。各部长和议员都可以做出提案，前者所做提案称政府案，后者所做提案称私人案。提案须经秘书向议会提交，如提案属宪法框架，还须事先征求总统的意见。如有其他议员反对提案，议长可视情况在正反双方陈述意见后由议会表决；如提案获得多数支持，则提案通过了第一阶段即"一读"。评议阶段往往较为漫长，提案可直接由议会全体评议，但实践中经常提交或常务委员会（Standing Committee）或特别委员会（Select Committee）评议，甚至先将提案在整个议会传阅，征求每个人的意见。议会对提案进行评议的初级阶段限于对其是否合乎法理及一般性条款的评议，随后进行逐条评议修改，最后投票通过即"二读"。立法的第三个阶段非常简短，议长经常不允许任何辩论即直接提交议会表决通过即"三读"。经"三读"通过的提案将由总统签批，签批后该法律正式生效。[2]

---

〔1〕 See Article 65, The Constitution of the People's Republic of Bangladesh, Laws of Bangladesh, http：//bdlaws. minlaw. gov. bd/act-367. html？hl = 1, April 12, 2020.

〔2〕 See Article 80, The Constitution of the People's Republic of Bangladesh, Laws of Bangladesh, http：//bdlaws. minlaw. gov. bd/act-367. html？hl = 1, April 12, 2020；Bangladesh Parliament, "Functions and Procedures of Parliament", https：//www. parliament. gov. bd/index. php/en/about-parliament/functions-and-procedures-of-parliament, April 12, 2020.

2. 行政机关

总统是孟加拉国的国家元首，每五年由立法机关选举一次[1]。同为深受英国西敏制传统影响的国家，一方面，孟加拉国的总统被赋予部分议会及立法权限[2]，在一定程度上与巴基斯坦实践相近；另一方面，孟加拉国的总统权力在很多方面都受到限制，又与印度总统情形同出一源。在通常情况下，总统为象征性职位，可任命总理及首席大法官，由其任命的总理领导政府并行使实质性权力[3]。

总理必须为议会成员，并获得议会成员的多数信任。由总理选出并由总统任命的各部部长组成内阁，其中 90% 应为议会成员，余下 10% 可为非议员专家（technocrats）。内阁是整个政府的集体决策机构，作为整体共同向议会负责[4]。

3. 司法机关

孟加拉国的司法体系由最高法院与一系列下级法院及法庭组成。其最高法院由上诉庭（Appellate Division）与高等法庭（High Court Division）组成，有权对宪法及其他国内法做出解释。其中，上诉庭有权审理高等法庭的相关判决及决定，并有权就其最高法院各分支及所有下级法院的审判实践包括审判程序制定相关规则。应总统要求，上诉庭还可就涉及公共利益的重大问题提供法律意见。而高等法庭既可以受理基于下级法庭及法庭判决的上诉请求，也可以对涉及公民基本权利行使的案件等进行初审管辖[5]。

在最高法院之下，孟加拉国还依据不同制定性文件设有民事系列法院、刑事系列法院及行政系列法院。其中，民事系列法院主要分为地区法官法院（Court of the District Judge）、附设地区法官法院（Court of the Additional District Judge）、联合地区法官法院（Court of the Joint District Judge）、高级助理法官法院（Court of the Senior Assistant Judge）、助理法官法院（Court of the

---

[1] See Article 48, The Constitution of the People's Republic of Bangladesh, Laws of Bangladesh, http://bdlaws. minlaw. gov. bd/act-367. html? hl = 1, April 12, 2020.

[2] 如非经总统同意，议会不得通过任何立法提案；或未经总统推荐，任何财政法案不得提交至议会等。See Bangladesh Parliament, "President and Parliament", http://www. parliament. gov. bd/index. php/en/about-parliament/president-and-parliament? csrt = 8936407970052653764, April 12, 2020.

[3] Md. Ershadul Karim, "UPDATE: The Legal System of the People's Republic of Bangladesh", https://www. nyulawglobal. org/globalex/Bangladesh1. html, April 12, 2020.

[4] See Article 55, The Constitution of the People's Republic of Bangladesh, Laws of Bangladesh, http://bdlaws. minlaw. gov. bd/act-367. html? hl = 1, April 12, 2020.

[5] See Article 44, 102, 103, 106, 110, The Constitution of the People's Republic of Bangladesh, Laws of Bangladesh, http://bdlaws. minlaw. gov. bd/act-367. html? hl = 1, April 12, 2020.

Assistant Judge）；而刑事系列法院则包括地区刑事法院（Courts of Sessions）与各类治安官法院（Courts of Magistrates）。除此之外，孟加拉国还设有大量特殊法院法庭，如环境法院（Environment Courts）、腐蚀酸犯罪刑庭（Acid Crime Tribunals）、劳动法院（Labour Courts）、妇女儿童法庭（Nari-O-Shishu-Nirjatan Daman Tribunals）、村级法院（Village Courts）等[1]。

（二）海洋管理的相关行政机构

1. 渔业和畜牧业部

孟加拉国的专属经济区面积约 9 万平方公里，拥有丰富的海洋资源。立足于此，渔业部门在外汇、创收和就业方面对国民经济做出了重大贡献。孟加拉国渔业和畜牧业部（Ministry of Fisheries and Livestock）成立于 1972 年，以增加渔业资源及生产、提高禽畜生产及生产力、增加鱼类及禽畜产品出口、维持生态平衡、保护生物多样性并促进公共健康、预防和控制相关疾病、提供就业以消除贫困为其宗旨和目标。渔业和畜牧业部下设畜牧业服务局、渔业局、孟加拉国畜牧业研究所、孟加拉国渔业研究所、孟加拉国渔业发展公司、渔业和畜牧业信息办公室、海洋渔业学院、孟加拉国兽医委员会等各机构。[2]

隶属于该部的渔业局早在东巴基斯坦时期即已成立。随着 1971 年孟加拉国独立，原属巴基斯坦中央渔业部的相关机构于 1975 年 4 月与孟加拉国渔业局合并。1984 年，中央海洋渔业部也并入渔业局，成为其海洋渔业的管理分支。渔业局现有 1 名局长、4 名副局长以及 2 名首席科学官，同时有 1500 余名不同级别的技术人员及后勤人员为渔业局的运行提供服务。除按各司、各地区的机构划分外，渔业局还设有海洋渔业站、渔业培训学院、渔业培训与推广中心以及鱼类孵化场。

渔业局的职能主要在于：第一，通过培训和示范推广改进的水产养殖技术，并向重点利益攸关方提供推广咨询服务；第二，通过制定养护和管理措施来壮大渔业资源；第三，协助行政部门制定相关政策、法规等；第四，实施可出口鱼类及鱼类产品的质量控制措施并签发健康证明；第五，进行渔业资源调查和种群评估，从而发展渔业数据库以进行合理规划；第六，为鱼虾养殖户、渔民、鱼类贸易商人及企业家提供机构信贷安排；第七，组织农村

---

〔1〕 See Md. Ershadul Karim, "UPDATE: The Legal System of the Peoples' Republic of Bangladesh", https://www.nyulawglobal.org/globalex/Bangladesh1.html, April 12, 2020; Banglapedia, "Judicial System", http://en.banglapedia.org/index.php? title = Judicial_System, April 12, 2020.

〔2〕 Bangladesh Minstry of Fisheries and Livestock, "About", https://mofl.gov.bd/, March 14, 2020.

贫困和失业人口的其他创收活动以减轻贫困；第八，制定和实施可持续利用渔业资源的发展项目，以确保粮食安全；第九，通过电子推广服务传播经改良的水产养殖技术。

与渔业局的工作紧密相连的姊妹机构还包括：孟加拉国渔业研究所（BFRI）、孟加拉国渔业发展公司（BFDC）、海洋渔业学院（BMFA）、渔业和畜牧业信息局（FLID）。其中，孟加拉国渔业研究所成立于1984年，是渔业和畜牧业部下设的自治性组织。该研究所在迈门辛（Mymensingh）、坚德布尔（Chandpur）等城市设有六大观测站点，就淡水水产、内陆渔业管理、湖泊管理、鱼类疾病、海洋渔业、半咸水养殖、鱼类遗传育种等进行基础及应用性研究，部分研究成果已经应用于渔业局的相关监管领域。而孟加拉国渔业发展公司早在1964年即已成立。作为渔业和畜牧业部下的又一自治性组织，该公司主要从事渔业资源的捕捞与国内市场设施的开发。通过建立渔港、卸货和配送中心、制冰厂、加工工厂等，该公司曾是孟加拉国国内市场鱼类供应品质安全的重要保障。海洋渔业学院则是在苏联协助下于1973年设立的人才培养机构，旨在通过研究海洋渔业的专业知识，保证对海洋渔产的适当和最佳管理。该学院的使命是通过现代化的技术和设备来训练学员，以迎接航运行业的千禧年挑战。在学院完成三年的学习和培训后，适格的学员将被授予国立大学学士学位。渔业和畜牧业信息局由渔业和畜牧业部于1986年建立，共有设于达卡、拉杰沙希、巴里萨尔与库米拉（Comilla）的四个分支。该信息局通过每月出版的简报、印制的宣传册或宣传页，不断传递有关渔业和畜牧业发展活动的最新信息、技术和资料。[1]

2. 航运部

孟加拉国水系发达、河道纵横，也由此决定了水路运输在其社会经济发展中的不可替代的作用。孟加拉国航运部（Ministry of Shipping）同时监管航运及港口行业，职责范围覆盖国家航道、内河运输、港口、远洋运输等部门，监督相关安全和环境事务，同时负责海运及海事相关教育的管理和规范。航运部的主要工作目标在于：第一，实现海港、河港与内陆港口的现代化；第二，保护可航行水道；第三，实现安全、经济的客货运输；第四，建立高效的海事工作队伍，从而为国际贸易提供便利。围绕上述目标，航运部将制定有关政策和规划，推动各项工程的尽快实施，同时维持和扩大可行、有效和可靠的水上交通和通信系统，推动航运成为城乡经济活动最经济的交

---

〔1〕　Bangladesh Minstry of Fisheries and Livestock, "About Department of Fisheries", http：//fisheries. gov. bd/site/page/43ce3767-3981-4248-99bd-d321b6e3a7e5/-, March 14, 2020.

通方式。[1]

航运部共下设十二大分支机构，与海洋运输相关的部门主要包括：航运局（Department of Shipping）、孟加拉国航运公司（Bangladesh Shipping Corporation）、孟加拉国海事学院（Bangladesh Marine Academy）、国家海事研究院（National Maritime Institution）、海员福利与移民局（Directorate of Seamen & Emigration Welfare）。[2]

（1）航运局

孟加拉国独立后，为进一步精简部门以贴合国际标准，并实现国家监管下安全可靠的航运，在原交通部下的港口、航运和外贸司内成立了"航运管理局"（Directorate of Shipping）。1976年，通过合并原"航运理事会"和"航运管理主任"（Controller of Shipping）的机构及职能，航运局正式成立。为实现将孟加拉国转变为具有全球竞争力的海洋国家的建设愿景，航运局力图通过对海事事务的有效管理、协调和监督，实现可持续的、安全和有保障的海上航运，同时保障海洋环境的清洁，并不断使国家海上能力得以加强。[3]

当前，作为孟加拉国航运部下设的重要组织机构之一，航运局根据《1983年孟加拉国商船运输条例》和《1976年内陆航运条例》，承担孟加拉国海事安全管理局和海事事务国际协调中心的双重职责：一方面，负责制定和实施相关国家政策和法律，以确保海上人命和船舶的安全，发展船舶工业，促进海事教育、相关认证及就业，保障海员福利及其他运输相关事项；另一方面，确保海洋事务相关国际公约在孟加拉国被遵守。除将总部设在达卡外，航运局在各地的分支机构均覆盖海上商船运输与内河运输两大领域。其涉及海上商船运输的分支机构主要包括：吉大港商船局、库尔纳商船办公室、吉大港政府航运办公室、吉大港海员福利局等。[4]

其中，吉大港商船局是航运局下设的对远洋及沿海船舶进行管理的主要

---

[1] See Bangladesh Mistry of Shipping, "Background", https：//mos. gov. bd/site/page/3c024802-0f-bf-4479-a977-b169d3d3cb9a/Background, March 14, 2020; Bangladesh Mistry of Shipping, "Vision and Mission", https：//mos. gov. bd/site/page/e554cf3c-a3a7-45a0-9818-028ed42c9eb1/Vision-and-Mission-, March 14, 2020.

[2] Bangladesh Mistry of Shipping, "About", http：//mos. gov. bd, March 15, 2020.

[3] See Bangladesh Department of Shipping, "Our History", http：//dos. gov. bd/site/page/8a8ee650-2011-4d1e-b3ef-ff46e0bd0bbd/-, March 15, 2020; Bangladesh Department of Shipping, "Mission & Vision", http：//dos. gov. bd/site/page/04f4a428-6596-4eac-a5c0-88f66e85b1a1/-, March 15, 2020.

[4] Bangladesh Department of Shipping, "About Us", http：//dos. gov. bd/site/page/e847ba4b-8b44-4fa1-8d6f-4d5a8292f5e2/-, March 15, 2020.

责任机关。其主要职能有：（1）执行《1983 年孟加拉国商船运输条例》；（2）负责远洋和沿海船舶的注册、核验和检查；（3）签发相关安全设备证书；（4）签发船舶适航证书；（5）为进出吉大港和勐拉港的船只签发无异议证明；（6）确保履行海上人命安全相关国际义务；（7）处理有关航运中伤亡的问询和调查等。[1]

（2）孟加拉国航运公司

孟加拉国航运公司于 1972 年根据孟加拉国 10 号总统令（已废除）设立。作为提供海上航运服务的国有公司，亦是孟加拉国的最大船东，其目标是为本地进出口商提供高效、安全、可靠和经济的运输服务，以减少对外国航运的依赖。[2]

孟加拉国航运公司的具体业务主要涉及：第一，一般客货运输，包括孟加拉国至巴基斯坦或西亚海湾班轮服务、孟加拉国或英国至非洲班轮服务、孟加拉国至远东或日本班轮服务、定期租船或航次租船服务、孟加拉国至新加坡、马来西亚、斯里兰卡的支线服务；第二，原油及粮食运输的专门业务，包括从中东和波斯湾地区运输原油至本国的业务、将孟加拉国石油公司原油从外锚地运输至东部炼油厂的原油轻质化业务、从澳大利亚和加拿大运输大宗粮食至本国或散运至港口仓库的业务、船舶代理业务、船舶维修业务等。

不过，由于孟加拉国国力较弱、造船能力与远洋航行能力低下，孟加拉国航运公司的业务量及业务范围始终维持在服务本国的基础水平，上述某些业务甚至已经处于停滞状态。如孟加拉国或英国至非洲班轮服务，由于散货船的快速集装箱化，海上贸易模式在过去十年发生了根本性的变化，传统散货船在该条航线上的班轮服务已无获利空间。此外，由于国际海事组织及欧盟相关条约条款和航运政策的出台，海上安全标准及欧洲港口的入港标准都愈加严苛。在孟加拉国老化的传统班轮已难以达到相应水平的情形下，孟加拉国航运公司不得不从 2000 年起暂停该航线的定期班轮服务。同时，由于孟加拉国至远东出口货物较少，孟加拉国至远东或日本班轮航线也自 1998 年起暂停营运。[3]

---

〔1〕 Bangladesh Department of Shipping, "Mercantile Marine Office", http：//dos. gov. bd/site/page/dbe01f14-0f6b-4def-b3d0-acb267037ec9/-, March 15, 2020.

〔2〕 Bangladesh Shipping Corporation, "History", http：//bsc. portal. gov. bd/site/page/76a22ff3-ea3f-4601-9aef-750f8f23b134/-, March 15, 2020.

〔3〕 Bangladesh Shipping Corporation, "Our Services", http：//bsc. portal. gov. bd/site/page/3c413fdb-4a24-4968-8eed-ef8d8f612598/-, March 15, 2020.

（3）孟加拉国海事学院

孟加拉国自认拥有世界上最大的河网、最大的海湾及三角洲，最长的不间断海滩和最古老的海港之一，作为既有古老的木制造船传统又有现代远洋造船动力的国家，其拥有悠久的海洋传统和相当的专业成就。

1952 年，在孟加拉国独立前的东巴基斯坦时期，在孟加拉湾旁边建立一所海事学院的计划即已提上日程。1962 年 9 月，当时的巴基斯坦"商船学院"开始正式运行，以训练 22 名航海见习军官和 22 名轮机见习军官为其初始人才培养目标。1972 年，新独立的孟加拉国在原巴基斯坦"商船学院"的基础上成立了孟加拉国海事学院，并于 1973 年启动"海事学院发展（1973—1980）"项目，致力于将该学院推升至南亚海事专业的领先水平[1]。

该学院以培养世界级海事领袖人才为使命，期望通过不断的创新和努力，成为航运界领先的海事教育、培训和研究设施的提供方。为不断提高人才培养的满意度，孟加拉国海事学院基于《1978 年海员培训、发证和值班标准国际公约》及其修订案中航海科学和海洋工程相关能力标准，遵照国家课程总体要求，持续推进各类型海事教育和培训课程的品质完善和改进，数十年来逐渐获得国际社会的认可。1990 年，该学院成为世界海事大学（World Maritime University，WMU）的分支之一；2013 年，成为国际海上人命救助联盟（International Maritime Rescue Federation，IMRF）的一员；2017 年，在南亚伙伴关系峰会上被评为"南亚最佳海事教育机构"；2019 年，升级为世界海事大学的"伙伴关系"（Partner Relation）；同时，从 2010 年起陆续与包括大连海事大学在内的中国、印度、澳大利亚、英国、越南、新加坡、菲律宾等国的高等专业院校建立起合作教育渠道[2]。

（4）国家海事研究院

国家海事研究院最初为 1952 年设立于吉大港的一个小型研究所，从 1959 年起即开始在吉大港哈奇营地（Hazi Camp）训练海员。1959 年到 1993 年，共有 9000 余名学员在该训练基地接受了出海前培训课程。2000 年，该海员训练中心被列入国际海事组织"白名单"[3]。2004 年 7 月，原海员训练

---

〔1〕 Bangladesh Marine Academy, "Historical Background", http：//macademy. gov. bd/historical-background/, March 16, 2020.

〔2〕 See Bangladesh Marine Academy, "Mission, Vision & Inspiration", http：//macademy. gov. bd/overview-mission-vision/, March 16, 2020; Bangladesh Marine Academy, "International Standing, Achievement & Awards", http：//macademy. gov. bd/strategic-alliances/, March 16, 2020.

〔3〕 国际海事组织"白名单"，是由国际海事组织公布的认为其船员培训已达到《经 1995 年修订的 1978 年海员培训、发证和值班标准国际公约》（STCW95）规定标准的国家名单。"白名单"首次公布于 2000 年，后每 5 年更新发布一次。

中心正式更名为国家海事研究院，致力于发展适任且优质的海上人力队伍，为世界各船队提供安全和有效的人手配备。2010 年 8 月，国际海事研究院被划归孟加拉国航运部。从 1994 年到 2012 年，该研究院共为 1862 名海员提供了出海前学习训练课程，为 8379 名海员提供了出海后学习训练课程。[1]

1993 年，在其本国和日本政府的财政及技术援助下，国家海事研究院新建了专属培训大楼，其中有多项现代化培训设施，包括：设备完善的实践和理论教室、阅兵场、训练池、救生艇下水平台、潜水平台、机舱及甲板模型室、急救班、电子导航、救生艇、计算机实验室、排球场地、消防室、厨房/食品储藏室、船艺设备等等。此外，还设有供在职海员和见习海员居住的海员宿舍区。[2]

（5）海员福利与移民局

在国际劳工组织的建议下，早在英国殖民统治期间，尚未分割独立的印度即已成立了水手福利总局，以适当施行相关建议并确保国内外港口水手的应有福利。1971 年，通过将"海员福利理事会"（Directorate of Seamen's Welfare）、"移民保护者"（Protector of Emigrants）及"国家就业局"（National Employment Bureau）三个机构合并，孟加拉国成立了海员福利与移民局，以执行国际劳工组织相关公约规定，促进海员及其他雇员福利，也由此获得宝贵的外汇支援。[3]

自成立以来，海员福利与移民局致力于为在海船上工作的在职或非在职海员提供必要的就业机会，并采取必要措施为其提供各项福利服务，以改善他们的工作及生活状况。同时，海员福利与移民局可根据《2006 年海事劳工公约》（Maritime Labour Convention 2006）的要求，就促进海员福利的措施向政府提供意见。当前，该机构下设一个海员中心、两个位于吉大港和蒙格拉港的地区办事处，共同履行以下职责：（1）管理、监督和协调国内外海员的福利事业；（2）从政府和海员福利基金处获得必要的资金以保障海

〔1〕 See Bangladesh National Marine Institute, "About the Institute", http：//www. nmi. gov. bd/site/page/0c442847-09fa-4b6e-ac27-5ce5e4511dc1, March 16, 2020；Bangladesh National Marine Institute, "History", http：//www. nmi. gov. bd/site/page/decc7fe7-6c59-41f9-9bf4-b8b9a2aec7be/-, March 16, 2020；Bangladesh National Marine Institute, "Mission Statement", http：//www. nmi. gov. bd/site/page/2a801366-549d-4dac-a34e-e62abc25aa9f/-, March 16, 2020.

〔2〕 Bangladesh National Marine Institute, "Training Facilities", http：//www. nmi. gov. bd/site/page/7f74ae7c-5d24-4fdb-99b2-397fe0ebfaf0/-, March 16, 2020.

〔3〕 Directorate of Seamen & Emigration Welfare, "Notice Board", https：//dsw. gov. bd/bn/% e0% a6% aa% e0% a6% b0% e0% a6% bf% e0% a6% 9a% e0% a6% bf% e0% a6% a4% e0% a6% bf/, March 16, 2020.

员福利；（3）就有关保养名册、招聘海员及为海员提供一般福利设施等提出建议；（4）选派海员就业委员会、海员纪律委员会、海员晋升委员会等委员会的法定成员；（5）就孟加拉国海员在孟加拉国及海外的就业与福利事宜拟订相关计划或方案，供航运部参考；（6）在发生粮食及储备、住宿、淡水、药品等相关纠纷时，对停靠在吉大港和勐拉港的船只执行登临检查[1]。

另外，1972 年成立的孟加拉国内陆水运公司（Bangladesh Inland Water Transport Corporation）尽管以内河运输为主营业务，但同时经营沿海运输业务。根据 1972 年 28 号总统令，孟加拉国内陆水运公司的职责是为沿海和内陆水路提供安全、有效的运输和水上运输服务，并开展与该水上运输有关的或辅助性的所有形式的活动。具体包括：取得、租赁、持有或处置相应船只；经营内陆和沿海油轮；在沿海和内陆水域经营客运、货运以及渡轮服务；建立和维护船坞及维修车间等[2]。

3. 电力、能源和矿产资源部

电力、能源和矿产资源部（Ministry of Power, Energy & Mineral Resources）负责对孟加拉国的能源进口、分销、勘探、贮存、价格调整等制定相关政策，并进行分析与监管。作为孟加拉国能源管理的主要行政部门，其下共有两个职能分支，即电力司（Power Division）及能源和矿产资源司（Energy & Mineral Resources Division）。其中，能源和矿产资源司负责对石油、天然气和煤炭等能源进行勘探、开发、采购、分销，其职能亦由此覆盖了海上油气资源的开发利用活动[3]。

根据相关规划，能源和矿产资源司的当前建设目标在于：确保石油、天然气、煤炭等初级燃料的供应；同时虑及以石油、天然气和煤炭为代表的能源安全问题，大力推动风能、水力和太阳能等替代能源的开发。由于石油、天然气和煤炭是孟加拉国发电的主要燃料来源，为满足其日益增加的发电量需求，能源和矿产资源司也在不断推进海上区块的天然气勘探、开发和生产。当前，孟加拉国第三轮海上天然气勘探招标已经完成，区块招标的结果已经生效。为了

---

[1] See Directorate of Seamen & Emigration Welfare, "Mission & Vision", https://dsw. gov. bd/bn/% e0% a6% ae% e0% a6% bf% e0% a6% b6% e0% a6% a8-% e0% a6% 93-% e0% a6% ad% e0% a6% bf% e0% a6% b6% e0% a6% a8/, March 16, 2020; Directorate of Seamen & Emigration Welfare, "Seamen Welfare & Emigration Directorate", http://dos. gov. bd/site/page/35d31a9e-938a-4f86-ad5a-8b8759e1b7bb/-, March 16, 2020.

[2] Bangladesh Code: "Bangladesh Shipping Corporation Order, 1972 (president's order)", http://bdcode. gov. bd/upload/bdcodeact/2020-11-10-10-38-27-401_ PO_ 10_ 1972_ 1990_ fina_ li_ sh_ E_ final. pdf, March 16, 2020.

[3] Ministry of Power, "Energy & Mineral Resources", https://mpemr. gov. bd/, March 16, 2020.

加强孟加拉国石油勘探与生产有限公司的生产能力，该国建成了一个新的钻井平台，以确保天然气的输送，并辅助陆上勘探活动的开展。[1]

能源和矿产资源司下设孟加拉国石油、天然气与矿产公司（Bangladesh Oil, Gas and Mineral Corporation）、孟加拉国石化公司（Bangladesh Petroleum Corporation）、孟加拉国地质调查局（Geological Survey of Bangladesh）、孟加拉国石油学院（Bangladesh Petroleum Institute）、矿产开发局（Bureau of Mineral Development）、爆破物管理局（Department of Explosives）、孟加拉国能源管理委员会（Bangladesh Energy Regulatory Commission）等多个机构。[2] 其中，孟加拉国石油、天然气与矿产公司以加强天然气勘探开发，为所有地区和社会群体提供本土初级能源，使本土能源资源多样化，改善国家环境，确保未来的能源安全等为目标；而孟加拉国地质调查局是为孟加拉国培训地质科技人才的全国性组织，并于1972年即获授权勘探除石油和天然气外的矿物资源，其实验室等研究设施的建设对国家在地球科学领域的发展至关重要，尤其有助于定位关键的自然资源；孟加拉国石油学院国家石油、天然气和矿产资源部门的研发单元，旨在满足不同单位对石油、天然气和矿产资源的勘探、生产和销售环节的人员培训需求，并可与本国及国外的私营企业合作发展。[3] 上述机构均从不同层面服务于孟加拉国包括海上能源开发在内的能源及矿产资源活动。

4. 水利部

水利部（Ministry of Water Resources）是孟加拉国开发和管理全国水资源的最高政府机关，负责制定与水资源开发和管理有关的政策、战略计划、指导方针、行为规章及条例等，并负责管理和指导向其报告的下属单位。根据1999年的《国家水政策》（National Water Policy），其具体职责还包括：第一，筹划和推行与防洪及排水有关的发展计划；第二，施行防洪、排水和灌溉相关的具体措施；第三，控制河岸的侵蚀；第四，负责三角洲开发及填海

〔1〕 Minsty of Power, Energy and Mineral Resource, "Energy and Mineral Resources Division", https: //mpemr. gov. bd/power/details/80, March 16, 2020.

〔2〕 See Minsty of Power, Energy and Mineral Resource, "Energy & Mineral Resources Division", https: //mpemr. gov. bd/energy-mineral, March 16, 2020; Minsty of Power, Energy and Mineral Resource, "Agencies", https: //emrd. gov. bd/#, March 16, 2020.

〔3〕 See Banglades Oil Gas and Mineral Corporation, "Vision and Mission", http: //www. petrobangla. org. bd/site/page/0ca3cd73-7e26-4634-bd89-4a73aeb12858/-, March 17, 2020; Banglades Oil Gas and Mineral Corporation, "Geological Survey Of Bangladesh", https: //mpemr. gov. bd/power/details/25, March 17, 2020; Minstry of Power, Energy and Mineral Resource, "Bangladesh Petrolium Institute", https: //mpemr. gov. bd/power/details/52, March 17, 2020.

工程；第五，在河岸及海岸修建堰坝、调压器、水闸、运河、大坝、堤防（海堤）等，以提供灌溉、排涝、防汛、防冲、复垦等设施；第六，编制具体的干旱监测和应急计划，查明缺水地区并在关键时期确定水分配的优先次序；第七，监督相关水利制度及条例的执行等。

为有效履行上述职能，水利部下设有：作为主要执行机构的孟加拉国水利开发委员会（Bangladesh Water Development Board）；作为宏观规划机构的水资源规划组织（Water Resources Planning Organization）；作为研究及协调机构的河流研究所（River Research Institute）、孟加拉国豪尔与湿地发展委员会（Bangladesh Haor and Wetland Development Board）、联合河流委员会（Joint Rivers Commission）等。[1]

其中，水资源规划的编制可追溯至 1964 年。在经历了 1954 年及 1955 年的严重洪灾之后，由当时的孟加拉国水利开发委员会主导水利部门 20 年发展总体计划的编制进程。至 1970 年，为取得世界银行的资金支持，孟加拉国决定立足于对资源和需求的系统评估进一步编制国家水利计划。该规划项目的编制对地表水和地下水资源以及包括航海、渔业和环境在内的所有相关资源需求都进行了综合评价。随着该规划编制的完成，将水资源规划和长期水资源管理制度化的建议被提上日程。根据这一建议，水资源规划组织于 1992 年正式成立。

当前，水资源规划组织已经完成了多项国家水资源政策、海岸带政策、国家水资源管理计划的编制，并开始了国家各类水资源数据库的建设。其中海洋区域水资源利用有关的工作成果主要包括：2005 年的《海岸资源综合数据库》（Integrated Coastal Resources Database）、2005 年的《海岸带政策》（Coastal Zone Policy）、2006 年的《海岸带战略》（Coastal Zone Strategy）、2013 年的《海岸带气候变化影响评估》（Impact Assessment of Climate Changes in the Coastal Zone）。[2]

5. 民航和旅游部

在孟加拉国建立初期，其民航及旅游相关管理职能曾在不同中央机关间被多次移转。1971 年，通信及旅游相关事务被分派到商务部；1972 年，航

---

[1] The Ministry of Water Resources, "Brief-History", https: //mowr. gov. bd/site/page/328c56b4-a102-48bc-be1c-bbc6a99c902d/Brief-History, March 17, 2020.

[2] See Water Resource Planning Organization, "Background", http: //www. warpo. gov. bd/site/page/3ee10cbe-3fb6-41a6-bde8-5a8c8d8f16b7/-, March 17, 2020; Water Resource Planning Organization, "Major Achievements", http: //www. warpo. gov. bd/site/page/f5e29c81-3794-4fd2-837f-1e57f6e78f42/-, March 17, 2020.

运、内河运输与民航部之下创立民航局；1975 年 8 月，独立的民航和旅游部（Ministry of Civil Aviation and Tourism）首次建立；后于 1976 年及 1982 年分别被划归通信部及国防部；最终自 1986 年起重归民航和旅游部至今。[1]

孟加拉国旅游局是民航和旅游部下设的行业监管组织，在其对旅游名胜的介绍中，海滩旅游是除古迹、特色节日、特色食品、田园生活以外的重要类别之一。[2] 考克斯巴扎、圣马丁（Saint Martin）、库卡塔（Kuakata）、婆坦加（Potenga）、帕基海滩（Parki Sea Beach）是旅游局重点推介的六大海滩资源。如考克斯巴扎为世界最狭长海滩，也是孟加拉国最引人注目的风景名胜；圣马丁以椰子树、丰富的海洋生物及海鲜闻名；而库卡塔则被谓为世界上唯一能够同时观看日出与日落的海滩。[3]

除上述行政机构外，孟加拉国的某些部门虽未被直接赋予海洋管理职能，其工作范围仍可能与海洋事务有所关联。如，隶属于孟加拉国环境、森林和气候变化部（Ministry of Environment, Forest and Climate Change）的环境署，其职责范围之一就包括：采取必要步骤，在国内、区域和国际各级遵守并履行有关环境的各种区域和国际公约、条约和议定书。据此，基于《联合国海洋法公约》（United Nations Convention on the Law of the Sea，以下简称《公约》）及其他相关条约的海洋环境保护行动也在此部门的职责范围之内。

（三）海上武装执法机构

孟加拉国武装力量由正规军和准军事力量组成。总统是武装部队最高统帅，但由总理掌握军队实权。该国陆、海、空三军分立，三军的作战指挥权分别由三军参谋长掌握，实行志愿兵役制。三军总兵力约 15.5 万人，其中陆军约 12 万人、海军约 1 万人、空军约 1 万人、准军事组织约 1.5 万人。其准军事力量主要包括边境卫队、乡村卫队、海岸警卫队、国家学员团和警察部队等。[4]

1. 孟加拉国海军

孟加拉国海军（Bangladesh Navy）是在 1971 年孟加拉国对巴基斯坦的解

---

[1] Ministry of Civil Aviation and Tourism, "Background", https://mocat. gov. bd/site/page/7c990d 63-87d4-4558-9f5b-9f6e738ef589/Background, March 18, 2020.

[2] Bangladesh Tourism Board, "Tourism Attraction", http://tourismboard. gov. bd/, March 18, 2020.

[3] Bangladesh Tourism Board, "Beaches", http://tourismboard. gov. bd/site/page/6d1a7bdd-85b0- 48be-9e19-2872185d6337/Sea-Beaches, March 18, 2020.

[4] Ministry of Defence, "Overview", https://mod. gov. bd/site/page/a220acbc-c20c-4eca-8288-e8d e1a0138f6, March 18, 2020.

放战争中作为孟加拉国部队的一部分而创建的。孟加拉国政府在独立后深感有必要建设一支强大的海军，但直至 1976 年孟加拉国海军舰队中仍没有一艘真正的海上作战舰艇。从 20 世纪 80 年代起，孟加拉国开始陆续从中国引进导弹护卫舰，并由此进入导弹时代。2012 年及 2015 年，孟加拉国海军分别从中国购买了 2 艘新建造的大型导弹巡逻艇（LPC）及 2 艘护卫舰，均装备系列现代化武器、传感器和其他设备。2013 年，孟加拉国在库尔纳造船厂成功建造了 5 艘巡逻艇，为孟加拉国海军自主建造战舰注入巨大信心。

经过数十年的发展，孟加拉国海军不仅在规模和形态上不断成长壮大，在角色、使命和愿景上也发生了变化。到目前为止，孟加拉国海军拥有超过 80 艘不同类型和能力的舰艇，包括导弹护卫舰、护卫舰、导弹舰、炮舰、大型导弹巡逻艇、轻型巡逻艇、近岸巡逻艇、扫雷舰等，并从特种作战潜水和打捞部队（Special Warfare Diving and Salvage）、海军航空部队和潜艇部队三个维度的建设提升国家安全保障。[1]

孟加拉国海军的主要职责在于：（1）保卫国家领海；（2）在战争期间保持海上交通顺畅；（3）在战争期间保证孟加拉国海港继续开放航运；（4）保护孟加拉国捕鱼船队；（5）承担海岸巡逻警卫职责；（6）在国内河流水域巡逻；（7）进行海上搜救；（8）在公海上保护孟加拉国商船；（9）在有需要时协助民政当局维持国内安全与和平；（10）在有需要时协助民政部门处理洪水、旋风、潮汐、地震等自然灾害；（11）海洋学调查等。立足于此，除常规性的军事行动以外，当前孟加拉国海军在海上搜索与救援、国内及国外的人道主义救助与灾难救济、打击海盗及走私、保护渔业捕捞、参与联合国相关行动、协助民事部门处理紧急事态、开展海军外交、发展蓝色经济等方面都有积极投入和良好表现。[2]

2. 孟加拉国海岸警卫队

孟加拉国 90% 以上的进出口通过吉大港和勐拉港两个海港进行，连接此两港的海上交通线已经成为其经济生命线。1982 年《联合国海洋法公约》的通过则使孟加拉国看到了其在专属经济区及更远海域勘探和开发生物和非生物资源的主权权利与广阔前景。与此同时，大量各类型船舶在孟加拉国沿海及外海上从事贸易、捕鱼、科研以及石油、天然气和矿产勘探开采等活动。为保障海上安全，保护国家及国际海洋利益，有效施行各项国内立法并履行

---

[1] Bangladesh Navy, "History of Bangladesh Navy", https：//www. navy. mil. bd/BN-HISTORY, March 18, 2020.

[2] See Bangladesh Navy, "Role of BN", https：//www. navy. mil. bd/Role-of-BN; Bangladesh Navy, "Operation", https：//www. navy. mil. bd/, March 18, 2020.

国际条约义务，有必要在孟加拉国相关海域建立起强有力的管制力量。[1]

在孟加拉国海岸警卫队（Bangladesh Coast Guard）成立之前，所有的海上防卫责任都由孟加拉国海军承担。随着孟加拉国独立后经济实力的攀升，海洋重要性的显现，海军除自身责任外很难在沿海地区再有效履行额外的职责。鉴于此，孟加拉国依《1994 年海岸警卫队法》（Coast Guard Act 1994）成立了作为"海上护卫者"的海岸警卫队，并通过 2016 年修订《海岸警卫队法》（Coast Guard Act 2016）对海岸警卫队的组成及职责进行了调整与发展。当前，海岸警卫队归属孟加拉国内政部下辖的公共安全司（Public Security Division），作为海上执法的准军事力量，承担孟加拉国涉海环境下几乎所有层面的军事及民事管控职责。海岸警卫队现有 3000 余名成员、57 艘不同类别的舰艇，管辖区域包括达卡区、东大区、西大区、南大区及 1 个基地（CG Base Agrajatra），并有 18 个驻地及 10 个前哨站。[2]

海岸警卫队的工作目标在于：通过打击海盗和非法贩运，保护孟加拉国水域及沿海地区的渔业、石油、天然气、森林资源和环境，做好对沿海港口进行安全救援，并承担沿海地区自然灾害抢险救灾工作，以有效维护国家和社会的长治久安。其主要职责包括：（1）维护国家海上利益；（2）保护渔业生产与捕捞；（3）防止来自海上的非法移民；（4）防控海上污染；（5）打击海盗；（6）防范非法武器、毒品和麻醉品的走私贩运；（7）执行救灾任务；（8）执行搜救任务；（9）保持对孟加拉国海域的监控等。另外，作为其次要职责，海岸警卫队在战争期间还承担协助孟加拉国海军的作战角色。[3]

---

〔1〕　Bangladesh Coast Guard，"Aim and Purpose"，http：//coastguard. gov. bd/site/page/e47f5581-c68f-4584-8867-970e1a34a0f6/-，March 18，2020.

〔2〕　Bangladesh Coast Guard，"Background"，http：//coastguard. gov. bd/site/page/120b3e36-81a6-489b-9241-885b76fcc27b/-，March 18，2020.

〔3〕　Bangladesh Coast Guard，"Aim and Purpose"，http：//coastguard. gov. bd/site/page/e47f5581-c68f-4584-8867-970e1a34a0f6/-，March 18，2020.

三、国内海洋立法

作为自 20 世纪 70 年代才从巴基斯坦独立的国家，孟加拉国与巴基斯坦乃至印度的法律体系具有高度的同源性。受到普通法系的深远影响，孟加拉国的法律主要采取了制定法的形式，由立法机构颁布并由最高法院解释。孟加拉国最高法院不仅有权解释议会制定的法律，亦可以在议会立法与宪法条款不符时宣布其无效，并督促公民基本权利的落实。[1]

依据孟加拉国的宪法，"法律"意指"法"（act）、"法令"（ordinance）、"命令"（order）、"规则"（rule）、"条例"（regulation）、"规章"（bye-law）、"通告"（notification）或其他法律文件以及习惯（custom）或惯例（usage）。[2] 其中，议会的"法""法令"及总统的"命令"是基本立法，而规则及条例等是次级立法。依据孟加拉国当前的法律编纂成果，有 7 项在英国统治时期由时任总督所颁布的条例也被视为基本立法。同时，孟加拉国最高法院还可公布对所有下级法院均有拘束力的法律规范。[3]

作为世界上第二大伊斯兰国家，伊斯兰法在孟加拉国宪法中被赋予极高地位。尽管刑法、民法、合同法、公司法及刑事与民事诉讼程序法等都与英国普通法一脉相承，但其家事相关法律仍然大多立足于宗教条规。[4] 如 1937 年颁布的《穆斯林人身法（伊斯兰教法）适用法》［Muslim Personal Law（Shariat）Application Act, 1937］在孟加拉国适用至今。就孟加拉国当前实践来看，宪法所赋予公民的宗教信仰自由，未能改变伊斯兰教在其官方及民间的强势影响，伊斯兰教以外的少数教派公民往往无法有效得到基于法律规定的应有帮助与保护。[5]

---

〔1〕 See Articles 7（2）and 44, The Constitution of the People's Republic of Bangladesh, Laws of Bangladesh, http：//bdlaws. minlaw. gov. bd/act-367. html？hl = 1, April 12, 2020.

〔2〕 See Article 152, The Constitution of the People's Republic of Bangladesh, Laws of Bangladesh, http：//bdlaws. minlaw. gov. bd/act-367. html？hl = 1, April 12, 2020.

〔3〕 See Article 111, The Constitution of the People's Republic of Bangladesh, Laws of Bangladesh, http：//bdlaws. minlaw. gov. bd/act-367. html？hl = 1, April 12, 2020.

〔4〕 ORG LEGAL, "Legal System of Bangladesh", https：//resource. ogrlegal. com/legal-system-bangladesh/, April 12, 2020.

〔5〕 Md. Ershadul Karim, "UPDATE：The Legal System of the Peoples' Republic of Bangladesh", https：//www. nyulawglobal. org/globalex/Bangladesh1. html, April 12, 2020.

（一）划定管辖海域的法

1. 《孟加拉人民共和国宪法》中的基本规定

《孟加拉人民共和国宪法》（Constitution of the People's Republic of Bangladesh，以下简称《孟加拉国宪法》）于 1972 年 11 月 4 日获得通过，至今已经过十余次修订，是孟加拉国法律体系的基础。

根据该宪法第 2 条，孟加拉国的领土即为 1971 年其宣布独立前的东巴基斯坦以及经与印度谈判交换飞地及确定边界后所包含的其他领土。[1] 而其第十一部分"杂项"第 143 条对"共和国财产"作出如下规定："（1）除合法拥有的其他土地或财产外，共和国应拥有以下财产：（a）孟加拉国土地下的所有矿产和其他有价值的物（things of value）；（b）孟加拉国领水或大陆架上覆海域范围内的所有土地、矿产和其他有价值的物；和（c）位于孟加拉国的没有合法所有者的任何财产。（2）议会可以适时通过法律以确定孟加拉国领土以及孟加拉国领水和大陆架的边界。"[2]

一方面，《孟加拉国宪法》第 2 条未能就孟加拉国领土中的领海范围作出明确规定，其第 143 条第 1 款更多是立足于将海洋资源纳入国家财产的考量；但另一方面，第 143 条第 2 款却为其进一步划定相关主权权利覆盖的管辖海域提供了实现路径，并使得孟加拉国较印度及巴基斯坦更早地完成了对本国管辖海域的专门性立法。

2. 关于领海及领海基线的划定

（1）《1974 年领水及海洋区域法》

在其《宪法》第 143 条第 2 款的背书之下，孟加拉国国民议会于 1974 年颁布了《领水及海洋区域法》（Territorial Waters and Maritime Zones Act，以下简称《1974 年海域法》），对包括领海、毗连区、大陆架等在内的相关海域作出初步规定。根据该法第 3 条，政府可以在"政府公报"（Official Gazette）中以发布通告的方式，宣布孟加拉国陆地领土和内水以外的海洋边界，并在该通告中明确测算孟加拉国领海的基线。根据该条第 2 款，若构成孟加拉国领土部分的某一单独岛屿、岩礁或其组成的岛礁群位于其主海岸或基线的向海一侧，则其领水将从该岛屿、岩礁或其组成的岛礁群的沿岸低潮线量起并延伸至相关通告所确定的边界。同时，孟加拉国的主权也延伸至领水及

---

〔1〕　See Article 2, The Constitution of the People's Republic of Bangladesh, Laws of Bangladesh, http：//bdlaws. minlaw. gov. bd/act-367/section-24548. html，April 12，2020.

〔2〕　See Article 143, The Constitution of the People's Republic of Bangladesh, Laws of Bangladesh, http：//bdlaws. minlaw. gov. bd/act-367. html？hl＝1，April 12，2020.

其上空与海床底土。[1]

(2)《1974 年外交部第 LT-I/3/74 号通告》

基于上述《1974 年海域法》第 3 条第 1 款的授权，孟加拉国政府于同年 4 月发布《外交部第 LT-I/3/74 号通告》（Notification No. LT-I/3/74 of the Ministry of Foreign Affairs，以下简称《1974 年通告》），就领海宽度及领海基线进行了划定，并由此取代该国此前一切领海相关声明。

根据《1974 年通告》，孟加拉国的领海宽度为 12 海里，其领海基线为连接 8 个基点的直线线段。该 8 个基点的地理坐标参见第 I 部分 表 1。

第 I 部分 表 1　《1974 年通告》所确定的基点坐标[2]

基点	基点地理坐标	
	纬度（北）	经度（东）
1	21° 12′00″	89° 06′45″
2	21° 15′00″	89° 16′00″
3	21° 29′00″	89° 36′00″
4	21° 21′00″	89° 55′00″
5	21° 11′00″	90° 33′00″
6	21° 07′30″	91° 06′00″
7	21° 10′00″	91° 56′00″
8	20° 21′45″	92° 17′30″

(3)《2015 年外交部通告》

2015 年 11 月，孟加拉国政府发布《外交部通告（S. R. O. No. 328-Law/ 2015/MOFA/UNCLOS/113/2/15）》（以下简称《2015 年通告》）以更新其管辖海域界限，对原单纯的直线基线划定方法以及领海及专属经济区范围作出调整或进一步明确。

在这一通告下，孟加拉国采取了直线基线与低潮线构成的正常基线相混合的基线测定方式：其直线基线部分所连接的基点从原有的 8 个删减为 4 个；而从基点 4 开始直至代格纳夫（Teknaf）与圣马丁岛（St. Martin's Island）的

---

[1] UN Office of Legal Affairs, "Territorial Waters and Maritime Zones Act 1974, Act No. XXVI of 1974", https：//www. un. org/Depts/los/LEGISLATIONANDTREATIES/PDFFILES/BGD_ 1974_ Act. pdf， April 12, 2020.

[2] UN Office of Legal Affairs, "Notification No. LT-I/3/74 of the Bangladesh Ministry of Foreign Affairs, Dacca, of 13 April 1974", https：//www. un. org/Depts/los/LEGISLATIONANDTREATIES/PDF-FILES/BGD_ 1974_ Notification. pdf， April 12, 2020.

基线部分均为低潮线。[1] 上述直线基线所连接基点的地理坐标如第 I 部分表 2 所示。

第 I 部分 表 2 《2015 年通告》所确定的基点坐标[2]

基点	基点标识	纬度（北）	经度（东）
1	陆地边界终点（LBT）	21°38′40.2″	89°09′20.0″
2	帕特尼岛（Putney Island）	21°36′39.2″	89°22′14.0″
3	达克因哈桑查（Dakhin Bhasan Char）	21°38′16.0″	90°47′16.5″
4	考克斯巴扎（Cox's Bazar）	21°25′51.0″	91°57′42.0″

对于孟加拉国通过《2015 年通告》所更新公布的领海基线，与其海岸相邻的印度与缅甸相继发表反对立场。2017 年 8 月，印度致信联合国秘书长表示：（1）孟加拉国划定直线基线所用基点与两国间 2014 年"孟加拉湾海洋边界仲裁案"的仲裁裁决不符；（2）从当前基点 2 与基点 5 所测算的孟加拉国专属经济区存在向海洋方向的移位，导致对印度在"灰色地带"（Grey Area）专属经济区的侵占，而印度依据前述仲裁裁决在此拥有主权权利；（3）2014 年的仲裁裁决是终局裁决，对双方均有拘束力。[3]

与印度相似，缅甸也尤其对孟加拉国更新后的基点 2 与基点 5 表示异议。在其 2019 年 2 月提交至联合国的声明中，缅甸批评孟加拉国的直线基线调整与国际海洋法法庭（ITLOS）在"孟加拉国与缅甸间在孟加拉湾的海洋划界争端案"中的判决不符，并由此侵占了缅甸的专属经济区，从而使上述判决中的"灰色地带"被最小化。[4]

3. 关于领海的无害通过

根据《1974 年海域法》，外国船舶可以在遵守孟加拉国的法律及相关规

---

[1] Division for Ocean Affairs and The Law of The Sea Office of Legal Affairs, "Bangladesh Ministry of Foreign Affairs Notification, 2015", *The Law of the Sea Bulletins*, 90, United Nations, 2017, p. 48.

[2] 有关《2015 年通告》所划定的领海基线的示意图，参见 Division for Ocean Affairs and The Law of The Sea Office of Legal Affairs, "Bangladesh Ministry of Foreign Affairs Notification, 2015", *The Law of the Sea Bulletins*, 90, United Nations, 2017, p. 47。

[3] UN Office of Legal Affairs, "Communication from the Permanent Mission of India Dated 3 August 2017 with Respect to The Deposit by Bangladesh (M. Z. N. 118. 2016. LOS of 7 April 2016) of A List of Geographical Coordinates", https：//www. un. org/Depts/los/LEGISLATIONANDTREATIES/PDFFILES/2017_ 08_ 03_ IND_ UN. pdf, April 12, 2020.

[4] UN Office of Legal Affairs, "Communication from the Permanent Mission of Myanmar Dated 15 Februaryruary 2019 with Respect to The Deposit by Bangladesh (M. Z. N. 118. 2016. LOS of 7 April 2016) of A List of Geographical Coordinates", https：//www. un. org/Depts/los/LEGISLATION-ANDTREATIES/PDFFILES/NV57 − 030945%28corrected%29. pdf, April 12, 2020.

则的前提下无害通过其领海。但外国军舰的通过需要获得孟加拉国政府的事先许可。该法特别就"军舰"作出解释，将一切以海上作战为目的的海面航行或水下航行的船舶或舰艇纳入其中。根据该法，孟加拉国对领海无害通过还可作出以下限制：（1）出于国家安全的需要，可发布政府公报暂停在领海任何特定区域或任何船舶的无害通过权；（2）可采取措施阻止任何不享有无害通过权的船舶通过其领海；（3）对外国船舶行使无害通过权时违反孟加拉国法律或规则的行为，可采取预防及惩处措施；（4）可对任何损害国家安全或利益的行为采取预防及惩处措施。[1]

4. 关于毗连区的划定

根据《1974 年海域法》第 4 条，孟加拉国的毗连区为邻接其领水的公海区域，其宽度为从其领海外部界限量起的 6 海里。对于在该区域内或与该区域有关的涉及国家安全、移民、卫生以及海关和其他财政事项，孟加拉国可行使相应权力、采取必要措施以预防或惩处任何违反或意图违反相关法律或规章的行为。[2]

5. 关于专属经济区的划定

与其对领海的划定历程相似，《1974 年海域法》并未明确孟加拉国专属经济区的宽度，甚至没有使用"专属经济区"（Exclusive Economic Zone）这一术语，而采用了"经济区"（Economic Zone）的表述，并意图通过"保护区"（Conservation Zone）的划定对其"经济区"地位有所补充。

依据《1974 年海域法》第 5 条，孟加拉国的"经济区"为邻接其领水的公海区域；该区域内的所有自然资源，无论生物性还是非生物性资源，无论位于海床底土还是位于海水表面或海水之中，都专属于孟加拉国。但上述规定不影响任何孟加拉国国民在此区域内利用非机动船舶的捕鱼活动。

而《1974 年海域法》第 6 条所载之"保护区"亦为邻接领水的海域，由孟加拉国发布政府公告建立。该特定区域以维护海洋生物资源的再生产能力为目标，通过采取相关养护措施，保护海洋生物资源免遭滥用、耗竭或破坏。这一"经济区"加"保护区"的设立动机与法律地位，明显与此后

---

〔1〕 UN Office of Legal Affairs, "Territorial Waters and Maritime Zones Act 1974, Act No. XXVI of 1974", https：//www. un. org/Depts/los/LEGISLATIONANDTREATIES/PDFFILES/BGD_ 1974_ Act. pdf, April 12, 2020.

〔2〕 UN Office of Legal Affairs, "Territorial Waters and Maritime Zones Act 1974, Act No. XXVI of 1974", https：//www. un. org/Depts/los/LEGISLATIONANDTREATIES/PDFFILES/BGD_ 1974_ Act. pdf, April 12, 2020.

《公约》中的"专属经济区"有所趋同。[1]

随着《1974 年通告》的颁布，孟加拉国"经济区"的起算线也得以确定，其宽度为从该通告中所确立的直线基线量起的 200 海里。至 2015 年 11 月，《2015 年通告》修正了 1974 年的直线基线，同时正式明确《1974 年海域法》中"经济区"为"专属经济区"，将区域范围调整为从 2015 年的混合基线量起的 200 海里范围。[2]

6. 关于大陆架的划定

按照《1974 年海域法》第 7 条第 1 款，孟加拉国的大陆架范围包括：（1）邻接孟加拉国海岸的其领海界限以外的海底区域的海床和底土，直至位于大洋盆地或深海海床的大陆边缘外部界限；（2）邻接构成孟加拉国领土一部分的任何岛屿、岩礁或其组成的岛屿岩礁群的海床、底土及类似的海底区域。非经政府许可或授权，任何人不得勘探或开发大陆架上的资源，也不得从事探索、挖掘或其他研究性活动；但孟加拉国公民使用非机动船的捕鱼行为仍然不受此限。[3]

尽管《1974 年通告》与《2015 年通告》均未对孟加拉国的大陆架范围作出进一步明确，孟加拉国仍于 2011 年 2 月向大陆架界限委员会（CLCS）提交了其 200 海里外大陆架划界案。该划界案中的大陆架外部界限由长度不超过 60 海里的直线段连接 120 个定点划出。[4]

孟加拉国的 2011 年外大陆架划界案同样引发利益关切国印度与缅甸的质

〔1〕 UN Office of Legal Affairs, "Territorial Waters and Maritime Zones Act 1974, Act No. XXVI of 1974", https：//www. un. org/Depts/los/LEGISLATIONANDTREATIES/PDFFILES/BGD_ 1974_ Act. pdf, April 12, 2020.

〔2〕 See UN Office of Legal Affairs, "Communication from the Permanent Mission of India Dated 3 August 2017 with Respect to The Deposit by Bangladesh（M. Z. N. 118. 2016. LOS of 7 April 2016）of A List of Geographical Coordinates", https：//www. un. org/Depts/los/LEGISLATIONANDTREATIE-S/PDFFILES/2017_ 08 _ 03 _ IND _ UN. pdf, April 12, 2020; UN Office of Legal Affairs, "Communication from the Permanent Mission of Myanmar Dated 15 Februaryruary 2019 with Respect to The Deposit by Bangladesh（M. Z. N. 118. 2016. LOS of 7 April 2016）of A List of Geographical Coordinates", https：//www. un. org/Depts/los/LEGISLATIONANDTREATIES/PDFFILES/NV57-030945% 28corrected% 29. pdf, April 12, 2020.

〔3〕 UN Office of Legal Affairs, "Territorial Waters and Maritime Zones Act 1974, Act No. XXVI of 1974", https：//www. un. org/Depts/los/LEGISLATIONANDTREATIES/PDFFILES/BGD_ 1974_ Act. pdf, April 12, 2020.

〔4〕 有关孟加拉国 2011 年提交大陆架界限委员会外大陆架界限的示意图，参见 UN Office of Legal Affairs, "Submission by the People's Republic of Bangladesh（Executive summary）", https：//www. un. org/Depts/los/clcs_ new/submissions_ files/bgd55_ 11/Executive% 20summary% 20final. pdf, April 12, 2020。

疑。印度提出，孟加拉国的领海基线不符合《公约》第 7 条的规定；且在两国间的海洋争端仲裁程序尚在进行的情形下，孟加拉国所申请的划界案不应妨害该仲裁程序对两国海洋边界的划分；同时重申据印度《1976 年海域法》，印度与他国间的海洋边界争端只能通过协议解决。[1] 而缅甸的反对立场更为强硬：（1）除否认孟加拉国领海基线的合法性外，缅甸更直接否认孟加拉国拥有大陆架的权利，无论是从"合法"基线量起的 200 海里内还是 200 海里外；（2）缅甸否认两国已通过协议划定了彼此间的领海边界；（3）缅甸同样强调孟加拉国的划界案不应妨害两国提交至国际海洋法法庭的划界争议的司法解决，并不能影响两国间其他海洋边界的划定，同时保留缅甸的相关权利。[2]

值得注意的是，自《1974 年海域法》颁布之后，孟加拉国对海洋权益的重视程度逐渐提升，对海洋主权的宣示也日益鲜明。随着孟加拉国于 2001 年批准加入 1982 年《公约》，在其国内法层面上，全文仅 9 条的《1974 年海域法》已经不能满足国家在维护发展其海洋权益方面的要求。为了进一步确认对海洋的主权范围与主权权利，孟加拉国内阁于 2019 年 11 月 25 日批准了《2019 年领水及海洋区域法（修正案）》的草案［The draft of Territorial Waters and Maritime Zone Act（Amendment）2019］。该草案能否成为孟加拉国的正式法律还需等待提交议会后的审议结果。

从当前这一草案的相关内容来看，一旦该草案获得议会通过，孟加拉国将进一步明确其管辖海域的界限及所能行使的主权权利。其中，大陆架宽度将扩展至 350 海里。同时，该草案特别引入了对海盗等海上暴力犯罪的刑事条款，孟加拉国将积极应对并遏制海盗、海上恐怖主义、海洋污染等海上犯罪，并有效控制非法船只的各项活动。此外，草案条款也为开展海洋科学研究提供协助与保障，以促使孟加拉国从海洋管理和海洋资源中获益。[3]

---

〔1〕 UN Office of Legal Affairs, "India: Note Verbale Dated 20 June 2011", https://www.un.org/Depts/los/clcs_new/submissions_files/bgd55_11/ind_nv_un_001_20_06_2011.pdf, April 12, 2020.

〔2〕 UN Office of Legal Affairs, "Myanmar: Note Verbale Dated 31 March 2011", https://www.un.org/Depts/los/clcs_new/submissions_files/bgd55_11/mmr_nv_un_001_08_04_2011.pdf, April 12, 2020.

〔3〕 See Bangladesh Post, "Draft of Maritime Zones Act-2019 Approved", https://www.bangladeshpost.net/posts/draft-of-maritime-zones-act-2019-approved-18380, April 12, 2020; Bangladeshinfo, "Territorial Waters and Maritime Zone（Amendment）Act 2019", April 12, 2020; https://bangladeshinfo.com/article/4843/cabinet-approves-draft-territorial-waters-and-maritime-zone-act-2019; NTV Online, "Draft Bill Okayed with Death Penalty Provision for Piracies in Sea", https://en.ntvbd.com/bangladesh/187749/Draft-bill-okayed-with-death-penalty-provision-for-piracies-in-sea, April 12, 2020.

（二）海上安全相关立法

1. 《1950 年海军（延长服役）法》

孟加拉国保留了原东巴基斯坦时期所颁布的《1950 年海军（延长服役）法》［Navy（Extension of Service）Act］，从而为在孟加拉国海军服役的特定人保留服役权。该法仅含 3 条，前两条分别涉及该立法的简称、生效时间、服役到期后的服役延长期限。与巴基斯坦当前有效的同名立法一样，其第 2 条规定：从政府根据本法进行通知的日期起，任何人在被招募加入孟加拉国海军时，如果由于其受雇服役期限届满而不再负有服役义务的，即使该期限届满，也应继续保持在孟加拉国海军的服役状态，直至孟加拉国海军总司令命令其退役；但此类人员的服役期限自其本应终止服役之日起计算，不得超过 5 年。[1]

2. 《1961 年海军条例》

1961 年，孟加拉国颁布《海军条例》（Navy Ordinance）以巩固政府与海军之间的联系并强化海军纪律。该条例共有 27 章 181 条，除适用范围、术语界定、与陆军及空军间的关系及借调程序等基本内容外，对海军纪律规则及其实施保障作出了立法确认，主要包括：（1）入伍资格、招募任命与佣金、入伍后法律地位与入伍宣誓；（2）服役期限、服役责任、国外服役终止等；（3）服役期间的特权与豁免、相关权利救济等；（4）军事犯罪行为，如通敌、失职、叛乱、违背军令、擅离职守、航行或飞行失当、违法拿捕等；（5）对上述行为的惩处措施、惩处机关、审前逮捕程序、军事法庭的组建及程序、刑罚的减免、刑罚的执行等；（6）死亡、叛逃或精神失常士兵的财产处置等。其中，第 12 条（关于入伍及低级军官委任）、第 179 条（基于该法授权的下级规则制定）、第 180 条及第 181 条（过渡性条款）已经由 2016 年《海军（修正）法》［Navy（Amendment）Act］删除或废止。[2]

（三）海洋渔业相关立法

1. 孟加拉国独立前的相关立法

同为对英印时代立法的继承，孟加拉国对 1889 年颁布的《私人渔业保

---

［1］　Laws of Bangladesh, "The Navy（Extension of Service）Act, 1950", http：//bdlaws. minlaw. gov. bd/act-details-235. html, April 12, 2020.

［2］　Laws of Bangladesh, "The Navy Ordinance, 1961（Ordinance NO. XXXV Of 1961）", http：//bdlaws. minlaw. gov. bd/act-310. html, April 15, 2020.

护法》（Private Fisheries Protection Act）采取了与印度及巴基斯坦类似的举措，即保留主体条款，但基于国家主体变化对相关名称及表述进行更新替换。根据《1973 年孟加拉法律（修订与声明）法》［The Bangladesh Laws（Revision And Declaration）Act］，除该法第 3 条将相关罚款的货币单位"卢比"（rupees）替换为"塔卡"（Taka）外，原 6 项法条至今仍然生效。立法体现了对私人渔业权利的较集中保护，主要涉及对侵犯私人渔场、渔权的处罚认定及处罚方式，如罚款、没收或拆卸固定发动机，依《1989 年刑事诉讼法典》纳入刑罚等。[1] 虽然这部法律并无与海洋渔业直接相关的条款，但从其第 2 条对"鱼类"的定义包含"贝壳类水生动物"及"龟类"（shell-fish and turtles）来看，该法仍可为涉海相关渔业权益保护提供一定依据。

1950 年，孟加拉国颁布《鱼类养护法（东孟加拉法）》［Protection and Conservation of Fish Act，1950（East Bengal Act）］，旨在为本国水域的鱼类养护提供法律依据。该法共 10 条，除第 10 条已被废止外，其余 9 条分别就所保护鱼类的范围、有权制定相应规则的政府机关、有权禁止鱼类销售的管理机关、特定捕鱼设备的禁止、违背本法的处罚措施及可能刑罚、可能面临逮捕等强制性手段、执行该法人员的公务地位及法律保障等作出了规定。该法经《1982 年鱼类养护（修订）条例》［Protection and Conservation of Fish（Amendment）Ordinance，1982］、《1995 年鱼类养护（修订）法》［Protection and Conservation of Fish（Amendment）Act］、《2002 年鱼类养护（修订）条例》［Protection and Conservation of Fish（Amendment）Ordinance，2002］就规范名称、所涉对象及范围进行了修正或补充，包括删除"东孟加拉"一词，将"东巴基斯坦"替换为"孟加拉国"，将"网"（net）明确为"渔网"（fish net），添加禁止使用单丝合成尼龙纤维渔网条款等。[2]

1959 年，孟加拉国进一步颁布《政府渔业（保护）条例（东巴基斯坦条例）》［Government Fisheries（Protection）Ordinance，（East Pakistan Ordinance）］以划定政府监管的专门渔场，从而保护从事小规模捕捞的底层渔民利益。根据该条例，政府可发布政府公报将相关区域宣布为"卡斯监管渔场"（Khas managed fishery），任何未经授权进入此类渔场及任何其他由政府管理或控制的渔场的捕捞相关行为都不被许可。除同样在关键地名、货币单位等表述上进行修订外，该条例中的 10 项规定主要涉及：条例适用范围、重要术语解释、政府规定

---

［1］ Laws of Bangladesh，"The Private Fisheries Protection Act，1889"，http：//bdlaws. minlaw. gov. bd/act-details-61. html，April 15，2020.

［2］ Laws of Bangladesh，"The Protection and Conservation of Fish Act，1950（East Bengal Act）"，http：//bdlaws. minlaw. gov. bd/act-details-233. html，April 15，2020.

区域内非授权行为的禁止、合法的捕鱼及加工许可的获得、非法捕捞的政府监管授权、豁免对象、刑事处罚条款、相关下级规则的制定等[1]。

2. 孟加拉国独立后的相关立法

（1）《1973 年孟加拉国渔业发展公司法》

1973 年，孟加拉国颁布《孟加拉国渔业发展公司法》（Bangladesh Fisheries Development Corporation Act，以下简称《渔业公司法》）以建立孟加拉国渔业发展公司，并推进孟加拉国的渔业捕捞及相关产业的发展。随着《1973 年渔业公司法》的生效，原《1964 年渔业发展公司条例》（Fisheries Development Corporation Ordinance）、《1973 年孟加拉国渔业发展公司条例》（Bangladesh Fisheries Development Corporation Ordinance）均因无法反映国内渔业的发展现状及立法技术的更新而被废止。

《渔业公司法》共有 23 条，主要围绕渔业公司的成立、职能、管理、董事会、利润、年度预算表、账目和审计等事项作出规定。根据该法，孟加拉国渔业发展中的"鱼类"包括生活在"咸水"或"淡水"中的所有种属的鱼及其他水生动植物，从鲸、海豹、海豚至贝类、蛙类、卵等都涵盖其中；而其"水产行业"则指鱼类的捕捞、养护、分配及销售，包括鱼类及其副产品的生产加工、渔船渔网等捕捞工具的生产及生产方营运、渔业市场、渔港及渔业码头管理等。其个别条款由《1984 年孟加拉国渔业发展公司（修订）条例》[Bangladesh Fisheries Development Corporation（Amendment）Ordinance]进行了修改或删除[2]。

（2）《1983 年海洋渔业条例》

孟加拉国于 1983 年颁布《海洋渔业条例》（Marine Fisheries Ordinance），就"孟加拉国渔业水域"（Bangladesh fisheries waters）中海洋渔业的管理、养护与开发作出专门性规定。该条例共 11 个部分 55 条，主要涉及：（1）条例的适用范围、适用主体及对象；（2）专门性监管机构的授权与运行；（3）海洋捕捞相关执照的颁发与管理；（4）分别针对本国渔船与外国渔船的法律地位与监管措施；（5）被禁止的捕捞方式；（6）海洋生物资源保护的一般制度；（7）获授权监管人员的职能范围与职权行使；（8）违法行为与相应法律程序；等等。

根据该条例，其海洋渔业监管所称的"孟加拉国渔业水域"是指由孟加拉国政府依据《1974 年海域法》宣布的领水及经济区，也包括任何海洋生物资源

---

[1]　Laws of Bangladesh，"Government Fisheries（Protection）Ordinance，1959（East Pakistan Ordinance）"，http：//bdlaws. minlaw. gov. bd/act-details-288. html，April 15，2020.

[2]　Laws of Bangladesh，"Bangladesh Fisheries Development Corporation Act，1973"，http：//bdlaws. minlaw. gov. bd/act-details-436. html，April 15，2020.

管理、养护及开发相关立法基于《1974 年海域法》所覆盖或主张的管辖水域。而该条例指称的"鱼类"则指一切鱼类或非鱼类水生动物，包括贝类、蟹类、龟类、水生哺乳动物以及其卵、鱼苗、幼生体等。而"渔船"则是指任何用于捕捞或运输存储鱼类的船只，包括对捕捞作业提供支持辅助的船只，但仅有部分货物为鱼货的件杂货船不算在其中。可以看到，《海洋渔业条例》所涵盖的"鱼类"范围相对前述的《渔业公司法》较为狭窄，明确将水生植物排除在外，但对参与捕捞作业的船舶类型、吨位等作出了更为细致的划分与认定，同时在海洋资源养护和海洋环境保护方面的专章规定具有较强的时代意义[1]。

（3）其他相关立法

为了对鱼类及相应加工产品的质量进行有效控制，孟加拉国于 1983 年颁布《鱼类和鱼类制品（检验和质量控制）条例》[Fish and Fish Products（Inspection and Quality Control）Ordinance]。该条例共 15 条，主要针对制定和实施关联规则的权力机关、条例执行情况的监督保障、鱼类出口及鱼类制品的处理、鱼类加工和包装厂的建立和运行、违反该条例的处罚措施、相关诉讼的管辖级别等内容作出规定。该条例以孟加拉国首席军法执行官名义发布，在一定程度上体现了孟加拉国对渔业产量增加与渔业产品质量保障的并重立场[2]。

值得一提的是，孟加拉国曾于 1984 年颁布《渔业研究所条例》（Fisheries Research Institute Ordinance）。该条例共 19 条，分别就渔业研究所的成立依据及成立方式、组织结构、主要职能、董事会组建、成员管理、职能委员会、官员任命、经费预算、年度报告等问题作出规定，以实现对原有的地方渔业研究机构的整合和替代。尽管该条例由《1996 年孟加拉国渔业研究所（修订）法》[Bangladesh Fisheries Research Institute（Amendment）Act]进行了修订且当前已被废止，但仍体现出孟加拉国对渔业科研事业的较早关注与投入[3]。

（四）海洋能源相关立法

1923 年颁布的《矿业法》（Mines Act）旨在对矿山监管检查相关法律进行修订和完善。该法共有 9 章 50 条及一项附表，分别就矿山监察员的任命、职能、权限及执行职务所需设施，矿业理事会和委员会的组建、职权及经

---

[1] Laws of Bangladesh, "Marine Fisheries Ordinance, 1983", http://bdlaws. minlaw. gov. bd/act-details-646. html, April 15, 2020.

[2] Laws of Bangladesh, "Fish and Fish Products（Inspection and Quality Control）Ordinance, 1983", http://bdlaws. minlaw. gov. bd/act-details-640. html, April 15, 2020.

[3] Laws of Bangladesh, "The Fisheries Research Institute Ordinance, 1984", http://bdlaws. minlaw. gov. bd/act-details-676. html, April 15, 2020.

费，矿山开采经营与矿山管理，健康及安全规条，劳动时间及雇佣限制，违法行为处罚及程序等作出规定。该法在英印及东巴基斯坦时期分别经 1928年、1935 年、1936 年、1940 年、1945 年、1946 年、1951 年等多个矿业修订法或条例进行修订，并在孟加拉国独立后经《1973 年孟加拉法律（修订与声明）法》、《2005 年矿业（修订）法》［Mines（Amendment）Act］对相关表述及细则进行调整，至今仍为孟加拉国的生效法律文件。《矿业法》并无与海洋矿产开发利用相关的明确规定，但从其第 1 条所指的适用范围来看，在该法适用于孟加拉国全境的情形下，孟加拉国主权海域的矿产资源开发和管理并未被排除在该法适用之外。[1]

《1974 年孟加拉国石油法》（Bangladesh Petroleum Act，以下简称《1974年石油法》）是孟加拉国为便利石油的勘探、开发、开采、生产、加工、提炼和销售等而颁布的专门性立法。该法共 12 条，从石油勘探开发的范围、政府勘探开发利用石油及石油制品的专属性权利、石油开采授权协议、石油勘探开发的监管检查、石油行业从业人员的职责、石油业运营的土地占用、违法行为的处罚措施等方面提供基本规范和指导。该法一经颁布，《1948 年矿山、油田和矿产开发（政府管制）法》［Regulation of Mines，Oil-fields and Mineral Development（Government Control）Act］和《1974 年石油条例》（Petroleum Ordinance）即随之废止。

孟加拉国至今尚无海洋能源开发相关的专门性立法，其对海洋自然资源永久主权的宣示在《1974 年石油法》中已得到明确体现。该法第 1 条特别指明，其适用范围应包含孟加拉国的"经济区"及大陆架，而这一"经济区"及大陆架则与其《1974 年海域法》中划定的管辖海域相一致，同时在第 3 条中就孟加拉国政府在其领土、大陆架及"经济区"内的勘探、开发、利用、生产、加工、提炼及销售石油的专属性权利进行了申明和强调。孟加拉国对其海洋石油资源专属性权利的重视可见一斑，但遗憾的是，除《1976 年孟加拉国石油（修订）条例》［Bangladesh Petroleum（Amendment）Ordinance］对该法作出零星修改外，《1974 年石油法》未见有体现海洋能源开发后续的立法推进。[2]

1985 年，《孟加拉国石油、天然气和矿产公司条例》（Bangladesh Oil，Gas and Mineral Corporation Ordinance）颁布，以设立孟加拉国石油、天然气和矿产公司并对相关附带事项作出规定。该条例共 24 条，主要就公司成立

〔1〕Laws of Bangladesh，"Mines Act，1923"，http：//bdlaws. minlaw. gov. bd/act-details-126. html，April 15，2020.

〔2〕Laws of Bangladesh，"Bangladesh Petroleum Act，1974"，http：//bdlaws. minlaw. gov. bd/act-details-480. html，April 15，2020.

依据及程序、注册资本、董事会组建及职权、相关委员会、公司的职能、下级公司的成立、股份持有及分红、年度预算表、投资基金等创建及运营事项作出安排。[1] 随着这一条例的颁布，此前据《1961 年石油和天然气开发公司条例》（Oil and Gas Development Corporation Ordinance）成立的石油和天然气开发公司、据《1972 年孟加拉国矿产勘探和开发公司令》（Bangladesh Mineral Exploration and Development Corporation Order）成立的孟加拉国矿产勘探和开发公司（Bangladesh Mineral Exploration and Development Corporation）、据《1972 年孟加拉国工业企业（国有化）令》[Bangladesh Industrial Enterprises（Nationalisation）Order]成立的孟加拉国油气公司（Bangladesh Oil and Gas Corporation）、据《1976 年孟加拉国石油公司条例》（Bangladesh Petroleum Corporation Ordinance）成立的相应实体均被解散，其相应业务被全部或部分移交至孟加拉国石油、天然气和矿产公司的管理之下。[2]

（五）海上运输相关立法

1. 《1925 年海上货物运输法》

作为对海上货物运输提单规则重要国际立法成果（《1924 年统一提单若干法律规定的国际公约》，即《海牙规则》）的国内转化，孟加拉国对英印时期的《1925 年海上货物运输法》作出了与巴基斯坦相同的承袭立场。相较于巴基斯坦的历次修订行动，孟加拉国独立后对该法的改动极为有限，除依据《1973 年孟加拉法律（修订与声明）法》对"印度""锡兰""巴基斯坦""中央政府"等涉及主权实体变更的表述有所修正之外，原《1925 年海上货物运输法》的实体性条款得到了全面保留。该法适用于孟加拉国全境，其所附提单相关规则适用于从孟加拉国任何港口至孟加拉国境内或境外任何其他港口的海上货物运输。[3]

---

〔1〕 Laws of Bangladesh, "Bangladesh Oil, Gas and Mineral Corporation Ordinance, 1985", http: // bdlaws. minlaw. gov. bd/act-details-683. html, April 15, 2020.

〔2〕 See Laws of Bangladesh, "Oil and Gas Development Corporation (Repeal) Act, 1974", http: // bdlaws. minlaw. gov. bd/act-details-481. html, April 15, 2020; Laws of Bangladesh, "The Bangladesh Petroleum Corporation Ordinance, 1976", http://bdlaws. minlaw. gov. bd/act-details-538. html, April 15, 2020; Laws of Bangladesh, "Bangladesh Oil, Gas and Mineral Corporation Ordinance, 1985", http://bdlaws. minlaw. gov. bd/act-details-683. html, April 15, 2020.

〔3〕 Laws of Bangladesh, "Carriage of Goods by Sea Act, 1925", http://bdlaws. minlaw. gov. bd/act-details-137. html, April 15, 2020. 关于该法正文及附表内容详见本丛书《印度、巴基斯坦海洋法律体系研究》"印度海洋法律体系"中"海上运输相关立法"部分《1925 年印度海上货物运输法》。

2. 《1983 年孟加拉国商船运输条例》

1983 年，孟加拉国颁布《孟加拉国商船运输条例》（Bangladesh Merchant Shipping Ordinance，以下简称《1983 年商船条例》），与 1976 年颁布的《内陆航运条例》（The Inland Shipping Ordinance）形成互补。在排除军事及政府公务船舶的前提下，《1983 年商船条例》适用于：（1）除《1976 年内陆航运条例》第 2 条下"内陆船"（inland ship）外的所有孟加拉国船舶；（2）孟加拉国境内外所有应依据《1983 年商船条例》注册登记的船舶；（3）所有经《1983 年商船条例》获得沿海航运贸易许可的非孟加拉国船舶；（4）位于孟加拉国领水内的港口或其他位置的所有船舶。

施行至今的《1983 年商船条例》含 13 部分 45 章，共 513 项条文及 1 项附表，其主要内容包括：（1）航运管理机构的组建及分工，航行监管各专门职位的选任与职务；（2）船舶登记与国籍，包括申请程序、登记机关、登记前的检验与测量、船舶不同权属的登记、登记档案的管理、登记证书的签发、船舶转让或抵押或优先权下的临时登记、国籍标志的恰当使用等；（3）租船运输的监管、沿海及远洋航运执照的颁发、无执照时的港口限制、特定船舶使用的限制、船舶管理局登船检查的权力等；（4）船舶航行的适格证书，包括船长及船员证书的认证与颁发、无适格证书或伪造适格证书或遗失适格证书时的处理及违法处罚、外国船员的雇佣、年轻船员的雇佣、船员解雇的情形与条件及补偿、船员的工资待遇、死亡船员的财产处置、船员纪律规则、针对船员的诉讼等；（5）客运船舶的监管规则，包括客运船舶的检验、客船安全证书的核验、对特定旅客的登船限制、特殊客运船舶的专门性规定等；（6）船舶安全相关规范，包括船舶及安全设施建造、无线电设备及无线电服务、基于安全公约的相关认证、载重线及载重线证书、不适航或不安全的船舶的处理等；（7）船舶碰撞或其他航行事故，包括基本航行规则、航行危险的报告义务、接收到遇难船舶信号时的救助义务、碰撞事故的报告与记录、船长在碰撞事故中的协助义务、碰撞损害的判定、碰撞中的人身损害等；（8）船东的责任与海上留置权，包括船东的责任限制、海上保险的一般规则、海上留置权的行使及优先性等；（9）航行中的爆炸、火灾与伤亡；（10）沉船处理与海难救助；（11）渔船或帆船的专门规定；（12）航海日志相关规定；等等。

随着《1983 年商船条例》的生效，1894 年至 1937 年各《商船运输法》（Merchant Shipping Act）、《1900 年商船运输（船东及其他方责任）法》〔Merchant Shipping（Lieability of Ship-owners and Others）Act〕、《1914 年商船运输（证书）法》〔Merchant Shipping（Certificates）Act〕、《1940 年商船运输

（救助）法》［Merchant Shipping（Salvage）Act］等 20 项英印时期的相关立法，以及《1947 年商船船员（诉讼）法》［The Merchant Seamen（Litigation）Act］、《1982 年孟加拉国商船（登记）条例》［The Bangladesh Merchant Ships（Registration）Ordinance］等 4 部孟加拉国法律均被废止。尽管孟加拉国先后于 1988 年、1995 年及 2004 年出台《孟加拉国商船运输（修订）法》［Bangladesh Merchant Shipping（Amendment）Act］对《1983 年商船条例》中的部分术语、时限、金钱数额等作出修改，但时至今日，这一"条例"层级的立法成果仍然是该国在海商事领域最为重要且全面的法典性文件[1]。

值得一提的是，依据《1976 年内陆航运条例》第 2 条，该法所称"内陆水域"既包括在孟加拉国境内的运河、河流、湖泊及其他可通航水域，也包括通过政府公报被该国宣布为符合该条例所指"内陆水域"的部分潮汐水域。由此，《1976 年内陆航运条例》也可能在特定情形下因涉及与海相通的潮汐水域而适用于海上航运[2]。

3. 港口管理相关立法

（1）《1908 年港口法》与《1948 年港口保护（特别措施）法》

与巴基斯坦相同，孟加拉国《1908 年港口法》也是在继承原《1908 年印度港口法》（Indian Ports Act）基础上的部分修正与更新。一方面，孟加拉国保留了英印时期 1923 年及 1925 年《印度港口（修订）法》［Indian Ports（Amendmnet）Act］在第 6 条中对船舶港口油污排放及运油船舶特别管理规定的增补；另一方面，同样依据《1973 年孟加拉国法律（修订与声明）案》对国家、政府、货币等名称或单位进行替换，同时就所涉港口范围、时限规定等作出调整[3]。

《1948 年港口保护（特别措施）法》则是对东巴基斯坦时期巴基斯坦立法的承袭。除将"巴基斯坦""中央政府"等措辞删除替换外，孟加拉国并未对该法的主体条款作出修改，只是在第 1 条中明确将该法优先适用于吉大港港口，同时通过政府公报的方式为该法延展适用于其他港口留下余地[4]。

---

［1］ Laws of Bangladesh, "The Bangladesh Merchant Shipping Ordinance, 1983", http：//bdlaws. min-law. gov. bd/act-details-642. html, April 15, 2020.

［2］ Laws of Bangladesh, "The Inland Shipping Ordinance, 1976", hhttp：//bdlaws. minlaw. gov. bd/act-details-531. html, April 15, 2020.

［3］ Laws of Bangladesh, "Ports Act, 1908", http：//bdlaws. minlaw. gov. bd/act-details-89. html, April 15, 2020. 有关该法当前 8 章共 69 条规定的具体内容，详见本丛书《印度、巴基斯坦海洋法律体系研究》"印度海洋法律体系"中"海上运输相关立法"部分《1908 年印度港口法》。

［4］ Laws of Bangladesh, "The Protection of Ports（Special Measures）Act, 1948", http：//bdlaws. minlaw. gov. bd/act-details-226. html, April 15, 2020.

这与其《1908 年港口法》所规定的港口适用范围基本一致。根据《1908 年港口法》所载附表，其修订后所适用的孟加拉国主要港口仅有吉大港与查尔纳港（Chalna）两处。[1]

（2）《1976 年吉大港港口管理局条例》与《勐拉港港口管理局条例》

《1976 年吉大港港口管理局条例》（Chittagong Port Authority Ordinance）的颁布，意在为吉大港港口设立一个负责其监管、维护和发展及相关事项的管理机构。该条例共有 7 章 53 条，主要内容包括管理局的设立程序、基本权力与应有职能、管理局内部官员的选任与管理局主席的权力、管理局基金的成立与使用、违背本条例相关规定的处罚及相应程序等。原英印时期的《1914 年吉大港港口法》随之被该条例所取代。孟加拉国于 1995 年颁布《吉大港港口管理局（修订）法》［Chittagong Port Authority（Amendment）Act］，主要就 1976 年条例中部分细则的准确性及可适用性作出修订，如将第 25 条关于货物交由管理局保管的起计期限从原来"1 个月"的表述修改为更为准确的"30 天"。[2]

孟加拉国于同年颁布了《勐拉港港口管理局条例》（Mongla Port Authority Ordinance），从而为管理勐拉港相关事务并维持该港口有效运作设立专门性管理机构。该条例从篇幅、结构到宗旨、内容都与《吉大港港口管理局条例》别无二致，同样以 7 章 53 条就在勐拉港设置专门管理机构的组织结构、人员构成、职务职能、基金运转、执行保障等作出相应规定。该条例同样于 1995 年，经由《勐拉港港口管理局（修订）法》［Mongla Port Authority（Amendment）Act］，基于几乎完全一致的考量对相似条款进行了调整与完善。[3]

---

[1] Laws of Bangladesh, "The First Schedule", http：//bdlaws. minlaw. gov. bd/upload/act/89 _ _ _ Schedule. pdf, April 15, 2020. 有关该法当前共 9 条规定的具体内容，详见本丛书《印度、巴基斯坦海洋法律体系研究》"巴基斯坦海洋法律体系"中"海上运输相关立法"部分《1948 年港口保护（特别措施）法》。

[2] Laws of Bangladesh, "Chittagong Port Authority Ordinance, 1976", http：//bdlaws. minlaw. gov. bd/act-details-527. html, April 15, 2020.

[3] Laws of Bangladesh, "Mongla Port Authority Ordinance, 1976", http：//bdlaws. minlaw. gov. bd/act-details-528. html, April 15, 2020.

四、缔结和加入的国际海洋法条约

（一）联合国框架下的海洋法公约

孟加拉国未签署 1958 年日内瓦海洋法公约体系下的《领海及毗连区公约》、《公海公约》、《捕鱼及养护公海生物资源公约》和《大陆架公约》中的任何一项。

2000 年 7 月 21 日，孟加拉国批准了《联合国海洋法公约》，并于同日批准了《关于执行 1982 年 12 月 10 日〈联合国海洋法公约〉第十一部分的协定》。2012 年 12 月 5 日，孟加拉国亦对《执行 1982 年 12 月 10 日〈联合国海洋法公约〉有关养护和管理跨界鱼类种群和高度洄游鱼类种群的规定的协定》作出批准。但孟加拉国未加入《国际海底管理局特权和豁免议定书》，也非《关于国际海洋法法庭特权和豁免的协定》的缔约方。[1]

2009 年 12 月，孟加拉国进一步就《公约》提出了长达 10 项的声明，表示：第一，依据孟加拉国政府之理解，《公约》从未授权任何其他国家在未经沿岸国同意的情形下，在沿岸国的专属经济及大陆架进行军事训练或演习，尤其是在其中使用武器或爆炸物。第二，任何他国的国内立法或基于签署或批准《公约》所提出的声明都不能对孟加拉国政府产生拘束力。孟加拉国保留在适当时候对所有此类立法或声明发表其立场的权利。在他国的海洋主张与相关国际法规则不符并损害孟加拉国在海洋区域的主权权利及管辖时，孟加拉国对《公约》的批准绝不构成对其他已签署或批准《公约》国家的海洋主张的承认。第三，军舰行使在他国领海的无害通过权应该是和平的。有效且迅捷的交流方式的获取并不困难，因而要求军舰在行使无害通过权之前进行通知是合理的，也并不与《公约》相悖。某些国家已经对此类通知作出了要求。孟加拉国保留就此问题立法的权利。第四，孟加拉国认为，

---

〔1〕 See UN Treaty Collection, "Chronological Lists of Ratifications of, Accessions and Successions to the Convention and the related Agreements", https：//www. un. org/depts/los/reference_ files/ chronological_ lists_ of_ ratifications. htm#The% 20United% 20Nations% 20Convention% 20on% 20the% 20Law% 20of% 20the% 20Sea, April 25, 2020; UN Treaty Collection, "Protocol on the Privileges and Immunities of the International Seabed Authority", https：//treaties. un. org/pages/ ViewDetails. aspx? src = TREATY&mtdsg_ no = XXI-9&chapter = 21&clang = _ en, April 25, 2020.

对于核动力船或运载有核材料或其他本质上危险及有毒物质的船舶，上述的通知要求是必需的。并且，此类船舶在无必要授权时将不被允许进入孟加拉国水域。第五，对于由军舰、海军辅助舰船、其他由国家所有或营运的船舶或飞机以及用于非商业性政府服务的船舶或飞机所造成的海洋环境污染，孟加拉国认为，该国将不得因《公约》第236条所规定的主权豁免而减轻其应承担的国家责任或对损害的赔偿责任。第六，孟加拉国对《公约》的批准并不意味着对其他《公约》当事方领土主张的事实承认或接受，也并不意味着对任何陆地或海洋边界的自动承认。第七，孟加拉国政府不受其他国家在签署、接受、批准或加入《公约》时所做任何声明或宣告的约束，并保留在任何时候对此类声明发表立场的权利。第八，孟加拉国声明，在不违背《公约》第303条的前提下，非经事先通知及许可，任何在本国主权及管辖权覆盖范围内发现的考古及历史性器物都不应被转移。第九，孟加拉国政府将在适当的时候就第287条及298条所规定的争端解决作出声明。第十，孟加拉国政府将对本国法律及法规进行全面审查，从而使其与《公约》规定相一致。

孟加拉国随后依据《公约》第287条第1款，就与印度及缅甸间的海洋争端作出专门声明，表示对孟加拉国与印度间以及孟加拉国与缅甸间在孟加拉湾的海洋划界，接受国际海洋法法庭的管辖。[1]

（二）国际海事组织框架下的相关公约

孟加拉国于1976年3月27日签署《1948年国际海事组织公约》，该公约于同日对孟加拉国生效。随后，孟加拉国在国际海事组织框架下加入了总计20多项国际海事条约，主要涉及船舶管理、防治海洋污染、海上航行安全、海员管理等海事安全及合作事宜。[2]

其中，与船舶管理有关的条约主要包括：于1978年8月10日对孟加拉国生效的《1966年国际船舶载重线公约》、于2003年3月18日对孟加拉国生效的《〈1966年国际载重线公约〉1988年议定书》、于1982年7月18日对孟加拉国生效的《1969年国际船舶吨位丈量公约》等。

---

〔1〕　UN Treaty Collection，"Declarations and Reservations"，https：//treaties. un. org/Pages/ViewDe-tailsIII. aspx？ src ＝ TREATY&mtdsg_ no ＝ XXI-6&chapter ＝ 21&Temp ＝ mtdsg3&clang ＝ _ en # EndDec，April 25，2020.

〔2〕　International Maritime Organization，"Status of IMO Treaties"，https：//wwwcdn. imo. org/localre-sources/en/About/Conventions/StatusOfConventions/Status% 20-% 202021. pdf，January 23，2021.

与防治海洋污染有关的条约主要包括：2018 年 9 月 7 日对孟加拉国生效的《控制船舶有害防污底系统国际公约》、于 1982 年 2 月 14 日对孟加拉国生效的《1969 年国际干预公海油污事故公约》、于 2004 年 10 月 23 日对孟加拉国生效的《1990 年国际油污防备、反应和合作公约》、于 2003 年 3 月 18 日对孟加拉国生效的《关于 1973 年国际防止船舶造成污染公约的 1978 年议定书》及其附则Ⅲ、Ⅳ、Ⅴ[1]、于 2005 年 5 月 19 日对孟加拉国生效的《经1978 年议定书修订的 1973 年国际防止船舶造成污染公约的 1997 年议定书》。

与海上航行安全有关的条约主要包括：于 1978 年 5 月 10 日对其生效的《1972 年国际海上避碰规则公约》、于 1978 年 12 月 10 日对其生效的《1971年特种业务客船协定》及其 1973 年议定书、分别于 1981 年 12 月及 2002 年12 月对其生效的《1974 年国际海上人命安全公约》及其 1988 年议定书、于1993 年 9 月 17 日对其生效的《国际海事卫星组织公约》、于 2000 年 9 月 21日对其生效的《1965 年便利国际海上运输公约》、于 2001 年 8 月 8 日对其生效的《1979 年国际海上搜寻救助公约》、于 2005 年 9 月 7 日对其生效的《制止危及海上航行安全非法行为公约》、于 2005 年 9 月 7 日对其生效的《制止危及大陆架固定平台安全非法行为议定书》等。

与船员管理有关的条约主要包括：于 1981 年 12 月 6 日签署、1984 年 4月 28 日对其生效的《1978 年海员培训、发证和值班标准国际公约》等[2]。

（三）对外缔结的其他条约

1. 《建立印度洋金枪鱼委员会协定》

《建立印度洋金枪鱼委员会协定》于 1996 年 3 月 27 日生效，其旨在设立一个政府间组织——印度洋金枪鱼管理委员会以统筹印度洋地区的海洋生物资源，并通过促进缔约国与非缔约国之间合作的方式，实现保护海洋资源与各个国家可持续发展的目标[3]。孟加拉国于 2018 年 4 月 24 日批准该协定，

---

[1] 其中，附则Ⅲ于 2003 年 3 月 1 日对孟加拉国生效，附则Ⅳ于 2003 年 9 月 27 日对孟加拉国生效，附则Ⅴ于 2003 年 3 月 18 日对孟加拉国生效。

[2] See International Maritime Organization, "Status of IMO Treaties", https：//wwwcdn. imo. org/localresources/en/About/Conventions/StatusOfConventions/Status% 20-% 202021. pdf, January 23, 2021.

[3] Indian Ocean Tuna Commission, "The Commssion", https：//www. iotc. org/node/1, August 12, 2020.

成为该协定当事方。[1]

2. 双边海事条约

孟加拉国与印度双边关系良好，印度积极帮助孟加拉国推进国家建设。2019 年 6 月，孟加拉国与印度签署《沿岸航运协定》（Costal Shipping Agreement）以加强两国间的沿海贸易及航运的协作与发展。同年 10 月 5 日，孟加拉国与印度签署《标准操作程序协定》（Standard Operation Procedure Agreement），以期实现两国船舶地位的平等对待与规则对接，从而密切两国间沿海贸易交往，有效改善两国的海上货物运输的现状。[2]

---

[1] Ecolex, "The Agreement for the Establishment of the Indian Ocean Tuna Commission", https://www. ecolex. org/details/treaty/agreement-for-the-establishment-of-the-indian-ocean-tuna-commission-tre-001227/? q = + Indian + Ocean + Tuna + Commission, April 25, 2020.

[2] The Dollarbusiness, "India, Bangladesh to Enhance Bilateral Trade through Costal Shipping", https://www. thedollarbusiness. com/news/india-bangladesh-to-enhance-bilateral-trade-through-coastal-shipping/34564, April 25, 2020.

五、海洋争端解决

位于印度洋东北部、面积约为 217 万平方公里的孟加拉湾，是孟加拉国主张其海洋权利的首要目标。孟加拉国与印度、缅甸呈三角形之势，分别处于孟加拉湾的北部、西部和东部。这一特殊的地理分布使得三国围绕孟加拉湾地区的海洋划界、海洋资源权属等问题多有龃龉。尽管三国都表现出利用国际仲裁或司法机制解决海洋争端的开放立场并积极实践，但裁决结果的遗留问题仍然令人困惑，并使国家的后继海洋开发实践面临障碍。

（一）与印度间通过国际仲裁解决的海洋争端

孟加拉国人口稠密，同时自然资源又十分有限。依据《公约》，孟加拉国有权主张 12 海里的领海和 200 海里的专属经济区，但相关海洋主张均与其邻国印度和缅甸相重叠。为最大限度也最高效率地占有并利用海洋资源，孟加拉国和印度自 1974 年以来即着手与海洋边界划定相关的谈判。至 2009 年，尽管已经历了 10 轮的漫长谈判，两国间的海洋争议解决仍未获实质进展。2009 年 10 月 8 日，两国同意组成《公约》附件七下的仲裁庭，依据《公约》第 15 条、第 74 条及第 83 条相关规定就两国在孟加拉湾的领海、专属经济区、200 海里以内及以外的大陆架界限作出划定。[1]

孟加拉国及印度均对本次仲裁庭的裁决结果表示认同。[2] 孟加拉国外交大臣阿里（Abul Hassan Mahmood Ali）称其为"孟加拉国和印度人民友谊的胜利和双赢局面"，而印度外交部则表示这一"长期悬而未决问题"的裁定，"进一步增进了印度和孟加拉国之间的相互了解和善意"。[3] 就孟加拉国而言，尽管其在大陆架上的权利主张基本未获仲裁庭承认，却将专属经济区的面积扩展了近 1.9 万平方公里，同时使本国关键主张之一的大陆架延伸出口获得了确认。

---

〔1〕 Permanent Court of Arbitration, "Bay of Bengal Maritime Boundary Arbitration between Bangladesh and India", https://pca-cpa.org/cn/cases/18/, March 25, 2020.

〔2〕 有关两国在"孟加拉湾海洋边界仲裁案"中的争端背景、双方主张、争议焦点及仲裁结果，详见本丛书《印度、巴基斯坦海洋法律体系研究》"印度海洋法律体系"中"六、印度海洋争端的解决实践"下的"（二）通过国际仲裁解决的海洋争端"部分。

〔3〕 Durham University, "Boundary News-Arbitral Tribunal Delimits Bangladesh-India Maritime Boundary", https://www.dur.ac.uk/ibru/news/boundary_news/?itemno=21685&rehref=%2Fibru%2Fnews%2F&resubj=Boundary+news+Headlines, March 25, 2020.

总体而言，一方面，该仲裁裁决为两国间海上边界的位置及走向提供了法律指引，有助于明晰两国渔民的捕捞范围并减少越境行为，从而减少双方海军和海警力量的对峙，同时两国在各自管辖海域的渔业和海洋资源的勘探和开发活动都得到保障，孟加拉湾油气开采的整体前景得以开辟。但另一方面，"灰色区域"的划定难免对两国在特定范围内厘定海洋权益界限产生阻碍，同时随着海平面上升、海洋地理标志消失、海岸线不稳定等问题的凸显，亦可能为两国海洋边界的争端再起埋下隐患。[1]

（二）与缅甸间通过国际司法解决的海洋争端

孟加拉国于 1971 年独立时继承了巴基斯坦与缅甸签订的《1966 年纳夫河边界协定》（Naaf River Boundary Agreement），但该协定所划边界仅及于纳夫河三角洲，止于通向孟加拉湾的河口处。自 1974 年起，两国就领海、专属经济区、大陆架界限的划定陆续进行了多轮谈判，其中于 1974 年至 1986 年共开展了 8 轮双边谈判，后于 2008 年至 2010 年再度开展了 6 轮双边谈判。

在前后两阶段的系列谈判中，两国分别于 1974 年 11 月及 2008 年 4 月达成了《孟加拉国代表团与缅甸代表团关于两国间海洋边界划定的协议纪要》（Agreed Minutes between the Bangladesh Delegation and the Burmese Delegation regarding the Delimitation of the Maritime Boundary between the Two Countries，以下简称《1974 年协议纪要》）及《孟加拉国代表团与缅甸代表团关于两国间海洋边界划定会议的协议纪要》（Agreed Minutes of the Meeting held between the Bangladesh Delegation and the Myanmar Delegation regarding the Delimitation of the Maritime Boundaries between the Two Countries，以下简称《2008 年会议纪要》）。《1974 年协议纪要》所附的"专门地图 114 号"（Special Chart 114）将两国海洋边界初步标注为一条与缅甸若开邦（Rakhine）海岸平行、与该海岸及圣马丁岛距离相等的线。《2008 年会议纪要》则对上述边界进行重申和明晰，进一步为其设定了具体的经纬度坐标，同时对划界所涉海洋地形的岛屿地位作出识别和确认。[2]

2002 年至 2007 年，孟加拉湾地区被探明存在丰富的烃气。这一方面成为两国于 2008 年重启海洋边界谈判的契机与动力，另一方面却也令两国在谈

---

〔1〕 American Society of International Law, "Annex VII Arbitral Tribunal Delimits Maritime Boundary Between Bangladesh and India in the Bay of Bengal", https：//www.asil.org/insights/volume/18/issue/20/annex-vii-arbitral-tribunal-delimits-maritime-boundary-between#_ edn10, March 25, 2020.

〔2〕 Judgement of 14 March 2012, Dispute Concerning Delimitation of The Maritime Boundary between Bangladesh and Myanmar in the Bay of Bengal (Bangladesh/Myanmar), ITLOS, p. 21, pp. 24-27.

判中的利益交锋更为尖锐，且难以满足于谈判的缓慢推进。从能源需求来看，孟加拉国国内受困于频繁的能源断供问题，急需寻求新的能源来缓解国内的能源短缺，而缅甸则致力于向中国、印度、泰国等周边国家出口更多的能源。就在《2008 年会议纪要》出台数月后，缅甸派海军护卫 4 艘考察船前往圣马丁岛西南约 50 海里处的争议海域进行勘探性钻井作业。孟加拉国则呼吁缅甸在两国海洋边界划定前暂停钻井，并出动 3 艘军舰对缅方实施武力威胁。[1] 2009 年 10 月，孟加拉国要求依据《公约》附件七启动仲裁程序，但缅甸倾向于将争端提交至国际海洋法法庭，同时继续展开双边谈判。2009年年底，两国分别依据《公约》第 287 条提交声明，同意将其海洋划界争端提交至国际海洋法法庭解决。

1. 海洋划界方法的适用

争端双方对应适用何种方法划定其领海、专属经济区及大陆架的分界线存在重大分歧。孟加拉国主张适用角平分线法，尤其应在专属经济区及大陆架划界时适用 215 度方位角线；而缅甸要求适用"等距离/相关情况"法划定一条通用的分界线。法庭认为：（1）角平分线法无法使孟加拉湾海岸向南突出的地形得到充分考虑，而"等距离/相关情况"法才是应适用于两国专属经济区及大陆架划界的适当方式；（2）法庭有义务对两国间的 200 海里外大陆架界限作出划定，且《公约》第 83 条对 200 海里外大陆架的划界应同等适用，200 海里外大陆架的划界方法不应区别于 200 海里内大陆架，因此"等距离/相关情况"法也同等适用于两国间 200 海里外大陆架的划定。[2]

由此，法庭采用了与国际法院在"黑海海洋划界案"中如出一辙的划界步骤：第一步，基于两国海岸地形及数学计算划定一条临时的等距离线；第二步，判断是否存在要求调整临时等距离线的相关情况，并据之调整至更为公平的结果；第三步，审查调整后的分界线是否会造成两国相关海岸线长度及海洋区域分配在比例上的明显失衡。[3]

2. 关于领海的划界

为使《公约》第 15 条得以适用，法庭认为在适用等距离原则之前，应

〔1〕 Ravi A. Balaram, "Case Study: The Myanmar and Bangladesh Maritime Boundary Dispute in the Bay of Bengal and Its Implications for South China Sea Claims", https://journals.sagepub.com/doi/full/10.1177/186810341203100304, March 3, 2020.

〔2〕 Judgement of 14 March 2012, Dispute Concerning Delimitation of The Maritime Boundary between Bangladesh and Myanmar in the Bay of Bengal (Bangladesh/Myanmar), ITLOS, pp. 62-64, pp. 101-103, p. 117.

〔3〕 Judgement of 14 March 2012, Dispute Concerning Delimitation of The Maritime Boundary between Bangladesh and Myanmar in the Bay of Bengal (Bangladesh/Myanmar), ITLOS, pp. 67-68.

先考虑是否存在与本区域相关的"历史性所有权或其他特殊情况"。这一做法似乎与"先确定等距离线、再考虑特殊情况"的顺序相悖,但法庭未能阐述其背离国际法院"卡塔尔和巴林之间海洋划界和领土问题案"在先实践的原因。法庭未能发现任何"历史性所有权",就对圣马丁岛是否构成特殊情况进行了分析。在否定圣马丁岛构成《公约》第15条"特殊情况"的结论下,法庭以一条等距离线划定了两国间的领海边界,该边界走向与《1974年协议纪要》的附图基本一致。[1] 所划定领海界限的基点坐标如第Ⅰ部分表3所示。[2]

第Ⅰ部分 表3 孟加拉国与缅甸领海界限基点坐标

序号	纬度(北)	经度(东)
1	20° 42′15.8″	92°22′07.2″
2	20° 40′45.0″	92°20′29.0″
3	20° 39′51.0″	92° 21′11.5″
4	20° 37′13.5″	92° 23′42.3″
5	20° 35′26.7″	92° 24′58.5″
6	20° 33′17.8″	92° 25′46.0″
7	20° 26′11.3″	92° 24′52.4″
8	20° 22′46.1″	92° 24′09.1″

3. 关于专属经济区与大陆架的划界

按照前述确定的"等距离/相关情况"法,法庭展开的步骤及作出的判定如下:

首先,法庭立足于缅甸择定的5个基点及法庭所择定的1个新基点划定了一条临时等距离线。法庭认为,由于圣马丁岛位于双方陆地边界的缅甸一侧的大陆的正前方,将该岛作为基点将导致分界线阻碍缅甸海岸向海洋方向的延伸。鉴于其可能导致分界线的不当扭曲,法庭排除了圣马丁岛转而寻求

---

〔1〕 Judgement of 14 March 2012, Dispute Concerning Delimitation of The Maritime Boundary between Bangladesh and Myanmar in the Bay of Bengal (Bangladesh/Myanmar), ITLOS, pp. 43-47.

〔2〕 有关该领海界限的位置及走向的示意图,参见 Judgement of 14 March 2012, Dispute Concerning Delimitation of The Maritime Boundary between Bangladesh and Myanmar in the Bay of Bengal (Bangladesh/Myanmar), ITLOS, p. 52。

其他的基点定位。[1]

其次，法庭在审查是否存在影响公平结果的"相关情况"时发现，由于孟加拉国的海岸在整体上呈现"明显的内凹"，临时等距离线确实会对孟加拉国的海洋延伸产生截断效应，若不经调整将无法达到《公约》第74条及第83条所要求的公平结果，孟加拉国海岸的内凹因此可构成需要调整的"相关情况"。这一"相关情况"被认为同时影响了200海里外大陆架的划界结果，因而需要与200海里内专属经济区及大陆架界限同步调整。[2] 在这一阶段，法庭再次否定了圣马丁岛在划界中的效力，认定其阻碍缅甸向海洋延伸的结果在12海里外将更为严重，因而无法作为"相关情况"被纳入考量。[3]

为应对孟加拉国海岸的内凹情况，法庭认为，双方在200海里内的专属经济区及大陆架的临时分界线应从坐标点11（X）（20°03′32.0″N，91°50′31.8″E）起调整为215度方位角线，直至从孟加拉国领海基线量起的200海里处；而双方在200海里外大陆架的临时分界线应调整为一条以215度方位角继续延伸的测地线，直至可能影响第三国权利的区域为止。[4]

最后，法庭就是否存在比例失衡进行了考察。依据法庭的裁判，双方相关海岸线长度的比例为1∶1.42，略有利于缅甸；而双方所获分配的海洋区域比例约为1∶1.54，略有利于缅甸。因而，在法庭看来，并不存在明显的比例失衡，也无须就所划界限进行调整。[5]

值得注意的是，法庭在处理"相关情况"时所适用的215度方位角线恰恰是被法庭所否定的、由孟加拉国早前基于角平分线法所主张的分界线。[6]法庭未能阐明其采用这一方位角数值的原因，也未就该方位角线的划界过程

---

[1] Judgement of 14 March 2012, Dispute Concerning Delimitation of The Maritime Boundary between Bangladesh and Myanmar in the Bay of Bengal (Bangladesh/Myanmar), ITLOS, p. 73.

[2] Judgement of 14 March 2012, Dispute Concerning Delimitation of The Maritime Boundary between Bangladesh and Myanmar in the Bay of Bengal (Bangladesh/Myanmar), ITLOS, pp. 81-82, p. 87, p. 118.

[3] Judgement of 14 March 2012, Dispute Concerning Delimitation of The Maritime Boundary between Bangladesh and Myanmar in the Bay of Bengal (Bangladesh/Myanmar), ITLOS, p. 86.

[4] Judgement of 14 March 2012, Dispute Concerning Delimitation of The Maritime Boundary between Bangladesh and Myanmar in the Bay of Bengal (Bangladesh/Myanmar), ITLOS, pp. 88-90.

[5] Judgement of 14 March 2012, Dispute Concerning Delimitation of The Maritime Boundary between Bangladesh and Myanmar in the Bay of Bengal (Bangladesh/Myanmar), ITLOS, p. 126.

[6] 有关调整后的分界线位置及走向的示意图，参见 Judgement of 14 March 2012, Dispute Concerning Delimitation of The Maritime Boundary between Bangladesh and Myanmar in the Bay of Bengal (Bangladesh/Myanmar), ITLOS, p. 91。

作出解释，甚至在 200 海里外大陆架划界时排除了任何其他地质或地形情况而直接适用了这一方位角。这一可能前后矛盾的做法以及判决中未能明晰的理据，都使得法庭在本案中对"等距离/相关情况"法的适用遭受一定的批评和质疑。[1]

4. 关于"灰色区域"的划定

法庭在本案中的划界也创造了所谓的"灰色区域"。这一"灰色区域"在距孟加拉国海岸 200 海里以外，但距缅甸海岸 200 海里以内的范围，且位于所划分界线的孟加拉国一侧。这导致孟加拉国大陆架权利与缅甸专属经济区权利在该区域的重叠，即对于这一超出孟加拉国专属经济区但仍在缅甸专属经济区内的"灰色区域"，海洋分界线划分的是双方有关大陆架海床和底土的权利，但并不限制缅甸有关专属经济区的权利，尤其是其对上覆水域的权利。[2] 在法庭看来，大陆架制度总是与其他海洋区域制度并存的，比如公海制度及其他国家在公海的自由。因而，在沿海国履行《公约》有关"适当顾及"他国权利及义务的前提下，这一海洋区域的权利重叠也可以在双方协商下得到较好解决。[3]

但法庭的这一乐观期待并不能完全消除"灰色区域"所带来的有关判决执行的困难以及使局势更为复杂的风险。一则，公海上并不存在所谓"专属性"的权利，但沿海国对专属经济区及大陆架都享有"专属性"的主权权利，非经其许可他国不得勘探和开发其内的自然资源。二则，依据《公约》第 56 条，专属经济区的权利也涉及海床和底土。在专属经济区的范围同时包含海床及其上覆水域的情形下，"灰色区域"的存在将导致概念上的困境。三则，"灰色区域"的存在也无疑将带来沿海国的管辖权冲突，并由此引发在判决执行中的进一步争端。四则，该"灰色区域"与前述孟加拉国和印度两国在"孟加拉湾海洋边界仲裁案"中所划定的"灰色区域"存在重叠，从

[1] See Separate Opinion of Judge Cot, Dispute Concerning Delimitation of The Maritime Boundary between Bangladesh and Myanmar in the Bay of Bengal (Bangladesh/Myanmar), ITLOS, p. 189; Separate Opinion of Judge Gao, Dispute Concerning Delimitation of The Maritime Boundary between Bangladesh and Myanmar in the Bay of Bengal (Bangladesh/Myanmar), ITLOS, pp. 208-209; Dispute Concerning Delimitation of The Maritime Boundary between Bangladesh and Myanmar in the Bay of Bengal (Bangladesh/Myanmar), ITLOS, p. 139.

[2] 有关该"灰色区域"的示意图，参见 Judgement of 14 March 2012, Dispute Concerning Delimitation of The Maritime Boundary between Bangladesh and Myanmar in the Bay of Bengal (Bangladesh/Myanmar), ITLOS, p. 122。

[3] Judgement of 14 March 2012, Dispute Concerning Delimitation of The Maritime Boundary between Bangladesh and Myanmar in the Bay of Bengal (Bangladesh/Myanmar), ITLOS, p. 463, pp. 474-475.

而可能在事实上使孟加拉湾周边海洋局势更为复杂。[1]

总体而言，孟加拉国与缅甸间的该海洋划界案是国际海洋法法庭受理的第一个海洋划界案，也是经由国际法庭划定200海里外大陆架界限的第一个国际海洋争端。尽管法庭未完全肯定两国在《1974年协议纪要》及《2008年会议纪要》中初步协定的界限，也未接受双方默示或事实上同意的界限，但两国都表示了对国际海洋法法庭判决的接受和支持，并声明将进行油气资源的合作开发。

但正如国际社会对该判决留白及"灰色区域"实践的担忧，孟缅两国近年来在该海域有再起争端的征兆。2018年10月，缅甸政府在其官网公布的地图上把圣马丁岛标注为己国领土。尽管后来网站删除了该地图，孟加拉国外交部仍于2019年2月紧急召见了缅甸驻达卡代办，并递交了措辞强烈的外交信函，严厉谴责缅甸政府将圣马丁岛不当标注为本国领土的行为。[2] 与此同时，尽管孟加拉国和缅甸的能源需求目标各有不同，但两者对天然气等自然资源的需要规模仍然与日俱增，两国对内补缺与对外输出的能源需求也使得围绕专属经济区及大陆架的能源开发摩擦无可避免且难以降温。

---

〔1〕 Yoshifumi Tanaka, *Predictability and Flexibility in the Law of Maritime Delimitation* (Second Edition), Oxford, Hart Publishing, 2019, pp. 134-135.

〔2〕 Dhaka Tribune, "Myanmar Again Shows Saint Martin's As Its Territory", https：//www. dhakatribune. com/bangladesh/foreign-affairs/2019/02/14/myanmar-again-shows-st-martin-s-as-its-territory, March 25，2020.

六、国际海洋合作

（一）海洋防务合作

孟加拉国海军于 1972 年 4 月 7 日成立，最初仅有 12 名军官和 1000 名海员，其中大部分曾在巴基斯坦海军服役。从仅有 6 艘缴获的快艇和部分小型武器艰难开局，孟加拉国海军逐渐发展成为一支 2 万人左右服务于沿海及内河安全的防御力量。

由于在地理上并未跨越任何海上主航道，国际社会并未对孟加拉国海域的海盗活动给予较多关注。事实上，从偷窃渔民的渔货和渔网，到盗窃系泊缆绳、锌阳极板等船舶设施配件及其他价值较高的船上储备，再到劫持渔船甚至绑架渔民以索取赎金，孟加拉国海域的犯罪行为有不断升级恶化的风险。鉴于孟加拉国的海上安保力量在防范和遏制相关海上犯罪时收效甚微，有学者提出，如同索马里海盗的成形轨迹，上述对小型渔船的袭击可能最终演变成对超级油轮的海盗行为。2006 年，国际商会的国际海事局（International Maritime Bureau，IMB）也将孟加拉国吉大港列为"世界上最危险的港口"。[1] 由此，通过与他国的海洋防务合作以加强对自身海军的实力建设、应对海上犯罪的猖獗态势，已成为孟加拉国海洋建设战略中的重要一环。

1. 与印度的合作

尽管孟加拉国并非印度所划定的"首要海洋利益区"，但对孟加拉国而言，无论是出于地缘关联还是基于立国背景，印度都无疑是其寻求海洋防务合作和信赖关系的首选目标。除了通过参谋人员会谈及其他交流媒介定期互动，印度海军现役军官和退役军官还每年派员参加为纪念 1971 年解放战争而在孟加拉国举行的胜利日庆祝活动。[2]

2014 年，孟加拉国受邀参加了由印度举办的"米兰"（Milan）海上军演，并在军演中的人道主义援助和救灾国际讨论会（HADR）上分享了本国在处理飓风、地震和海啸等灾难中的第一手经验。作为印度的"品牌"军演项目，

---

〔1〕 Global Security. org, "Bangladesh Navy", https：//www. globalsecurity. org/military/world/bangla-desh/ navy. htm, May 13, 2020.

〔2〕 India Today, "India Navy Chief Admiral Sunil Lanba Visits Bangladesh for Multilateral Naval Exer-cise：Highlights", https：//www. indiatoday. in/education-today/gk-current-affairs/story/navy-chief-visits-to-bangladesh-for-naval-exercise-1095081-2017-11-27, May 13, 2020.

"米兰"军演于 1995 年开始举办，旨在建立一个有效的论坛，以讨论印度洋地区共同关切的问题，并加强友好海军之间更深层次的合作。孟加拉国积极利用这一平台加强与印度及参演各国在海上防卫力量建设专业能力及文化领域的交流，以巩固彼此间的友谊，同时提升国家间海上协调作业的信心。[1]

2016 年 9 月，孟加拉国派遣海军训练中队的两艘汉密尔顿级巡逻舰"索穆德拉·阿维扬"号（Somudra Avijan）和"索穆德拉·乔伊"号（Sumudra Joy）前往印度布莱尔港（Port Blair），与印度海军舰船一起参加了"通航训练"演习（Passage Exercise, Passex）。[2] 2017 年，孟加拉国更是成为由印度海军发起、由印度洋海军论坛（IONS）主持的"国际多边海上搜救演习"（IMMSAREX）的举办地。2017 年度的"国际多边海上搜救演习"于 2017 年 11 月 26 日至 28 日在孟加拉国举行，印度海军派出"南维尔"号（Ranvir）、"希亚德里"号（Sahyadri）、"恒河鳄"号（Gharial）和"苏坎亚"号（Sukanya）舰艇以及海上巡逻机"P-8I"参加了这次演习，并视之为巩固印度和孟加拉国之间的双边海军关系、探索海军合作的新途径。[3]

2018 年 7 月，孟加拉国总理谢赫·哈西娜到访印度，并与印度签署了两项重大国防协议，成为印度首次签署此类协议的南亚邻国。这一关于国防关系的总体协议不但涵盖了一切现有的国防合作事务，包括联合演习和培训项目，还规定由印度向孟加拉国提供价值 5 亿美元的信贷额度，用以从印度购买国防设备。印度此举意在通过上述国防协定减少孟加拉国对中国的依赖。作为孟加拉国武装部队一直以来的主要国防装备供应商，中国在印度周边地区影响力的扩大为印度所高度警惕。与孟加拉国进行包括海上防务合作在内的军事合作，正是印度政府限制中国在南亚区域扩张的努力之一。[4]

2. 与美国的合作

孟加拉国和美国长期以来都保持着多项海上军事演习合作关系，双方在包括"海蝙蝠"（Sea Bat）联合军演、"虎鲨"（Tiger Shark）联合军演、"卡拉

---

〔1〕 Indian Navy, "Milan 2014: An Unequivocal Success", https://www.indiannavy.nic.in/content/milan-2014-unequivocal-success, May 13, 2020.

〔2〕 Daily News, "Bangladesh Naval Ships Somudra Joy and SomudraAvijan in Colombo", http://www.dailynews.lk/2016/09/30/law-order/94565, May 13, 2020.

〔3〕 GKTOADY, "Bangladesh hosts 2017 International Multilateral Maritime Search and Rescue Exercise (IMMSAREX)", https://www.gktoday.in/news-today/bangladesh-hosts-2017-international-multilateral-maritime-search-and-rescue-exercise-immsarex/, May 13, 2020.

〔4〕 The Economic Time, "India to Sign Two Major Defence Deals with Bangladesh", https://economictimes.indiatimes.com/news/defence/india-to-sign-two-major-defence-deals-with-bangladesh/articleshow/58068508.cms, May 13, 2020.

特"（CARAT）联合军演在内的各项海上军演活动中持续进行紧密的防务合作。

其中，"海蝙蝠"军演于 1992 年、1993 年、1994 年、1995 年及 1998 年在孟加拉国和美国海军间联合举行，每届持续时间从 4 天到 11 天不等，联合演习地点均在孟加拉国专属经济区的海域范围之内[1]。

"虎鲨"军演则是由孟加拉国海军和美国特种部队举行的联合演习。第一届"虎鲨"军演于 2009 年在孟加拉国的吉大港举行，孟加拉国海军和美国特种部队在演习中接受以反恐、打击海盗及海上和沿海威胁为目标的训练，孟加拉国海军的特种作战潜水和打捞部队特别参与其中，与美军培养协同作战能力[2]。此后，"虎鲨"系列在两国间实现了每年 1 次或多次的常规演练。2010 年，两国在吉大港密集举行了合计共 86 天的"虎鲨-2""虎鲨-3""虎鲨-4""虎鲨-5"演习。在该年度的系列"虎鲨"演习中，孟加拉国陆军第一伞兵突击旅和美国陆军部队进行了反恐、射击和城市作战方面的专门演练[3]。至 2019 年 9 月，孟加拉国陆军第一伞兵突击旅（PCB）和美国特种部队共同参与了"虎鲨-37"联合军事演习，继续以系列危机应对和反恐演习科目为重心，并邀请英国联合反恐训练和咨询小组的成员伞兵突击旅第一指挥官参与观察讨论，以探讨三国间军事部门的未来多边训练前景并强化国家间的关联[4]。正如美国驻孟加拉国大使所申明的，美国政府支持孟加拉国政府建立能力更强的军事部门，美国政府将继续协助孟加拉国政府满足其安全需要，通过促进整个亚太地区的军事互动，对孟加拉国及区域安全作出了坚定承诺，同时不断加强两国政府之间的合作，并深化友谊[5]。

除"海蝙蝠"及"虎鲨"系列的双边军演外，孟加拉国也积极参与由美国所主办的其他地区军演项目。2011 年，孟加拉国第一次参加了"卡拉特"演习。该演习全名为"海上战备合作及联训"（Cooperation Afloat Readiness and Training），是由美国海军西太平洋后勤补给群（第 73 任务特遣队）统筹

〔1〕　Bangladesh Navy, "Exercises with Foreign Navies", https：//www. navy. mil. bd/NAVAL-DIPLO-MACY, May 13, 2020.

〔2〕　The Daily Star, "Bangladesh-US joint military exercises in November", https：//www. thedaily-star. net/news-detail-108534, May 13, 2020.

〔3〕　Bangladesh Navy, "Naval Diplomacy", https：//www. navy. mil. bd/Exercises-with-Foreign-Navies, May 13, 2020.

〔4〕　U. S. Embassy in Bangladesh, "U. S. Ambassador Visits Sylhet", https：//bd. usembassy. gov/u-s-ambassador-visits-sylhet/, May 13, 2020.

〔5〕　Embassy of The United Sates of America, "Joint U. S. - Bangladesh Military Exercise Concludes in Sylhet ", https：//photos. state. gov/libraries/bangladesh/19452/pdfs/13-may-10-pr-joint-us-ban-gladesh-military-exercise-Tiger-Shark2-Closing-sylhet. pdf, May 13, 2020.

的、在美国与东南亚国家间举办的年度演习，参演国包括马来西亚、菲律宾、印度尼西亚、泰国、新加坡、文莱、柬埔寨。由于该军演地点及目标设定为南海及南海区域的军事协同，也被视为美国介入南海主权纷争的战略布局之一。[1] 孟加拉国在 2011 年的加入，成为南亚国家参演的第一步，使该演习规模得到进一步扩充。

在 2011 年的第 17 届"卡拉特"演习中，孟加拉国演习部分在孟加拉国专属经济区海域进行，美方派出包括"基德"号导弹驱逐舰（DDG 100）、"福特"号护卫舰（FFG 54）、"卫士"号反水雷舰（MCM 2）以及"美国海军安全保障"号潜水救援舰（T-ARS 50）在内的 4 艘海军舰艇及约 500 名美方人员参演。演习将岸上和海上的培训科目相结合，前者集中于潜水培训、内河战、登船培训以及医疗和社区服务项目，后者则主要聚焦于美国和孟加拉国海军舰船之间的直升机操作、舰载通信和机动演习、水面炮兵演习和战术自由活动。[2] 此后"卡拉特"演习成为孟加拉国与美国间海上军事合作演练的常态项目。在 2018 年的演习中，来自孟加拉国海军的导弹护卫舰和巡逻艇以及来自美国海军的海上巡逻机和前线运载船继续就沿岸及海上项目进行系列联合演练，以涵盖和应对孟加拉湾的复杂情况为目标，通过协调部署水面舰艇和海上巡逻飞机提高海军共同跟踪和追击目标的能力，通过加强舰船通信的划分策略进行复杂的机动航行，同时进行掩护演习以提高船舶防御潜在威胁的能力。[3] 在 2019 年的演习中，其内岸演练阶段主要为领域专家围绕反潜作战及飞机的维护操作等主题的广泛交流，并开放 P-8A 波塞冬反潜巡逻机（Poseidon aircraf）供孟加拉国服役人员参观学习；海上演练阶段则主要通过机动反潜训练目标演习（EMATTEX），测试两国海军跟踪和追击目标的能力，以提高海上作战部队之间的沟通效率。[4]

3. 与中国的合作

一直以来，中国都是孟加拉国的最大军事装备供应国，孟加拉国与中国的海洋防务合作也因而首先体现在军备供应方面。早在 1989 年，孟加拉国就向中国购买了 053H1 型导弹护卫舰，以满足其海上行动与军备升级的应急需求。根据瑞典斯德哥尔摩国际和平研究所相关数据，在 2010 年至 2016 年，

〔1〕 Naval Technology, "Exercise CARAT 2011 Begins", https://www.naval-technology.com/news/newsexercise-carat-2011-begins/, May 13, 2020.

〔2〕 Naval Today, "Bangladesh, US Navies Begin First CARAT Naval Exercise", https://navaltoday.com/2011/09/20/bangladesh-us-navies-begin-first-carat-naval-exercise/, May 13, 2020.

〔3〕 U. S. Embassy in Bangladesh, "U. S. -Bangladesh Navy Commence CARAT Exercise", https://bd. usembassy. gov/u-s-bangladesh-navy-commence-24th-carat-exercise/, May 13, 2020.

〔4〕 Seaman Thomas Higgins, "CARAT Bangladesh", https://www. dvidshub. net/news/351020/carat-bangladesh, May 13, 2020.

中国共向孟加拉国提供了 5 艘海上巡逻舰、2 艘轻型巡洋舰、44 辆坦克、16架战斗机，以及地对空导弹和反舰导弹。[1] 如 2014 年购买 2 艘 053H2 型护卫舰，2016 年购买 2 艘 1350 吨 056 型轻巡洋舰等。2016 年后，孟中两国间的海军军备合作更迈向一个新阶段。2016 年 11 月，孟加拉国向中国购买的035G "明"级柴电潜艇在中国大连港正式交付，于 2017 年 3 月由孟加拉国总理谢赫·哈西娜主持仪式后正式入海军服役，成为孟加拉国海军史上首次装备的常规潜艇，引发较多的国际关注。2017 年 11 月，孟中两国联合建造的 2 艘大型巡逻艇正式列装，孟加拉国总统和海军参谋长出席其服役典礼。作为首次在孟加拉国本土建造的大型军舰，这 2 艘巡逻艇的成功建造及入列服役均对该国具有里程碑意义。2019 年 12 月，中国再次向孟加拉国交付了 2艘其于 2018 年购买的导弹护卫舰。[2]

除了军事装备领域的硬件输入，孟加拉国和中国也有着较为活跃的海上军演实践。在 2014 年 4 月中国海军承办的第 14 届西太平洋海军论坛（Western Pacific Naval Symposium）年会上，孟加拉国作为观察员国派出海军护卫舰 "阿布·巴卡尔"号（Abu Bakar）参演，而该护卫舰则由中国原 "黄石"号 053H2 型护卫舰升级改造而来。[3] 该论坛成立于 1987 年，是目前西太平洋地区唯一定期开展的多边对话与合作的海军论坛，当前已有 20 余个成员国，影响力超出 "西太平洋"地域范围。[4] 2017 年 5 月，中国海军远航编队访问孟加拉国时，两国海军在孟加拉湾举行海上联合演习，并由此创造了两国海军交往史上的多个之 "最" ——两国间联演课目最多、持续时间最长、交流范围最广。[5] 2017 年 11 月，由印度洋海军论坛（IONS）发起的 "国际多边海上搜救演习"在孟加拉国附近海域举行，应此次演习承办方孟

〔1〕 "India 'Watching' Chinese Defence Minister's Dhaka Visit Closely"，https：//bdnews24. com/bangladesh/2016/05/24/india-watching-chinese-defence-minister-s-dhaka-visit-closely，May 13，2020.

〔2〕 参见《中国售孟加拉战舰换新导弹 物美价廉变废为宝》，载环球网，https：//mil. huanqiu. com/article/9CaKrnJE4E2，最后访问日期：2020 年 5 月 13 日；《日媒：中印争夺孟加拉湾盟友 中国出口多艘军舰》，载环球网，https：//mil. huanqiu. com/article/9CaKrnJZvyk，最后访问日期：2020 年 5 月 13 日；李彦彬：《2017 年南亚军情：巴铁涨军费孟加拉国或买中国无人机》，载新浪军事网，http：//mil. news. sina. com. cn/2018-02-02/doc-ifyremfz3518534. shtml? from = wap，最后访问日期：2020 年 5 月 13 日。

〔3〕 "Bangladesh Joins Chinese Naval Exercise"，https：//bdnews24. com/bangladesh/ 2014/04/21/bangladesh-joins-chinese-naval-exercise，May 13，2020.

〔4〕 范江怀、柳刚：《第 14 届西太平洋海军论坛年会在青岛举行》，载搜狐网，http：//news. sohu. com/20140422/n398621287. shtml，最后访问日期：2020 年 5 月 13 日。

〔5〕 许寿明、刘春涛：《中国海军远航访问编队离开孟加拉国 中孟海军举行海上联合演习》，载新华网，http：//www. xinhuanet. com/politics/2017-05/27/c _ 1121048942. htm，最后访问日期：2020 年 5 月 13 日。

加拉国的邀请，中国海军首次派舰艇与印度海军共同参加了该论坛框架下的多边演习项目，意义与效应不言而喻。[1]

另外，孟加拉国也与中国维系着较大规模的军事交流。两国在 2014 年 6 月发表的《关于深化更加紧密的全面合作伙伴关系的联合声明》中表示："双方对中孟两国在防务领域的合作水平表示满意，同意进一步加强有关合作。"[2] 在 2016 年 10 月发表的"关于建立战略合作伙伴关系的联合声明"中进一步明确："双方同意保持和加强两军各层级交流与合作，深化在人员培训、装备技术、联合国维和等领域的合作。"[3]

4. 与其他国家的合作

马来西亚的兰卡威国际海事和航空展览（Langkawi International Maritime and Aerospace Exhibition，LIMA）每两年举办一次，是亚太地区同类展览中规模最大的活动，以亚洲国家国内安全、国防装备、海洋及航空航天制造产业为重心。自 1991 年举办以来，其已吸引了超过 16 万名贸易商代表及公众参与相关会展和航展项目，并为包括航空器、船舶在内的制造商提供在亚洲各国军政部门的领导人前展示其产品的大型平台，其国际影响力和受欢迎程度不断提高。[4] 2015 年 3 月 17 日至 25 日，孟加拉国海军派出"阿布·巴卡尔"号军舰参加该年度展览，以此显示与周边国家增进国防军备、海上防务交流与合作的开放立场。[5]

同年 5 月，卡塔尔举办第四届"凶猛猎鹰"（Ferocious Falcon）军事演习，美国、英国、德国和法国等 27 个国家派遣观察员参与此次演习。孟加拉国派出了由 236 名海军军官及其当时最大舰艇"索穆德拉·乔伊"号（Somudra Joy）组成的近 350 人的代表团，全程参与了从 5 月 11 日开始的全部活动环节。演习内容涵盖了在恐怖袭击、人质劫持、自然灾害、重要设施受威胁时的快速反应以及提供关键服务期间的危机管理。孟加拉国武装部队在

---

〔1〕 王天傛：《台媒：印度称 11 月将与中国在孟加拉湾参加演习》，载参考消息网，http：//news. sina. com. cn/w/2017-08-15/doc-ifyixipt1732331. shtml，最后访问日期：2020 年 5 月 13 日。

〔2〕 《中华人民共和国与孟加拉人民共和国关于深化更加紧密的全面合作伙伴关系的联合声明》，载中国政府网，http：//www. gov. cn/xinwen/2014-06/10/content_ 2698374. htm，最后访问日期：2020 年 5 月 13 日。

〔3〕 《中华人民共和国和孟加拉人民共和国关于建立战略合作伙伴关系的联合声明》，载人民网，http：//world. people. com. cn/n1/2016/1016/c1002-28781678. html，最后访问日期：2020 年 5 月 13 日。

〔4〕 Langkawi-Insight, "Langkawi International Maritime and Aerospace Exhibition（LIMA）", https：// www. langkawi-insight. com/langkawi_ 0000f0. htm, May 13, 2020.

〔5〕 Bangladesh Navy, "Exercises with Foreign Navies", https：//www. navy. mil. bd/Exercises-with-Foreign-Navies, May 13, 2020.

灾害管理方面，尤其是在经常遭受的飓风袭击应对方面，积累了较具价值的专门知识与经验。孟加拉国军方将此次演习视为向世界展示其能力的重要机会，也增强了其在维持全球和平中发挥更大作用的信心。[1]

而在随后的 5 月 19 日至 21 日，亚洲国际海防展（IMDEX Asia）在新加坡樟宜开展，受到多国高级海军官员、海事机构和行业代表的高度关注。孟加拉国海军亦派出"托莱索里"（Dhaleshwari）号军舰，与来自美国、俄罗斯、中国、澳大利亚、印度、韩国、文莱等 11 个国家的 18 艘军舰同台展示，从而在这一亚太地区最具代表性的国际海防展上，再次表达出孟加拉国欲进入并维系该海洋防务"朋友圈"的强烈期待。[2]

除上述以军备交易、联合军事演习为主的海上防务合作外，军舰友好互访作为孟加拉国海军外交的内容之一，也成为其近年来拓展国际防务合作的重要渠道。从孟加拉国海军官网所公布的相关数据来看，印度洋及东南亚周边国家成为孟加拉国海军互访的首要目标。2016 年至 2017 年，孟加拉国共派军舰出访 22 次，分别对马来西亚、印度、斯里兰卡、印度尼西亚、泰国、新加坡、缅甸等国进行了友好访问，其中 5 次前往马来西亚、3 次前往印度、3 次前往斯里兰卡。而在 2015 年至 2017 年，共有印度、中国、印度尼西亚、美国、法国等国先后 15 次派军舰访问孟加拉国港口，其中印度到访 8 次、中国到访 2 次。[3]

（二）海洋油气资源合作

孟加拉国以天然气和生物质能为其主要能源。根据国际能源署（IEA）的国别数据，在孟加拉国的一次能源消费[4]中，55% 为天然气、27% 为生物质能、15% 为石油、3% 为煤，水电和太阳能占比不足 1%。[5] 而在能源生产方面，天然气同样是孟加拉国最主要的能源产出。一方面，孟加拉国已发现 27 个天然气田含 39 万亿立方英尺（约合 1.1 亿立方米）的天然气储量，

[1]　"Bangladesh displays military capabilities in Qatar 'Ferocious Falcon' drills", https：//bd-news24. com/bangladesh/2015/05/13/bangladesh-displays-military-capabilities-in-qatar-ferocious-fal-con-drills, May 13, 2020.

[2]　Naval Today, "IMDEX Asia 2015 Attracts Strong International Interest", https：//navaltoday. com/2015/04/22/imdex-asia-2015-attracts-strong-international-interest/, May 13, 2020.

[3]　Bangladesh Navy, "Good Will Visit", https：//www. navy. mil. bd/Good-will-Visit, May 13, 2020.

[4]　一次能源是指自然界现实存在，可供直接利用的能源，如煤、石油、天然气、风能、水能等；二次能源则指由一次能源直接或间接加工、转换而来的能源，如电、蒸汽、焦炭、煤气、氢等。参见黄素奕、林一歆：《能源与节能技术》（第三版），中国电力出版社 2016 年版，第 5 页。

[5]　IEA,"Total Energy Supply（TES）by Source, Bangladesh 1990－2018", https：//www. iea. org/countries/bangladesh, May 13, 2020.

其中已探明的可开采储量为 27.12 万亿立方英尺（约合 7679 亿立方米），其天然气年生产量也已达到 1.04 万亿立方英尺（约合 294 亿立方米），由此成为亚太地区的第八大天然气生产国。但另一方面，截至 2017 年，孟加拉国已完成了所探明储量中 15.22 万亿立方英尺（约合 4098 亿立方米）天然气的开采，剩余不足 12 万亿立方英尺（约合 3398 亿立方米）的储量将只能支撑孟加拉未来 10 到 12 年的能源需求。[1] 这使得孟加拉国巨大的能源短缺一直未能得以改善，至今仍只有 85% 的人口能够获得电力供应。[2] 当前，孟加拉国正积极推进风能、水力及太阳能等可再生能源的部署，同时通过多种优惠措施大力鼓励私人资本和外国资本投资电力和油气领域，其中也包括针对海上油气资源开发的投资吸引与合作努力。

1. 与俄罗斯的合作

俄罗斯与孟加拉国的能源合作历史可以追溯到 20 世纪 70 年代初，孟加拉国从原东巴基斯坦获得独立之时。为促进国家的经济独立，开辟经济现代化的道路，孟加拉国必须寻求本国堪以负担的能源资源。在 1970 年至 1990 年，苏联为年轻的孟加拉人民共和国提供了包括军事、政治、工业、能源勘探等在内的大量支持。正是在被调派该国的苏联地质学家和地球物理学家的支持之下，孟加拉国完成了其第一幅地质地图的绘制，为该国未来的石油和天然气工业铺平了道路。然而，由于国际局势的急剧变化，苏联和孟加拉国之间的积极合作态势被中断搁置了近 20 年。

为推动十年未有进展的新油田的勘探和开发、建造新的生产井，孟加拉国于 2010 年向俄罗斯发出提议，邀请其在政府钻井计划中参与本国境内油气田的勘探和开发以及单一天然气供应系统的建设。自 2012 年以来，俄罗斯天然气工业股份公司 EP 国际（Gazprom EP International）参与了孟加拉国 8 个气田中 17 口评价、勘探和生产井的设计和建造，仅 2013 至 2018 年总钻井深度就超过 50000 米，钻井总流量每年约达 70 亿立方米，从而将孟加拉国的天然气总产量提高了 10% 以上。2020 年 1 月，俄罗斯天然气工业股份公司 EP 国际和孟加拉国石油勘探与生产公司再度于达卡签署了两份备忘录，分别是为期 5 年的"战略合作谅解备忘录"（Memorandum of Understanding for Strategic Cooperation）以及前瞻性的"波拉岛气田评估谅解备忘录"（Memorandum of Understanding on Bhola Island Fields Evaluation）。依据后者，双方将基于相

---

〔1〕 M. Hassan Shetol et al., "Present Status of Bangladesh Gas Fields and Future Development: A Review", *Journal of Natural Gas Geoscience* 6, 2019, pp. 347-354.

〔2〕 IEA, "Bangladesh", https://www.iea.org/countries/bangladesh, May 13, 2020.

关评估结果所证实的勘探前景，考虑建立合资企业开发该岛屿及周边海域气田的可行性。[1]

2. 与美国的合作

美国是孟加拉寻求能源生产设备建设投资的又一主要目标。作为"浮式存储再气化装置"（FSRU）项目的专家级机构，美国卓越能源公司（Excelerate Energy）协同国际金融公司（IFC），于2017年起共同开发了孟加拉国的"莫哈什卡利浮式液化天然气"项目（Moheshkhali Floating LNG project, MLNG）。该项目位于孟加拉湾的莫哈什卡利岛海域，耗资约1.8亿美元，通过部署1座浸没型输送转塔作为接入点向孟加拉国输送再气化后的液化天然气。作为孟加拉国第一个液化天然气（LNG）进口终端，这一项目是该国从全球市场获取天然气的关键性基础设施，也由此成为孟加拉国能源设施建设历史上的一个里程碑。[2] 2018年8月，美国卓越能源孟加拉国有限公司（Excelerate Energy Bangladesh Limited）完成了"莫哈什卡利浮式液化天然气"项目接收站的调试，正式开始向孟加拉国吉大港地区输送天然气，标志着孟加拉国正式成为全球第42个液化天然气进口国。[3] 2019年5月，由该公司建设的第二个离岸液化天然气终端"顶峰液化天然气"（Summit LNG）开始运营。该终端位于考克斯巴扎附近海域，距离"莫哈什卡利浮式液化天然气"项目接收站约1.25英里，其投入运行将有望使孟加拉国的液化天然气的进口能力增加1倍。[4] 值得一提的是，根据相关协议，美国卓越能源公司将仅在15年内拥有并运营上述天然气进口终端，意即孟加拉国石油、天然气与矿产公司将得以在15年后获得上述能源设施的所有权。[5]

---

〔1〕 Gazprom EP International, "Bangladesh", https：//gazprom-international. com/en/operations/country/bangladesh, May 13, 2020.

〔2〕 See CDC Group Plc, "Bangla Offshore LNG", https：//www. cdcgroup. com/en/our-investments/investment/bangla-offshore-lng/, May 13, 2020; Offshore Energy, "Moheshkhali LNG terminal given thumbs up", https：//www. offshore-energy. biz/moheshkhali-lng-terminal-given-thumbs-up/, May 13, 2020.

〔3〕 《孟加拉国复制巴基斯坦LNG进口模式》，载搜狐网，https：//www. sohu. com/a/259543097_99912085，最后访问日期：2020年5月13日。

〔4〕 Chron, "Excelerate Begins Operations at Second Offshore LNG Facility in Bangladesh", https：//www. chron. com/business/energy/article/Houston-area-company-begin-operations-at-second-13811865. php, May 13, 2020.

〔5〕 Excelerate Energy, "Print Friendly, PDF & Email Moheshkhali Floating LNG Terminal Flowing Natural Gas into Bangladesh", https：//excelerateenergy. com/excelerate-energy-commissions-bangladeshs-first-lng-import-terminal/, May 13, 2020.

3. 与中国的合作

中国在油气资源方面与孟加拉国一直保持较为紧密的合作关系。早在 20世纪 90 年代初，中国企业就开始以工程承包形式进入孟加拉国发电市场，在吉大港地区建设了两座燃气电站。2000 年后，更多中国企业借孟加拉国优渥的政策环境大举进军其能源市场。如 2002 年开工建设巴拉普库利亚（Barapukuria）燃煤电站，并于 2006 年正式移交；2009 年至 2012 年再签署电厂承建合同 13 份，包括重油电厂和燃气电厂；同时，中国企业在 200 兆瓦以上大型发电机组上也取得了突破。[1]

在油气资源开发方面，2010 年 3 月，孟加拉国总理谢赫·哈西娜访华期间，孟加拉国油气矿产公司及孟加拉国石油公司与中国石油天然气集团公司签署了《石油天然气领域合作谅解备忘录》。[2] 2016 年 10 月，中国石油天然气集团公司与孟加拉国石油公司代表在达卡交换了《孟加拉单点系泊及双管道项目 EPC 合同》签署文本。这一合作协议的签署，被视为两国共建"一带一路"重大战略构想在能源领域合作的务实推进。根据协议，中国石油管道局将以 EPC 工程总承包模式建设孟加拉国石油公司东方炼厂单点系泊及双管道项目。该项目位于孟加拉湾东部吉大港入海口，是东方炼厂扩建改造工程的重要组成部分，建成后将大幅提升炼厂原油和成品油接卸速度，显著降低运营成本及漏油环境污染事故风险，从而有效服务于两国能源合作领域的互利共赢与共同发展目标。[3]

4. 与其他国家的合作

作为缓解国内油气资源紧张及改变单一陆上油气田现况的主要举措，自 2008 年起孟加拉国即开始就孟加拉湾的海上油气区块进行国际招标。但出于对其与印度、缅甸间海洋边界争议的担忧，大多数国际油气公司放弃了该轮投标。尽管自 2012 年 3 月与缅甸、2014 年 7 月与印度通过第三方裁决初步解决海上边界争端以来，孟加拉国政府已着手开展新一轮的国际招标，但其仍未在海上天然气勘探方面取得重大突破。[4]

---

〔1〕《孟加拉能源概况和中孟能源合作建议》，载中华人民共和国商务部网站，http：//bd. mofcom. gov. cn/article/ztdy/201605/2016 0501310457. shtml，最后访问日期：2020 年 5 月 13 日。

〔2〕《中华人民共和国与孟加拉人民共和国联合声明》，载中华人民共和国驻塞尔维亚共和国大使馆网站，http：//rs. chineseembassy. org/chn/xwdt/t674101. htm，最后访问日期：2020 年 5 月 14 日。

〔3〕《中国石油天然气集团公司与孟加拉石油公司交换合作项目签署文本》，载石油圈网，http：//www. oilsns. com/article/99202，最后访问日期：2020 年 5 月 13 日。

〔4〕《孟加拉能源概况和中孟能源合作建议》，载中华人民共和国商务部网站，http：//bd. mofcom. gov. cn/article/ztdy/201605/2016 0501310457. shtml，最后访问日期：2020 年 5 月 13 日。

当前，孟加拉国的天然气区块总数为 48 个，包括 22 个陆上区块及 26 个海上区块，而海上区块中的 11 个为浅海区块、15 个为深海区块。从 2012 年放出 9 个浅海区块和 3 个深海区块至今，孟加拉国仅批准授予 4 个海上区块的开发。其中，印度石油天然气公司下属的维德希公司（ONGC Videsh）和印度石油公司（Oil India）于 2014 年分别获得了浅海区块 SS - 04 及 SS - 09；新加坡克里斯能源公司（Kris Energy）与澳大利亚桑托斯公司（Santos）于同年联合获得了浅海区块 SS - 11；韩国大宇公司（Posco-Daewoo Corporation）于 2017 年获得了深海区块 DS - 12。[1] 除此之外，挪威国家石油公司（Statoil）、韩国大宇公司和新加坡克里斯能源公司还曾于 2016 年就浅水区块 SS - 10、深水区块 DS - 10 及 DS - 11 向孟加拉国提交了开发兴趣函。该 3 个区块的面积分别为 3381 平方公里、3693 平方公里和 4696 平方公里。根据竞标条款，承包商将承担所有开发成本，成本回收情况将取决于油气发现程度。[2]

2018 年，孟加拉国政府开始着手对相关油气生产及利益分享合同的示范性条款进行修订与更新，以便在新一轮的国际招标中对外国石油公司发出更具吸引力的邀约。但为了保证本国能源缺口的有效填补，孟加拉国一直在海上油气资源的合作开发中坚持，所有浅海区域的天然气开发都将全部供孟加拉国本国使用，仅深海区域的产出可以在其份额限制内且孟加拉国无购买需求的情形下被输出国外。[3]

（三）海洋渔业合作

1. 与印度的合作

2011 年 9 月 6 日，孟加拉国与印度达成了《孟加拉国与印度有关渔业领域合作的谅解备忘录》（Memorandum of Understanding between the Government of the Republic of India and the Government of the People's Republic of Bangladesh on Co-Operation in the Field of Fisheries）。该备忘录第 1 条即指出："缔约双方应通过联合行动、多种项目方案以及科研资料、信息和人员的交换，促进两国渔业

---

〔1〕 Dhaka Tribune, "Bangladesh Moves to Go for Auction to Explore Offshore Gas", https：//www. dhakatribune. com/bangladesh/power-energy/2018/08/26/bangladesh-moves-to-go-for-auction-to-explore-offshore-gas, May 13, 2020.

〔2〕 《三家国际石油公司竞标孟加拉海上油气区块》，载中华人民共和国商务部网站，http：//bd. mofcom. gov. cn/article/jmxw/2016 11/20161101557208. shtml，最后访问日期：2020 年 5 月 13 日。

〔3〕 Dhaka Tribune, "Bangladesh Moves to Go for Auction to Explore Offshore Gas", https：//www. dhakatribune. com/bangladesh/power-energy/2018/08/26/bangladesh-moves-to-go-for-auction-to-explore-offshore-gas, May 13, 2020.

和水产养殖合作及相关活动的发展。"其第2条进一步强调："联合行动的内容由双方共同确定，并通过相互商定的程序执行。"这些联合行动须符合环保和可持续发展的要求，行动领域应包括：（1）水产种质资源的交换（aquaculture germplasm exchange）；（2）鱼类种群评估、收获后技术、淡水珍珠养殖、云鲥渔业管理等相关培训；（3）与渔业发展有关的生物多样性保护；（4）鱼产品的生产、配送和贸易；（5）生物安全的国际标准等。[1]

2016年12月，来自孟加拉国渔业部下属的迈门辛市孟加拉国渔业研究所（Bangladesh Fisheries Research Institute in Mymensingh）和吉大港大学海洋科学与渔业研究所（Institute of Marine Science and Fisheries，University of Chittagong）的12名中层官员在印度中央海洋渔业研究所（The Central Marine Fisheries Research Institute）总部接受了培训。研究所主任表示，本次培训旨在帮助他们培养海洋鱼类种群评估所需的人才，提高专业技术，并鼓励该领域的研究，这将有助于发展用于渔业生产和生物性投入的数据收集系统，以促进海洋渔业资源的养护和可持续发展。[2]

为维系两国的传统友谊并促进相关渔业合作，孟加拉国已经连续两年向印度特许出口云鲥。云鲥是最受孟加拉国民众欢迎的珍贵水产，被视为孟加拉国的"国鱼"。为保护这一珍贵鱼种，孟加拉国政府近年来采取了严格的捕捞限制和监管措施，并于2012年禁止云鲥出口。但为在印度一年一度的杜尔迦节（Durga Puja）上表达善意，孟加拉国政府曾于2019年9月28日至10月10日暂时解除了云鲥出口禁令，并向印度赠送了500吨云鲥作为杜尔迦节的礼物。2020年9月，1475吨云鲥再次被许可运送至印度。两国在渔业贸易与渔业合作上的亲密态势可见一斑。[3]

2. 与美国的合作

诚如前述，云鲥是孟加拉国最重要的海洋鱼类之一，为保证此种鱼类的

---

〔1〕 India Minstry of External Afairs，"MOU between India and Bangladesh on Co-operation in The Field of Fisheries"，https：//mea. gov. in/bilateral-documents. htm？dtl/5189/MOU + between + India + and + Bangladesh + on + cooperation + in + the + field + of + fisheries，May 12，2020.

〔2〕 Business Line，"CMFRI Offers Training to Bangla Fisheries Officials"，https：//www. thehindu-businessline. com/economy/agri-business/cmfri-offers-training-to-bangla-fisheries-officials/article9429129. ece，May 12，2020.

〔3〕 See Sutanuka Ghosal，"Bangladesh Gives Traders Special Permission for Hilsa Export to India"，https：//economictimes. indiatimes. com/news/economy/foreign-trade/bangladesh-gives-traders-special-permission-for-hilsa-export-to-india/articleshow/78059441. cms，May 12，2020；The Daily Star，"Bangladesh to Export 1，475 Tonnes of Hilsa to India for Durga Puja"，https：//www. thedailystar. net/business/news/bangladesh-export-1475-tonnes-hilsa-india-durga-puja-1960757，May 12，2020.

可持续发展，孟加拉国采取了较为严格的云鲥捕捞限制。但每年云鲥捕捞禁令期，也令许多以捕捞云鲥为生的渔民的生活遭受巨大影响。为应对该问题，美国国际开发署（United States Agency for International Development）特别设立了"加强孟加拉国沿海渔业项目"（Enhanced Coastal Fisheries in Bangladesh Project）以资助受影响的孟加拉国渔民。该项目的主要工作内容包括：通过支持云鲥的可持续渔业管理来帮助孟加拉国打击沿海和河口地区的非法、不报告和不管制捕捞，提高政府和渔业社区的能力，加强政府的执法能力，建立对渔业管理和生物多样性保护至关重要的海洋保护区和禁捕区等。[1] 在 2014 年 7 月至 2019 年 6 月的五年间，该项目已在孟加拉国的 81 个村庄建立了 280 个云鲥保护小组，并通过培训渔民从事蔬菜种植等其他生计活动以改变对云鲥捕捞的依赖。[2]

3. 与中国的合作

2008 年 7 月，由孟加拉国渔业和畜牧部副部长担任团长的孟加拉国农业考察团一行专程赴江苏省金坛市，对多处水产养殖场进行了为期 3 天的实地考察，并在当地就渔业技术交流和共建水产养殖基地签署合作协议，希望在水产养殖技术上得到中国的支持和帮助，同时欢迎金坛市渔业技术人员和养殖户到孟加拉国推广技术，援建"金坛渔业村"。[3]

2015 年 4 月 23 日，中国国家海洋局副局长陈连增应孟加拉国外交部邀请，率团访问孟加拉国，就构建双边海洋合作机制、推动海洋领域务实合作、共建"21 世纪海上丝绸之路"进行了沟通与交流，并达成重要共识。陈连增在访问期间指出，中孟两国都是海洋国家，中方愿与孟方共同建设"21 世纪海上丝绸之路"，推动双方海洋合作，适时签署海洋领域合作文件，通过构建海洋合作伙伴关系，开展海洋政策、法律管理、科学研究、观测预报与防灾减灾、人才培训等领域的合作。孟加拉国外交部副部长表示，孟方支持中国"一带一路"倡议，愿意加强对华全方位海洋领域合作，分享海洋科学研究和资源开发的成果、经验，希望通过技术援助升级孟加拉国的海洋基础设施和装备，提高本国海洋综合管理水平和开发能力，并加强科技人员交流和培训。陈连增还在会见孟加拉国渔业与畜牧部

〔1〕 World Fish，"Enhanced Coastal Fisheries in Bangladesh（ECOFISH-BD）"，https：//www. worldfishcenter. org/content/enhanced-coastal-fisheries-bangladesh-ecofish-bd，May 12，2020.

〔2〕 World Fish，"Conserving Hilsa and Building Livelihoods in Bangladesh"，https：//www. worldfishcenter. org/video/conserving-hilsa-and-building-livelihoods-bangladesh，May 12，2020.

〔3〕《金坛高效渔业与孟加拉国签合作协议》，载中国水产养殖网，http：//www. shuichan. cc/news_ view-7980. html，最后访问日期：2020 年 5 月 18 日。

部长、科技部副部长和达卡大学副校长时，分别与其就推动中孟海洋领域合作深入交换了看法。[1]

2018年8月，孟加拉国计划部部长在会见中国驻孟加拉国大使张佐时表示，欢迎中方加大对孟投资，实现互利共赢，期待中方加大对孟加拉国海洋经济、渔业捕捞、农产品加工、新能源发电、服装等领域的投资。孟加拉国计划部愿同中国使馆建立政策沟通协调机制，推动孟中经贸领域务实合作再上新台阶。[2]

2018年10月，由中国商务部主办、自然资源部国家海洋技术中心和福建海洋研究所协办的中国援孟海洋空间规划海外技术培训班在孟加拉国首都达卡开班，旨在通过双边合作促进孟加拉国的蓝色经济发展。孟加拉国政府主管部门的官员、技术专家、相关企业负责人和技术人员参加了培训。来自中国国家海洋技术中心的专家，结合孟方培训需要和当地海洋空间规划管理领域实际情况，以专题讲座与实践教学相结合的形式展开为期20天的培训。内容涉及海洋功能区划技术方法、海洋资源评价与管理、海洋综合观测技术与防灾减灾、海洋可再生能源、蓝色经济发展、海水养殖技术和中国海洋功能区划进展及成果等，目的在于将海洋空间规划的先进理论、技术及实践介绍给孟加拉国的参训学员。此外，中国培训师们还有针对性地安排了实地考察，带领学员参观了中国造船厂、捕捞厂，并造访相关研究所，进行了实地踏勘讲解和分析等。[3]

2019年9月6日，孟加拉国贾格纳特大学（Jagannath University）执行校长一行访问上海海洋大学，与上海海洋大学签署了学术交流合作协议。贾格纳特大学规划在现有的动物学系的基础上，建立渔业和水产养殖系，期待上海海洋大学支持其相关专业发展，并与孟加拉国积极开展水产养殖、生物多样性保护以及海洋生态环境监测等方面的研究合作。[4]

在随后的16日至29日，中国农业农村部2019年扬帆出海人才培训工程——"丝路国家海水养殖技术培训班"在中国青岛顺利举办。本次培训班

〔1〕 王安涛：《陈连增副局长访问孟加拉国外交部和缅甸交通部》，载搜狐网，http：//roll.sohu.com/20150429/n412129189.shtml，最后访问日期：2021年3月18日。

〔2〕 刘春涛：《中国对孟加拉国的巨额投资惊动印度》，载新华网，http：//www.xinhuanet.com/world/2018-08/09/c_1123248430.htm，最后访问日期：2020年5月18日。

〔3〕 朱彧、滕欣：《携手推进海洋空间规划》，载中国水产科学研究院黄海水产研究所网站，http：//www.ysfri.ac.cn/info/1111/33161.htm，最后访问日期：2020年5月18日。

〔4〕 《上海海洋大学与孟加拉国贾格纳特大学签署学术交流合作协议》，载中国教育在线网，https：//www.eol.cn/shanghai/shanghainews/201909/t20190909_1682292.shtml，最后访问日期：2020年5月18日。

由中国农业农村部国际合作司主办，中国水产科学研究院黄海水产研究所承办，中国海洋试点国家实验室海洋渔业科学与食物产出过程功能实验室、中国农业农村部海洋渔业可持续发展重点实验室、中国水产学会海水养殖分会、中国农村专业技术协会海水养殖专业委员会协办。来自孟加拉国、马来西亚等八国的 20 名政府官员、优秀青年科学家和渔业企业负责人参加了本次培训。培训内容涵盖了海水养殖苗种繁育、水产育种技术、生态健康养殖模式、营养饲料、水产疫病防控和水产品加工与质量安全等多个方向，同时安排学员赴寻山集团有限公司、荣成褚岛水产有限公司、青岛瑞兹海珍品发展有限公司等水产知名企业和黄海水产研究所海水鲆鲽鱼类遗传育种中心现场考察，使学员对中国先进的海水养殖技术和产业发展规模有更为深入全面的了解。此外，培训班还组织学员集体参加了"丝路国家水产养殖国际论坛暨 2019 年绿色养殖发展研讨会"，了解和交流水产养殖可持续发展的先进理念、技术和模式[1]。

2019 年 11 月，由中华人民共和国商务部主办，福建海洋研究所承办的中国对外援助培训项目"2019 年孟加拉国海水养殖与水产品加工技术培训班"在福建厦门举办。孟加拉国渔业与畜牧部渔业司、渔业研究所、渔业发展公司的高级渔业官员、生物化学家和政府官员共 30 人参加了此次为期 40 天的培训[2]。在福建省淡水水产研究所的养殖示范合作基地参观学习时，研究所人员围绕山塘高效生态养殖模式，向孟加拉国渔业与畜牧部渔业司及其所属渔业研究所、渔业发展公司官员详细介绍了大水面立体增氧综合解决方案、水质综合调控技术、风送投喂技术、肠道保健技术和机械化高效捕捞技术等内容，分享了系统运营下实现零排水和增质增效等成果的经验，并介绍了福建省淡水水产研究所在淡水特色品种大刺鳅方面的研究成果和进展。现场参观交流后，孟加拉国渔业与畜牧部渔业司代表赞赏了我国的淡水养殖技术和生态调控技术水平，介绍了孟加拉国山塘的开发利用情况及大刺鳅在孟加拉国的产业发展情况，并希望加强双方技术合作和交流，提升孟加拉国的淡水养殖技术水平，促进经贸关系发展[3]。

---

〔1〕《农业农村部 2019 年扬帆出海人才培训工程——"丝路国家海水养殖技术培训班"举办结业仪式》，载青岛海洋科学与技术试点国家实验室网站，http：//www.qnlm.ac/hyyykxyswc-cgc/page? a=0&b=5&c=51&p=detail，最后访问日期：2020 年 5 月 18 日。

〔2〕《联鲲集团专家应邀为中国对外援助培训孟加拉和泰国项目授课》，载搜狐网，https：//www.sohu.com/a/352851054_678981，最后访问日期：2020 年 5 月 18 日。

〔3〕《孟加拉国渔业与畜牧部渔业司官员参观淡水所养殖示范基地》，载海峡风，http：//www.fishexpo.cn/contact.asp，最后访问日期：2020 年 5 月 18 日。

4. 与其他国家或机构的合作

2015 年 3 月 25 日，孟加拉国与菲律宾两国外长签署了《关于建立孟加拉国与菲律宾外交政策磋商机制的谅解备忘录》（Memorandum of Understanding Establishing Foreign Policy Consultations between the Philippines and Bangladesh）。同日，两国代表团成功举行首次外交政策磋商，讨论了两国关系的发展，并讨论了在渔业、水产养殖、教育、通信技术和体育等领域进一步加强两国关系的可能举措。[1]

2016 年 7 月，孟加拉国与冰岛两国外长举行了双边会谈，一致同意加强在两国具有共同利益的领域的合作，尤其是渔业管理领域的合作。双方同意探索改善贸易和投资关系的新途径，包括鼓励在孟加拉湾海洋资源管理方面建立公私伙伴关系（public-private partnerships）。冰岛外长接受了率领代表团访问孟加拉国的邀请，该代表团主要由渔业部门和地热能业的专家和企业家组成。孟加拉国外长对冰岛渔业部门正在进行的高附加值工作表现出极大兴趣，包括将鱼皮用于皮革和衣服制造、将鱼肠用于制药和人类皮肤移植等多个领域。[2]

2019 年 4 月，孟加拉国和文莱两国总理举行了双边会议。会议结束后，孟加拉国渔业和畜牧部部长同文莱代表签署了《关于渔业领域合作的谅解备忘录》（Memorandum of Understanding on Cooperation in The Field of Fisheries）和《关于牲畜领域合作的谅解备忘录》（Memorandum of Understanding on Cooperation in The Field of Livestock）。[3]

（四）海洋研究合作

为实现其总理提出的 2041 年发展愿景，孟加拉国将有效利用和科学管理海洋资源的能力建设作为国家支持的重心之一。[4] 仅就当前合作实践

---

〔1〕 Philippines Department of Foreign Affairs, "Philippines, Bangladesh Move toward Closer Relations with Signing of MoU Establishing Foreign Policy Consultations", https：//www. dfa. gov. ph/dfa-releases/5995-philippines-bangladesh-move-toward-closer-relations-with-signing-of-mou-establishing-foreign-policy-consultations, May 18, 2020.

〔2〕 "Bangladesh, Iceland agree to strengthen collaboration in fisheries management", https：//bdnews24. com/economy/2016/09/09/bangladesh-iceland-agree-to-strengthen-collaboration-in-fisheries-management, May 18, 2020.

〔3〕 Thedailystar, "Bangladesh, Brunei Sign Seven Instruments", https：//www. thedailystar. net/business/dhaka-bangladesh-brunei-sign-seven-instruments-1732972, May 18, 2020.

〔4〕 DhakaTribune, "Bangladesh Calls for Strategic Partnership for Marine Scientific Research in Deep Sea", https：//www. dhakatribune. com/bangladesh/2020/11/18/bangladesh-calls-for-strategic-partnership-for-marine-scientific-research-in-deep-sea, May 18, 2020.

来看，孟加拉国的海洋研究合作尚属起步阶段，国际合作的直接成果有限。

1. 与印度的合作

作为孟加拉国从东巴基斯坦独立的历史盟友，印度与孟加拉国一直保持着紧密的合作关系。两国在海洋科研合作领域的最近发展主要包括 2019 年的 7 项双边合作协议以及 2020 年的新兴领域合作计划。2019 年 10 月，两国签署 7 项双边合作协议，同意：（1）为孟加拉国提供一套沿海监控系统；（2）制定从孟加拉国吉大港、勐拉港进出口货物到印度的标准作业程序；（3）从孟加拉国芬尼（Feni）河以每秒 1.82 立方英尺（约 0.05 立方米）的水量抽取河水，以供应印度东北部特里普拉邦某些城镇的日常用水；（4）印度向孟加拉国承诺相应信贷额度并予以落实；（5）印度海得拉巴（Hyderabad）大学与孟加拉国达卡大学建立合作关系，并维持青年事务的交流合作项目。[1]

2020 年 8 月，孟加拉国与印度进一步展开科研合作以探索新的合作领域。这些合作领域将海洋灾害管理、人工智能运用、海洋生态及保护等内容涵盖其中，同时将继续推进包括港口、电力、铁路和公路等在内的基础设施的改善。为呼应两国蓬勃发展的双边关系，使孟加拉国的投资环境得到持续性的改善，两国均强调应大力倡导更多的青年人才参与到新兴领域的科研合作中来。[2]

2. 与中国的合作

2010 年 3 月，孟加拉国与中国发表《中华人民共和国与孟加拉人民共和国联合声明》，两国同意在"雅鲁藏布江/布拉马普特拉河水文报汛和防洪减灾领域"进行持续合作，继续加强在水资源管理、水文报汛和防洪减灾领域的合作，同时在应对国际金融危机、气候变化、能源和粮食安全以及其他涉及发展中国家诉求和挑战的重大国际问题上保持密切协调与配合。

2016 年 10 月，基于两国发展友好合作的强烈意愿和两国合作的广阔前景，孟加拉国与中国一致同意将中孟关系提升为战略合作伙伴关系。鉴于两国在海洋事务中存在较大的合作潜力，双方一致同意建立海上合作对话机

---

〔1〕　孙静波：《孟加拉国与印度签署 7 项双边合作文件》，载中国新闻网，http：//www. chinanews. com/gj/2019/10-05/8972056. shtml，最后访问日期：2020 年 5 月 14 日。

〔2〕　Dipanjan Roy Chaudhury, "India, Bangladesh Explore New Areas of Cooperation in Advanced Tech, AI, Ecology & Vaccines", https：//economictimes. indiatimes. com/news/politics-and-nation/india-bangladesh-explore-new-areas-of-cooperation-in-advanced-tech-ai-ecology-vaccines/articleshow/77626437. cms, May 18, 2020.

制，中国愿帮助孟加拉国发展蓝色经济并加强相关领域的能力建设。在应对海平面上升、填海造地、保护农田和森林（包括红树林和海藻）免受盐碱化等气候变化问题上，中国愿同孟加拉国加强合作，为其在各层面的努力提供助力。除支持孟加拉国推进城市化和工业化建设外，中国愿意为孟加拉国加强灾害管理能力、提高城市和工业区的垃圾管理和污水处理水平、建设抗震基础设施等提供支持和帮助。[1]

2017 年 7 月，中国—孟加拉国首轮海上合作对话在北京举行。[2] 2018 年 11 月，中国自然资源部第三海洋研究所主办的"中国—孟加拉海洋合作与交流研讨会"在中国召开。孟加拉国国立海洋研究所、达卡大学海洋管理国际交流中心参加了此次研讨会。该研讨会为加强中孟海洋领域的交流与合作，提升双方海洋科技水平和管理能力，建立长期和稳定的合作机制奠定了基础。

2019 年 5 月，应孟加拉国吉大港大学邀请，中国自然资源部第三海洋研究所下的海洋环境管理与可持续发展研究中心、海洋与海岸地质实验室、海洋生物与生态实验室以及自然资源部第一海洋研究所的 12 位科研人员，赴孟加拉国吉大港开展孟加拉湾海岸带联合调查，并赴吉大港大学进行学术研讨和访问交流。双方科学家围绕"一带一路"、孟加拉湾气候变化、海洋空间规划、孟加拉流域—海域污染状况、污染物的源汇过程、红树林生态系统、白海豚保护等领域开展了学术交流。吉大港大学进一步提出，希望与自然资源部第三海洋研究所建立长期合作伙伴关系，加强双方在海洋领域科学研究和人才培养方面的合作。[3]

2019 年 7 月，孟加拉国总理哈西娜访问中国期间，在孟中两国总理的共同见证下，中国商务部部长与孟加拉国财政部秘书共同签署《中华人民共和国商务部和孟加拉人民共和国财政部关于建立投资合作工作组的谅解备忘录》，将海洋经济发展、海洋科研设施建设相关项目也涵盖其中。[4]

---

〔1〕《中华人民共和国和孟加拉人民共和国关于建立战略合作伙伴关系的联合声明》，载新华网，http：//www. xinhuanet. com/politics/2016-10/15/c_ 1119721775. htm，最后访问日期：2020 年 5 月 4 日。

〔2〕《中国同孟加拉国举行首轮海上合作对话》，载中华人民共和国外交部网站，https：//www. fmprc. gov. cn/web/wjbxw_ 673019/t1480243. shtml，最后访问日期：2020 年 5 月 14 日。

〔3〕《中孟 2019 年孟加拉湾海岸带联合调查暨学术交流顺利开展》，载中国自然资源部第三海洋研究所网站，http：//www. tio. org. cn/OWUP/html/zhxw/20190614/845. html，最后访问日期：2020 年 5 月 14 日。

〔4〕《中国与孟加拉国建立投资合作新机制》，载中华人民共和国商务部网站，http：//www. mof-com. gov. cn/article/ae/ai/201907/20190702879065. shtml，最后访问日期：2020 年 5 月 14 日。

（五）区域性国际合作

1. 环印度洋联盟

与印度相同，孟加拉国也是环印度洋联盟（IORA）的成员国之一。这一成立于 1997 年的政府间国际组织，吸纳了印度洋沿岸从大洋洲的澳大利亚到非洲南非共 22 个成员国。巴基斯坦是南亚五国中唯一未加入该组织的国家。[1]

孟加拉国于 1999 年加入环印度洋联盟，积极履行自己的成员义务并参与环印度洋联盟开展的计划与项目。[2] 2014 年，环印度洋联盟组织"第一届环印度洋联盟旅游业部长级会议"。孟加拉国与澳大利亚、印度、印度尼西亚等国接受了根据《塞舌尔宣言》（Seychelles Declaration）拟定的 16 项措施，以促进各成员国间旅游业的可持续发展。2019 年 9 月 4 日至 5 日，孟加拉国在其首都达卡举办第三届环印度洋联盟"蓝色经济"部长级会议，与会代表围绕"促进可持续发展的蓝色经济"主题进行磋商。[3] 为实现"海上安全与安保""贸易和投资便利化""渔业管理""灾难风险管理""旅游和文化交流""学术、科学和技术""蓝色经济""女性的经济自主"等八大优先领域的组织目标，此次会议的议程主要包括：（1）以"可持续渔业及水产养殖"加强海水养殖和渔业能力的区域性合作；（2）寻求海洋收获的可持续性，通过海洋治理确保成员国的"蓝色机遇"；（3）促进对未开发的潜在能源的勘探利用，尤其就海床底土上的资源开发及研究展开探索；（4）加强海上物流设施、海岸运输及港口网络的互通性，从而使各国的"蓝色经济门户"相连接。[4]

2. 环孟加拉湾多领域经济技术合作倡议

环孟加拉湾多领域经济技术合作倡议（BIMSTEC）是孟加拉国与印度协同创建的又一国际组织。该组织以孟加拉湾周边国家为主要成员方，但巴基

---

〔1〕　The Indian Rim Association，"About IORA"，https：//www. iora. int/en/about/about-iora，October 25，2019

〔2〕　The Indian Rim Association，"Member-states"，https：//www. iora. int/en/about/about-iora，May 12，2020.

〔3〕　The Indian Rim Association，"About-Milestones"，https：//www. iora. int/en/milestones，May 13，2020.

〔4〕　The Indian Rim Association，"Events"，https：//www. iora. int/en/events-media-news/events/priorities-focus-areas/blue-economy/2019/the-3rd-iora-blue-economy-ministerial-conference-bec-iii-on-promoting-sustainable-blue-economy-making-the-best-use-of-opportunities-from-the-indian-ocean，May 13，2020.

斯坦仍然被排除在外。

孟加拉国分别于 1997 年至 1999 年、2005 年至 2006 年两度担任该组织主席国。[1] 同时兼任组织框架下"贸易与投资"及"气候变化"两个领域的主导国。[2] 在贸易与投资领域，孟加拉国促成了各成员国于 2004 年 2 月 8 日在泰国签署《构建环孟加拉湾多领域经济技术合作倡议自由贸易区框架协议》（The Framework Agreement on the BIMSTEC Free Trade Area）。该协议于同年 6 月 30 日生效，为成员国间消减关税壁垒、构建促进贸易和服务自由的自由贸易区提供基础和依据。[3] 在气候变化领域，孟加拉国积极响应印度倡导的构建服务于农业和灾害管理的远程信息共享系统的倡议，起草在成员国间建立气候变化合作框架的意向文件，同时在达卡举办气候变化专家研讨会。[4] 2014 年 9 月 13 日，该组织将其常设秘书处设在孟加拉国达卡。[5]

3. 《亚洲地区反海盗及武装劫船合作协定》

孟加拉国是《亚洲地区反海盗及武装劫船合作协定》（ReCAAP）的发起国及缔约国之一。作为亚洲第一个关于加强反海盗和武装抢劫船舶合作的区域性政府间协定，印度及巴基斯坦均为该条约的当事国。[6] 根据这一合作协定，亚洲地区反海盗及武装劫船合作协定信息共享中心（ISC）于 2006 年 11 月在新加坡正式成立，旨在通过信息共享、能力建设及合作安排以加强区域协调，从而更有效打击海盗及海上武装抢劫行为。[7]

通过与信息共享中心的协同工作，孟加拉国海岸警卫队自 2010 年起已处理了 13 起海上劫持案件，展现了在该协定机制下信息共享及跨机构合作的显著成果。[8] 2011 年 10 月 11 日至 13 日，信息共享中心联合其在孟加拉国设

---

〔1〕 BIMSTEC, "About BIMSTEC-Chairmanship", https：//bimstec. org/? page_ id =1759, May 13, 2020.

〔2〕 BIMSTEC, "About BIMSTEC-Areas of Cooperation", https：//bimstec. org/? page_ id =199, May 14, 2020.

〔3〕 BIMSTEC, "About BIMSTEC-Areas of Cooperation-Trade and Investment", https：//bimstec. org/? page_ id =264, May 14, 2020.

〔4〕 BIMSTEC, "About BIMSTEC-Areas of Cooperation-Climate Change", https：//bimstec. org/? page_ id =290, May 14, 2020.

〔5〕 BIMSTEC, "Home- Secretariat", https：//bimstec. org/? page_ id =743, May 14, 2020.

〔6〕 《Recaap 发布亚洲海盗和武装抢劫船报告》，载国际船舶网，http：//www. eworldship. com/html/2016/ship_ inside_ and_ outside_ 1211/122869. html，最后访问日期：2020 年 5 月 14 日。

〔7〕 ReCAAP, "Vision & Mission", http：//www. recaap. org/vision_ mission_ of_ ReCAAP-ISC, May 14, 2020.

〔8〕 ReCAAP, "Incident Alert", https：//www. recaap. org/resources/ck/files/alerts/2010/Incident% 20Alert% 2015% 20Aug% 2010% 20（Hong% 20Kong% 20Star）. pdf, May 14, 2020.

立的分部（Focal Point）在达卡和吉大港举办了第二届联席会议。该会议的举办，意在加强信息共享中心及其分部与各国政府机构、航运业间的合作，从而更妥善地处理针对船舶的海盗和武装抢劫行为。孟加拉国政府派其航运部部长与会，同印度、缅甸、斯里兰卡等国政府人员围绕妥善解决孟加拉湾地区的海盗及海上暴力犯罪等问题展开了专门性的经验分享与路径探讨。[1]

（六）全球性国际组织框架下的合作

1. 国际海事组织

孟加拉国于 1976 年加入国际海事组织。[2] 对于这一负责全球海上航行安全、防止船舶污染的联合国专门机构，孟加拉国表现出高度的关注与信赖，就其在促进航运技术合作、促进海上安全、提高船舶航行效率、防止和控制船舶污染海洋等方面的标准制定与规则制定都表示配合与欢迎。孟加拉国已加入国际海事组织下 20 多项国际条约，涉及国际海洋污染防治、海员管理、船舶管理、港口管理、海上航行安全、海事赔偿和责任等多项内容。[3]

2. 联合国粮食及农业组织及其下属机构

联合国粮食及农业组织以提高人民的营养水平和生活标准为目标，致力于改进农产品的生产和分配，改善农村和农民的经济状况，促进世界经济的发展并保证人类免于饥饿。[4] 作为联合国粮食及农业组织的 194 个成员国之一，孟加拉国在该组织所获得的援助聚焦于减少贫困，加强粮食安全和营养；多样化、集约化和可持续地管理自然资源、农业机械化生产；加强与市场的联系，增强粮食安全和质量。[5]

（1）亚太渔业委员会

在联合国粮食及农业组织第三届大会的建议下，亚太渔业委员会（Asia-Pacific Fishery Commission，APFIC）于 1948 年 11 月正式成立。该委员会通常每两年举行一届会议，旨在通过发展和管理捕捞及养殖活动以及通过符合成

---

〔1〕 ReCAAP, "Press Statement", https：//www. recaap. org/resources/ck/files/news/2011/2011-10-14% 20Press% 20Statement. pdf, May 14, 2020.

〔2〕 International Maritime Organization, "Memberstates", http：//www. imo. org/en/About/Membership/Pages/MemberStates. aspx, October 29, 2020.

〔3〕 International Maritime Organization, "The GEF-UNDP-IMO GloBallast Programme", http：//www. imo. org/en/About/Events/Rio2012/Documents/Report% 20card% 20leaflet% 20GloBallast% 20Rio. pdf#search = India, October 29, 2019.

〔4〕 FAO, "About FAO", http：//www. fao. org/about/en/, May 14, 2020.

〔5〕 FAO, "Bangladesh", http：//www. fao. org/countryprofiles/index/en/? iso3 = BGD, May 14, 2020.

员目标的相关加工和销售活动，促进水生生物资源的全面、适当应用。[1] 目前该委员会有 21 个成员，孟加拉国是成员之一。[2]

亚太区域渔产品销售信息及技术咨询服务政府间组织（INFOFISH）最初为联合国粮食及农业组织于 1981 年启动的试点工程。自 1987 年以来，该组织逐渐成长为一个专门针对亚太地区及其他地区的渔业行业提供市场信息和技术咨询服务的政府间国际组织，共有包括孟加拉国在内的 13 个成员国。亚太地区存在数个世界最大的渔业国，而总部设在马来西亚吉隆坡的亚太区域渔产品销售信息及技术咨询服务政府间组织，已经成为该地区渔业生产及出口最重要的市场营销后援力量。[3]

（2）亚太水产养殖中心网络

亚太水产养殖中心网络（Network of Aquaculture Centres in Asia-Pacific，NACA）最初是联合国粮食及农业组织的一个区域性项目，于 1990 年 1 月依据《亚太水产养殖中心网络协定》（Agreement on the Network of Aquaculture Centres in Asia and the Pacific）转变为由其成员国拥有并管理的区域性自治组织，总部设于泰国曼谷。当前，该组织共有包括澳大利亚、中国、伊朗等在内的 17 个成员国，印度、巴基斯坦、斯里兰卡、马尔代夫等其他南亚国家都加入其中。[4] 作为以可持续水产养殖和水产资源管理促进农村发展并减少贫困为目标的区域性组织，亚太水产养殖中心网络持续关注的工作主题涉及：水生动物健康、气候变化、食品安全与认证、行业性别平等、遗传学及生物多样性、可持续性农业、人才培训与教育等七大方面。孟加拉国已于 1990 年加入该组织，是最早加入该组织的成员之一，并在各主题的建设与推进中都表现出积极姿态。[5]

〔1〕 FAO, "About the Asia-Pacific Fishery Commission", About the Asia-Pacific Fishery Commission, May 14, 2020.

〔2〕 FAO, "Membership", http：//www. fao. org/apfic/background/about-asia-pacific-fishery-commission/membership/en, May 14, 2020.

〔3〕 InfoFish, "Member Countries", http：//infofish. org/v3/index. php/about-us, May 14, 2020.

〔4〕 NACA, "Governing council", https：//enaca. org/? id = 34&title = naca-governing-council, May 14, 2020.

〔5〕 FAO, "Network of Aquaculture Centres in Asia-Pacific（NACA）", http：//www. fao. org/3/AD089E/ad089e06. htm#：~：text = NETWORK% 20OF% 20AQUACULTURE% 20CENTRES% 20IN% 20ASIA-PACIFIC% 20% 28NACA% 29% 201, programme% 20on% 20aquaculture% 20education. % 20... % 20More% 20items... % 20, May 14, 2020.

七、对中国海洋法主张的态度

（一）对"南海仲裁案"的态度

2016 年 4 月，中国外交部部长王毅会见出席亚洲相互协作与信任措施会议第五次外长会议的孟加拉国外交国务部长阿拉姆。王毅介绍了中方在南海问题上的原则立场，阿拉姆表示，中方在南海问题上的立场和做法是符合国际法的，孟方对此予以充分理解，并认同域外国家的介入不利于问题的解决。[1]

2016 年 6 月，中共中央对外联络部部长助理会见了孟加拉国人民联盟青年政治领袖代表团相关人员。中方代表介绍了中国在南海问题上的原则立场，孟方则指出，各国根据国际法在南海享有的航行自由不存在任何问题，中国对此作出了积极贡献。孟方代表再次表示，南海问题应由中国和有关当事国通过双边渠道协商解决，反对域外国家干涉本地区事务。[2]

值得注意的是，虽然在"南海仲裁案"最终裁决结果公布前夕，中国政府通过外交努力争取到了孟加拉国的支持，但是孟加拉国仅表达了其对"南海仲裁案"的基本立场，并未对该问题做深入表述。在"南海仲裁案"最终裁决公布后，孟加拉国也始终未在国内和国际的正式外交场合公开表达其对"南海仲裁案"最终裁决的态度。

（二）对《南海各方行为宣言》的态度

2018 年 3 月 5 日，越南总统对孟加拉国进行国事访问，并与孟加拉国总理哈西娜发表《孟加拉国—越南联合声明》（Bangladesh-Vietnam Joint Statement）。双方在该声明第 19 条强调维护和平稳定和海洋法治秩序的重要性，维护航行安全并保证符合国际法的航行和飞越自由。双方也一致同意，应根据包括《公约》在内的国际法，和平解决包括领土和海洋争端在内的所有国际争端。同理，双方均明确表示继续支持《南海各方行为宣言》，并期待早

---

[1]《王毅会见孟加拉国外交国务部长阿拉姆》，载中华人民共和国外交部网站，https：//www.fmprc.gov.cn/web/zyxw/t1358968.shtml，最后访问日期：2020 年 3 月 1 日。

[2]《李军会见孟加拉国人民联盟青年政治领袖代表团》，载中国中共中央对外联络部网站，https：//www.idcpc.gov.cn/lldt/201912/t20191216_ 114253.html，最后访问日期：2020 年 3 月 1 日。

日达成更具实质意义的"南海行为准则"。[1]

总体而言，尽管孟加拉国在正式外交场合中对《南海各方行为宣言》鲜有提及，但从其与越南发表的《联合声明》中可以看出，不同于某些国家的谨慎刻意，孟加拉国不仅对《南海各方行为宣言》持支持态度，还表达出支持有关各方依照《南海各方行为宣言》早日达成具有国际法效力的"南海行为准则"的明确意愿。

（三）在"一带一路"框架下与中国合作的态度

孟加拉国一直是区域合作的积极倡导者，20 世纪 80 年代初其便提出了成立南盟的构想。同时，孟加拉国也是 1999 年中印缅孟地区经济合作国际研讨会后"昆明倡议"的初始成员方以及 2013 年"孟中印缅经济走廊"的创始成员国。"一带一路"倡议一经提出，便得到孟加拉国官方和民间的大力支持。[2]

2016 年 10 月 14 日，孟加拉国总理哈西娜同中国国家主席习近平举行会谈。双方积极评价孟中传统友谊和两国各领域合作取得的进展，在就双边关系及共同关心的国际地区问题深入交换意见并达成广泛共识后，一致决定建立孟中战略合作伙伴关系，使两国关系在更高层次上持续向前发展。哈西娜表示，孟加拉国对中国的发展成就深感钦佩，愿在实现"金色孟加拉"梦想过程中加强同中方合作。孟方愿积极参加"一带一路"建设，支持"孟中印缅经济走廊"建设，以推动孟加拉国电力、能源、技术、农业、水利、投资、交通基础设施、互联互通等领域的发展。[3] 会谈结束后，两国签署了共建"一带一路"以及产能、能源、信息通信、投资、海洋、防灾减灾、人文等领域的多份合作文件，并发表《中华人民共和国和孟加拉人民共和国关于建立战略合作伙伴关系的联合声明》。

孟加拉国首先在该声明第 6 条表示了对"'丝绸之路经济带'和'21 世纪海上丝绸之路'（'一带一路'）倡议"的赞赏，认为这一倡议"将为孟方实现 2021 年建成中等收入国家和 2041 年成为发达国家的目标带来重要机遇"。双方同意，"加强两国发展战略对接，充分挖掘各领域合作潜力，推进

---

〔1〕 Thedailystar，"Bangladesh-Vietnam Joint Statement"，https：//www. thedailystar. net/country/bangladesh-vietnam-joint-statement-1543768，May 14，2020.

〔2〕 ［孟］基肖尔·库梅尔·班萨克等：《孟加拉国视角下的"一带一路"及孟中印缅经济走廊建设》，载《南亚东南亚研究》2018 年第 3 期，第 65—70 页。

〔3〕 《习近平同孟加拉国总理哈西娜举行会谈》，载中国政府网，http：//www. gov. cn/xinwen/2016-10/14/content_ 5119314. htm，最后访问日期：2021 年 2 月 5 日。

'一带一路'建设，实现两国可持续发展和共同繁荣"。双方在该联合声明第18条重申"孟中印缅经济走廊对于促进四国务实合作及地区整体发展的重要作用"，强调"愿意就推进孟中印缅经济走廊加强沟通与协调，推动各方尽快就四方联合研究总报告达成一致，建立四国政府间合作框架，早日启动早期收获项目"。同时，就双边海洋事务的合作，该声明第11条明确："两国在海洋事务中存在广泛合作潜力，一致同意建立海上合作对话机制。中方愿帮助孟方发展蓝色经济并加强相关领域的能力建设。"[1]

2017年5月14日至15日，孟加拉国积极参与首届"一带一路"国际合作高峰论坛，并与中国在"一带一路"建设框架下达成众多新的合作成果，包括两国间的经贸合作协议以及中国进出口银行与孟加拉国有关企业间的电网升级改造、燃煤电站、煤矿改造、轮胎厂等项目的贷款协议等[2]。

2018年11月8日，孟中两国代表进行了第十一轮外交磋商。孟方表示，孟加拉国坚定奉行对华友好政策，视中国为孟方信任和依赖的重要伙伴。孟加拉国愿加强同中国的全面合作，积极参与"一带一路"建设，推动孟中各领域合作项目稳步落实，实现互利共赢，共同发展。双方代表全面探讨了经贸、投资、产能、农业、海洋、安全、防务、人文等领域的交流合作，并就国际地区形势及共同关心的问题交换了意见[3]。

2019年4月，孟加拉国出席了第二届"一带一路"国际合作高峰论坛并与中国和其他国家达成众多新的合作成果。如孟加拉国农业部与中国农业农村部、柬埔寨农林渔业部、缅甸农业部、尼泊尔农业部、巴基斯坦食品与农业部、菲律宾农业部、泰国农业部、斯里兰卡农业部、越南农业和农村发展部共同发布了《促进"一带一路"合作共同推动建立农药产品质量标准的合作意向声明》；中国美术馆与孟加拉国、俄罗斯、韩国、希腊、白俄罗斯、哈萨克斯坦、越南、斯里兰卡、乌克兰、立陶宛、保加利亚、匈牙利、土耳其、摩尔多瓦、亚美尼亚、波兰等18个国家的21家美术馆和重点美术机构共同成立了"丝绸之路国际美术馆联盟"；中国进出口银行与孟加拉国财政

---

[1]　《中华人民共和国和孟加拉人民共和国关于建立战略合作伙伴关系的联合声明（全文）》，载中华人民共和国外交部网站，https：//www.mfa.gov.cn/web/ziliao_674904/1179_674909/t1405952.shtml，最后访问日期：2020年3月1日。

[2]　《"一带一路"国际合作高峰论坛成果清单》，载中国政府网，http：//www.gov.cn/xinwen/2017-05/16/content_5194255.htm? gs_ws = tsina_636305323348716746，最后访问日期：2020年3月1日。

[3]　《中国—孟加拉国举行第十一轮外交磋商》，载中华人民共和国外交部网站，https：//www.fmprc.gov.cn/web/wjbxw_673019/t1611989.shtml，最后访问日期：2020年3月1日。

部再次签署多份桥梁、管道项目贷款协议等〔1〕

2019 年 7 月，中国商务部部长钟山与孟加拉国财政部秘书莫诺瓦·艾哈迈德共同签署《中华人民共和国商务部和孟加拉人民共和国财政部关于建立投资合作工作组的谅解备忘录》。鉴于近年来中国对孟加拉国投资及双方合作的良好发展势头，中国企业在孟加拉国交通、电力、通信等领域实施了多个重大项目，为两国经济社会发展作出了积极贡献。如中国帮助孟加拉国建设了位于该国最大港口吉大港的卡纳普里河（Karnaphuli）河底隧道工程。该项目连接孟加拉国吉大港卡纳普里河东西两岸，全长 9293 米，是孟加拉国第一座水下隧道，更是"孟中印缅经济走廊"的重要组成部分，亦是"一带一路"建设的重要一环。双方通过本次谅解备忘录所建立的投资合作工作组将成为携手拓展合作空间、提升合作水平的重要举措。随着这一投资合作机制的建立，中国商务部与孟加拉国有关部门将以共建"一带一路"为引领，引导企业、行业组织、金融机构和地方政府等投资合作相关方加强政策层面的沟通交流和项目推介，并重点就改善投资环境和保障企业合法权益开展磋商，着力研究解决具体合作项目中存在的障碍和问题，推动两国投资合作实现高质量发展。〔2〕 根据孟加拉国计划部部长的相关表态，孟加拉国尤其欢迎中方加大对孟新能源发电、海洋经济、渔业捕捞、农产品加工、服装等领域的投资与帮助。〔3〕

由上，就孟中两国在"一带一路"框架下达成的具体合作项目的数量来看，孟加拉国对"一带一路"的实际参与程度较印度明显活跃，但较巴基斯坦稍显保守，对于"一带一路"倡议总体上持支持态度。这既显示出孟加拉国寻求高质量国际合作的迫切需求与开放立场，也体现出其在历史性盟友与地区大国的印度与中国间平衡求存的谨慎姿态。因而，在推进包括"孟中印缅经济走廊"在内的"一带一路"未来建设中，孟加拉国与中国间无论是经济纽带的强化还是政治互信的增进都将十分重要。

---

〔1〕 《第二届"一带一路"国际合作高峰论坛成果清单》，载中华人民共和国外交部网站，https://www.fmprc.gov.cn/web/ziliao_674904/zt_674979/dnzt_674981/qtzt/ydyl_675049/zyxw_675051/t1658760.shtml，最后访问日期：2020 年 3 月 1 日。
〔2〕 《中国与孟加拉国建立投资合作新机制》，载中华人民共和国商务部网站，http://www.mofcom.gov.cn/article/ae/ai/201907/20190702879065.shtml，最后访问日期：2020 年 5 月 14 日。
〔3〕 《聚焦中国与孟加拉国建立投资合作新机制，助力"金色孟加拉"》，载搜狐网，https://www.sohu.com/a/325104345_731021，最后访问日期：2020 年 3 月 1 日。

结　语

就地理位置而言，位于南亚次大陆东部的孟加拉国并非是孟加拉湾最具地理优势的沿岸国，且受国土面积所限，其海岸线长度亦相当有限。尽管如此，孟加拉国仍然不失为扼守印度洋航线与北方内陆国入海口的战略要点。

孟加拉国国内法在深受英国普通法影响 200 余年后，发展出其独特的内容，海洋相关权益在其国内也较早地得到了关注。孟加拉国宪法在 20 世纪 70 年代初即将孟加拉国领水及大陆架上的资源纳入国家财产之列，并为其进一步划定相关主权权利覆盖的管辖海域提供了实现路径，使得孟加拉国较印度及巴基斯坦更早地完成了对本国管辖海域的专门性立法。就孟加拉国当前海洋法律体系而言，其海上安全相关立法还停留在海军相关的零星立法上，而其早期的渔业、能源、海上运输相关立法都出于历史原因基本与印度及巴基斯坦同源，且尚无海洋能源开发、海洋环境保护等方面的专门立法出台。在加入《公约》20 年后，孟加拉国正在积极推动对其现行海洋立法的更新与完善，以适应海洋权益与海洋安全的新阶段态势与需求。

在缔结国际海洋法条约方面，孟加拉国的倾向性明显，仅缔结了 1982 年《公约》及与之相关的两项议定书，且在 2001 年批准加入时就《公约》提出了 10 项声明，显示出对管辖海域内的军事活动、海洋文物保护、海洋争端解决等特定事项的重点关注。

在处理与邻国的海洋争端上，孟加拉国首先采取友好协商并缔结协定的做法，也在谈判陷入僵局或分歧重大时，主动寻求国际海洋争端司法机制的帮助。孟加拉国虽然没有在正式的外交场合公开发表对"南海仲裁案"的态度，但是对《南海各方行为宣言》，孟加拉国不仅表明其支持态度，而且表达了对各国早日达成"南海行为准则"的希冀。孟加拉国积极参与中国推进的国家间合作，是 1999 年"昆明倡议"和"孟中印缅经济走廊"的创始成员国，更积极响应中国提出的"一带一路"倡议。作为印度洋及孟加拉湾的重要沿岸国、伊斯兰人口大国，孟加拉国对区域稳定、经济繁荣及海洋治理的发展无疑都独具战略意义。

斯里兰卡海洋法律体系研究

一、斯里兰卡海洋基本情况

斯里兰卡民主社会主义共和国（The Democratic Socialist Republic of Sri Lanka，以下简称"斯里兰卡"），是南亚次大陆以南印度洋上的岛国。2500年前，来自北印度的雅利安人移民至锡兰岛（Ceylon）建立僧伽罗王朝。公元前247年，印度孔雀王朝的阿育王派其子来岛弘扬佛教，受到当地国王欢迎，从此僧伽罗人摒弃婆罗门教而改信佛教。随着公元前2世纪南印度的泰米尔人逐步迁徙并定居锡兰岛，岛内的僧伽罗王国和泰米尔王国在数个世纪中彼此征战不断。16世纪起，锡兰岛先后被葡萄牙人和荷兰人统治，至18世纪末成为英国殖民地。1948年2月，锡兰作为英联邦自治领正式独立，于1972年5月22日改国名为斯里兰卡共和国，又于1978年8月16日改称斯里兰卡民主社会主义共和国，首都为科伦坡（Colombo）。[1]

（一）地理位置

斯里兰卡是印度洋上的岛国，位于北纬5°55′到北纬9°51′、东经79°41′到东经81°53′之间，全岛最长处为268英里（约432公里），最宽处为139英里（约224公里），陆地领土面积共65610平方公里，西北隔保克海峡（Palk Strait）与印度半岛相望。斯里兰卡地势中高周低，绝大部分河流都呈放射状流向大海。[2]

（二）政治概况

根据斯里兰卡1978年《宪法》的规定，斯里兰卡实行总统制。总统是国家元首和政府首脑，由人民选举产生，任期6年。国家行政权属于总统，并由内阁协助其实施。现任总统为戈塔巴雅·拉贾帕克萨（Gotabaya Rajapaksa），于2019年11月当选。内阁主要负责与国家经济和发展有关的各种重要事项。

斯里兰卡的立法权由议会行使，议会为一院制，由225名议员组成，由人民按比例选举产生。由人民选举产生的省议会是省级的管理机构，地方当

---

〔1〕 参见刘兴武编著：《斯里兰卡》，上海辞书出版社1984年版，第62—63页；《斯里兰卡国家概况》，载中华人民共和国外交部网站，https://www.fmprc.gov.cn/web/gjhdq_676201/gj_676203/yz_676205/1206_676884/1206x0_676886/，最后访问日期：2020年4月20日。

〔2〕 何道隆主编：《当代斯里兰卡》，四川人民出版社2000年版，第1页。

局负责分别管理其国内的 9 省、25 区。斯里兰卡建立了独立于行政和立法的司法制度，维护国家法律秩序，解决公民法律纠纷。[1]

（三）经济概况

斯里兰卡是一个以农业为主的国家，主要农作物为水稻，基本能够自给自足。茶叶、橡胶和椰子是该国的重要经济作物，茶叶更是主要外汇收入来源。此外，其他重要作物还包括可可和各种香料，如肉桂、豆蔻、胡椒和丁香等。由于纬度较低，气温较高，斯里兰卡盛产各类热带水果和蔬菜。斯里兰卡也是宝石和半宝石的主要出口国之一。经过 30 多年的发展，旅游业已经成为斯里兰卡重要的产业，但受政局及恐怖活动的影响，旅游业在近年的发展也出现波折。与此同时，其制造业正在迅速发展，石油产品、皮革制品、成衣和电子设备等都是其主要出口产品。而在国外工作的斯里兰卡人的侨汇，则在过去数年中占据了斯里兰卡外汇的较大部分。[2]

根据斯里兰卡央行发布的 2019 年度报告，斯里兰卡当年度的国内生产总值（GDP）总额为 150160 亿卢比（约 840 亿美元），同比增长 2.3%，第一、第二、第三产业占其国内生产总值的份额分别为 7.0%、26.4%、57.4%，人均国内生产总值为 3852 美元。2019 年，斯里兰卡通货膨胀率为 4.3%，失业率为 4.8%。斯里兰卡外债为 559 亿美元，占其国内生产总值的 66.6%，偿债率为 29.7%。贸易逆差为 79.97 亿美元，其中出口总额 119.4 亿美元，进口总额 199.37 亿美元。截至 2019 年年底，斯里兰卡官方外汇储备为 76.42 亿美元，可维持 4 至 5 个月的进口。[3]

（四）外交关系

1. 外交概况

斯里兰卡奉行独立和不结盟的外交政策，支持和平共处五项原则，反对各种形式的帝国主义、殖民主义、种族主义和大国霸权主义，维护斯里兰卡独立、主权和领土完整，不允许外国对其国家内政和外交事务进行干涉。长期以来，斯里兰卡积极推动南亚区域合作，并在联合国和南盟等组织内呼吁

---

[1] Government of Sri Lanka, "Services & Information", https：//www. gov. lk/index. php, April 20, 2020.

[2] Government of Sri Lanka, "Services & Information", https：//www. gov. lk/index. php, April 20, 2020.

[3] 《斯 2019 年度经济数据快报》，载中华人民共和国商务部网站，http：//lk. mofcom. gov. cn/article/jmxw/202005/20200502962209. shtml，最后访问日期：2020 年 5 月 10 日。

加强国际反恐合作。目前，斯里兰卡已同 140 多个国家建立了外交关系。

2. 与印度的关系

斯里兰卡与印度有着悠久的历史和地缘联系，同印度保持友好关系是斯里兰卡外交政策的重点，两国高层互访频繁。双方重视经济合作，希望借此带动南盟合作。印度支持斯里兰卡和平解决民族冲突。[1]

3. 与中国的关系

斯里兰卡与中国友好交往的历史悠久。斯里兰卡于 1950 年宣布承认新中国，并于 1957 年与中国建交。自建交以来，两国长期保持友好关系，高层往来不断。两国在许多重大国际和地区问题上拥有广泛共识，保持良好合作，在重要国际问题上一贯给予中国坚定支持。[2]

（五）海洋资源利用情况

在海洋生物资源方面，斯里兰卡鱼类捕捞年产量自 2017 年起已超过 53 万吨，附加值超过 1300 万美元。其中，有约 45 万吨来自海洋渔业，包括在领海、专属经济区以及公海海域的渔业捕捞，占其鱼类捕捞总产量的 85%。鱼类产品是斯里兰卡人民获取蛋白质的主要来源。目前，其本国渔业生产满足了国内消费所需鱼类产品总量的 65% 左右，其余部分则依靠进口。与此同时，斯里兰卡也将本国 5% 左右的鱼类产品用于出口，出口种类包括金枪鱼、虾、龙虾、螃蟹和观赏鱼等，年收入超过 2.5 亿美元，从而利用特定鱼类的出口收入抵销食用鱼类进口的部分成本。[3]

在非生物资源方面，斯里兰卡蕴藏丰富的宝石、石墨、钛铁矿、铁矿石、石灰石、石英、云母和工业黏土等矿产资源。一些地方的海滩沙中含有少量但具有商业开采价值的有色金属和钛（titanium）、独居石（monazite）、锆石（zircon）等矿物。在化石燃料中，斯里兰卡唯一已探明的资源是在其西海岸一处沼泽地带发现的低品位泥炭（peat）。此外，特殊的地理位置使得海浪能资源（wave energy resource）成为斯里兰卡可利用的重要新型可再生能源。为了促进海浪能的开发，斯里兰卡可持续能源管理局（Sri Lanka Sus-

---

〔1〕《斯里兰卡国家概况》，载中华人民共和国外交部网站，https：//www. fmprc. gov. cn/web/gjhdq_ 676201/gj_ 676203/yz_ 676205/1206_ 676884/1206x0_ 676886/，最后访问日期：2020 年 4 月 20 日。

〔2〕《中国同斯里兰卡的关系》，载中华人民共和国外交部网站，https：//www. fmprc. gov. cn/web/gjhdq_ 676201/gj_ 676203/yz_ 676205/1206_ 676884/sbgx_ 676888/，最后访问日期：2020 年 4 月 2 日。

〔3〕 Mistry of Fisheries, "The National Fisheries and Aquaculture Policy", https：//www. fisheries. gov. lk/web/images/downloads/pdfs/fisheries_ policy_ e. pdf, April 20, 2020.

tainable Energy Authority）与佩拉德尼亚大学（University of Peradeniya）机械工程系合作开展了对本国海浪能资源的评估。该研究通过提供高质量的海浪能资源数据，评估和分析海浪能资源，从而确定最具前景的海浪能开发区域，并开展覆盖斯里兰卡的海浪能资源测绘。[1]

在海洋运输和港口建设方面，斯里兰卡的大部分海洋航运都经由科伦坡港进行，包括来自印度港口的转运。此外，亭可马里港（Trincomalee）和加勒港（Galle）也承担部分国际货运任务。[2]

---

〔1〕 Mistry of Fisheries, "Performance 2018 and Programmes for 2019", http：//powermin. gov. lk/sin-hala/wp-content/uploads/2019/03/03. -English. pdf, April 20, 2020.

〔2〕《中国同斯里兰卡的关系》，载中华人民共和国外交部网站，https：//www. fmprc. gov. cn/web/gjhdq_ 676201/gj_ 676203/yz_ 676205/1206_ 676884/sbgx_ 676888/，最后访问日期：2020 年 4 月 2 日。

二、海洋事务主管部门及其职能

（一）基本政治结构

斯里兰卡实行立法权、行政权、司法权三权分立的民主制度，其主要政党有统一人民自由联盟（United People's Freedom Alliance）、统一国民阵线（United National Front）、泰米尔全国联盟（The Tamil National Alliance）、民主全国联盟（Democratic National Alliance）等。

1. 立法机关

斯里兰卡的立法权由议会行使。议会为一院制，由 225 名议员组成，任期 5 年，其中 196 名议员从 22 个选区中选举产生，其余 29 名议员则是从分配给各政党和独立团体的全国名单中选举产生。议会职能设置以英国议会制为蓝本，议会为国家最高立法机关。[1]

2. 行政机关

斯里兰卡的行政机关由总统、总理及其领导的内阁组成。总统是国家元首、行政首长、政府首脑和武装部队总司令，行使国家最高行政权。总统由人民选举产生，并由内阁协助，任期 5 年。总统担任内阁首脑，主持内阁会议，并从当选的议会成员中任命总理。总统有权召集、停止和解散议会，并有权任命内阁部长和最高法院的法官。[2] 总理则可以与总统协商确定内阁人员，并向总统建议部长人选，以及与总统协商确定各部委职能。此外，总统领导下的内阁还负责与国家发展和经济建设有关的各类重要事项。[3]

3. 司法机关

斯里兰卡的司法机关层级由上至下为：最高法院、上诉法院、高等法院、地区法院及初审法院（First Instance Court），而初审法院有治安官法庭（Magistrate's Court）、初级法庭（Primary Court）和劳动法庭（Labour Tribunal）之分。

---

〔1〕 SriLanka Parliament, "Parliament", https：//www. president. gov. lk/parliament/, April 24, 2020.

〔2〕 President of SriLanka, "The Presidency", https：//www. president. gov. lk/presidency/, April 24, 2020.

〔3〕 Office of the Cabinet of Ministers, "Prime Minister and the Cabinet of Ministers", http：//www. cabinetoffice. gov. lk/cab/index. php? option = com_ content&view = article&id = 1&Itemid = 17&lang = en, April 24, 2020.

其中，最高法院为国家的最高级法院及最终上诉法院，其全部法官都由总统基于议会提名而任命。最高法院的职权在于：（1）对来自上诉法院及任何初审法院的民事及刑事上诉案件的最终管辖权；（2）对宪法的解释及对任何法律违宪的审查；（3）保护宪法所赋予公民的基本权利；（4）对总统选举中的呈请事项、违反议会权力等事项的管辖权。其下的上诉法院受理一切来自高等法院及初审法院的上诉请求，并有权纠正任何初审法院或法庭判决在事实上或法律上的错误。高等法院是斯里兰卡各省的最高司法机关，受理本省内的刑民事案件。地区法院则广泛设置于斯里兰卡各省下辖区，并以民事、经济及家事案件为主要管辖对象。初审法院则专门接受所涉金额或危害程度在一定标准之下的诉讼请求，是斯里兰卡的基层法院。[1]

（二）海洋渔业相关管理机构及协作部门

作为岛国，斯里兰卡主张拥有 21500 平方公里的领海，517000 平方公里的专属经济区。自 1948 年斯里兰卡独立以来，海洋捕捞活动逐渐从谋生活动发展为一项年产值数十亿卢比的产业。而内陆渔业与水产养殖则是近 75 年才在斯里兰卡发展起来。20 世纪 80 年代初，随着斯里兰卡西北省份养虾场的建立，近海水产养殖在全国沿海地区逐渐普及起来。至 2010 年，斯里兰卡深海水产养殖起步。当前，该国的渔业和水产资源业对国内生产总值的贡献约为 1.4%，为 60 万人（占该国劳动力的 3.7%）提供直接和间接就业。

鉴于渔业和水产养殖业的天然便利与发展前景，斯里兰卡组建渔业和水产资源部（Ministry of Fisheries and Aquatic Resources），下辖多个渔业和水产资源职能机构并形成了较为细致的专门性分工。其主要任务是：第一，利用先进科学技术改进渔业和水产养殖业，使其实现可持续发展，增加其产量；第二，完善渔业生产链条，减少捕捞后的加工损耗，增加渔业生产附加产值，从而扩大出口产值；第三，改善渔民的生存环境，通过优化产业结构，增加企业发展的机会，创造国民就业机会；第四，增加国民人均鱼产品和水产品消费量，通过改革渔业与水产行业使其与休闲行业相结合。[2]

---

[1] See Judicial Service Commission Secretariat, "Judicial Hierarchy", http：//www. jsc. gov. lk/web/index. php？option ＝ com＿ content&view ＝ article&id ＝ 51&Itemid ＝ 64&lang ＝ en, April 24, 2020; Hierarchy Structure, "Court Hierarchy of Sri Lanka", https：//www. hierarchystructure. com/court-hierarchy-sri-lanka/, April 24, 2020.

[2] Ministry of Fisheries and Aquatic Resources, "Overview", https：//www. fisheries. gov. lk/, April 24, 2020.

同时，渔业和水产资源部还负责港口发展项目（Harbour Development Projects）、亚投行项目（ADB Project）、潟湖开发项目（Lagoon Development Projects）的管理与运行。

港口发展项目启动于 2013 年。该项目包括渔港、锚地和登陆点的建设、开发与升级，渔业和水产资源部可以利用该项目建立经济发展中心，并吸引当地物力及人力资源建立商业企业，也可以协助渔业港口公司扩大业务。

亚投行项目的运行旨在振兴和发展斯里兰卡北部省份贾夫纳（Jaffna）、马纳尔（Mannar）、穆拉蒂武（Mulathivu）和基利诺奇（Kilinochchi）等的地方渔业。近年来，在斯里兰卡其余地区的渔业迅速发展之时，北方各省相关地区渔业却进步缓慢甚至凝滞。斯里兰卡全国共有 21 个渔港，没有一个渔港分布在北方省份。为加大对北方省份渔业部门的投资，最大限度地激发北方省份的经济潜力，渔业和水产资源部计划利用亚投行和政府的投资与本地机构合作，建设功能性港口、培训当地渔民以及与私营企业合资建立示范性渔业企业，从而增加北方省份的渔业生产和就业机会。

潟湖开发项目则以发展潟湖系统经济为目标。斯里兰卡有多个潟湖位于沿海地区，具有水产养殖潜力却未得到充分利用。在该项目下，渔业和水产资源部制定政策，鼓励投资者对该项目进行商业性投资，以增加鱼类产量，为国民创造就业机会，促进旅游业及其相关产业发展，从而提升斯里兰卡潟湖地区的经济价值。[1]

渔业和水产资源部下辖的相关职能机构包括：

1. 渔业和水产资源局

渔业和水产资源局（Department of Fisheries & Aquatic Resources）的建立旨在提升以渔业和水产养殖业为生的国民的社会经济地位，同时促进渔业和水产养殖业的可持续发展。该局的工作重点是引导国民按照国家法律和相关国际规章进行经济活动，通过增强渔民开发优质渔业产品的能力来提高渔民的生活水平。

渔业和水产资源局在沿海地区建立了 15 个办事处和 20 个渔港监测中心。此外，该局还建立了 133 个渔业检查员办公室。该局的主要任务为：第一，为造船厂、供应商以及船只提供注册服务；第二，为渔民提供登记服务，签发捕鱼作业许可证、船长身份许可证、潜水员许可证以及本地建造船舶销往海外的许可证；第三，为鱼类产品进出口机构或公司提供注册服务，为鱼类

---

〔1〕　Ministry of Fisheries and Aquatic Resources, "Projects", https：//www.fisheries. gov. lk/, April 24, 2020.

加工企业提供注册服务,签发进出口许可证、健康证明以及捕捞证书;第四,对本国船舶公海捕鱼情况进行监督管理,查处非法捕鱼活动,对船舶的进出境情况及船舶日志进行检查;第五,负责勘定潟湖。[1]

2. 国家水产资源研究开发署

国家水产资源研究开发署(National Aquatic Resources Research and Development Agency,以下简称"开发署")负责在斯里兰卡开展和协调水产资源相关研究、开发和管理活动。1981 年,斯里兰卡依据《公约》主张拥有约 50 万平方公里的专属经济区,为了实现和保障本国的相关海洋利益,政府通过 1981 年第 54 号法令(Act No. 54 of 1981)创设了开发署。

作为斯里兰卡国内首屈一指的水产资源保护、管理和开发机构,开发署致力于发展科学技术并将其运用到国家水产资源领域,为国家的经济发展提供创新路径和方案。为查明、评价、管理、养护和开发水产资源,开发署在以下方面开展研究活动:第一,海洋学和水文学;第二,改进渔船、渔具和相关设备,发展捕捞方法;第三,包括渔民及其家属福利在内的渔业的社会及经济考量;第四,鱼类和其他水产品的捕捞、加工、保存和销售;第五,就开发、管理和养护水产资源及相关科学、技术和法律事项提供咨询服务;第六,统筹从事开发、规划、研究、发展、保存及管理水产资源的各机构活动;第七,收集、整理、出版有关管理、养护和发展水产资源和渔业的数据和信息,为斯里兰卡政府和民众提供参考和指南。[2]

开发署下设的相关职能机构包括:

(1)内陆水产资源和水产养殖司(Inland Aquatic Resources and Aquaculture Division)。内陆水产资源和水产养殖司负责内陆和沿海水产养殖的研究和开发,以实现水产资源的可持续发展为研究目标,将研究重心集中在开发经济可行但现阶段尚不发达的水产品,如有鳍鱼类、双壳类水产、海参和海藻等。该司还承担着鱼饲料的研发、水产养殖部门的疾病防控以及对脆弱生态环境的保护等职能,并基于研究成果向民众和政府提供咨询服务。[3]

(2)海洋生物资源司(Marine Biological Resources Division)。海洋生物

[1] Department of Fisheries & Aquatic Resources, "Overview", https://www.fisheriesdept.gov.lk/web/index.php? option = com _ content&view = featured&Itemid = 101&lang = en, April 24, 2020.

[2] National Aquatic Resources Research and Development Agency, "About NARA", http://www.nara.ac.lk/? page_ id=33, April 24, 2020.

[3] Inland Aquatic Resources and Aquaculture Division, "Inland Aquatic Resources and Aquaculture Division-About Us", http://www.nara.ac.lk/? page_ id=437, April 24, 2020.

资源司有 16 名科学家、2 名开发人员以及 16 位研究助理。该司拥有生物实验室（biological laboratory）、珊瑚礁部、海洋博物馆以及生物技术部，并在生物技术部中设有生物技术实验室（biotechnology laboratory）。该司主要负责的事项包括：第一，海洋生物资源管理、开发和养护；第二，海洋生态系统的保护与管理；第三，渔业数据的收集和分析以及渔业数据库的建立；第四，海洋、微咸水物种的分子研究；第五，海洋生物种群的识别。该司还为斯里兰卡海军、海岸警卫队及渔民普及海洋知识。[1]

（3）社会经济与市场司（Socio-Economic & Marketing Division）。社会经济与市场司成立于 1997 年，其主要职能是：第一，研究渔业捕捞的社会和经济功能，为渔业及相关行业所涉及的广泛社会、经济和市场问题提供创新性见解和解决方案；第二，促进社会和经济发展并提升国民的生活质量；第三，分析不同鱼类的区域分布并编制《渔业年鉴》（Annual Fisheries Year Book）。[2]

（4）捕鱼技术司（Fishing Technology Division）。捕鱼技术司主要就渔具、捕鱼设施以及捕鱼技术的改进和完善展开研究。该司最近的研究成果是近海鱼类聚集装置，该装置将有助于增加渔获量和小规模捕捞下的渔民收入。[3]

（5）环境研究司（Environmental Studies Division）。环境研究司致力于进行内陆、沿海和海洋环境方面的研究，通过对内陆和沿海水域的水质进行检查和评估，确定污染源以及预估水质对海洋生物的影响。该司设有水质及废水监测实验室，为政府和私人提供经济可靠的水质测试服务。该司还承担环境影响评估（Environmental Impact Assessment）和初始环境检查（Initial Environment Examination）等渔业和水产资源部的主要开发项目，并向公众提供咨询服务。[4]

（6）收获后技术研究所（Institute of Post Harvest Technology）。收获后技术研究所致力于改进和发展水产资源收获后的加工处理技术。该所的主要职能包括：第一，改进传统鱼类产品加工技术；第二，引进先进的食品加工技术从而充分利用原本未利用或未充分利用的水产资源产品及副产品；第三，

---

〔1〕 Marine Biological Resources Division,"Marine Biological Resources Division-About Us", http：// www. nara. ac. lk/? page_ id =475, April 24, 2020.

〔2〕 Socio-Economic & Marketing Division,"Socio-Economic & Marketing Division-About Us", http：// www. nara. ac. lk/? page_ id =538, April 24, 2020.

〔3〕 Fishing Technology Division,"Fishing Technology Division-About Us", http：//www. nara. ac. lk/? page_ id =546, April 24, 2020.

〔4〕 Environmental Studies Division,"Environmental Studies Division-About Us", http：//www. nara. ac. lk/? page_ id =482, April 24, 2020.

改进水产品的保存、加工环节以提升水产品的品质，并对水产品进行微生物分析和化学评估；第四，发展改良从鱼类及鱼类废料中提取鱼油的技术，并对水产养殖饲料进行研究；第五，采取措施和改进技术从而减少水产品收获后的损失；第六，研究、改进新技术从而减少水产品中的化学残留物、抗生素、生物毒素和耐药病原体污染。[1]

（7）国家海洋科学研究所（National Institute of Oceanographic Marine Sciences）。国家海洋科学研究所旨在对国家海洋环境进行研究。该所的主要工作职责在于：第一，与国际海洋学机构在印度洋进行联合考察，研究本国专属经济区的内季风环流和其他海洋学参数；第二，在联合国周转基金（United Nations Revolving Fund）的协助下，在贝鲁韦拉（Beruwela）附近进行矿物勘探；第三，监测海平面变化，测量洋流、温度、波浪、潮汐和盐度，探明全国各地的海洋能源潜力；第四，调查海洋和沿海水域中养分、微量金属、有机物的分布、流转并进行其他生物学评估；第五，为渔民、农民、工业管理者等提供咨询服务，并协助相关机构对海洋活动进行监督。此外，该所正策划建立一个国家海洋学数据中心（National Oceanographic Data Centre）。[2]

（8）国家水文局（National Hydrographic Office）。国家水文局成立于1984年，被国际水文组织（International Hydrographic Organisation）认可为斯里兰卡水文学联络中心。该机构的主要职能包括：第一，对内陆水域和海洋水域进行水文测量并收集相关数据，从而支持国家的海上航行安全维护、海洋环境保护、国防以及资源勘探；第二，负责制作航海图、鱼类资源分布图以及其他的水文地图；第三，应用研究成果以支持国家的港口发展、海岸带管理、海洋污染控制、海岸保护以及海岸工程的建造。[3]

（9）技术转让司（Technology Transfer Division）。技术转让司负责引进渔业及水产资源相关先进技术，并对已有技术进行创新。该司的主要职能包括：第一，致力于新技术的开发，从而增加国家的水产资源产量并保持国家水产资源的可持续发展；第二，致力于促进现有企业、新兴企业采用新技术，并协助其他国家机构建立水产品安全、可持续发展的监督框架；第三，

---

〔1〕 Institute of Post harvestTechnology, "Institute of Post harvest Technology-About Us", http://www. nara. ac. lk/? page_ id =486, April 24, 2020.

〔2〕 National Institute of Oceanographic Marine Sciences, "National Institute of Oceanographic Marine Sciences -About Us", http://www. nara. ac. lk/? page_ id =490, April 24, 2020.

〔3〕 National Hydrographic Office, "National Hydrographic Office-About Us", http://www. nara. ac. lk/? page_ id =493, April 24, 2020.

负责向公众普及相关知识。[1]

（10）海洋和渔业信息中心（Center for Ocean and Fisheries Information）。海洋和渔业信息中心成立于2014年，下设有专门的气象站和实验室，以向民众提供渔业和海洋信息为工作目标。除作为一个信息中心外，该中心也参与协助其他部门制订有关观赏鱼出口的规划。[2]

（11）水产养殖研究中心（Aquaculture Research Center）。水产养殖研究中心旨在通过应用研究，提高本国食用鱼、观赏鱼和海洋无脊椎动物养殖业水平。该中心致力于引进先进的观赏鱼养殖技术，完善本国观赏鱼研究框架，并将技术成果运用到本国的观赏鱼产业中，提高观赏鱼养殖者的收入。该中心还向相关专业本科生及研究生开放学习和研究机会。[3]

3. 国家水产养殖发展管理局

国家水产养殖发展管理局（National Aquaculture Development Authority）于1999年根据《1998年第53号议会法》（Parliamentary Act No. 53 of 1998）成立，负责斯里兰卡的水产养殖和渔业的管理与开发。该管理局共有5个淡水养殖发展中心、3个沿海水产养殖发展中心、2个观赏鱼繁育发展中心以及1个虾类养殖发展中心。其主要任务为：扩大水产养殖规模，拓展水产养殖相关业务，增加斯里兰卡水产养殖生产量并提高本国的水产养殖业产值；通过发展内陆和海洋水产养殖业为国民创造就业机会；促进包括观赏鱼在内的高价值鱼类的养殖；通过生态友好的方式进行水产养殖，促进水资源环境的最佳利用；与其他部门协作创立良好的水产养殖业投资环境，从而促进国内外投资者对大中小型水产养殖企业的投资；恢复和养护因错误养殖方法而遭到破坏的水产养殖生态环境。[4]

国家水产养殖发展管理局下辖两个培训机构，分别为国家内陆渔业和水产养殖培训学院（National Inland Fisheries and Aquaculture Training Institute）及观赏鱼繁殖和培训中心（Ornamental Fish Breeding and Training Center）。其中，国家内陆渔业和水产养殖培训学院成立于2009年，隶属于渔业和水产资源部的水生资源开发和质量改善项目（Aquatic Resource Development and

---

〔1〕 Technology Transfer Division, "Technology Transfer Division-About Us", http：//www. nara. ac. lk/? page_ id = 8319, April 24, 2020.

〔2〕 National Aquatic Resources Research and Development Agency, "Center for Ocean and Fisheries In-formation-About Us", http：//www. nara. ac. lk/? page_ id = 1804, April 24, 2020.

〔3〕 Aquaculture Research Center, "Aquaculture Research Center-About Us", http：//www. nara. ac. lk/? page_ id = 9477, April 24, 2020.

〔4〕 National Aquaculture Development Authority, "Overview", http：//www. naqda. gov. lk/about-us/, April 24, 2020.

Quality Improvement Project）。该学院拥有一支高素质、经验丰富且训练有素的专家团队，专门从事水产养殖业和内陆渔业研究。[1] 而观赏鱼繁殖和培训中心的主要职能则包括：（1）提供观赏鱼养殖培训，为养殖户提供优质的观赏鱼孵化器，并协助养殖户保持鱼群健康；（2）为养殖户提供鱼类疾病的诊断和咨询服务；（3）提供优质的水生植物母本，对观赏性动植物文化进行适应性研究，并向公众提供不同的培训计划。[2]

4. 锡兰渔业公司

锡兰渔业公司（Ceylon Fisheries Corporation）于1964年根据《1957年国家工业公司法》（State Industrial Corporations Act）成立，并于1965年开始商务运作。作为国家全资成立的商业实体，锡兰渔业公司成立之初曾控制斯里兰卡的整个渔业部门，至今仍是在其国家渔业行业占据领导地位的商业组织。

以促进和指导鱼类的生产和贸易活动并服务于国民利益为目标，锡兰渔业公司不断利用现代技术促进、完善渔业的生产、加工和销售环节，提升渔民生产能力，增强渔民的社会经济地位，同时为国民提供稳定的蛋白质供应，并努力为国民生产总值增长作出更大贡献。该公司的主要任务为：直接或通过授权代理商使用拖网渔船进行深海捕捞作业以及从事鱼类产品、鱼类副产品的加工和生产；直接或通过授权代理商以批发和零售方式从事鱼类产品的分配和销售；对渔港和锚地进行建造和维护，建造、维修、保养用于渔业的船舶；管理渔业设备的生产和销售，为了支持本国渔业的发展引进外国先进的渔业相关设备；代行政府机构的某些渔业相关职能，以更好地发展渔业。[3]

5. 塞诺基金有限公司

塞诺基金有限公司（Cey-Nor Foundation Limited）是位于科伦坡的一家国有企业。该公司拥有两个船坞，也是斯里兰卡唯一一家政府所有的玻璃纤维船（fiberglass boats）制造公司，负责为渔业捕捞提供高质量的玻璃纤维产品。通过引入先进的造船设备、造船技术以及配备用于造船的专业软件，该公司的造船水平已经达到了国际水平。在该公司长期按照国际标准生产船舶、提供服务的严格要求之下，该公司的产品和服务已获得"劳氏认证"

---

[1] National Inland Fisheries and Aquaculture Training Institute, "Overview", http：//www. naqda. gov. lk/training/national-inland-fisheries-and-aquaculture-training-institute-nifati/，April 24，2020.

[2] Ornamental Fish Breeding And Training Center, "Overview", http：//www. naqda. gov. lk/training/ornamental-fish-breeding-and-training-center-rambadagalla/，April 24，2020.

[3] Ceylon Fisheries Corporation, "Overview", https：//www. cfc. gov. lk/web/index. php? option = com_ content&view = article&id = 15&ltemid = 149&lang = en，April 24，2020.

（Lloyds Certification）〔1〕。

除了生产玻璃纤维船，该公司的运营范围还包括：（1）联合渔业企业向客户提供渔网和各类捕鱼工具及设施；（2）通过合资项目向孟加拉国转让造船技术，为孟加拉国玻璃纤维船的建造奠定基石；（3）从 2013 年起涉足港口、锚地及离岸海上设施等大型海洋工程的建设工作。〔2〕

6. 国家渔业联合会

国家渔业联合会（National Fisheries Federation）成立于 2010 年，旨在同渔民群体和渔业部门协作，共同促进国家渔业的可持续发展。联合会也致力于引进国际先进渔业知识和技能，促进国家捕鱼行业的现代化，同时推动渔民社会和经济地位的提高。

7. 佩里亚戈达鱼类综合市场

佩里亚戈达国家综合鱼类市场（Fish Market Complex-Peliyagoda）由斯里兰卡政府于 2006 年建立并提供资金支持。近年来，亚投行也为该综合鱼类市场的发展提供了额外资金支持。作为斯里兰卡最先进的鱼类市场，该综合鱼类市场占地 3.17 公顷，拥有 148 个批发摊位、128 个零售摊位、3 个冷藏室以及 1 个制冰厂。

当前，该市场的工作目标主要为：（1）确保鱼类产品的质量和卫生，稳定鱼类产品的价格；（2）严格规范供应商，使鱼类产品的供应符合相关标准；（3）为消费者及商家提供足够的鱼货存储空间，并通过大型鱼类市场的集中交易缓解在科伦坡市内频繁运输的交通拥挤情况。〔3〕

（三）海洋能源及环境相关管理机构

1. 电力、能源与商业发展部

电力、能源与商业发展部（Ministry of Power, Energy and Business Development）负责为国家的经济繁荣提供优质、可靠及可持续的能源，确保国家能源安全。斯里兰卡已在全国范围内实现了 90% 以上的电气化率，并基本实

---

〔1〕 "劳埃德船级社"及其认证（劳氏认证）在造船业中因其公正、权威、独立而享有盛誉，甚至某些与"Lloyds"相关的短语已经成为质量的象征。See Lloyds Register, "Overview", https://www.lr.org/en/, April 24, 2020.

〔2〕 Cey-Nor Foundation Limited, "Overview", http://ceynor.gov.lk/about-ceynor-foundation, April 24, 2020.

〔3〕 Ministry of Fisheries and Aquatic Resources, "Overview", https://www.fisheries.gov.lk/web/index.php?option=com_content&view=article&id=26&Itemid=1^{30}&lang=en#national-fisheries-federation, April 24, 2020.

现了在《斯里兰卡国家能源政策与战略》（National Energy Policy & Strategies of Sri Lanka）中设定的战略目标。电力、能源与商业发展部的主要工作职责为：积极采取措施以实现农村电气化；制定合理的电力规章，规范国内的发电、输电及配电流程，对电力的供应和使用进行调控和监测；对地热、水力、风能以及太阳能等资源进行调查研究，规划发展相关设施和工程，实现能源来源的多样化；管理能源需求，确保能源效率，发展可再生资源，对能源研究领域进行资金投入；制定与电力和可再生资源有关的政策，对电力和可再生资源有关的计划及项目进行检测和评估，对电力、能源与商业发展部的下属机构进行监督和管理。[1]

斯里兰卡可持续能源管理局（Sri Lanka Sustainable Energy Authority）是电力、能源与商业发展部的下属机构之一。该局依据《第35号斯里兰卡可持续能源管理局法》（Sri Lanka Sustainable Energy Authority Act No. 35）于2007年成立。作为引导斯里兰卡可持续能源革命（sustainable energy revolution）的主要责任机关，该管理局承担着包括太阳能、风能、水能以及生物能等在内的可再生资源的开发推进任务，以提高国内能源效率、保证国家能源安全为首要工作目标。

其主要任务包括：（1）紧跟国际可再生资源的发展趋势，通过借鉴外国先进经验，开发与本国环境相契合的可再生资源技术，并制定适宜方案将技术运用到实际开发中去；（2）制定高效益的可再生资源开发方案，向国家提出资源结构改革建议，并做好相关宣传以吸引资金的投入；（3）通过不同的渠道与公众、企业以及相关科研机构等分享所收集掌握的数据、知识及见解观点。

依赖从外国进口化石燃料，不仅加重国家经济负担，加剧环境污染，更影响国家能源安全。为了改善这一状况，斯里兰卡可持续能源管理局在关注太阳能、风能、生物质能等传统可持续能源的开发之外，也将注意力放到了前景广阔但现阶段尚未商业化的海洋能源之上。现今，在斯里兰卡处于研发阶段的海洋能源主要包括：波浪能、潮汐能、盐度梯度能、海洋热能。[2]

2. 石油资源开发部

2005年12月，斯里兰卡政府颁布《第1422/22号特别公报》（Government Extraordinary Gazette No. 1422/22）设立石油和石油资源开发部（Ministry

---

〔1〕 Ministry of Power, Energy and Business Development, "Overview", http：//powermin. gov. lk/english/？ page_ id = 1222, April 24, 2020.

〔2〕 Sri Lanka Sustainable Energy Authority, "Other Forms of Energy", http：//www. energy. gov. lk/en/renewable-energy/technologies/other-forms-of-energy, April 24, 2020.

of Petroleum and Petroleum Resources Development），又于 2010 年 4 月颁布《第 1651/20 号政府特别公报》（Government Extraordinary Gazette Notification No. 1651/20）改组为石油工业部（Ministry of Petroleum Industries）。该部门仅负责石油产业的下游活动，而将石油产业的上游活动交由总统负责。2015 年 9 月 1 日，石油资源开发部（Ministry of Petroleum Resources Development）依据《第 1933 /13 号政府特别公报》（Government Extraordinary Gazette Notification No. 1933/13）正式成立，全权收拢斯里兰卡石油产业上下游活动的管控工作。

石油资源开发部的建立旨在以可持续且高效的方式利用石油资源，通过有序、科学地管理石油上下游产业，保证国家的能源需求，实现国家的能源安全。其主要职责包括：（1）使斯里兰卡变成能源上自给自足的国家；（2）增加国内的石油和天然气产量，增强本国加工石油产品的能力，提升本国的柴油和汽油质量水平；（3）开发、改进塑料废物转换为燃料的技术能力；（4）通过提升技术、制定政策保证燃料的贮存和运输安全；（5）促进全国范围的节油活动。

石油资源开发部的下辖机构和国有公司有：石油资源开发秘书处（Petroleum Resources Development Secretariat）、锡兰石油公司（Ceylon Petroleum Corporation）、锡兰石油储油码头有限公司（Ceylon Petroleum Storage Terminals Limited）、保利托公司（Polypto）。[1]

斯里兰卡的海上石油储藏主要集中于高韦里盆地（Cauvery Basin）和马纳尔盆地（Mannar Basin）。高韦里盆地位于北纬 9°—北纬 11°及东经 79°东经 81°之间，马纳尔盆地位于北纬 6°—北纬 9°度及东经 78°—东经 80°之间。当前，马纳尔盆地被分为 9 个勘探区块。2007 年 9 月，石油资源开发部将马纳尔盆地 3 个区块（SL2007 - 01 - 001 区块、SL2007 - 01 - 002 区块、SL2007 - 01 - 003 区块）的勘探权进行公开招标。因只有 001 区块收到足够数量的投标，石油资源开发部仅针对 001 区块的投资商进行了评估，并最终选择凯恩兰卡有限公司（Cairn Lanka Limited）为开发方。2008 年 7 月，斯里兰卡政府通过石油资源开发部与凯恩兰卡有限公司签订了《石油资源协议》（Petroleum Resources Agreement）。[2]

---

〔1〕　Ministry of Petroleum Resources Development，"Exploration History"，https：//www. petroleummin. gov. lk/web/index. php/en/，April 24，2020.

〔2〕　Petroleum Resources Development Secretariat，"Exploration History"，http：//www. prds-srilan- ka. com/exploration/origins. faces，April 24，2020.

3. 海岸保护及海岸资源管理部

海岸保护及海岸资源管理部（Coastal Conservation & Coastal Resources Management Department）旨在对沿海资源和沿海工程进行可持续管理，以优化斯里兰卡的社会、经济和环境状况。尽管沿海地区人口的快速增长带动了渔业、旅游业、航海事业的发展，也加速了沿海地区的工业化和城市化，但是人口增加也不可避免地造成了沿海自然环境的恶化，因此科学管理沿海地区的工程建设，将有助于斯里兰卡沿海地区的可持续发展。

1963 年之前，斯里兰卡的海岸防治工作分由不同的部门承担。为了实现对海岸侵蚀的全面控制，斯里兰卡政府于 1963 年建立隶属于科伦坡港口委员会（Colombo Port Commission）的海岸保护工程部（Coast Protection Engineering Unit）。1978 年，海岸保护工程部被归于渔业和水产资源部，改组为该部下设的海岸保护司（Coast Conservation Division）。1981 年，斯里兰卡议会颁布《海岸保护法》（Coast Conservation Act No. 57 of 1981），将海岸保护司升级为海岸保护局（Coast Conservation Department）。至 2009 年 7 月，海岸保护局独立并升级为海岸保护及海岸资源管理部。

海岸保护及海岸资源管理部主要有以下职责：第一，对沿海地区的开发活动进行合理规划，改善沿海环境状况，提高沿海地区居民的生活水平；第二，以沿海海洋资源为基础，促进经济的可持续发展；第三，发展和提升沿海地区的社会、经济和文化价值，提高沿海地区的生产力，实现环境友好型发展；第四，采取措施减少自然灾害对民众的影响。[1]

海岸保护及海岸资源管理部下设 6 大部门，除负责财务、行政及信息监测与评估的基础部门外，3 个特色职能机构分别为：（1）海岸工程司（Coast Works Division）。海岸工程司负责对沿岸工程建设进行管理，并维修现有的海岸防护设施，实现海岸保护及海岸资源管理部的基础职能。（2）海岸研究与设计司（Coastal Research & Designs Division）。海岸研究与设计司负责对海岸进行监测、调查和研究，具体包括：第一，通过监测和探索沿岸地区查找沿岸地区的社会、经济和环境问题，并通过针对性研究寻求解决方案；第二，利用水动力学和地貌学方法对海岸线进行调查，制定海岸线加固方案和沿海工程建设方案；第三，对沿海风险进行分析，针对日益增多的自然灾害，制定相应的防范、适应和缓解措施；第四，负责将收集到的海岸数据向社会公布。（3）海岸资源管理司（Coastal Resource Managemen Division）。海

---

[1] Coastal Conservation & Coastal Resources Management Department, "Overview", http：//www. coastal. gov. lk/index. php? lang = en, April 24, 2020.

岸资源管理司负责利用沿海地区资源协助社会发展，具体包括：第一，推行发展监管制度，对沿岸地区的开发活动进行评估和管理，以减轻对环境的影响并确保资源的可持续利用；第二，和其他相关机构共同推行特殊地区管理计划（Special Area Management Plans），严格遵照国家战略和政策解决沿海地区的社会、文化、经济和环境问题；第三，向民众普及保护沿海环境的重要性。[1]

（四）海洋运输相关管理机构

港口与航运部（Ministury of Ports & Shipping）是指导管理斯里兰卡海洋航运相关事务发展的主要国家行政机关。港口与航运部以将斯里兰卡发展为南亚最具竞争力的海事活动中心为目标，不断努力为国内外提供优质的海事服务。该部门通过制定适当、高效的政策架构和工作机制，提升本国港口、航运服务的竞争力，使本国的海事活动服务能满足国内外客户的需求，并协调本国的海事活动以满足国家经济发展的需要。港口与航运部的主要任务为：管理、监督、协调本部门下属机构的工作，与下属机构共同推进相关海事服务项目的开展；更新并完善港口与航运服务准则，为港口及航运客户提供更好的服务；构建高效的工作机制以实施国家相关港口及航运政策；对海运代理业务、集装箱出境业务、旅行代理业务等海事业务进行严格、高效的管理和监督；协助立法机构制定有利于海事机构运行的法律架构。[2]

港口与航运部下辖三个机构，分别为：

1. 商船秘书处

商船秘书处（Merchant Shipping Secretariat）是斯里兰卡的航运管理机构，全面负责监管海上运输事务，并根据《1971 年第 52 号商船法》（Merchant Shipping Act No. 52 of 1971）、《1972 年第 10 号船舶代理人执照法》（Licensing of Shipping Agents Act No. 10 of 1972）、《1983 年第 40 号海军法》（Admiralty Jurisdiction Act No. 40 of 1983）等有关法律行使权力。

该处的主要工作目标为：第一，进行船员身份登记，签发、认证船员能力证书，对船员进行考核并颁发相应技术证书，同时对船员纠纷进行仲裁；第二，调查、处理海上事故，对遇难船员进行救助，并制定政策以防范海上

〔1〕 Coastal Conservation & Coastal Resources Management Department，"Head Office Divisions"，http：//www. coastal. gov. lk/index. php? option = com_ content&view = article&id = 20&Itemid = 154&lang = en，April 24，2020.

〔2〕 Ministury of Ports &Shipping，"Overview"，http：//portcom. slpa. lk/minport/ministry-of-port-shipping/FUNCTIONS-OF-MINISTRY，April 24，2020.

事故的发生；第三，在遵守国际公约的同时，完善本国相应法律，并担任国际海事组织在斯里兰卡的联络机构；第四，对海事培训机构进行审核和监督，审核、批准海事培训课程，进行海员考试和认证；第五，规范买卖船舶行为并处理海事运输相关事务，对国内外船舶进行检查以及协调增加国内海员在外国船舶上的就业机会。[1]

2. 锡兰航运有限公司

锡兰航运有限公司（Ceylon Shipping Corporation Ltd）的历史可以追溯到20世纪60年代末。1969年，政府依据《1938年公司条例》（Company Ordinance No. 51 of 1938）以公私合营的形式建立了锡兰航运有限公司，并将总部设立在科伦坡。1970年4月，原锡兰海运有限公司（Ceylon Shipping Lines Ltd）并入锡兰航运有限公司。该公司曾于1971年被划归国有，至1992年，为了更好地应对国际市场的变化，斯里兰卡政府决定赋予该航运公司更多的商业独立性，但锡兰航运有限公司仍保留其国有企业身份。

锡兰航运有限公司拥有包括"锡兰微风"号（M. V. Ceylon Breeze）、"锡兰公主"号（M. V. Ceylon Princess）等在内的11艘船舶，其商务航线已延伸至印度、澳大利亚及欧洲、远东各国。作为南亚地区第一家提供从南亚到欧洲集装箱海上运输服务的公司，该公司不仅使很多非传统出口产品进入全球市场，还为国际航运提供了在南亚航线的立足点。同时，该公司为科伦坡港口的现代化作出了重大贡献，并为斯里兰卡培养了大批航运业人才。[2]

3. 港务局

港务局（Port Authority）的建立可以追溯到20世纪20年代末。1918年，科伦坡港由科伦坡港口委员会（Colombo Port Commission）管理，该委员会负责建设、维护货物装卸设备以及其他基础设施。其所有活动资金均由政府提供，但货物的搬运和装载业务由数家私营码头装卸公司分别承担。1958年，港口货运公司（Port Cargo Corporation）成立，以提供港口货运服务为主营业务。1967年，港口理货和防护服务公司（Port Tally and Protective Services Corporation）成立，为停靠装卸船舶提供港口理货和值班服务。1979年8月，政府根据《斯里兰卡港务局法》（Sri Lanka Ports Authority Act, No. 51 of 1979）将科伦坡港口委员会、港口货运公司、港口理货和防护服务公司合并成港务局。港务局不从政府获得财政拨款，而是依靠自己的收入和资源运作。

---

[1] Merchant Shipping Secretariat, "Overview", http://www. dgshipping. gov. lk/web/index. php? option = com_ content&view = article&id = 2&Itemid = 105&lang = en, April 24, 2020.

[2] Ceylon Shipping Corporation Ltd, "Overview", http://www. cscl. lk/, April 24, 2020.

为了应对来自国际贸易的机遇和挑战，港务局与工业、交通等主管部门协作，共同提升斯里兰卡港口物流整合能力、全球货物运输能力以及港口事务管理能力，致力于将斯里兰卡变为全球物流枢纽。在坚持服务高标准的同时，港务局也持续顾及海洋环境保护，不断发展提供环境友好型服务的能力。当前，港务局的主要职能为：在斯里兰卡建设最先进的商业港口，对港口设施进行维护，并提供高效、可靠的港口服务；通过制定切实可行的政策规章，保证港口运输业务的运行畅通无阻；确保客户人身和港口设施及一切与港口有关事项的安全，为客户及员工提供一个安全、舒心的业务及工作环境；为财政部提供资金，支持国家卫生、教育以及交通部门的基础设施建设。[1]

（五）其他海洋管理行政机构

1. 气象部

气象部（Department of Meteorology）按照国际标准向政府机构、社会企业和公众提供有关气象学、航空气象学、海洋气象学、水文气象学、农业气象学、气候学和天文学的服务。气象部的主要工作目标为：第一，根据世界气象组织的标准，观察和整理天气要素，并维护气候数据库；第二，根据世界气象组织和国际民用航空组织制定的技术规则，为国家和国际航空提供气象服务；第三，协助科研机构在气象学、气候学、气候变化及相关学科领域进行研究，并在这些专题领域组织和推动公众认知计划；第四，提供有限的天文及地磁服务，发出海啸以及与天气有关的事件预警。[2]

在海洋气象预报方面，气象部分别提供：（1）服务于渔民及海军的天气预报；（2）斯里兰卡所在岛屿周边海域天气预报；（3）服务于来往国际商船、国际舰队的天气预报；（4）覆盖斯里兰卡周边海域、孟加拉湾、阿拉伯海及南印度洋部分海域的多日气象预报。

2. 文化艺术事务部

文化艺术事务部（Ministry of Cultural and Art Affairs）在斯里兰卡历史上经历过多次分立重组。1994 年，斯里兰卡在 1956 年成立的文化事务部（Ministry of Cultural Affairs）中增设宗教事务机构，并将其改组为文化和宗教事务部（Ministry of Cultural and Religious Affairs）。在经历了宗教与文化管理

---

〔1〕　Port Authority, "Overview", https：//www. slpa. lk/port-colombo/vision-and-mission, April 24, 2020.

〔2〕　Department of Meteorology, "Overview", http：//meteo. gov. lk/index. php？lang = en, April 24, 2020.

职务的多次分离合并之后，斯里兰卡内阁于 2010 年将该部正式变更为文化艺术事务部。

文化艺术事务部致力于保护本国的珍贵文化遗产，制定文化遗产保护政策，执行文化遗产保护方案，并向海内外传播斯里兰卡文化。其主要任务包括：指导全国的文化建设，制定和实施文化认同和多元文化相关政策；通过科学系统地保护文化和自然遗产资源，建立并完善博物馆服务，满足公众对于文化艺术的欣赏、教育、娱乐需要；制定体现斯里兰卡文学、艺术元素的文化方案，向国内外弘扬斯里兰卡的优秀与特色文化。[1]

隶属于文化艺术事务部的中央文化基金会（Central Cultural Fund）在海洋考古、古代海洋文化遗产发掘中取得了一定成果。中央文化基金会根据《1980 年第 57 号国会法》（Act of Parliament，Act No. 57 of 1980）成立，于 2007 年划归文化艺术事务部管理。中央文化基金会的理事会由大约 12 名成员组成，由斯里兰卡总理担任主席，成员中包括至少 6 名内阁部长。中央文化基金会有权接受来自斯里兰卡国内外捐赠的资金，并将这些资金用于文物的保护和管理。该机构的主要工作包括考古调查、文物修复、有关文物的科学研究、文化资料的提供以及建造文物区中的游客基础设施等。

位于斯里兰卡西南部的加勒（Galle）遗址区，是由中央文化基金会管理保护的国内近 30 个文化遗址区之一。中央文化基金会以加勒港为中心，进行海洋考古研究，并在此设立海洋博物馆，展示该遗址的古代海洋遗产和文化遗产。该基金会为保护包括该区域在内的文化遗址所作出的杰出贡献，被联合国教科文组织赞誉为亚洲地区文化遗址保护的榜样。[2]

（六）海上武装执法机构

斯里兰卡的海上武装执法任务主要由海岸警卫队和海军承担，两者虽然均隶属于国防部，但在职责范围、执法方式等方面各有侧重。此外，斯里兰卡还有一家国有海上安保公司，可以提供优质的海上安保服务。

1. 斯里兰卡海岸警卫队

斯里兰卡海岸警卫队（Sri Lanka Coast Guard）的建立可以追溯到 20 世纪 90 年代末。1998 年，渔业和水产资源部部长向内阁提交报告，就斯里兰卡拥有本国海岸警卫队的必要性进行阐述，并在内阁许可下由政府着手建立

---

〔1〕 Ministry of Cultural and Art Affairs，"Overview"，https：//www. cultural. gov. lk/web/index. php? option = com_ content&view = article&id = 47&Itemid = 55&lang = en，April 24，2020.

〔2〕 Central Cultural Fund，"Overview"，http：//www. ccf. gov. lk/index. php? option = com_ content & view = article&id = 44&Itemid = 173&lang = en，April 24，2020.

海岸警卫队。1999 年，共有 75 名人员被招募到海岸警卫队任军官、士官和水手。2002 年，政府决定撤销海岸警卫队，将其所有资产和人员移交海岸保卫局（Coast Conservation Department）。2009 年，国防部长向内阁提交了重新建立海岸警卫队的报告，议会于同年 7 月 9 日通过了 2009 年第 41 号法令（Act. No 41 of 2009），组建新的斯里兰卡海岸警卫队。2010 年 3 月 4 日，斯里兰卡海岸警卫队正式开始海上执法活动。[1]

斯里兰卡海岸警卫队的主要职责是：第一，制止渔业相关犯罪。海岸警卫队在斯里兰卡各大渔港共设立了 24 个渔业监测点，对所有进出渔船进行全面的监测，确保一切捕鱼活动符合法律规定。第二，打击走私、贩毒和人口贩卖活动。海岸警卫队全年部署海上部队，防止印度南部邦的犯罪团伙将毒品以及其他违禁品通过保克海峡和马纳尔海湾走私到斯里兰卡。海岸警卫队还通过部署机动单位配合部队对可疑船只进行检查，打击人口走私活动。第三，打击海盗和海上恐怖主义。海岸警卫队与其他海上部队合作，通过持续监视和海上巡逻，确保斯里兰卡的专属经济区和邻近公海不受海盗和海上恐怖分子的侵害，以确保斯里兰卡的海上贸易畅通无阻。斯里兰卡海岸警卫队还通过信息共享和联合演习的方式与他国开展海上力量合作，以制止海盗活动。第四，致力于预防、控制和管理在斯里兰卡海域的石油、化学物品等物质的泄漏。除了加强对船舶的检查以及建立相关岸上监测站，海岸警卫队还计划配备与国际标准相匹配的技术设备来增强自身处理石油、化学物质等泄漏事件的能力。第五，与其他国家海上执法机构建立良好的关系，在海洋环境保护、海事安全等领域开展各种形式的合作。第六，根据与国际海事组织达成的协议对遭遇自然灾害和遇险的船舶进行救助。[2]

2. 斯里兰卡海军

斯里兰卡海军（Sri Lanka Navy）的建制可以追溯至 20 世纪 30 年代。为了配合宗主国英国的帝国防卫计划，斯里兰卡成立了锡兰海军志愿部队（Ceylon Naval Volunteer Force）。二战期间，锡兰海军志愿部队积极执行打击法西斯军队的作战任务，并于 1942 年被英国皇家海军吸收，更名为锡兰皇家海军志愿人员后备队（Ceylon Royal Naval Volunteer Reserve）。二战结束后，当时的锡兰政府恢复了对锡兰皇家海军志愿人员后备队的控制。1948 年斯里兰卡以英联邦自治领的身份独立，海军核心人员在数量和质量上都得到了全面提升。1950 年 12 月，斯里兰卡颁布《海军法》（Navy Act），成立皇家锡

---

〔1〕　Sri Lanka Coast Guard, "Overview", http：//www. coastguard. gov. lk/, April 24, 2020.

〔2〕　Sri Lanka Coast Guard, "Vision&Mission", http：//www. coastguard. gov. lk/, April 24, 2020.

兰海军（Royal Ceylon Navy）。1972 年，随着斯里兰卡完全脱离英国统治，从"锡兰自治领"成为"斯里兰卡民主社会主义共和国"，皇家锡兰海军也依据国家新宪法正式更名为斯里兰卡海军。[1]

斯里兰卡海军总部设在科伦坡，由海军司令行使斯里兰卡海军行政权和作战控制权。为了有效地对海军进行指挥和行政控制，根据斯里兰卡的地理状况和行政区划，斯里兰卡水域和沿海地区被分为 7 个海军区划，分别为：东部海军军区（Eastern Naval Area）、北部海军军区（Northern Naval Area）、西部海军司令部（Western Naval Command）、南部海军军区（Southern Naval Area）、西北部海军司令部（North Western Naval Command）、中北部海军军区（North Central Naval Area）、东南部海军军区（South Eastern Naval Area）。各军区都设有属于自己军区的港口、船舶维修中心、车辆维修中心、信号中心、医疗设施及建设局，确保海军后勤体系的有效运作。[2]

斯里兰卡海军舰队拥有 50 多艘舰船，除少量为本国建造外，大部分舰船来自美国、中国、印度及以色列等多国。斯里兰卡海军舰队拥有"加贾巴胡"号（SLNS Gajabahu）、"萨卢拉"号（SLNS Sayurala）、"辛杜劳拉"号（SLNS Sindurala）、"帕拉克拉玛巴胡"号（SLNS Parakramabahu）4 艘轻型近海巡逻舰；"塞杜拉"号（SLNS Sayura）、"塞姆杜拉"号（SLNS Samudura）、"萨加拉"号（SLNS Sagara）、"杰亚萨贾拉"号（SLNS Jayasagara）4 艘近海巡逻舰；2 艘南迪密特拉级（Nandimithra）快速导弹船；以及多艘快速攻击舰、沿海攻击艇、两栖战舰、辅助船等。[3]

斯里兰卡将海军视为本国最重要的防御力量以及国家安全和利益的有力保障。斯里兰卡海军以根据国家政策展开及时、连续的海上作战行动为使命，其主要职责为：第一，在公海上部署海军船舰进行巡逻，在商船协助下，对非法转移战争物资的行为进行监视；第二，对港口进行全天候的保护，使本国军舰和国内外商船免受恐怖组织袭击，维持港口的良好秩序；第三，协助陆军进行两栖作战，支持陆军执行地面作战任务，解放恐怖分子所占地区。[4]

3. 斯里兰卡国防安保公司

斯里兰卡国防安保公司（Rakna Arakshaka Lanka Limited）是斯里兰卡国

---

〔1〕 Sri Lanka Navy, "History", https：//www. navy. lk/history. html, April 24, 2020.

〔2〕 Sri Lanka Navy, "Tactical Area of Responsibility", https：//www. navy. lk/newtaor. html, April 24, 2020.

〔3〕 Sri Lanka Navy, "Fleet", https：//www. navy. lk/fleet. html#, April 24, 2020.

〔4〕 Sri Lanka Navy, "Mission", https：//www. navy. lk/, April 24, 2020.

防部于 2006 年 10 月创立的公司，既具有私人安保公司的营运资格，又得到了来自斯里兰卡国防部的专门性安保服务支持。该公司有能力提供一流的安全服务，以全面满足商业部门的安全需求，服务范围包括工业安全、商业安全、航空安全、海事安全以及提供安保服务培训等多方面。该公司现有 3000 名员工，通过和港口代理商、港口当局、军队以及警察局合作以获得武器和安保设备，同时吸纳众多包括陆军、海军、空军以及民防部队在内的退役军人和警察加入公司团队，以最大限度保障公司员工的专业性和纪律性。[1]

当前，该公司主要业务区域为红海、亚丁湾、阿拉伯海、印度洋以及莫桑比克海峡等海域，为商船航行提供武装或者非武装的海上安保人员以抵御海盗的侵扰。该公司的专业人员有能力提前做好应急规划，在护航途中及时发现海盗侵扰风险并迅速规避，或在不能规避时采取适当处理手段以最大限度地保全客户利益。[2]

---

〔1〕 Rakna Arakshaka Lanka Limited，"Rakna Arakshaka Lanka Limited（RALL）in Affiliation with the Ministry of Defence"，http：//rallsecurity. lk/index. php，April 24，2020.

〔2〕 Rakna Arakshaka Lanka Limited，"Maritime"，http：//rallsecurity. lk/index. php，April 24，2020.

三、国内海洋立法

一方面，斯里兰卡从 16 世纪起即先后被葡萄牙、荷兰、英国三个欧洲国家纳入殖民统治，它们在 400 多年里分别引入不同的法律体系，强烈地冲击着斯里兰卡的本土规则。另一方面，作为一个多民族和多语言的国家，斯里兰卡各个群体的不同习俗、惯例、观念及刑罚最终都通过相关法律得到了不同程度的反映和施行。

从英国殖民时代开始，多种渊源的法律制度即并行于斯里兰卡的土地上，包括由英国人引入的英国法原则、由荷兰人所引入的"罗马荷兰法"（Roman-Dutch）原则、适用于康提僧伽罗的"康提安法"（Kandyan Law）、适用于贾夫纳泰米尔的"特萨瓦拉迈法"（Thesavamalai Law）、适用于穆斯林的"穆斯林法"（Muslim Law）以及少量适用于佛教徒与印度教徒宗教财产及习俗的宗教法。

在斯里兰卡当前的法律体系中，"罗马荷兰法"普遍适用于其议会立法与本土法未能规制的问题。作为斯里兰卡所承继的法律传统，其与若干本土法律及英国普通法共同创造了一种大陆法系与普通法系混合的独特法律文化。英国普通法被适用于商事合同与商业财产，并经由议会立法等形式被引入该国的成文法。"特萨瓦拉迈法"与"康提安法"为适用于各自民族或宗教团体的人身法与地方法。而"穆斯林法"则在婚姻继承相关事项中适用于穆斯林群体。

同时，斯里兰卡也遵循判例法的原则。最高法院的判决对其他法院均有约束力。在与最高法院裁判不冲突的情形下，上诉法院的判决对初审法院具有约束力。自 1978 年斯里兰卡的新宪法生效以来，最高法院在 1978 年之前的判决以及英国枢密院作为斯里兰卡最终上诉法院时的判决都不再具有约束力。但是，早期的判例法仍然可作为审判机关的"指导"（guidence），这意味着，早期的判例法可作为有拘束力的证据（binding evidence）而非仅有说服性的证据（persuasive evidence）存在。同时，根据 1978 年所颁行宪法的第 168 条，斯里兰卡在 1978 年以前所通过的法律依然有效。[1]

---

〔1〕 See Ayomi Aluwihare, Shakthi Ratnakumaran, "Update: Legal Research and Legal System in Sri Lanka", https：//www. nyulawglobal. org/globalex/Sri_ Lanka1. html#_ 3._ Legal_ Constructs, April 25, 2020.

（一）划定管辖海域的法

1. 关于国家领土和管辖海域的基本规定

《斯里兰卡民主社会主义共和国宪法》（Constitution of The Democratic Socialist Republic of Sri Lanka，以下简称《斯里兰卡宪法》）于 1978 年颁布，并经过多次修正。2020 年 10 月，斯里兰卡通过了第 20 次宪法修正案，但所修正条款未涉及国家领土及管辖海域的相关规定[1]。

依据现行的《斯里兰卡宪法》第一章第 5 条，斯里兰卡民主社会主义共和国的领土由 25 个行政区（administrative districts）及其领水（territorial waters）组成。而据其第二十二章"术语解释"下第 170 条，"领水"包括斯里兰卡的领海和历史性水域（historic waters）。其余条款除第 27 条第 3 款、第 157 条有涉及维护国家领土完整、禁止任何个人及政党破坏国家领土完整相关内容外，再无条款与国家管辖海域直接相关[2]。

2. 关于领海基线及领海宽度的规定

（1）《1976 年第 22 号海洋区域法》

斯里兰卡于 1976 年 9 月 1 日颁布了《1976 年第 22 号海洋区域法》（Maritime Zones Law No. 22 of 1976，以下简称《第 22 号海域法》）。该法全文共 15 条，就领海基线、领海的无害通过权、毗连区、专属经济区、大陆架、污染防治区、历史性水域等不同海区及其制度作出规定。

《第 22 号海域法》对领海基线和领海范围的规定为：第一，斯里兰卡总统可以通过发布政府公报，宣布斯里兰卡陆地领土和内水以外的海洋界限（在本法中即斯里兰卡领海），并在该公告中指明测量该海域的基线。该基线向陆地一侧的水域，应构成斯里兰卡内水的一部分。第二，如构成斯里兰卡领土一部分的岛屿或岩石或一群岛屿和岩石位于从主海岸或基线向海的方向，领海应延伸至根据前述政府公报所宣布的界限，该界限从沿该岛屿或岩石或一群岛屿和岩石向海一侧边缘在通常满潮（spring tides）时的低潮水位线开始计算。第三，斯里兰卡的主权延伸至领海和领海上方的领空以及领海的海床和底土。

同时，《第 22 号海域法》分别对船舶和飞机在领海的通行权进行了规定：第一，各国船舶均享有无害通过斯里兰卡领海的权利，只要这种通过

---

[1] Parliament of Sri Lanka, "Twentieth Amendment", https://www.parliament.lk/en/constitution/twentieth-amendment, April 25, 2020.

[2] Parliament of Sri Lanka, "Constitution", https://www.parliament.lk/en/constitution/main, April 25, 2020.

不损害斯里兰卡的和平、良好秩序或安全，其通过就是无害的。外国军舰不得进入或通过领海，除非事先得到斯里兰卡总理的同意，并受到总理所规定条件的制约。第二，除非斯里兰卡现行的成文法律另有规定，任何外国飞机不得进入或通过其斯里兰卡领海上空；除事先获得总理的同意并遵守总理所规定的限制条件外，外国军用飞机不得进入或通过斯里兰卡领海上空。第三，外国船舶或者外国航空器违反该法相关规定的，应当予以没收。第四，为维护共和国的和平、良好秩序或安全，如认为有必要，总理可通过政府公报发布命令，在领海的某一区域或多个区域暂停任何船舶无害通过的权利。[1]

（2）《基于〈1976 年第 22 号海洋区域法〉的 1977 年总统公告》[2]

1977 年 1 月 15 日，斯里兰卡总统发布《基于〈1976 年第 22 号海洋区域法〉的 1977 年总统公告》（Presidential Proclamation of 15 January 1977 in pursuance of Maritime Zones Law No. 22 of 1 September 1976，以下简称《1977 年总统公告》），宣布斯里兰卡领海应当是从其领海基线量起 12 海里宽的海域。为测定这一领海基线：第一，若在测量领海宽度时不考虑任何低潮高地，则全部或部分位于 12 海里领海宽度之内的低潮高地应被作为岛屿对待。第二，延伸入海的永久性设施，若构成港口系统组成部分，应视为斯里兰卡大陆海岸的一部分。第三，在海岸存在较深的海湾及水曲或存在紧邻着海岸的一系列岛屿时，可采用直线基线法绘制基线，但该等基线不得明显偏离海岸的一般方向，且该基线向陆地一侧的海域须与陆地有充分紧密的联系，使其受内水制度的支配。[3]

该公告还进一步规定，在佩德罗点（Point Pedro）以北的海域的领海基线应是一条连接保克海峡中两点的弧线，连接点的坐标位置如第 Ⅱ 部分表 1 所示：

---

〔1〕 See Section 2, Section 3, Maritime Zones Law No. 22 of 1 September 1976, UN Office of Legal Affairs, https：//www. un. org/Depts/los/LEGISLATIONANDTREATIES/PDFFILES/LKA_ 1976_ Law. pdf, April 24, 2020.

〔2〕 UN Office of Legal Affairs, "Presidential Proclamation of 15 January 1977 in pursuance of Maritime Zones Law No. 22 of 1 September 1976 ", https：//www. un. org/Depts/los/LEGISLATION-ANDTREA TIES/PDFFILES/LKA_ 1977_ Proclamation. pdf, April 25, 2020.

〔3〕 See Article (1), Article (2), Presidential Proclamation of 15 January 1977 in pursuance of Maritime Zones Law No. 22 of 1 September 1976, UN Office of Legal Affairs, https：//www. un. org/Depts/los/LEGISLATIONANDTREATIES/PDFFILES/LKA_ 1977_ Proclamation. pdf, April 24, 2020.

第 Ⅱ 部分 表 1　佩德罗以北海域的基线坐标点[1]

序号	纬度（北）	经度（东）
1	09°49′8″	80°15′2″
2	10°05′0″	80°03′0″

3. 关于毗连区的基本规定

根据《第 22 号海域法》第 4 条，总统可以通过政府公报宣布毗连其领海、由领海外部界限向海洋延伸的海洋区域范围，即斯里兰卡的毗连区。对于违反斯里兰卡国家安全、移民、健康、卫生、海关及其他税收事宜相关成文法的行为，相关内阁部长应在毗连区采取必要措施，以确保上述法律的实施或防止对此类法律的违犯。《1977 年总统公告》第 3 条进一步确认，斯里兰卡的毗连区应自其领海基线量起向海延伸至 24 海里。

4. 关于专属经济区的基本规定

依据《第 22 号海域法》第 5 条，总统可以通过政府公报宣布与领海相邻的任何海域及其海床和底土为斯里兰卡的专属经济区。该区域的界限应由相关总统公告予以确定。

立足该条的相关表述，在其专属经济区内、海床上及海床下、底土内、水面上和水体内（water column）的所有自然资源，包括生物和非生物资源，均应归属于斯里兰卡。在该区域内，斯里兰卡享有以下权利：第一，就勘探、开发、养护和管理生物和非生物自然资源以及利用潮汐、风力和洋流生产能源或用于其他经济目的而享有的主权权利；第二，授权、管理和控制科学研究的专属权利和管辖权；第三，为方便航运或任何其他目的建造、维护或运营人工岛屿、离岸码头、设施以及勘探和开发该区域资源所必需的其他结构和装置的专属权利和管辖权；第四，国际法承认的其他权利。

《1977 年总统公告》第 4 条进一步确认，斯里兰卡的专属经济区应延伸至从领海基线量起 200 海里的海域。

5. 关于大陆架的基本规定

依据《第 22 号海域法》第 6 条，斯里兰卡大陆架应包括：第一，斯里兰卡领海以外依其陆地领土的自然延伸，扩展到大陆边外缘的海床与底土，如果从领海基线量起到大陆边外缘的距离不到 200 海里，则扩展至 200 海里；

---

[1]　See Article（2）（iii），Presidential Proclamation of 15 January 1977 in pursuance of Maritime Zones Law No. 22 of 1 September 1976，UN Office of Legal Affairs，https：//www. un. org/Depts/los/ LEGISLATIONANDTREATIES/PDFFILES/LKA_ 1977_ Proclamation. pdf，April 24，2020.

第二，与任何岛屿或岩石、岛屿群和岩石群、岛屿群或岩石群的海岸相邻的类似海底区域的海床和底土，构成斯里兰卡领土的一部分。

所有在海床上和海床下以及大陆架底土中的生物和非生物自然资源均应属于斯里兰卡。斯里兰卡在大陆架拥有以下权利：（1）为勘探、开发、养护和管理生物和非生物自然资源而享有的主权；（2）授权、规范和控制科学研究的专属权利和管辖权；（3）为勘探和开发大陆架资源、便利航运或任何其他目的而建造、维护或运营人工岛屿、离岸码头、设施和其他必要结构和装置的专属权利和管辖权；（4）国际法承认的其他权利。

斯里兰卡于 2009 年 5 月向大陆架界限委员会提交了其 200 海里外大陆架划界案。[1] 该划界案立刻引发了马尔代夫、印度及孟加拉国等周边国家的关注。马尔代夫首先于 2009 年 8 月提出，马尔代夫正在筹备本国的外大陆架界限提案，要求保留权利以便对斯里兰卡外大陆架案进行后续评估。[2] 印度则在 2010 年 5 月向联合国秘书长的致函中强调，斯里兰卡的划界案不应妨害其与海岸相邻或相向国家的海洋划界，也不得妨害印度与斯里兰卡的未来相关协定。[3] 孟加拉国则在 2010 年 10 月致信大陆架界限委员会时，指称斯里兰卡的外大陆架界限既超过了从领海基线量起 350 海里的宽度，也超过了 2500 米等深线外 100 海里的范围，因而与《公约》第 76 条不符；同时，鉴于孟加拉国也处于筹备本国外大陆架划界提案的过程之中，同样要求保留嗣后评估斯里兰卡划界案的权利。[4]

6. 关于污染防治区的基本规定

污染防治区（pollution prevention zone）是《第 22 号海域法》中较为独特的规定。根据该法第 7 条，总统可以通过政府公报，宣布邻接领海的任何海区及其海床和底土为斯里兰卡的污染防治区。这一区域的界限应在相关总统公告中作出规定。斯里兰卡相关内阁部长应采取必要措施，预防和控制对这一区域的污染，并保持该区域内的生态平衡。

《1977 年总统公告》第 5 条进一步确认，污染防治区应当延伸至从领海基线量起 200 海里的海域，由此使其污染防治区与专属经济区的实际范围相

---

〔1〕 CLCS, "Continental Shelf Submission of Sri Lanka", https：//www. un. org/depts/los/clcs_ new/ submissions_ files/lka43_ 09/lka2009executivesummary. pdf, April 25, 2020.

〔2〕 CLCS, "Maldives：Note dated 4 August 2009", https：//www. un. org/depts/los/clcs_ 43_ 2009_ los_ mal. pdf, May 20, 2020.

〔3〕 CLCS, "India：Note dated 10 May 2010", https：//www. un. org/depts/los/clcs_ new/submissions_ files/lka43_ 09/clcs_ 43_ 2009_ los_ ind. pdf, May 20, 2020.

〔4〕 CLCS, "Bangladesh：Note dated 20 October 2010", https：//www. un. org/depts/los/clcs_ new/ submissions_ files/lka43_ 09/clcs_ 43_ 2009_ los_ bgd. pdf, May 20, 2020.

重叠。[1]

7. 关于历史性水域的基本主张

依据《第 22 号海域法》第 9 条，总统可以通过政府公报宣布斯里兰卡历史性水域的界限。斯里兰卡对历史性水域及其内的岛屿、大陆架以及海床和底土行使主权、专属管辖权和控制权。

《1977 年总统公告》第 7 条进一步确认，斯里兰卡的历史性水域应为保克海峡、保克湾和马纳尔湾中的相关海域，其界限由以下四段构成：（1）斯里兰卡的大陆海岸；（2）《第 22 号海域法》第 8 条所划定的斯里兰卡和印度之间的海洋边界；（3）在马纳尔湾中连接两个坐标点的弧线（具体坐标位置如第Ⅱ部分 表 2 所示）；（4）在保克海峡中连接两个坐标点的弧线（具体坐标位置如第Ⅱ部分 表 3 所示）。

第Ⅱ部分 表 2　马纳尔湾中的基线坐标点[2]

序号	纬度（北）	经度（东）
1	08°15′0″	79°44′0″
2	08°22′2″	78°55′4″

第Ⅱ部分 表 3　保克海峡中的基线坐标点[3]

序号	纬度（北）	经度（东）
1	09°49′8″	80°15′2″
2	10°05′0″	80°03′0″

立足上述界限，保克海峡和保克湾的历史水域应构成斯里兰卡内水的一部分，而马纳尔湾的历史水域应构成斯里兰卡领海的一部分。

8. 关于与印度海洋边界的初步划定

鉴于与印度间的《1974 年协定》及《1976 年协定》，斯里兰卡随之在国

---

〔1〕 UN Office of Legal Affairs, "Presidential Proclamation of 15 January 1977 in pursuance of Maritime Zones Law No. 22 of 1 September 1976", https：//www. un. org/Depts/los/LEGISLATION-ANDTREA TIES/PDFFILES/LKA_ 1977_ Proclamation. pdf, April 25, 2020.

〔2〕 See Article (7) (c), Presidential Proclamation of 15 January 1977 in pursuance of Maritime Zones Law No. 22 of 1 September 1976, UN Office of Legal Affairs, https：//www. un. org/Depts/los/LEGISLATIONANDTREATIES/PDFFILES/LKA_ 1977_ Proclamation. pdf, April 25, 2020.

〔3〕 See Article (7) (d), Presidential Proclamation of 15 January 1977 in pursuance of Maritime Zones Law No. 22 of 1 September 1976, UN Office of Legal Affairs, https：//www. un. org/Depts/los/LEGISLATIONANDTREATIES/PDFFILES/LKA_ 1977_ Proclamation. pdf, April 25, 2020.

内法中对上述协定中的划界成果进行了确认。[1] 根据《第22号海域法》第8条的规定：

第一，从保克海峡到亚当桥的水域中，斯里兰卡和印度的边界应是连接以下各点的系列弧线，其坐标位置如第Ⅱ部分 表4 所示：

第Ⅱ部分 表4 印度与斯里兰卡在保克海峡的海上界限坐标点[2]

坐标点	纬度（北）	经度（东）
1	10° 05′	80° 03′
2	09° 57′	79° 35′
3	09° 40.15′	79° 22.60′
4	09° 21.80′	79° 30.70′
5	09° 13′	79° 32′
6	09° 06′	79° 32′

第二，斯里兰卡和印度在马纳尔湾的边界应为连接以下各点的系列弧线，其坐标位置如第Ⅱ部分 表5 所示：

第Ⅱ部分 表5 印度与斯里兰卡在马纳尔湾的海上界限坐标点[3]

坐标点	纬度（北）	经度（东）
1m	09°06.0′	79°32.0′
2m	09°00.0′	79°31.3′
3m	08°53.8′	79°29.3′
4m	08°40.0′	79°18.2′
5m	08°37.2′	79°13.0′
6m	08°31.2′	79°04.7′
7m	08°22.2′	78°55.4′
8m	08°12.2′	78°53.7′
9m	07°35.3′	78°45.7′
10m	07°21.0′	78°38.8′

---

〔1〕 参见本丛书《印度、巴基斯坦海洋法律体系研究》"印度海洋法律体系"第五部分"海洋争端解决"下"通过协议解决的海洋争端"中的相关内容。

〔2〕 See Section 8 (a), Maritime Zones Law No. 22 of 1 September 1976, UN Office of Legal Affairs, https：//www. un. org/Depts/los/LEGISLATIONANDTREATIES/PDFFILES/LKA ＿ 1976 ＿ Law. pdf, April 24, 2020.

〔3〕 See Section 8 (b), Maritime Zones Law No. 22 of 1 September 1976, https：//www. un. org/Depts/los/LEGISLATIONANDTREATIES/PDFFILES/LKA＿ 1976＿ Law. pdf, April 24, 2020.

续表

坐标点	纬度（北）	经度（东）
11m	06°30.8′	78°12.2′
12m	05°53.9′	77°50.7′
13m	05°00.0′	77°10.6′

第三，斯里兰卡和印度在孟加拉湾的边界应为连接以下各点的系列弧线，其坐标位置如第Ⅱ部分 表6所示：

第Ⅱ部分 表6　印度与斯里兰卡在孟加拉湾的海上界限坐标点[1]

坐标点	纬度（北）	经度（东）
1 b	10°05.0′	80°03.0′
1 ba	10°05.8′	80°05.0′
1 bb	10°08.4′	80°09.5′
2 b	10°33.0′	80°46.0′
3 b	10°41.7′	81°02.5′
4 b	11°02.7′	81°56.0′
5 b	11°16.0′	82°24.4′
6 b	11°26.6′	83°22.0′

（二）海上安全相关立法

1.《1950年海军法》及其修订

斯里兰卡于1950年颁布《海军法》（Navy Act）以组建国家海军部队，并就维持该部队的训练和发展事宜作出规定。该法共含15个部分163条，主要内容分别涉及：（1）皇家锡兰海军的组织结构，包括海军司令任命、预备役及志愿军储备、训练模式等；（2）海军各级军官的任命，包括任命方式、任职期限、人事登记、军官在船员入伍中的职责等；（3）海军舰员的相关规范，包括常规入伍及再录用要求、从志愿军或后备役中退伍的规定等；（4）服役要求，包括对海军各军事单位的部署、海军服役期限的延长、在共同服役时与陆空军的关系、与外国海军部队的合作、非海军职务的执行等；（5）适用于海军法

---

[1]　See Section 8 （c）, Maritime Zones Law No.22 of 1 September 1976, https://www.un.org/ Depts/los/LEGISLATIONANDTREATIES/PDFFILES/LKA_ 1976_ Law.pdf, April 24, 2020.

律的人员，包括人员范围界定、海军拘捕的行为主体与适用对象、对非现役海军军人的拘捕、检诉时限、对违法人员的审判与惩罚；（6）指挥人员的司法性权力，包括军官在军事法庭受审时的权利、指挥官对其司法性权力的授权、审判中的证人与记录要求等；（7）军事法庭相关规定，包括相应军事法庭的设立、权限、组织章程、法官的任命、法庭程序、庭审方式、法庭的解散等；（8）对敌时的海军不法行为，包括行动中的不当行为、未能追击敌军或援助友军、拖延或懈怠、间谍行为、通敌、渎职、叛乱、违抗命令、军事法庭相关的不当行为、人员拘押时的不当行为、财产相关不当行为等；（9）非海军对敌时的不法行为，包括非法招纳入伍人员、引诱或协助海军军人从事不法行为、妨碍海军军务等；（10）军事法庭对民事违法行为的惩处；（11）军事法庭及行使司法权的海军军官就相关惩罚所做裁决；（12）对军事法庭及行使司法权的海军军官所做裁决的变更或执行；（13）非军事法庭在本法下的管辖权行使、案件移交、案件审理等；（14）相关证据规则；（15）其他杂项规定。[1]

随着 1972 年原"锡兰自治领"独立为"斯里兰卡民主社会主义共和国"，《1950 年海军法》也基于国家发展状态及军队建设需求逐步修订完善。根据《1976 年海军法（修正案）》［Navy Law（Amendment），No. 83 of 1976］，前因隶属于英联邦海军体系而任命的锡兰"海军上校"（Captain of the Navy）全部修改为斯里兰卡"海军司令"（Commander of the Navy）。[2]而根据《1979 年海军和空军法（修正案）》［Navy and Air Force Act（Amendment），No. 21 of 1979］，"皇家锡兰海军"（Royal Ceylon Navy）一称全部由"斯里兰卡海军"（Sri Lanka Navy）取代，并明确该修改适用于斯里兰卡的所有议会立法或基于议会立法所发出、订立、规定或授权的任何通知、来文、表格及其他文件。[3]

此后，《1950 年海军法》又分别经《1986 年海军法（修正案）》［Navy（Amendment）Act，No. 24 of 1986］、《1993 年海军法（修正案）》［Navy（Amendment）Act，No. 11 of 1993］、《1999 年海军法（修正案）》［Navy（Amendment）Act，No. 53 of 1999］、《2011 年海军法（修正案）》［Navy（Amendment）Act，No. 32 of 2011］进行了数次修订，就其第 4 条、第 11 条、第 13 条、第 14

〔1〕 Lawnet，"Navy"，https：//www. lawnet. gov. lk/navy/，December 25，2020.

〔2〕 Lawnet，"Navy（Amendment）Law"，https：//www. lawnet. gov. lk/navy-amendment-law-2/，December 25，2020.

〔3〕 Lawnet，"Navy And Air Force（Amendment）"，https：//www. lawnet. gov. lk/navy-and-air-force-amendment-3/，December 25，2020.

条、第26—29条、第34—35条、第37条、第52条、第60—61条、第68—69条、第71条、第77条、第80条、第82条、第102条、第104—107条、第110条、第114条、第120条、第144条、第151条、第163条等作出一次或多次调整、重制或完善。[1]

2.《2009年海岸警卫队法》

为了确保本国沿海、领海及周边公海海域的安全，斯里兰卡于2009年通过《海岸警卫队法》（Department of Coast Guard Act，No. 41 of 2009），目的是在斯里兰卡海军之外设立一个更为灵活的多任务海上安全服务机关，以保护相关海域的国民经济和国家利益，确保斯里兰卡的领土完整和国家安全。作为创立海岸警卫队的规范性文件，该法除序言外共含4部分22条，分别就海岸警卫队的建立方式、海岸警卫队的职责及授权、咨询委员会的设立及其他相关或附带事宜作出规定。

一如前述"海上武装执法机构"部分所示，立足该法，斯里兰卡海岸警卫队的当前职能主要包括：制止渔业相关犯罪、保护本国渔民；打击走私、贩毒和人口贩卖活动；打击海盗和海上恐怖主义；参与自然灾害和海上事故的搜救，协助对船舶及货物的救助；协助执行和监测预防及控制海洋污染措施；协助保育海洋生物；利用无线电等方法发布自然灾害警告信息等。同时，该法授权斯里兰卡政府可随时向海岸警卫队指派或分配上述职能外的其他任务。[2]

3.《2000年制止危及海上航行安全非法行为法》

斯里兰卡于2000年通过《制止危及海上航行安全非法行为法》（Suppression of Unlawful Acts against the Safety of Maritime Navigation Act，No. 42 of 2000），从而为其加入《制止危及海上航行安全非法行为公约》完成国内立法的阶段性准备。斯里兰卡于当年9月向国际海事组织提交加入《制止危及海上航行安全非法行为公约》的相关文件，并于同年12月正式接受公约约束，开始立足上述立法履行公约相关义务。

该法共11条，主要内容包括：（1）对前述公约缔约国的不定期认定与

---

[1] See Lawnet, "Navy (Amendment)", https://www. lawnet. gov. lk/navy-amendment-2/, December 25, 2020; Lawnet, "Navy (Amendment)", https://www. lawnet. gov. lk/navy-amendment-3/, December 25, 2020; Lawnet, "Navy (Amendment)", https://www. lawnet. gov. lk/navy-amendment-4/, December 25, 2020; Department of Government Printing, "Navy (Amendment) Act", http://documents. gov. lk/files/act/2011/6/32-2011_ E. pdf, December 25, 2020.

[2] Department of Government Printing, "Department of Ciast Guard Act, No. 41 OF 2009", http://documents. gov. lk/files/act/2009/8/41-2009_ E. pdf, April 25, 2020.

通报；（2）所涉非法行为的界定与要件；（3）高等法院适用该法对相关非法行为的审理；（4）因该法所规定的非法行为而被逮捕的人的权利；（5）相关引渡规则的适用；（6）对其他公约缔约国的协助义务；（7）在僧伽罗语与泰米尔语解释不一致时以前者为作准文本。

适用于该法的非法行为主要有：（1）以武力或武力威胁或任何其他形式的恐吓夺取或控制船舶；（2）对船上人员实施暴力行为，以致危及该船舶的安全航行；（3）毁损或造成船舶或其货物的毁损，以致危及或可能危及该船舶的安全航行；（4）以任何方式安放可能毁损或造成船货毁损的设备或材料，或以任何方式造成此类设备或材料的安放危及或可能危及该船舶安全航行；（5）破坏或严重损坏海上航行设施或者严重干扰其作业，以致危及或者可能危及船舶航行安全；（6）传播明知是虚假的信息，以致危及船舶航行安全；（7）实施或企图实施上述任何罪行而使任何人受伤或死亡的行为。[1]

4.《2005 年海啸法（特别规定)》

《2005 年海啸法（特别规定)》〔Tsunami（Special Provisions）Act, No. 16 of 2005〕是针对重大自然灾害的救济性立法。2004 年 12 月 26 日发生的海啸给斯里兰卡人民造成了巨大的生命和财产损失。由于难以满足相关法律要求或认定标准，在这一灾害中遭受严重损害的民众往往无力基于现行法律享有相应权利或获得特定利益，因海啸而失去亲人的儿童及青少年，尤其需要在灾后得到相应的保护与照料。由此，为扫除相关法律障碍，解决现行法律困境，落实基本国策，斯里兰卡特为此次海啸的灾后救济进行专门性立法，以确保受灾民众的权利及利益得到充分切实的保障。

该法共有 6 大部分 33 条及 10 项附录，分别就死亡证明的签发、儿童及青少年的监护、对土地等不动产的占有时效在海啸影响下的状态与效力、相关法定期限在海啸影响下的理解与计算、不动产承租人的权利不因海啸而终止、涉及海啸救援财物的罪行等方面作出针对性规定。而所列 10 项附录则主要就海啸中死亡人口认定、文书出具及交验的各地方机关，以及儿童与青少年的监护、收养及其他保护事宜的监管机关等作出进一步明确。[2]

---

〔1〕 Lawnet, "Suppression Of Unlawful Acts Against The Safety Of Maritime Navigation", https://www.lawnet.gov.lk/suppression-of-unlawful-acts-against-the-safety-of-maritime-navigation-3/, April 20, 2020.

〔2〕 Department of Government Printing, "Tsunami（Special Provisions）", http://documents.gov.lk/files/act/2005/6/16-2005_E.pdf, April 25, 2020.

（三）海洋渔业相关立法

1. 《1941 年渔业条例》及其修订

1941 年，当时的锡兰政府颁布《渔业条例》（Fisheries Ordinance）就锡兰及其周边水域的渔业捕捞、渔业生产及鱼类资源保护等法律规定进行修订及整合，为本地渔船注册提供指导，以便更好地对渔业捕捞及其关联事项进行监管。尽管该条例已于 1996 年被斯里兰卡议会所废止，但其适用及其修订历程仍可被视为斯里兰卡早期海洋渔业相关立法的代表性实践。

该条例共有 37 条，主要内容包括：第一，咨询委员会的组建，如渔业部门部长及咨询委员会高级官员的委任、委员会的创立方式、委员会的职权和功能等；第二，捕捞许可与渔船登记相关规定，如营利性捕捞许可的形式、申请与颁发，禁止使用非登记渔船在锡兰水域从事捕捞等；第三，对鱼类资源的保护，对捕捞特定鱼类及鱼卵的限制，对非本土鱼类进口的限制，对使用毒药或爆炸物捕鱼的限制，对损害或破坏捕鱼设备的禁止，对捕捞特定非本土鱼类的专属性授权等；第四，渔业争议的解决，如渔业争议的含义、范围、基本解决程序等；第五，有关监管官员的权力及其对相关不法行为的规制，如检查权的行使，对捕捞设备的扣押，对非法手段捕捞的认定及推定，对相应不法行为的惩处等；第六，本法的适用说明，如与其他现行法律冲突时的适用优先等。

在该条例下所创建的咨询委员会的职责为：第一，就一切与渔业捕捞及渔业产业相关事宜或与本条例实施相关的行政事宜，向渔业部部长或本条例主管机关提供建议，渔业部部长也可主动向咨询委员会寻求建议；第二，行使本条例所规定或赋予咨询委员会的相应权力，履行相应职责。[1]

《1941 年渔业条例》在斯里兰卡独立后的 1973 年经历了 3 次密集的修订。根据三项《1973 年渔业法（修正案）》［Fisheries（Amendment）Law，No. 7 of 1973，Fisheries（Amendment）Law，No. 20 of 1973，Fisheries（Amendment）Law，No 46 of 1973］，《1941 年渔业条例》原第 2 条、第 3 条、第 15 条、第 20 条、第 22 条、第 23 条、第 26 条、第 27 条、第 30 条、第 32 条、第 33 条、第 35 条被删改、增补或替代，主要涉及渔船的转让和抵押、禁止使用毒药捕捞条款的适用、渔业争议中的临时措施、渔业部部长及副部长的任命等。[2]

---

〔1〕 Lawnet，"Fisheries"，https：//www. lawnet. gov. lk/fisheries-2/，April 25，2020.

〔2〕 See Lawnet，"Fisheries（Amendment）"，https：//www. lawnet. gov. lk/fisheries-amendment-2/，A-pril 25，2020；Lawnet，"Fisheries（Amendment）"，https：//www. lawnet. gov. lk/fisheries-amend-ment-law-3/，April 25，2020；Lawnet，"Fisheries（Amendment）"，https：//www. lawnet. gov. lk/fisheries-amendment-law-2/，April 25，2020.

此后,《1941年渔业条例》再经《1995年渔业法(修正案)》[Fisheries (Amendment) Act, No. 3 of 1995]作了最后一次修订,主要就第26条中的非法捕捞行为的罚金数额、第30条中的拉网捕捞行为的规范方式作出了调整。[1]

2.《1996年渔业和水产资源法》及其修订

斯里兰卡于1996年通过《渔业和水产资源法》(Fisheries and Aquatic Resources Act, No. 2 of 1996),意在为管理、规范、养护和开发渔业及水产资源提供法律依据。随着这一立法的颁布,《1941年渔业条例》、《1953年犬齿螺捕捞法》(Chank Fisheries Act)、《1925年珍珠捕捞条例》(Pearl Fisheries Ordinance)及《1936年捕鲸条例》(Whaling Ordinance)均告废止。

《渔业和水产资源法》共10部分67条,主要内容为:第一,管理渔业及水产资源的行政机关的组建,包括部门首长及其他官员的任命、渔业及水产资源咨询委员会的建立、咨询委员会的功能与职责、渔业监管与发展计划等;第二,渔业捕捞行业许可相关规定,包括经营捕捞业执照的适用范围、执照的申请及形式要求、执照有效期的更新与延长、执照的撤销、将结果通知申请人并说明理由、申请结果的申诉、不适用于外国渔船的相关规定等;第三,本国渔船的注册登记,包括本国渔船登记的基本程序与要求、渔船船东变更时的报告、渔船抵押时的登记及优先权、抵押权的行使方式、渔船转让或船东破产时抵押权的效力、登记文件的公开与证据效力等;第四,对鱼类及其他水产资源的保护,包括禁止使用或占有有毒或爆炸物、禁止在渔船上装备任何非法捕捞设备、禁止收揽或运输或买卖或收受非法捕捞的鱼货、捕捞产品进出口的禁止或限制、渔业监管区的设定、渔业委员会的建立、渔民的注册登记、休渔期的开始与结束、利用渔船进行科学研究等;第五,鱼类资源的养护,包括相关渔业养护规定的颁布、渔业养护中被禁止的行为等;第六,水产养殖的相关规定,包括为水产养殖而租赁国家土地、水产养殖企业的执照申请与形式要求、执照的续期与撤销等;第七,渔业争议的解决,包括解决渔业争议的行政机关与基本程序、渔业争议相关临时命令的发布等;第八,经授权的行政官员及其权力,包括获授权的行政官员的权力内容、范围及其获得授权的认定等;第九,渔业及水产养殖相关非法行为及其惩处,包括渔业及水产养殖相关的非法行为类别、有关团体从事的非法行为、对非法行为人财产的罚没、多种非法行为的竞合、被扣押船舶的释放、对相关非法行为的推定等;第十,其他一般性规定,包括各省级渔业主管部

---

〔1〕 Lawnet, "Fisheries (Amendment)", https://www.lawnet.gov.lk/fisheries-amendment-3/, April 25, 2020.

门的权限、相关奖励基金的设立与使用、对鱼类及水产品的进口的中止、本法与动植物保护等其他相关立法间的关系协调、相关术语解释及优先适用的作准文字等。

根据该法第 66 条，其所适用的"斯里兰卡水域"（Sri Lanka Waters）包括《第 22 号海域法》中所宣示的领海、毗连区、专属经济区、历史性水域及所有公共河流、湖泊、潟湖、溪流、水池、水塘、运河等一切公共内水及内陆水；"鱼类"是指任何水生生物，包括任何贝类、甲壳类动物、珍珠牡蛎、软体动物、海参类动物或水生哺乳动物及其幼鱼、鱼苗或卵，同时包括浮游动物；"水产资源"是指水生生物，包括在水生介质中发现的任何海藻、浮游植物或其他水生植物和非生物物质；"渔业争议"是指从事渔业捕捞的两个或两个以上个人或群体之间在斯里兰卡任意水域因捕鱼权、捕捞时间、方式或地点所发生的任何争议，也包括为水产养殖目的使用水域或土地的争端。

同时，该法就渔业监管区的设立进行了说明，即在渔业和水产资源部部长认为必要时，可采取特别措施，经与负责野生动物保护的部长协商，通过政府公报将斯里兰卡水域或与其相邻的任何土地或水域及其任何区域宣布为渔业监管区。设立这一监管区的目的在于：（1）对有灭绝危险的水生资源给予特别保护，以保全相关鱼类和水生资源的自然繁殖地和生存环境，特别是珊瑚生长环境及关联水生生态系统；（2）在水生生物枯竭的地区促进水生生物的再生；（3）促进该区域内水生生物相关的科学研究；（4）保护和增进该地区的自然之美。[1]

截至 2020 年，《1996 年渔业和水产资源法》已经陆续经历了 7 次修订，包括《2000 年渔业和水产资源法（修正案）》［Fisheries and Aquatic Resources（Amendment）Act, No. 4 of 2000］、《2004 年渔业和水产资源法（修正案）》［Fisheries and Aquatic Resources（Amendment）Act, No. 4 of 2004］、《2006 年渔业和水产资源法（修正案）》［Fisheries and Aquatic Resources（Amendment）Act, No. 22 of 2006］、《2013 年渔业和水产资源法（修正案）》［Fisheries and Aquatic Resources（Amendment）Act, No. 35 of 2013］、《2015 年渔业和水产资源法（修正案）》［Fisheries and Aquatic Resources（Amendment）Act, No. 2 of 2015］、《2016 年渔业和水产资源法（修正案）》［Fisheries and Aquatic Resources（Amendment）Act, No. 2 of 2016］、《2017 年渔业和

---

［1］　Lawnet, "Fisheries And Aquatic Resources", https：//www.lawnet. gov. lk/fisheries-and-aquatic-resources-2/, April 25, 2020.

水产资源法（修正案）》［Fisheries and Aquatic Resources（Amendment）Act, No. 11 of 2017］。所修订条款包括第2条、第3条、第15条、第27条、第28条、第29条、第31条、第39—43条、第46条、第49条、第52条、第61条、第66条，主要涉及渔业和水产资源部部长及官员的任命、非法捕鱼手段的范围与内容、保释条款、水产养殖企业的执照管理、渔业捕捞企业的许可与执照、相关非法行为的司法管辖权、行政执法机构及程序、罚金数额、术语解释等内容的调整与完善。[1]

3. 《1979 年渔业法（外国渔船管理)》及其修订

《1979 年渔业法（外国渔船管理)》［Fisheries（Regulation of Foreign Fishing Boats）Act，No. 59 of 1979］是规范、控制和管理外国船舶在斯里兰卡水域的渔业捕捞及相关活动的立法。该法共分4个部分，其28项条文所及内容主要包括：第一，实施本法的主管机关，包括负责执行与落实本法规定的行政机关首长、配合本法执行与落实的军队指挥官职责等。根据本法第3条，武装部队指挥官应提供一切必要形式的协助，以确保该法规定得到适当执行，从而有效建立和维持针对在斯里兰卡水域活动的外国渔船的监管体系。第二，对在斯里兰卡水域从事渔业捕捞及相关活动的外国船舶的管控，包括原则上禁止外国渔船在斯里兰卡水域从事渔业捕捞及相关活动、未经许可进入斯里兰卡水域的外国渔船应保持设备处于收束状态、可划设保留给本国渔民及渔船的捕捞区、准许外国渔船进入斯里兰卡水域的条件与程序、对外国渔船许可的暂停或吊销、对渔业部门首长决定的申诉、基于科研目的的捕捞等。第三，经授权的官员的权力，包括拦截、登临、搜查外国渔船、要求出具航行日志等文件文书并接受核验，检查船上捕捞设备，检查船上船员身份及行为，可不出具逮捕令即行逮捕事宜，经授权官员行使权力的行为受国家特别保护等。第四，与本法相关的不法行为，包括违法船舶的船东或船长及

---

〔1〕 See Lawnet, "Fisheries And Aquatic Resources（Amendment)", https：//www. lawnet. gov. lk/fisheries-and-aquatic-resources-amendment-2/, April 25, 2020; Lawnet, "Fisheries And Aquatic Resources （Amendment)", https：//www. lawnet. gov. lk/fisheries-and-aquatic-resources-amendment-3/, April 25, 2020; Lawnet, "Fisheries And Aquatic Resources（Amendment)", https：//www. lawnet. gov. lk/fisheries-and-aquatic-resources-amendment-4/, April 25, 2020; Department of Government Printing, "Fisheries And Aquatic Resources（Amendment)", http：//documents. gov. lk/files/act/2013/11/35-2013_ E. pdf, April 25, 2020; Department of Government Printing, "Fisheries And Aquatic Resources （Amendment)", http：//documents. gov. lk/files/act/2015/3/02-2015_ E. pdf, April 25, 2020; Department of Government Printing, "Fisheries And Aquatic Resources（Amendment)", http：//documents. gov. lk/files/act/2016/2/02-2016_ E. pdf, April 25, 2020; Department of Government Printing, "Fisheries And Aquatic Resources（Amendment)", http：//documents. gov. lk/files/act/2017/7/11-2017_ E. pdf, April 25, 2020.

租船人都将被视为负责人、不遵守许可条件的不法行为、阻挠经授权官员的不法行为、法院发布没收命令的权力、对没收货物的处置、不法行为竞合时的处理、在收到保证金或其他担保时释放被扣押船舶、在未收到罚金时对船舶的扣留、相关法院的管辖权、文书送达等事宜、渔业部门部长进一步制定细则的权力等。[1]

《1979 年渔业法（外国渔船管理）》分别经《1982 年渔业法（外国渔船管理）（修正案）》［Fisheries（Regulation of Foreign Fishing Boats）（Amendment）Act，No. 37 of 1982］、《2018 年渔业法（外国渔船管理）（修正案）》［Fisheries（Regulation of Foreign Fishing Boats）（Amendment）Act，No. 1 of 2018］对其中第 3 条、第 13 条、第 15 条、第 16—19 条、第 20 条、第 21 条、第 23—24 条、第 26 条、第 28 条进行了修订，内容主要涉及：（1）代表国家执行该法的行政机关首长的名称、职位及权力；（2）扣押外国船舶的通知、扣押过程中的费用和损害赔偿责任；（3）所涉不法行为中不可保释的范围；（4）被遗弃的外国渔船的认定与处置；（5）行政及司法程序调查行动的专家小组的任命；（6）为施行本法的奖励基金的设立等。[2]

4. 《1990 年渔民养老金和社会保障福利计划法》

《1990 年渔民养老金和社会保障福利计划法》（Fishermen's Pension and Social Security Benefit Scheme Act，No. 23 of 1990）的颁布旨在为斯里兰卡的渔民提供养老金和社会保障福利相关的法律保障。该法共有 5 大部分 33 项条文，内容分别涉及：第一，渔民养老金和社会福利保障计划的启动与基本规则，包括该养老金与社会福利保障计划的实施目标与实施范围，加入该计划的资格，该计划可给予渔民的收益，相关福利保障可支付的时限，养老金缴纳的减免，在部分残疾、完全残疾以及死亡时的福利保障支付等；第二，对渔民养老金和社会福利保障计划的管理规定，包括由农业保险局负责该计划的实施，农业保险局及其代表在实施该计划时的权力与职责，相关保单的签发与没收，社会福利分红的确定，由该计划产生的养老金及津贴不得被分配或征收，相关申诉程序等；第三，咨询委员会的设立，包括咨询委员会的组建，咨询委员会的权力，咨询委员会成员的酬劳，总理对该咨询委员会的权力等；第四，渔民和社

---

［1］　Lawnet，"Fisheries（Regulation Of Foreign Fishing Boats）"，https：//www. lawnet. gov. lk/fisheries-regulation-of-foreign-fishing-boats-2/，April 25，2020.

［2］　See Lawnet，"Fisheries（Regulation Of Foreign Fishing Boats）（Amendment）"，https：//www. lawnet. gov. lk/fisheries-regulation-of-foreign-fishing-boats-amendment-2/，April 25，2020；Department of Government Printing，"Fisheries（Regulation Of Foreign Fishing Boats）（Amendment）Act，No. 1 of 2018"，http：//documents. gov. lk/files/act/2018/2/01-2018_ E. pdf，April 25，2020.

会福利保障基金的建立，包括该基金的创建方式与资金来源，该基金的投资许可，农业保险局从该基金借贷的条件，该基金的财年规定等；第五，其他一般性规定，包括总理作出进一步规定的权力，对于在本法下或农业保险委员会指示下采取相关行动的保护，相关不法行为及解释条款等。

根据该法第 5 条，其所适用的"渔民"是指在斯里兰卡的海洋、潟湖及内水中以渔业捕捞或渔业养殖为生的人。通过施行该法，斯里兰卡政府将：（1）为年老或残疾的渔民提供社会保障；（2）在渔民死亡时，为依赖其生存的人提供社会救济；（3）鼓励渔民坚持从事这一职业；（4）吸引年轻人进入渔业行业；（5）引导渔民的储蓄习惯并厉行节俭。[1]

（四）海上运输相关立法

1. 港口相关立法

（1）《1958 年港口（货运）公司法》

《1958 年港口（货运）公司法》［Port（Cargo）Corporation Act，No. 13 of 1958］是为服务在科伦坡港以及由总理通过政府公报所确定的其他类似港口设立公司而颁布的立法，旨在使由此设立的公司能够强制收购或征用其所需的不动产或动产，并对相关港口从业者的业务终止作出相应规定。

该法全文共 80 条，分属 7 大部分，主要内容包括：（1）港口（货物）公司及其董事会的章程、权力和职责；（2）公司财务相关规定；（3）公司业务的开展、财产的收购和征用；（4）对该公司收购、征用及投资行为的补偿；（5）公司雇员的相关规定；（6）公司可能收取的费用以及公司销售某些货物的权力；（7）其他一般性规定，如违反相关规定的不法行为，董事会主席的权力，公司抵押与租赁条款，禁止向公司成员及财产签发法院令状，港口企业在终止雇佣未妥当通知时应受到保护，相关术语解释等。[2] 需要明确的是，尽管曾为斯里兰卡海港的早期建设提供了较为集中的法律支持，这一立法已于 1979 年为新法所取代。

（2）《1979 年斯里兰卡港务局法》

斯里兰卡于 1979 年颁布《斯里兰卡港务局法》（Sri Lanka Ports Authority Act，No. 51 of 1979），合并原科伦坡港口委员会、港口货运公司、港口理货和防护服务公司，成立新的斯里兰卡港务局，从而为科伦坡港、加勒港和亭

---

〔1〕 Lawnet, "Fishermen's Pension and Social Security Benefit Scheme", https：//www. lawnet. gov. lk/fishermens-pension-and-social-security-benefit-scheme-3/, April 25, 2020.

〔2〕 Lawnet, "Port（Cargo）Corporation", https：//www. lawnet. gov. lk/port-cargo-corporation-3/, April 25, 2020.

可马里港以及其他由总理通过政府公报所确定适用该法的港口的发展、维护、营运等提供综合性服务。根据这一立法，斯里兰卡港务局将执行、落实及履行原港口委员会、港口货运公司及其他由该法所移交和赋予的权力、职责及义务。前述各机构的公职人员、雇佣人员及其财产、权利、责任等也由该立法一并予以调整。

随着该法的颁布，《1951 年科伦坡港（行政）法》［Port of Colombo（Administration）Act］、《1958 年港口（货运）公司法》、《1967 年港口理货和防护服务公司法》（Port Tally And Protective Services Corporation Act，No. 10 of 1967）均被废止；《1870 年海关条例》（Customs Ordinance，1870）及其修正案中适用于科伦坡港、加勒港和亭可马里港及其他由总理通过政府公报所确定港口的条款，因本法而被更新、修改或替代；与船员、船舶、引航员、关税及治安相关的其他法律中涉及上述港口权力、职责、义务，以及原港口委员会、港口货运公司、港口理货和防护服务公司的权力、职责、义务亦都转由斯里兰卡港务局执行和承担。

该法全文共计 38 条，分为 5 个部分，主要内容包括：（1）斯里兰卡港务局的组织章程及其权力、责任和职能；（2）斯里兰卡港务局职员的相关规定，包括港务局总经理及财务经理的任命，对科伦坡港口委员会雇员的临时雇佣及长期雇佣，科伦坡港口委员会雇员的退休金支付，对港口货运公司及港口理货和防护服务公司雇员的安排、其他公职人员的任命等；（3）斯里兰卡港务局财产的处置，包括从所替代港务机构中的财产转移，总理对港务局的土地授权，港务局对其他动产和不动产的收购和征收等；（4）斯里兰卡港务局的财政及经费问题，包括港务局的资金来源、股票发行、政府保证、税收减免等；（5）相关费用及费用的回收及补收，港务局相关收费的确定与调整，在费用拖欠时对货物的留置，货物留置时与海关等机构的协调，出售滞留在中转站的货物的权力，在未缴费时扣押船舶的权力及其他强制性措施和程序性要求等。[1]

《1979 年斯里兰卡港务局法》分别经《1984 年斯里兰卡港务局法（修正案）》［Sri Lanka Ports Authority（Amendment）Act］、《1984 年斯里兰卡港务局法（修正案）》［Sri Lanka Ports Authority（Amendment）Act，No. 35 of 1984］、《1992 年斯里兰卡港务局法（修正案）》［Sri Lanka Ports Authority（Amendment）Act，No. 2 of 1992］对其中第 7 条、第 8 条、第 11 条、第 14—17 条、

---

[1] Lawnet，"Sri Lanka Ports Authority"，https：//www. lawnet. gov. lk/sri-lanka-ports-authority-6/，April 25，2020.

第 21 条、第 24 条、第 25 条、第 38 条、第 39 条、第 42 条、第 46 条、第 65 条、第 68—70 条、第 80 条、第 86 条、第 89 条及附录作出修订，主要涉及港口局董事会的组织结构、终止港口服务及收回港口费用的程序、港务局的财政义务、对违反本法行为的惩处方式、对没收或留置货物的拍卖或变卖方式、港口安保人员的职责、对相关船舶的援助与强制性权力、港务局对引航员的责任等内容的更新、补充和调整。[1]

除上述修订外，斯里兰卡还于 1990 年通过《斯里兰卡港务局法（特别规定）》[Sri Lanka Ports Authority（Special Provisions）Act，No. 36 of 1990]，专门为工作岗位被斯里兰卡港务局所吸收、却未获资格领取养老金的原科伦坡港务委员会雇员作出救济性规定，明确相关雇员及其继承人在满足相应条件的前提下，将有资格领取斯里兰卡港务局所发放的养老金。[2]

2. 船舶相关立法

（1）《1971 年锡兰航运公司法》

根据《1971 年锡兰航运公司法》（Ceylon Shipping Corporation Act，1971）所设立的锡兰航运公司（现改称"锡兰航运有限公司"），至今仍是斯里兰卡最为重要且居于主导地位的国有全资航运公司。该立法共有 44 条，分别对锡兰航运公司的成立，公司的目标与宗旨，公司及公司高级管理人员的权力，公司董事会的设立与职权，公司的资金来源与财务管理，国家总理对该公司相关事项作出进一步规范的权力，公司官员及职员在特定范围内被视同公务人员等作出了规定。

根据该法，锡兰航运公司的宗旨是：（1）经营货物、邮件和旅客的海上运输业务；（2）从事船东、租船人、船舶经纪人、船舶代理人相关及其他附属业务；（3）承担对船舶的建造、维护、修理和翻修工作。锡兰航运公司有权：（1）购买、承租或出租、建造、收购、交换或以任何其他方式处置任何船舶；（2）建立、维护并运营航运业务及所有关联服务；（3）出于承担公司工作的需要而任命、雇用或辞退任何官员、雇员、代理人或专家，并决定雇佣条款及条件；（4）作为国内外的其他公司或个人的船舶代理人或船舶经纪人；

---

〔1〕 See Lawnet, "Sri Lanka Ports Authority（Amendment）", https：//www. lawnet. gov. lk/sri-lanka-ports-authority-amendment-3/, April 25, 2020; Lawnet, "Sri Lanka Ports Authority（Amendment）", https：//www. lawnet. gov. lk/sri-lanka-ports-authority-amendment-2/, April 25, 2020; Lawnet, "Sri Lanka Ports Authority（Amendment）", https：//www. lawnet. gov. lk/sri-lanka-ports-authority-amendment-4/, April 25, 2020.

〔2〕 Lawnet, "Sri Lanka Ports Authority（Special provisions）", https：//www. lawnet. gov. lk/sri-lan-ka-ports-authority-special-provisions-2/, April 25, 2020.

（5）承担一切与公司宗旨相关的财务、商业、贸易、科技及其他业务往来；（6）利用一切手段提升雇员技能、提高设备效率、改进工作方法；（7）在政府许可下，促进国内外分支机构直接或间接贡献于公司的收益；（8）组建咨询委员会以及类似地方委员会，其功能及相应条款由公司视其需要确定。[1]该公司当前的运营状况参见本书"第Ⅱ部分 斯里兰卡海洋法律体系研究"部分"二、海洋事务主管部门及其职能"下"（四）海洋运输相关管理机构"中"2. 锡兰航运有限公司"相关内容。

（2）《1971年商船运输法》及其修订

1971年，即将独立的斯里兰卡通过《商船运输法》（Merchant Shipping Act，No. 52 of 1971）以归拢并修订当时已有的商船运输相关法律，同时就其关联及附带事项作出进一步规定。该法全文共计333条，分为12个部分，主要内容包括：

第一，有关本法的基本说明。如该法的适用范围、施行时间，对商船运输部门部长及其他官员的任命，总理作出进一步指示的权力，商船运输部门相关官员或职员的职责，商船运输部门的机构及职权划分，监察员及登记官的任命等。

第二，有关运输的管控。如对船舶租赁的登记，海上运输船舶的许可与续期或撤销，无许可时不得离港，相关管理部门部长在船舶登记中的权力，航运规划委员会（Shipping Allocation Board）及运费率咨询委员会（Shipping Rates Advisory Board）的组建，对违反航运许可行为的处罚，对海上货物运输的限制，总理就航运事项进一步制定规则的权力等。

第三，有关船舶的登记。如斯里兰卡（锡兰）船舶的登记资格，登记船舶的义务，船舶登记的豁免，登记证书的签发，临时登记证书的适用，船舶所有权的转移及其登记，船舶抵押及其登记，已登记船舶的优先权的产生与行使，船舶相关事项的变更与登记，在本国水域的内国及外国船舶的权利与义务，不适用本部分规定的特殊情形等。

第四，船长及船员相关规定。如对船员驾船及管理资质的审查，对正式船员以外其他在船人员的工作条件的规范，船舶相关文书的要求及出生死亡等事项的登记与移交，对偷渡及非经许可登船的违法认定，船长的逮捕权，对未登记的本国船舶进行处罚，为海员组建国家福利委员会（National Welfare Board）等。

---

〔1〕 Lawnet，"Ceylon Shipping Corporation"，https：//www. lawnet. gov. lk/ceylon-shipping-corpora-tion-6/，April 25，2020.

第五，有关船舶建造、船舶设备与船舶检验。如总理在船舶安全方面的权力，货运船及客运船的船舶检验要求，船舶检验机构及检验证书的签发，检验证书在斯里兰卡外的承认，斯里兰卡船舶在国外的检验以及外国船舶在斯里兰卡的检验，信号灯的使用，违反船舶检验行为的惩处等。

第六，载重线相关规定。如对在本国登记船舶的载重线检验及要求，在外国登记船舶的载重线核验及要求，对特定国际航行船舶及单程运输船舶的豁免规定、豁免权的行使主体与条件，相关术语解释等。

第七，航行安全相关规定。如防止船舶碰撞的相关规定，对船舶事故及船舶损失的报告，有关破坏灯塔的防范与处罚，防止灯塔发出错误信号并消除错误信号影响，对事故船舶的协助与救援，对不适航船舶的责任认定与处罚等。

第八，航运调查法院（Court of Survey）的组建。如航运调查法院的建立方式与人员构成，该法院的权力与基本程序，要求该法院向总理提交报告，该法院审理规则的制定，向科技专家咨询疑难案件的规则，费用及救济等。

第九，海难与海难救助。如对遇难船舶的接收义务，接收遇难船舶的权力机关及其相关行动规则，发现海难残骸时应遵守的规则，对船舶残骸的处理程序，处理海难中货物的相关义务，无人主张的海难残骸的处理与归属，海难残骸的清除，有关残骸处理的违法行为等。

第十，相关法律程序。如航运中涉及人身伤亡的相关程序，处理本法相关法律问题的法院及其管辖权，对船舶的扣押的权力主体及程序等。

第十一，其他补充问题。如督察员的任命与权力，相关文档的形式要求与报告存档，对船员及其他船上人员的死亡调查，对航运管理官员及公职人员的保护等。

第十二，与涉及关联事项的其他法律的协调。如对特定法律的废止、替代以及过渡期的法律适用等。

该立法体系全面、内容庞杂，可谓斯里兰卡海商事单行法典。但除其第二部分明确规定只适用于"海上航行"（sea-going）的船舶外，其他部分并未就船舶航行水域作出限定，由此与传统的海商事法律的适用范围有所差别。[1]

《1971年商船运输法》分别经《1988年商船运输法（修正案）》［Merchant Shipping（Amendment）Act，No. 36 of 1988］、《2006年商船运输法（指

---

〔1〕 Lawnet, "Merchant Shipping", https：//www. lawnet. gov. lk/merchant-shipping-8/，April 25, 2020.

派变更）》［Merchant Shipping（Change of Designation）Act，No. 3 of 2006］、《2019 年商船运输法（修正案）》 ［Merchant Shipping（Amendment）Act，No. 17 of 2019］对其第 2 条、第 3 条、第 123 条、第 138 条、第 139 条、第 143 条、第 144 条、第 152 条、第 155 条、第 156—160 条、第 164 条、第 166—169 条、第 171—175 条、第 205 条、第 207 条作出修订，涉及船舶并行登记、船舶抵押登记及其解释、商船运输部门负责人的指派及权限、国际航行的界定、国际公约的适用、相关处罚的实施标准及惩罚力度、专家小组的建立、相关豁免权、防止船舶污染等内容的修改与补充。[1]

（3）《1972 年船舶代理执照法》及其修订

《1972 年船舶代理执照法》（Licensing of Shipping Agents Act，No. 10 of 1972）旨在引入及实施执照制度来规范和管控船舶代理人的业务，并就关联或附带事宜制定相关条文。

该法全文共计 14 条，内容主要包括：（1）禁止无执照经营船舶代理业务；（2）禁止船舶代理业务执照的转让；（3）执照的中止或吊销；（4）向货运代理人发出指示的相关要求；（5）船舶代理人入境及检查的权力；（6）在指定日期前以船务代理人身份经营业务而未能获发执照者，其所引致的任何损失概不赔偿；（7）对相应违法行为的认定与处罚；（8）法人团体或非法人团体所犯罪行的法律责任；（9）船舶代理执照颁发的相关记录与报告等。同时，该法第 2 条明确规定，其不适用于据 1971 年《锡兰航运公司法》成立的锡兰航运公司。[2]

《1972 年船舶代理执照法》分别经《1981 年船舶代理执照法（修正案）》［Licensing of Shipping Agents（Amendment）Act，No. 9 of 1981］、《1982 年船舶代理执照法（修正案）》 ［Licensing of Shipping Agents（Amendment）Act，No. 16 of 1982］、《2002 年船舶代理执照法（修正案）》 ［Licensing of Shipping Agents（Amendment）Act，No. 18 of 2002］对其第 2 条、第 3 条、第 13 条、第 15 条作出修订，主要涉及船舶代理业务经营资格的申请、船舶代理业务经营的期限、代理人资格的转让、对雇员过失责任的承担、船舶代理

---

〔1〕　See Lawnet，"Merchant Shipping（Amendment）"，https：//www. lawnet. gov. lk/merchant-ship-ping-amendment-2/，April 25，2020；Lawnet， "Merchant Shipping（Change of Designation）"，https：//www. lawnet. gov. lk/merchant-shipping-change-of-designation-3/，April 25，2020；Department of Government Printing，"Merchant Shipping（Amendment）Act"，http：//documents. gov. lk/files/act/2019/10/17-2019_ E. pdf，April 25，2020.

〔2〕　Lawnet，"Licensing of Shipping Agents"，https：//www. lawnet. gov. lk/licensing-of-shipping-a-gents-6/，April 25，2020.

人业务范围的界定与表述等内容的替换或修改。[1]

（五）海洋能源相关立法

1. 石油资源相关立法

（1）《1961 年锡兰石油公司法》及其修订

斯里兰卡于 1961 年通过《锡兰石油公司法》（Ceylon Petroleum Corporation Act，No. 28 of 1961），以成立一家专门经营石油相关业务的国有公司。成立该公司的目的在于：第一，作为石油的进口商、出口商、销售商、供应商或分销商经营业务；第二，经营石油的勘探、开采、生产和精炼业务；第三，经营附带的或有助于实现第一和第二款所述宗旨的任何其他业务。

为实现上述目的，该法涵盖了 6 大部分 74 项条文，主要内容包括：（1）锡兰石油公司及其董事会的章程；（2）锡兰石油公司的权力和职责；（3）该公司的资金来源和财务管理规定；（4）为该公司运营目的而强制征收及使用任何不动产或动产；（5）为征用土地或其他财产设立赔偿法庭；（6）相关赔偿事项及方式；（7）进一步制定细则、术语解释等其他一般性规定。[2]

该法分别经《1973 年锡兰石油公司法（修正案）》［Ceylon Petroleum Corporation（Amendment）Law，No. 50 of 1973］、《1976 年锡兰石油公司法（修正案）》［Ceylon Petroleum Corporation（Amendment）Law，No，2 of 1976］对其第 6 条、第 8 条、第 17 条、第 18 条、第 22 条、第 34 条、第 36 条、第 37—39 条、第 47 条、第 48 条、第 54 条、第 55 条、第 57—59 条、第 67 条、第 69 条、第 70 条、第 78 条进行修订，主要涉及公司的权力，董事会组建与董事选任，董事会主席及总经理的选任，对索赔案件赔偿条款的接受条件，赔偿法庭酬金及法庭开支，董事会主席预付薪酬的权力，赔偿法庭的开庭程序，对在特定行政命令生效后归属公司或被公司征用的财产的赔偿，赔偿的最终支付，在地表下发现的石油归公司所有，土地相关文书的报送，特定情

---

〔1〕 See Lawnet, "Licensing Of Shipping Agents（Amendment）", https：//www. lawnet. gov. lk/licensing-of-shipping-agents-amendment-2/, April 25, 2020；Lawnet, "Licensing Of Shipping Agents（Amendment）", https：//www. lawnet. gov. lk/licensing-of-shipping-agents-amendment-3/, April 25, 2020；Lawnet, "Licensing Of Shipping Agents（Amendment）", https：//www. lawnet. gov. lk/licensing-of-shipping-agents-amendment-4/, April 25, 2020.

〔2〕 Lawnet, "Ceylon Petroleum Corporation", https：//www. lawnet. gov. lk/ceylon-petroleum-corporation-4/, April 25, 2020.

形下的豁免等。[1]

此外，为就组建锡兰石油公司所征用或收购土地或资产提供救济途径，斯里兰卡分别于 1965 年及 1968 年通过了《锡兰石油赔偿法（外国索赔）》[Ceylon Petroleum Compensation（Foreign Claims）Act，No. 19 of 1965]、《锡兰石油公司（赔偿认定）特别规定法》[Ceylon Petroleum Corporation（Determination of Compensation）Special Provisions Act，No. 22 of 1968]。前者共计 5 条，意在就因《锡兰石油公司法》而被划归锡兰石油公司或为其征用的某些外国石油资产进行赔偿。根据该法，政府因国有化或征用与外国公司所订立的任何赔偿协议均应受这一立法的约束。[2]后者全文共计 17 条，旨在就外国石油公司以外的主体因划归锡兰石油公司或为锡兰石油公司征用的土地所提出的赔偿要求作出裁定，并就索赔请求的提出对象与程序、支付赔偿的方式、对索赔要求进行调查、对赔偿裁定的上诉、违反赔偿裁定的后果等关联或附带事项作出规定。[3]

（2）《2003 年石油资源法》

斯里兰卡于 2003 年通过《石油资源法》（Petroleum Resources Act，No. 26 of 2003），以就斯里兰卡石油资源的勘探开发及相关事项的管控作出必要规定。随着这一立法的施行，《1961 年锡兰石油公司法》第 5D 条、第 5F 条、第 5G 条、第 34A 条即告废止，斯里兰卡曾赋予锡兰石油公司有关石油进出口、销售、供应、分配的专属性权利就此终止。

该法全文共计 34 条，分为 6 个部分，内容主要涉及：第一，石油资源所有权的明确，包括明确石油资源的所有权应归于国家，国家将参照国际实践开发石油资源，石油资源开发协议的订立等；第二，石油资源开发委员会的设立，包括石油资源开发委员会的设立主体与组织机构，该委员会的权力与职能等；第三，有关石油资源开发协议、开发区块及开发许可，包括石油业经营行为的限制，进入协议相关开发区块的申请，石油资源开发协议的签订，石油资源开发许可的颁发，石油开发中附带的条件，协议方违反开发许

[1] See Lawnet，"Ceylon Petroleum Corporation（Amendment）Law"，https：//www. lawnet. gov. lk/ceylon-petroleum-corporation-amendment-law-2/，April 25，2020；Lawnet，"Ceylon Petroleum Corporation（Amendment）Law"，https：//www. lawnet. gov. lk/ceylon-petroleum-corporation-a-mendment-law-3/，April 25，2020.

[2] Lawnet，"Ceylon Petroleum（Foreign Claims）Compensation"，https：//www. lawnet. gov. lk/cey-lon-petroleum-foreign-claims-compensation-3/，April 25，2020.

[3] Lawnet，"Ceylon Petroleum Corporation（Determination of Compensation）Special Provisions"，ht-tps：//www. lawnet. gov. lk/ceylon-petroleum-corporation-determination-of-compensation-special-pro-visions-3/，April 25，2020.

可条件时的通告，开发许可的中止或撤销，开发许可下的协议方权利，开发许可中参与股权的转让，项目分包方的许可，联合单位开发协议的签订，对协议方资产的收购等；第四，关于秘书处的职能，包括石油资源部门部长领导下的秘书处的建立，公职人员的借调任用等；第五，财务相关规定，包括石油产品份额的相关条款，税负增加时对相关条款的调整，对利润与收入的确定，石油资源特许权使用费，关税减免等；第六，其他一般性条款，包括总理制定进一步细则的权力，进入石油行业的权力，相关不法行为的认定与处罚，在涉及相同事项时与其他法律的关系，相关术语解释等。

根据该法第 2 条，斯里兰卡对其陆地"地表以下"以及"内水、历史性水域、领海、毗连区、大陆边缘和专属经济区"中的石油资源都拥有绝对所有权，而无论他人是否对发现石油资源的土地有所有权或其他权利。而该法所称"领海""毗连区""专属经济区""历史性水域"都与《1976 年第 22 号海域法》所主张水域一致，所称"大陆边缘"则指《公约》第 76 条所界定的海床及底土。由此，《2003 年石油资源法》可覆盖适用于海上石油资源的勘探开发活动，斯里兰卡政府亦有意于以此为海上能源开发提供基本法律支撑。[1]

（3）石油产品相关立法

《1979 年石油产品（供应管控）法》［Petroleum Products（Regulation and Control of Supplies）Act，No. 34 of 1979］是为确保石油产品的公平分配而对石油产品的供应及其关联或附带事项作出的相应规定，意在管理、控制和保证石油产品的合理分配和有效利用。该法共计 9 个部分 44 条，分别就相应行政管理机关及管理人员任用、汽油销售的限制、煤油销售的限制、汽车柴油销售的限制、重柴油销售的限制、液化石油气销售的限制、航空涡轮燃料销售的限制等作出规定。[2]

《2002 年石油产品（特别规定）法》［Petroleum Products（Special Provisions）Act，No. 33 of 2002］意在为锡兰石油公司外的其他石油进出口、销售、供应和分配途径提供法律依据，由此赋予能源供应委员会某些权力，并就其他关联或附带事项作出规定。该法全文共计 9 条，分别就锡兰石油公司的权力不受减损、能源供应委员会依法享有的权力、《锡兰石油公司法》某些规定的中止适用、进出口石油许可证的签发、石油销售许可证的签发、本

---

[1] Lawnet, "Petroleum Resources", https：//www. lawnet. gov. lk/petroleum-resources-3/, April 25, 2020.

[2] Lawnet, "Petroleum Products（Regulation And Control Of Supplies）", https：//www. lawnet. gov. lk/petroleum-products-regulation-and-control-of-supplies-4/, April 25, 2020.

法与其他现行法律的关系、法律解释时的作准文本等作出规定。[1]

2. 一般性矿业立法

（1）《1973 年矿山和矿产法》

《1973 年矿山和矿产法》（Mines and Minerals Law, No. 4 of 1973）是斯里兰卡有关矿产开采、勘探、收集、加工、销售和出口的基本立法，意在保护矿山工人的健康、安全和福利，将特定矿产的所有权完全归属于国家，赋予为发展矿产工业而成立的公司强制取得或征用不动产或动产的权利，同时就与上述事项有关或附带的其他事项制定条文。该法全文共计 77 条，分为 6 个部分，分别就矿物的所有权和许可证的颁发、行政管理规章、矿业公司的发展、牌照持有人及管理人的一般职责、矿山工人的安全和福利等作出规定。[2] 该法已于 1992 年随下述立法的通过而被废止。

（2）《1992 年矿山和矿产法》

1992 年，斯里兰卡颁布新的《矿山和矿产法》（Mines and Mineral Act, No. 33 of 1992），旨在建立地质勘探和矿产局以管理矿物的勘探、开采、运输、加工、贸易或出口，将原地质勘探部相关职能移交至地质勘探和矿产局，同时就其他关联或附带事项作出规定。随着该法的颁布，《1890 年盐业条例》（The Salt Ordinance）、《1968 年放射性矿物法》（The Radio Active Minerals Act, No. 46 of 1968）及前述《1973 年矿山和矿产法》均告废止。全文共计 70 条，分为 4 个部分，分别就①地质勘探局的建立、权力和职能，②矿物的所有权和许可证的签发，③矿山工人的健康、安全和福利，④相关不法行为的认定与惩罚、总理作出进一步规定的权力、地方议会的征税权、术语解释等一般性事项等作出规定。

根据该法，在斯里兰卡的土地之上、之中、之下所发现的任何矿产的所有权都归于国家，无论该土地相关的其他权利归属为何。任何人在发现矿物时，都须通知地质勘探和矿产局局长。而专为矿产开发所设立的地质勘探和矿产局的主要职能在于：①承担斯里兰卡系统地质填图和地质准备工作；②确定和评估斯里兰卡的矿产资源；③评估相关矿物开采、加工和出口的商业可行性；④颁发执照管控相关矿产的勘探和开采，管理特定矿物的加工、

---

[1] Lawnet, "Petroleum Products（Special Provisions）", https：//www. lawnet. gov. lk/petroleum-products-special-provisions-2/, April 25, 2020.

[2] Lawnet, "Mines and Minerals", https：//www. lawnet. gov. lk/mines-and-minerals-5/, April 25, 2020.

贸易和出口；⑤基于商业目的就矿物开采和生产的促进措施向部长提出建议。[1]

《1992 年矿山和矿产法》经《2009 年矿山和矿产法（修正案）》[The Mines and Minerals（Amendment）Act，No. 66 of 2009] 对其第 4—6 条、第 8 条、第 12 第、第 13 第、第 27—31 条、第 33 条、第 35 条、第 37 条、第 42 条、第 44 条、第 46 条、第 48—49 条、第 51 条、第三部分标题、第 55 条、第 57—58 条、第 61 条、第 63 条、第 64 条、第 68 条、第 70 条进行了修订，主要就地质勘探和矿产局的成员构成，地质勘探和矿产局局长的任命及权力，这一机构的权力与职能，矿产开采执照的颁发及其限制与范围，在执照所限定范围内采矿的权利，占有执照所限定区域的权利，该法所适用的"矿工"范围的限定，对雇用女性矿工的限制，童工及成年矿工的工作时间，采矿作业的环境保护，相关不法行为的认定，地方议会对矿产征税的限制，对"采矿"术语的进一步解释等内容作出调整和补充。[2]

根据该法第 65 条，《1949 年王国土地条例》（The Crown Lands Ordinance）第 63 条因该立法而作出修订，允许经《1992 年矿山和矿产法》而获得采矿执照者在"海床"上进行矿产勘探和开发。同时根据其第 66 条，《1981 年海岸保护法》（Coast Conservation Act，No. 57 of 1981）中所有矿产开发有关的执照均指依据《1992 年矿山和矿产法》所获得的执照，且已获这一执照者无须就在海岸保护区所占有的海滩或海床获取额外许可。可以认为，尽管该立法未直接就海洋矿产资源的勘探开发作出规定，但其可涵盖或延展适用于斯里兰卡管辖海域的资源开采活动。

另外，就与其他特定矿产资源开发立法的关系而言，该法明确规定，其条款不适用于《1961 年锡兰石油公司法》及《1971 年国家宝石公司法》下所涉矿物资源，但所有与碳氢化合物及宝石类矿产的调查勘探相关的数据及报告都应提交地质勘探和矿产局。[3]

---

[1] Lawnet，"Mines and Minerals"，https：//www. lawnet. gov. lk/mines-and-minerals-6/，April 25，2020.

[2] Department of Government Printing，"Mines And Minerals（Amendment）"，http：//documents. gov. lk/files/act/2009/11/66-2009_ E. pdf，April 25，2020.

[3] Lawnet，"Mines and Minerals"，https：//www. lawnet. gov. lk/mines-and-minerals-6/，April 25，2020.

（六）海洋环境相关立法

1.《1981 年海洋污染防治法》

《1981 年海洋污染防治法》（Marine Pollution Prevention Act，No. 59 of 1981）意在预防、减少和控制斯里兰卡水域污染，促使海洋污染防治相关国际公约在斯里兰卡的生效，并为其他关联或附带事项提供法律依据。立足于该法，斯里兰卡政府所推动加入或施行的国际公约主要包括：《1969 年国际油污损害民事责任公约》、《1954 年国际防止海上油污公约》（International Convention on the Prevention of Pollution of the Sea by Oil，1954）、《1971 年设立国际油污损害赔偿基金国际公约》（International Convention on the Establishment of an International Fund for Compensation for Oil Pollution Damage，1971）、《1969 年国际干预公海油污事故公约》及《1973 年国际防止船舶造成污染公约的 1978 年议定书》。

　　该法全文共计 37 条，分为 8 个部分，内容主要涉及：（1）海洋污染防治署的设立，包括其设立主体、组织结构、人员选任及职权等；（2）海洋污染相关的刑事责任，包括向斯里兰卡水域排放或泄漏油污或其他污染物的情形，向斯里兰卡水域倾倒油污或其他污染物的情形，特殊情形下的抗辩等；（3）海洋污染相关的民事责任，包括此类民事责任的范围，特殊情形下的抗辩，责任限制的情形与认定，强制保险条款等；（4）海洋污染的防治措施，包括有关油类及其他污染物的记录簿，石油转移的限制，在向斯里兰卡水域排放油污或其他污染物时的报告义务等；（5）接收设施与在船设备，包括排放或处置油污或其他污染物的接收设施的安排，防止污染的在船设备的安装等；（6）海上事故导致污染的情形，包括海上事故导致污染时的处置措施，相关措施与实际或可能的损害的相称性要求等；（7）对相关国际公约的施行，包括总理施行国际公约的权力，基于国际公约规定的额外抗辩等；（8）其他杂项规定，包括海洋污染防治署的检查与调查权，进入海洋邻近土地或住所以执行职务的权力，船长或海上设施负责人配合相关机构的义务，扣押船舶或禁止船舶入海的权力，相关领事义务的履行，相关法院的管辖权，逮捕和起诉的权力，总理制定进一步细则的权力，不得对海洋污染防治署官员或雇员基于本法采取的善意行为提起法律程序等。

　　根据该法第 37 条的解释，其所称"船舶"是指在海洋环境中作业的任何类型的船舶，包括拖网渔船、水翼船、气垫船、潜水器、驳船、浮式船和固定或浮动平台，无论其动力方式如何，但军用船舶除外；而该法所适用的"斯里兰卡水域"包括其领海、毗连区、专属经济区、大陆架以及《1976 年第22号海域法》特别规定的污染防治区。[1]

2.《1981年海岸保护法》及其修订

斯里兰卡于1981年颁布《海岸保护法》(Coast Conservation Act, No. 57 of 1981),以服务于以下目标:第一,对本国海岸带进行勘测,从而为海岸带管理方案的制订做好准备;第二,规范和控制海岸带内的开发活动;第三,在海岸带内制订并执行海岸保护工作计划;第四,对相关成文法作出必要修订。

该法全文共计42条,分为5个部分,主要内容包括:第一,海岸带的行政管理相关规定。如海岸带的管理、控制、养护与运行相关权力都归于国家,海岸保护总负责人的任命,总负责人的职责与职能,海岸保护咨询委员会的建立,该咨询委员会的职能,该咨询委员会成员的任命,该咨询委员会的会议召开等。第二,海岸带管理相关规定。如海岸带的勘测,海岸带的管理措施,总理可以就特许权发放的标准作出规定等。第三,特许权发放的程序。如特许权的发放、特许权发放的条件,环境影响评价,特许权的其他附带条件,特许权的期限及续期,特许权条件的变更,海岸保护计划的执行,申诉要求与程序,不适用于通航运河的维护或疏浚等。第四,其他一般性规定。如过渡性条款的适用,对占有海滩或海床的特别许可,防止废弃物或外来物侵入海岸带的指示,违反本法构成犯罪的行为,对未经授权设施的拆除,国家相关权利的保留,对国家相关公职人员善意行为的保护等。第五,对现行立法的修改或修正。如其他现行立法在海岸带的适用,其他现行立法条款的废除或增补,相关术语的解释等。

根据该法第42条,其中的"海岸"(coast)是指邻接海洋但未被海水覆盖的陆地边缘;而"海岸带"(Coastal Zone)是指位于平均高潮水位线(Mean High Water line)向陆地方向300米界限与平均低潮水位线(Mean Low Water line)向海洋方向2000米界限之间的区域,若有河流、溪流、潟湖及其他水体暂时或长期与海洋相通,其向陆地方向的边界将为从自然入海口的直线基线垂直延伸至2000米的界限,从而将上述连接海洋的河流、溪流、潟湖及其他水体包含其中。

随着该法的施行,《1915年住房与城镇改善条例》(Housing and Town Improvement Ordinance)第56条、《1946年城镇与乡村规划条例》(Town and Country Planning Ordinance)第29条、《1973年矿山和矿产法》第13条均作

---

[1] Lawnet, "Marine Pollution Prevention", https://www.lawnet.gov.lk/marine-pollution-prevention-3/, April 25, 2020.

出修订，《1968 年旅游业发展法》（Tourist Development Act，No. 14 of 1968）第 7 条及第 8 条被废止，《1951 年土壤养护法》（Soil Conservation Act）则由此增补第 11A 条。[1]

《1981 年海岸保护法》分别经《1988 年海岸保护法（修正案）》［Coast Conservation（Amendment）Act，No. 64 of 1988］、《2011 年海岸保护法（修正案）》［Coast Conservation（Amendment）Act，No. 49 of 2011］就其第 3—5 条、第 10 条、第 12 第、第 13 条、第 15—21 条、第 24—31 条、第 35 条、第 42 条作出修订，主要涉及对海岸保护总负责人的权力委托，违反相关规定而扣押交通工具，禁止在海岸带内开采及收集珊瑚，由总负责人出具的证明书可作为初步证据，海滩的所有权不能通过占有或使用而获得，沙子和贝壳的运输，罚款与警方奖励，在没有逮捕令的情况下进行逮捕的权力，相关人员的豁免，海岸资源管理咨询委员会的设立，海岸带资源调查，未经许可的填海行为，保释规定等内容的修改、删除或增补。[2]

（七）海洋科研相关立法

1. 《1999 年国家渔业与航海工程研究所法》

《1999 年国家渔业与航海工程研究所法》（National Institute of Fisheries and Nautical Engineering Act，No. 36 of 1999）的颁布，旨在建立国家渔业与航海工程研究所，提高从事或准备从事渔业的相关人才的技术和管理技能，并就相关联或附带的事项制定相应法律规则。该法分为序言和正文，正文共计 36 条，分为 4 个部分，分别就国家渔业与航海工程研究所的建立、该研究所所长和研究所工作人员的任命、该研究所的资金来源与财政管理、其他一般事项等作出规定。

根据该法第 3 条，斯里兰卡国家渔业与航海工程研究所的职能为：第一，制订渔业和航海工程的学习课程和培训方案，以提高从事或准备从事渔业的相关人才的技术和管理技能；第二，提供渔业和航海工程的课程和培训方案，以便颁发证书、文凭和其他学术荣誉；第三，在国家和国际组织的协助下，举办或安排举办有关渔业和航海工程教育的会议、研讨会和专题讨论会；第四，就渔业和航海工程领域的教育和推广训练进行或推进研究和调

---

〔1〕　Lawnet，"Coast Conservation"，https：//www. lawnet. gov. lk/coast-conservation-3/，April 25，2020.

〔2〕　See Lawnet，"Coast Conservation（Amendment）"，https：//www. lawnet. gov. lk/coast-conserva-tion-amendment-2/，April 25，2020；Department of Government Printing，"Coast Conservation（Amendment）"，http：//documents. gov. lk/files/act/2011/11/49-2011 _ E. pdf，April 25，2020.

查；第五，通过交换教师和学生及其他方式，与斯里兰卡国内外具有类似目标的机构合作；第六，就有关渔业和航海工程的事项向渔业部部长提供咨询意见。[1]

2. 《2014 年斯里兰卡海洋大学法》

《2014 年斯里兰卡海洋大学法》（Ocean University of Sri Lanka Act, No. 31 of 2014）的颁布，旨在为建立、维持和管理斯里兰卡海洋大学提供必要的法律基础，同时就其他关联或附带事项作出法律安排，从而为斯里兰卡海洋大学的高等教育提供便利。随着该法的正式施行，前述《1999 年国家渔业与航海工程研究所法》由此废止。该法分为序言和正文，正文共计 71 条，分为 13 个部分，主要就斯里兰卡海洋大学的建立，该大学的宗旨和权力，总理执行本法的责任以及管理指导该大学的权力，大学校长及教职员的任命及职责，该大学的主管机关及其职责，校园的建设与管理，大学集会的事由与要求，申诉委员会成立及程序，财务管理，学生会和其他社团，术语解释等内容作出规定。

据该法规定，斯里兰卡海洋大学的宗旨是：第一，在渔业、海洋科学、海事技术和相关领域提供大学教育；第二，提供渔业及相关领域的职业及技术课程，以配合各地区的人力需求；第三，向渔业及相关领域的从业人员传播有关渔业、海洋和海事部门的知识；第四，为渔业、海洋科学、海事技术及相关领域的持续专业发展提供延伸课程；第五，以入学为目的，为渔业及其相关领域的人员提供职业及技术课程；第六，根据学生在渔业、海洋科学、海事技术及相关领域的才能和能力，促进他们在工程、科学、技术和职业教育及培训体系方面的逐步发展；第七，为有国家职业资格的人提供学习课程，协助他们提高资质并获取在渔业、海洋科学、海事技术及相关领域的学历认证。[2]

---

[1] Lawnet, "National Institute Of Fisheries And Nautical Engineering", https：//www. lawnet. gov. lk/national-institute-of-fisheries-and-nautical-engineering-3/, April 25, 2020.

[2] Department of Government Printing, "Ocean University of Sri Lanka Act, No. 31 of 2014", http：//documents. gov. lk/files/act/2014/9/31-2014_ E. pdf, April 25, 2020.

四、缔结和加入的国际海洋法条约

（一）联合国框架下的海洋法公约

斯里兰卡于 1958 年 10 月 30 日签署了日内瓦海洋法体系下的《领海及毗连区公约》《公海公约》《捕鱼及养护公海生物资源公约》《大陆架公约》，却均未予批准。但斯里兰卡仍于同日以最终签署方式成为 1958 年《关于强制解决争端之任择签字议定书》的缔约国，表示对于所签订的海洋法各条约之任何条款因解释或适用而发生涉及本国的一切争端，愿接受国际法院之强制管辖。[1]

斯里兰卡于 1982 年 12 月 10 日签署了《联合国海洋法公约》，随后于 1994 年 7 月 19 日批准生效，且未就《公约》条款作出特别声明。[2] 1994 年 7 月 29 日，斯里兰卡签署了《关于执行 1982 年 12 月 10 日〈联合国海洋法公约〉第十一部分的协定》，并自 1994 年 11 月 16 日起对该协定予以临时适用，后于 1995 年 7 月 28 日同意接受该协定约束。[3]

斯里兰卡于 1996 年 10 月 9 日签署《执行 1982 年 12 月 10 日〈联合国海洋法公约〉有关养护和管理跨界鱼类种群和高度洄游鱼类种群的规定的协定》，随后于同月 24 日批准该协定;[4] 1999 年 6 月 30 日，斯里兰卡签署了《国际海洋法法庭特权和豁免协定》，但至今未就其作出批准。[5]

---

〔1〕 UN Treaty Collection, "Optional Protocol of Signature concerning the Compulsory Settlement of Disputes", https: //treaties. un. org/Pages/ViewDetails. aspx? src = TREATY&mtdsg _ no = XXI-5&chapter = 21&clang = _ en, April 22, 2020.

〔2〕 UN Treaty Collection, " United Nations Convention on the Law of the Sea ", https: //treaties. un. org/Pages/ViewDetailsIII. aspx? src = TREATY&mtdsg _ no = XXI-6&chapter = 21&Temp = mtdsg3&clang = _ en, April 22, 2020.

〔3〕 UN Treaty Collection, " Agreement relating to the implementation of Part XI of the United Nations Convention on the Law of the Sea of 10 December 1982", https: //treaties. un. org/Pages/ViewDetails. aspx? src = TREATY&mtdsg_ no = XXI-6-a&chapter = 21&clang = _ en, April 22, 2020.

〔4〕 UN Treaty Collection, " Agreement for the Implementation of the Provisions of the United Nations Convention on the Law of the Sea of 10 December 1982 relating to the Conservation and Management of Straddling Fish Stocks and Highly Migratory Fish Stocks", https: //treaties. un. org/Pages/ViewDetails. aspx? src = TREATY&mtdsg_ no = XXI-7&chapter = 21&clang = _ en, April 22, 2020.

〔5〕 UN Treaty Collection, " Agreement on the Privileges and Immunities of the International Tribunal for the Law of the Sea", https: //treaties. un. org/Pages/ViewDetails. aspx? src = TREATY&mtdsg_ no = XXI-8&chapter = 21&clang = _ en, April 22, 2020.

（二）海上安全相关条约

在海上航行安全方面，斯里兰卡于 1978 年 1 月 4 日加入《1972 年国际海上避碰规则公约》，该公约于同日对斯里兰卡生效；于 1983 年 8 月 30 日签署了由国际海事组织于 1974 年通过的《国际海上人命安全公约》，该公约于同年 11 月 30 日对斯里兰卡生效；于 2000 年 9 月 4 日加入了《1988 年制止危及海上航行安全非法行为公约》，该公约于同年 11 月 3 日对斯里兰卡生效。

在改善海上救险安全通信、提高海陆空运输效率方面，斯里兰卡于 1976 年 9 月 3 日签署了经修订的《国际移动卫星组织业务协定》，并分别于 1986 年 6 月 10 日、2000 年 2 月 4 日对该协定 1985 年以及 2000 年的修正案作出赞同；于 1981 年 11 月 15 日接受了《国际移动卫星组织公约》，并陆续接受了该公约 6 部修正案中的 1985 年修正案和 1998 年修正案。[1]

（三）海洋环境保护相关条约

为保护海洋环境，促进海洋资源开发的可持续发展，斯里兰卡曾于 1983 年加入《1954 年国际防止海上油污公约》（International Convention for the Prevention of Pollution of the Sea by Oil），于 1983 年接受《1969 年国际油污损害民事责任公约》和《1971 年设立国际油污损害赔偿基金国际公约》（International Convention on the Establishment of an International Fund for Compensation for Oil Pollution Damage，1971），后分别于 1997 年 9 月 24 日及 2000 年 1 月 22 日退出。[2]

当前对斯里兰卡生效的相关条约主要包括：（1）1997 年 6 月 24 日签署的《关于 1973 年国际防止船舶造成污染公约的 1978 年议定书》。该议定书于 1997 年 9 月 24 日起对其生效。斯里兰卡在签署该议定书的同日，接受了该议定书的 3 个附件，分别是：《1973 年国际防止船舶造成污染公约附件三》、《1973 年国际防止船舶造成污染公约附件四》以及《1973 年国际防止船舶造成污染公约附件五》。其中，"附件三"与"附件五"于 1997 年 9 月

---

[1] International Maritime Organization, "Status of IMO Treaties", https：//wwwcdn. imo. org/localresources/en/About/Conventions/StatusOfConventions/Status% 20-% 202021. pdf，December 22，2020.

[2] See ECOLEX, "International Convention for the Prevention of Pollution of the Sea by Oil, 1954, as amended in 1962 and 1969", https：//www. ecolex. org/details/treaty/international-convention-for-the-prevention-of-pollution-of-the-sea-by-oil-1954-as-amended-in-1962-and-1969-tre-000135/，April 22，2020.

24 日起对斯里兰卡生效,"附件四"于 2003 年 9 月 27 日起对斯里兰卡生效。
(2) 1983 年 4 月 12 日接受的《1969 年国际干预公海油污事故公约》,该公约于同年 7 月 11 日起对其生效。(3) 1999 年 1 月 22 日接受的《修正〈1969年国际油污损害民事责任公约〉的 1992 年议定书》(Protocol of 1992 to Amend the International Convention on Civil Liability for Oil Pollution Damage, 1969),该议定书于 2000 年 1 月 22 日对其生效。(4) 1999 年 1 月 22 日加入的《修正〈1971 年设立国际油污损害赔偿基金国际公约〉的 1992 年议定书》,该议定书于 2000 年 1 月 22 日对其生效。[1]

(四) 船舶及船员相关条约

在船舶管理方面,斯里兰卡于 1974 年 5 月 10 日接受了《1966 年国际船舶载重线公约》,并于 1980 年 11 月 27 日批准了国际海事组织对该公约第 49条第 4 款 b 项的修正案,该公约于 1998 年 5 月 5 日起对斯里兰卡生效;于1975 年 6 月 30 日最后签署了《1974 年联合国班轮公会行动守则公约》,该公约自 1983 年 10 月 6 日对斯里兰卡生效;于 1981 年 11 月 10 日接受了《1971年特种业务客船协定》,该协定自 1982 年 3 月 10 日对斯里兰卡生效;于1982 年 3 月 10 日接受了《1973 年特种业务客船舱室要求议定书》(Protocol on Space Requirements for Special Trade Passenger Ships, 1973),该议定书自同年 6 月 10 日起对斯里兰卡生效;于 1992 年 3 月 11 日接受了《1969 年国际船舶吨位丈量公约》,该公约自 1992 年 6 月 11 日起对斯里兰卡生效;于 1998年 3 月 6 日加入了《1965 年便利国际海上运输公约》,该公约自同年 5 月 5日起对斯里兰卡生效,以确保船舶运输相关程序标准尽可能与国际一致。

在船员管理方面,为保障国际海上人命和财产安全,斯里兰卡于 1987 年1 月 22 日以接受方式加入了《1978 年海员培训、发证和值班标准国际公约》,该公约于同年 4 月 22 日对其生效。[2]

---

〔1〕 International Maritime Organization, "Status of IMO Treaties", https：//wwwcdn. imo. org/localresources/en/About/Conventions/StatusOfConventions/Status% 20-% 202021. pdf, December 22, 2020.

〔2〕 See UN Treaty Collection, "Convention on a Code of Conduct for Liner Conferences", https：// treaties. un. org/Pages/ViewDetails. aspx? src = TREATY&mtdsg_ no = XII-6&chapter = 12&clang = _ en, April 24, 2020；International Maritime Organization, "Status of IMO Treaties", https：//wwwcdn. imo. org/localresources/en/About/Conventions/StatusOfConventions/Status% 20-% 202021. pdf, December 22, 2020.

（五）渔业管理相关条约

斯里兰卡渔业资源丰富，为发展本国渔业，其接受或批准了的渔业相关协定主要包括：于 1949 年 2 月 21 日加入的《1948 年关于设立印度洋—太平洋渔业理事会的协定》[1]，于 1994 年 7 月 13 日加入的《建立印度洋金枪鱼委员会协定》[2]，于 1989 年 1 月 5 日批准的《亚洲—太平洋水产养殖中心网协议》[3]，于 2001 年 6 月 23 日加入的《养护和管理印度洋和东南亚海龟及其栖息地的谅解备忘录》（Memorandum of Understanding concerning Conservation and Management of Marine Turtles and their Habitats of the Indian Ocean and South East Asia)[4]，于 2011 年 1 月 20 日加入的《关于港口国预防、制止和消除非法、不报告、不管制捕鱼的措施协定》（Agreement on Port State Measures to Prevent, Deter and Eliminate Illegal, Unreported and Unregulated Fishing)[5]。

（六）与周边国家缔结的划定管辖海域的条约

在海洋水域划界问题方面，斯里兰卡主要与印度以及马尔代夫于 20 世纪 70 年代就保克海峡至亚当桥的历史水域界限、在马纳尔湾和孟加拉湾的两国海上界限及三国海上交界点等协商签署了多项双边或三边划界协定。有关各划界协定的具体内容，详见下节"海洋争端解决"部分。

---

〔1〕 印度洋—太平洋渔业理事会已于 1994 年经粮农组织理事会第 107 届会议决议更名为"亚洲—太平洋渔业委员会"。参见 FAO, "Agreement for the Establishment of the Indo-pacific Fisheries Council", http://www.fao.org/fileadmin/user_upload/legal/docs/001s-e.pdf, April 22, 2020; FAO, "About the Asia-pacific Fishery Commission", https://www.fao.org/apfic/background/about-asia-pacific-fishery-commission/en/, January 19, 2022.

〔2〕 Indian Ocean Tuna Commission, "Structure", https://www.iotc.org/about-iotc/structure-commission, April 23, 2020.

〔3〕 Ecolex, "Agreement for the Establishment of the Network of Aquaculture Centres in Asia and the Pacific", https://www.ecolex.org/details/treaty/agreement-for-the-establishment-of-the-network-of-aquaculture-centres-in-asia-and-the-pacific-tre-001112/? q = Agreement + on + the + Network + of + Aquaculture + Centres + in + Asia + and + the + Pacific% 2C&xdate_min = &xdate_max = , April 23, 2020.

〔4〕 CMS, "IOSEA Marine Turtles", https://www.cms.int/en/legalinstrument/iosea-marine-turtles, April 23, 2020.

〔5〕 FAO, "Agreement on Port State Measures (PSMA)", http://www.fao.org/port-state-measures/background/parties-psma/en/, April 23, 2020.

五、海洋争端解决

作为印度洋上的岛国,斯里兰卡已通过谈判与隔海相望的南北近邻印度与马尔代夫达成了海洋划界协定,有效防范或平息了可能存在的重叠海域争端。当前,斯里兰卡尚无通过国际司法或仲裁方式解决海洋争端的实践。

(一)斯里兰卡与印度之间的划界协定

斯里兰卡与印度间的海域中岛屿众多、浅滩密布,长期以来只能容纳较小的船舶穿过,特别是保克海峡与马纳尔湾之间的亚当桥一带,基本上仅斯里兰卡和印度两国渔船可通行。同时,这一海域因散落着狭长的石灰岩沉积带和细密的珊瑚礁群,汇聚了多样的渔业资源,海产极为丰富,是两国沿岸人民重要的生存依靠。

为划定该区域的海洋边界,两国将该海洋区域划分为3段。第一段:斯里兰卡北部的塔莱曼纳尔港(Talaimannar)和印度南部泰米尔纳德邦的拉梅斯沃勒姆岛之间的海域带。该海域的东北端为保克海峡,其西南端则为保克湾;该海域内坐落着归属斯里兰卡的众多岛屿,其中部分组成了亚当桥。第二段:斯里兰卡西海岸和印度东南端之间的科罗曼德尔海岸(Coromandel Coast)海域带,亦即坐落于亚当桥以南的马纳尔湾。第三段:保克海峡和马纳尔湾以外位于孟加拉湾的剩余交界海域。两国间的海洋划界协定也围绕上述3段海域相继展开谈判,并先后完成了3个相关协定的签署。

1.《1974年斯里兰卡与印度两国间关于历史性水域边界及相关事项的协定》

卡此沙提武岛的归属是两国在保克海峡中确定海上边界的关键问题。为此,两国总理于1974年签署了两国历史上第一份海洋边界划界协定——《斯里兰卡与印度两国间关于历史性水域边界及相关事项的协定》(以下简称《1974年协定》)。有关《1974年协定》的背景、谈判过程、协定内容及所确定的海上边界的位置与走向,详见本丛书《印度、巴基斯坦海洋法律体系研究》"印度海洋法律体系"部分"海洋争端解决"一节中"印度与斯里兰卡之间的划界协定"相关内容。[1]

---

[1] See Article 1, Agreement between Sri Lanka and India on the Boundary in Historic Waters between the two Countries and Related Matters, 26 and 28 June 1974, UN Office of Legal Affairs, https://www.un.org/Depts/los/LEGISLATIONANDTREATIES/PDFFILES/TREATIES/LKA-IND1974BW.PDF, April 24, 2020.

对斯里兰卡而言，该协定的重要成果是将卡此沙提武岛正式划归该国。一方面，两国划定界限后，各自依照《1974 年协定》，对其一侧的水域、岛屿、大陆架及其底土拥有主权、专属管辖权和控制权，并对特殊跨界矿藏的开发利用进行协商。另一方面，印方的渔民和朝圣者将一如既往地享有前往卡此沙提武岛参加宗教仪式的权利。斯里兰卡官方将不能因此而要求此类渔民和朝圣者提供旅行证件或签证。同时，斯里兰卡和印度两国的船舶也将继续在对方水域享有传统上应有之权利。

尽管依据《1974 年协定》第 8 条，缔约双方应在交换批准文书之后使其尽快施行，但由于印度国内势力的阻挠，《1974 年协定》未能在其议会获得通过，因此未对印度生效。[1] 对此结果，斯里兰卡并不认同。斯里兰卡提出，印度法院不能单方废除《1974 年协定》，在斯里兰卡境外的法院所做判决对斯里兰卡没有拘束力，此类法院的命令或判决将不能影响两个主权国家之间所订立的条约。除此之外，《1974 年协定》对于两国渔民在卡此沙武提岛上的具体权利未做清晰界定。如根据其第 6 条，印度沿海居民拥有不持签证前往卡此沙提武岛参加宗教仪式的权利，但是后续实践却只限于参加相关教派的年度集会；而赋予两国渔民的出入权也仅限于晒网和捕鱼，无法体现两国在该海域居民的真实需求，也导致此协定的贯彻实施时常陷入困境。[2]直到现在，由于传统及现代渔业利益的冲突，斯里兰卡和印度渔民在卡此沙提武岛附近海域仍多有摩擦。

2. 《1976 年斯里兰卡与印度两国间在马纳尔湾和孟加拉湾的海上边界及相关事项的协定》

马纳尔湾历来以丰富的生物资源而闻名，被称为"具有全球意义的海洋生物多样性宝库"。[3] 对马纳尔湾海洋资源的开发以及对其生物圈的保护都在两国的海洋战略中得到了高度关注。而在马纳尔湾另一侧的孟加拉湾则有着独特的热带海洋生态系统，拥有丰富的水系、大量的沼泽湿地以及成片的红树林，为两国的近海渔业提供了稳定的出口来源。在订立《1974 年协定》

---

[1] 根据 1960 年印度最高法院对贝鲁贝里联盟案（Berubari Union Case）的裁定，印度宣称放弃对其领土的控制时，必须经由印度议会通过宪法修正案来加以批准，所以未经批准的协定是无效的。See Lawfare, "Throwback Thursday: The Indo-Bangladesh Enclaves and the Indian Con stitution, Reprise", https: //www. lawfareblog. com/throwback-thursday-indo-bangladesh-encl a ves-and-indian-constitution-reprise, April 24, 2020.

[2] MFA, "India and Sri Land Boundary", https: //www. mfa. gov. lk/si/1396-the-maritime-bounda-ry-between-sri-lanka-and-india-stands-settled-minister-bogollagama/, April 24, 2020.

[3] UNESCO, "Gulf of Mannar Biosphere Reserve, India", https: //en. unesco. org/biosphere/aspac/ gulf-mannar, April 24, 2020.

之后，两国就马纳尔湾和孟加拉湾的海上边界进行了新一轮的积极磋商，并于 1976 年 3 月在印度新德里签署了《斯里兰卡与印度两国间在马纳尔湾和孟加拉湾的海上边界及相关事项的协定》（以下简称《1976 年协定》）。[1] 有关《1976 年协定》的背景、谈判过程、协定内容及其分别于马纳尔湾及孟加拉湾上所确定的海上边界的位置与走向，详见本丛书《印度、巴基斯坦海洋法律体系研究》"印度海洋法律体系"部分"海洋争端解决"一节中"印度与斯里兰卡之间的划界协定"相关内容。[2]

随着《1974 年协定》和《1976 年协定》的相继签订，斯里兰卡和印度两国的海洋边界全线得以基本厘定。在该两项条约达成之后，两国官员还举行了数次双边会谈以讨论协定所提及的对误入对方水域的渔民的处置。两国在执行上述协定中的摩擦与冲突也在会谈中被不时提及。如印度曾指控斯里兰卡海军参与在卡此沙提武岛对印度船只的袭击，斯里兰卡则否认此项指控，宣称从未介入此类行动，并提交了其多次援助在临近海域遇险的印度渔民的证据。[3]

3. 《1976 年斯里兰卡与印度两国间在马纳尔湾从 13 号位置至斯里兰卡、印度及马尔代夫三国交界点（点 T）的海上边界延伸的补充协定》

1976 年 11 月 22 日，斯里兰卡、印度就两国与马尔代夫之间的三国交界点（点 T）的具体适用问题在科伦坡签署了补充协定。[4] 作为《1974 年协定》、《1976 年协定》及《1976 年斯里兰卡、印度和马尔代夫间关于确定在马纳尔湾的三国交界点的协定》的补充性文件，该协定仅以两项条文就相关海上边界作出进一步明确。有关该补充协定的具体条文及所涉交界点位置，

〔1〕　UN Office of Legal Affairs，"Agreement between Sri Lanka and India on the Maritime Boundary between the two Countries in the Gulf of Mannar and the Bay of Bengal and Related Matters 23 March 1976"，https：//www.un.org/Depts/los/LEGISLATIONANDTREATIES/PDFFILES/TREATIES/LKA-IND1976MB.PDF，April 24，2020.

〔2〕　See Article 1，Article 2，Agreement between Sri Lanka and India on the Maritime Boundary between the two Countries in the Gulf of Mannar and the Bay of Bengal and Related Matters，23 March 1976，UN Office of Legal Affairs，https：//www.un.org/Depts/los/LEGISLATIONANDTREATIES/PDF-FILES/TREATIES/LKA-IND1976MB.PDF，April 24，2020.

〔3〕　MFA，"India and Sri Land Boundary"，https：//www.mfa.gov.lk/si/1396-the-maritime-boundary-between-sri-lanka-and-india-stands-settled-minister-bogollagama/，April 24，2020.

〔4〕　UN Office of Legal Affairs，"Supplementary Agreement between Sri Lanka and India on the Extension of theMaritime Boundary between the two Countries in the Gulf of Mannar from Position 13 m to the Trijunction Point between Sri Lanka，India and Maldives（Point T）22 Novemberember 1976"，https：//www.un.org/Depts/los/LEGISLATIONANDTREATIES/PDFFILES/TREATIES/LKA-IND1976TP.PDF，April 24，2020.

详见本丛书《印度、巴基斯坦海洋法律体系研究》"印度海洋法律体系"部分"海洋争端解决"一节中"印度与斯里兰卡之间的划界协定"相关内容。

(二) 斯里兰卡与印度、马尔代夫之间的划界协定

根据《1976 年协定》第 2 条的规定，对于从所确立的第 13 号点（05°00′00″N、77°10′06″E）向外延伸的边界，需要在嗣后谈判中作出进一步明确。由此，借印度和马尔代夫协商确定两国在阿拉伯海的海上边界的契机，斯里兰卡、印度和马尔代夫分别于 1976 年 7 月 23 日、24 日及 31 日签署了《斯里兰卡、印度和马尔代夫间关于确定在马纳尔湾的三国交界点的协定》，为划定三国之间的海上交界点确立法律基础[1]。

根据该协定第 1 条的规定，以等距离线方式划定的斯里兰卡、印度和马尔代夫的三国海上界限交会于马纳尔湾之外的点 T（04°47.04″N、77°01.40″E）。有关点 T 的确定方式、具体位置及划界走向详见本丛书《印度、巴基斯坦海洋法律体系研究》"印度海洋法律体系"部分"海洋争端解决"一节中"印度涉及的多国间划界协定"相关内容。

---

[1] UN Office of Legal Affairs, "Agreement between Sri Lanka, India and Maldives concerning the De-termination of the Trijunction Point between the three Countries in the Gulf of Mannar 23, 24 and 31 July 1976", https：//www. un. org/Depts/los/LEGISLATIONANDTREATIES/PDFFILES/TREA-TIES/LKA-IND-MDV1976TP. PDF, April 24, 2020.

六、国际海洋合作

（一）海洋防务合作

1. 与周边国家的合作

（1）与印度的合作

斯里兰卡国土面积小、人口少，经济和军事力量薄弱，接受邻近大国印度的支持和援助成了斯里兰卡外交策略的自然走向。斯里兰卡与印度的关系较为曲折：1948 年至 1956 年，斯里兰卡在外交上亲近西方，戒备印度；1956 年至 1977 年，斯里兰卡采取不结盟的外交方针，使两国关系得以改善；1977 年至 1994 年，斯里兰卡再次偏重亲西方的外交政策，与印度的关系亦因斯里兰卡内战而趋于紧张；1994 年至 2005 年，斯里兰卡政府一度将建立并发展与印度的良好关系作为外交重心，但波折仍不断；2015 年大选后，斯里兰卡政府再次调整外交政策，着力修复和改善在前政府时期总体恶化的两国关系[1] 总体而言，斯里兰卡和印度有着较悠久的安全合作历史，两国军事交流合作近年来稳步加强。

在海上联合军演方面，斯里兰卡与印度多次展开或共同参与"米特拉·夏克提"（Mitra Shakti）联合军事演习和 SLINEX 海上军事演习。印度、斯里兰卡和马尔代夫间的"多斯蒂"（Dosti）海军演习自 1991 年开始，至 2019 年已成功完成了 14 次三国联合演习。在区域一级，两国都利用孟加拉湾多部门技术与经济合作组织（BIMSTEC）平台加强安全联系，并参加了 2018 年 9 月孟加拉湾多部门技术与经济合作组织成员国的联合军事演习[2]

在高层交流互访方面，2016 年 11 月 3 日，斯里兰卡和印度举行了第四次年度防务对话。两国防长及国防部、外交部和武装部队官员组成的代表团共同参加了会议，联合审查了正在进行的各项国防合作倡议，确定了新的合作路径，同时就地区安全形势和海上安全问题展开讨论。同年 11 月 27 日，印度海军总司令抵达科伦坡进行为期 5 天的访问，旨在巩固和加强印度和斯里兰卡之间的双边海上安全关系。在访问期间，其与斯里兰卡总统、总

---

〔1〕 刘耀辉、简天天：《1948 年以来斯里兰卡外交政策的演变》，载《东南亚南亚研究》2018 年第 1 期，第 83—91 页。

〔2〕 有关 SLINEX 及"多斯蒂"军演中的合作参见"印度海洋法律体系"部分"国际海洋合作"一节中"海洋防务合作"相关内容。

理以及包括国防参谋长和 3 名军中首长在内的高级政要举行了双边讨论，参加了在科伦坡举行的"加勒对话"，并就印度对战略海洋伙伴关系的立场发表讲话。[1]

2019 年 4 月 10 日，印度国防部长对斯里兰卡进行了为期两天的正式访问。访问期间，双方会谈同意加强区域安全合作，包括在人口贩卖和毒品走私等非传统安全问题上的合作。作为访问的一部分，印度代表团参加了第六次印度—斯里兰卡国防对话（Indo-Sri Lankan Defence Dialogue）。自 2012 年以来，这一对话已成为评估讨论两国安全与防务合作问题的重要平台。印度在对话中表示，希望加强与邻国的区域安全合作，以此作为其"邻国优先"（neighbourhood first）政策的一部分，并改变斯里兰卡的政治和安全环境，为进一步加强两国在安全领域的合作提供了机会。[2]

2020 年 1 月 19 日，斯里兰卡总统在总统秘书处会见了印度国家安全顾问，以加强两国在国家安全、情报共享、海上安全等方面的区域合作为会谈重点。通过会谈，战略位置优越的斯里兰卡与地区大国印度之间的紧密防务合作得到了加强。两军间的合作，特别是以印度洋区域安全为重点的合作成为会谈的主要议题。两国均意识到海上安全的重要性以及两国海岸警卫队之间密切合作和交互活动的可行性，强调共同行动对于制止走私、贩毒、非国家行为者的枪支贩运及非法捕捞行为至关重要。印度代表还提出，印度、斯里兰卡和马尔代夫应确立并评估海域感知（Maritime Domain Awareness）制度，并将其他国家作为观察员。[3] 同年 2 月 7 日，斯里兰卡总理对印度进行了为期四天的国事访问，与印度总统、总理和外交部长举行了会晤，再次就双边年度国防对话及涉及马尔代夫的三边海上安全合作等国防和海上安全倡议下的关键领域问题展开讨论。[4]

在军备合作及人员训练方面，印度分别于 2006 年、2008 年及 2018 年向

---

[1] Hindustan Times, "Navy Chief on 5-day Visit to Sri Lanka to Boost Maritime Security Ties", https: //www. hindustantimes. com/india-news/navy-chief-on-5-day-visit-to-sri-lanka-to-boost-maritime-security-ties/story-qJQbA8Cm2IuY2YvnLoBHiO. html, May 15, 2020.

[2] Air World Service, "India Steps Up Defence Cooperation With Sri Lanka", http: //airworldservice. org/ourblog/2019/04/10/india-steps-up-defence-cooperation-with-sri-lanka/, May 15, 2020.

[3] Daily News, "Indo-Lanka Defence Co-operation Cemented", http: //www. dailynews. lk/2020/01/20/local/208886/indo-lanka-defence-co-operation-cemented, May 15, 2020.

[4] One India, "Lankan PM Rajapaksa to Visit India from Friday: Trade, Defence, Maritime Talks on Agenda", https: //www. oneindia. com/international/lankan-pm-rajapaksa-to-visit-india-from-friday-trade-3028645. html, May 15, 2020.

斯里兰卡出售或赠送了3艘海岸警卫队近海巡逻舰[1]同时，两国一直将斯里兰卡军队的能力建设和训练作为两国军事合作的核心领域，并于2019年再次同意增加印度在斯里兰卡的军事培训人员数量。此外，斯里兰卡与印度、马尔代夫还签署了一项三边海上安全合作协定，以提高在印度洋地区的监控效率、加强反海盗行动并减少海洋污染[2]

（2）与泰国的合作

泰国与斯里兰卡已建交60余年，海上防务及安全也在两国的对外交往中获得推进。在高层交流互访方面，2013年5月，泰国总理访问斯里兰卡，与斯里兰卡总统展开双边会谈，两国领导人呼吁加强国防和海上安全合作以应对恐怖主义，并同意借访问之机与斯里兰卡分享更多相关情报[3]斯里兰卡表示，泰国方面所分享的经验和专业知识将有助于消除该地区的恐怖主义和其他安全威胁[4]

2018年8月，斯里兰卡与泰国共同出席了在新加坡举行的第25届"东盟区域论坛"（ASEAN Regional Forum）部长级会议。该论坛于1994年在泰国成立，是亚太地区安全对话的主要论坛，旨在促进区域发展与繁荣，应对对区域和平、安全与繁荣造成的挑战。斯里兰卡在论坛上发表声明，强调斯里兰卡对外合作的重点包括：海事安全、灾害管理、建立与国防有关的信任措施、预防性外交以及其他维持本区域日益增长的经济活力和繁荣的重要领域[5] 2018年10月，应泰国政府邀请，斯里兰卡国防部长对泰国进行了为期四天的正式访问。在会见泰国国防部长时，斯里兰卡代表重申了加强两国防务合作的重要性，并特别强调了斯里兰卡作为未来海上枢纽的潜力以及斯

---

〔1〕　Economic Times，"China Gifts Warship to Sri Lanka"，https：//economictimes. indiatimes. com/news/defence/china-gifts-warship-to-sri-lanka/articleshow/70255526. cms，May 15，2020.

〔2〕　Drishti IAS，"India-Sri Lanka Relations"，https：//www. drishtiias. com/to-the-points/Paper2/india-sri-lanka-relations，May 15，2020.

〔3〕　Yahoo News，"Sri Lanka, Thailand Agree on Defence Cooperation"，https：//sg. news. yahoo. com/sri-lanka-thailand-agree-defence-cooperation-192822419. html？ guccounter = 1&guce＿ referrer = aHR0cH M6Ly9tMi5jbi5iaW5LmNvbS8&guce＿ referrer＿ sig = AQAAACqUQeIsnUDR5fuMR9YcsGL MWO4fA Xl73mObrF0pZO5WaC-U2sMH8bCfae＿ dmUvzHYzkI8mKWeUPrsDfFOPkVjHL8-Z0kUgyB IYB98aip 8FxtfM9q51kqxGRwmCWF8DqNETeWndETXNAekwGJoxU2kZjtENQ-RMSiP9-Fo5jAEhp，May 15，2020.

〔4〕　Colombo Gazette，"Thailand, Lanka to Enhance Maritime Security"，https：//colombogazette. com/2013/05/31/thailand-and-lanka-hold-bilateral-talks/，May 15，2020.

〔5〕　Colombo Gazette，"Sri Lanka Discusses Maritime Security at ARF Conference"，https：//colombogazette. com/2018/08/05/sri-lanka-discusses-maritime-security-at-arf-conference/，May 15，2020.

里兰卡在印度洋区域有利于国际贸易和运输的地缘战略位置。[1]

在海上联合军演方面，斯里兰卡于 2017 年起开始与泰国共同参加"东南亚合作与训练"（Southeast Asia Cooperation and Training，SEACAT）年度军事演习。该军事演习由美国自 2002 年发起和提供支持，于 2012 年由原"东南亚反恐合作"演习更名为"东南亚合作与训练"，并将演习范围扩大至区域内海军外的海警部队。在 2017 年第 16 届"东南亚合作与训练"演习中，斯里兰卡同时参加了新加坡多国行动和演习中心以及菲律宾马尼拉演习点的联合行动，包括 7 项海上登陆演练。[2] 2020 年 7 月，包括斯里兰卡与泰国在内的来自亚洲、欧洲、大洋洲、北美洲的 22 个国家共同参与了第 19 届"东南亚合作与训练"演习。在新冠肺炎疫情影响下，各国参训代表通过线上方式就如何提高海域感知等问题进行了研讨，尤其围绕海域感知的信息分享、联合跨部门的特遣部队行动、多国部队标准作业程序、基于网络的海上态势感知工具等开展了学习与演练。[3]

2. 与域外大国的合作

（1）与美国的合作

为加强在印太地区的影响力，促进该区域的安全和繁荣，美国与斯里兰卡的双边军事合作一直都以海上安全合作为重心。自斯里兰卡 2015 年大选以来，美国和斯里兰卡的军事和海上合作显著增加，主要活动包括：美国海军访问斯里兰卡港口，与斯里兰卡海军建立伙伴关系，协助建立斯里兰卡海军陆战队，与斯里兰卡海军和空军开展演习，开展人道主义援助、救灾和海上安全合作，以实现印太地区的安全和繁荣。两国政府都有意在海上安全保障方面进一步促进经济合作与交流，并同意继续采取联合行动，提升安全、稳定、透明度，并增进有利于双方的经济机会。[4]

在高层交流互访方面，斯里兰卡和美国于 2019 年 5 月发表联合声明，表示："美国和斯里兰卡决心立足基于规则的秩序，确保尊重国际法及相关规范，共同努力促进和平与安全，确保印度洋和太平洋的海洋安全"；"双方对

---

〔1〕 Daily FT, "Sri Lanka Seeks to Strengthen Defence Cooperation with Thailand", http：//www. ft. lk/news/Sri-Lanka-seeks-to-strengthen-defence-cooperation-with-Thailand/56-664650, May 15, 2020.

〔2〕 NavalToday, "Southeast Asian Naval Drill SEACAT Kicks Off", https：//www. navaltoday. com/ 2017/08/21/southeast-asian-naval-drill-seacat-kicks-off/, May 15, 2020.

〔3〕 Gregory Johnson, "SEACAT 2020 Puts Regional Cooperation First on Agenda", https：//www. dvi dshub. net/news/374412/seacat-2020-puts-regional-cooperation-first-agenda, May 15, 2020.

〔4〕 U. S Department of State, "U. S. Relations With Sri Lanka", https：//www. state. gov/u-s-relations -with-sri-lanka/, May 15, 2020.

斯里兰卡于 2018 年 10 月举办的印度洋会议表示满意", "愿进一步推动海上安全合作与交流", "同意继续共同努力, 加强安全性、稳定性、透明度", 并为双方提供互利的经济机会。美国表示愿意继续扩大与斯里兰卡在反恐及海上和陆上边境安全方面的合作。[1]

在海上联合军演方面, 除从 2017 年起参加前述由美国发起并支持的东南亚合作与训练多国联合演练项目外, 斯里兰卡与美国还开展"联合海上战备与训练"(Cooperation Afloat Readiness and Training, CARAT)双边军演。该军演于 2017 年在斯里兰卡首次举办, 是斯里兰卡长达 25 年的内战结束后的重要国际军事合作。在 2019 年的第二届联合海上战备与训练演习中, 美国派出了"斯普鲁恩斯"号导弹驱逐舰(USS Spruance)、"密尼诺克"号联合高速运输舰(USNS Millinocket)以及约 100 名海军官兵, 与斯里兰卡海军共同演练, 以建立两国武装力量之间的操作联动并强化作战单位间的纽带。尽管原定为期一周的演习因 2019 年科伦坡复活节爆炸案而中断, 但本次演习的海上演练环节已经完成, 两国在该演习中的筹备及协作仍然得到了肯定。[2]

在军备援助与合作方面, 美国国务院政治军事事务局(Bureau of Political-Military Affairs)曾于 2004 年根据美国国防部"富余国防物品"(Excess Defense Articles, EDA)计划, 将美国海岸警卫队快艇"勇敢"号移交斯里兰卡海军。2019 年, 美国再次根据"富余国防物品"计划向斯里兰卡移交原美国海岸警卫队快艇"谢尔曼"号(USCGC Sherman)。斯里兰卡将"富余国防物品"计划下所获得的海上军备视为其海上安全能力建设的重要成果, 并积极寻求更多美国海军舰艇在未来的成功移交, 以通过合作推进本国军队的现代化建设, 充实执行边境和海上安全及禁毒等任务所需的军备物资, 从而支持两国的共同利益, 改善区域安全情势。[3] 美国在 2018 年 8 月举行的东盟地区论坛(ASEAN Regional Forum)上宣布提供约 3 亿美元的安全援助, 以改善印度—太平洋地区的安全关系。这些援助将用于包括斯里兰卡、孟加

---

〔1〕 Economic Times, "US, Lanka to Work Together for Peace, Security in Indo-Pacific Region", https://economictimes.indiatimes.com/news/defence/us-lanka-to-work-together-for-peace-security-in-indo-pacific-region/articleshow/69384593.cms, May 15, 2020.

〔2〕 See Amy Forsythe, "U. S., Sri Lanka Navy Partnership Strong during CARAT 2019", https://www.dvidshub.net/news/322938/us-sri-lanka-navy-partnership-strong-during-carat-2019, May 15, 2020; "US-Sri Lanka Naval Exercise at Port Managed by China", https://news24onlin e.com/news/World/us-sri-lanka-naval-exercise-port-managed-china-f81e334a/, May 15, 2020.

〔3〕 U.S Department of State, "U.S's Strategy", https://www.state.gov/new-missions-and-stronger-partnerships-how-u-s-excess-defense-articles-help-promote-a-free-and-open-indo-pacific-region/, May 15, 2020.

拉国、印度尼西亚、菲律宾、蒙古等在内的南亚、东南亚及东北亚国家，用以加强海上安全、人道主义援助及救灾与维持和平能力的外国军事融资，以及建立用于打击跨国犯罪及国际麻醉品贩运的执法基金。同时，斯里兰卡也是美国"孟加拉湾方案"（Bay of Bengal Initiative）下安全援助基金的受援合作方，该方案旨在提高印度洋地区军民海事行动的能力，加强对重点海域的探测、信息共享和应对新出现问题的能力。[1]

（2）与澳大利亚的合作

自 1947 年建交以来，斯里兰卡与澳大利亚在 70 多年间一直保持着较为密切的双边关系，合作领域涉及包括移民、走私、高等教育、体育等在内的政治、经济多个层面。其中，保护海洋资源、打击非法捕鱼、打击海上犯罪网络等都是双方合作的重点领域。如为实现两国战略关系发展的重要目标、打击人口走私犯罪，澳大利亚协同斯里兰卡成立了贩运人口及其他跨国犯罪问题联合工作组，并于 2013 年向斯里兰卡赠送了 2 艘湾级（Bay-class）舰艇，以增强斯里兰卡海军在本国水域拦截人口走私的能力，不断推进在这一问题上的多边合作。[2]

在高层交流互访方面，两国已建立起常态化的"高官对话"（Senior Officials' Talks）机制。该对话每两年举行一次，是斯里兰卡和澳大利亚评估现有双边关系和据两国政策优先事项加强未来合作的主要平台。[3] 2017 年 5 月，澳大利亚和斯里兰卡表示应加强两国海上安全合作。斯里兰卡总统保证，斯里兰卡政府将全力支持打击人口走私和海盗活动，为加强海上安全合作付出最大努力。澳大利亚国防部长则对斯里兰卡在遏制人口走私中的良好合作表示感谢，澳大利亚将进一步在毒品走私领域与斯里兰卡密切合作，并向斯里兰卡海军和海岸警卫队提供一切可能的援助。澳大利亚当时已经向斯里兰卡的军校学员提供培训，澳大利亚国防部长也同意斯里兰卡总统的要求，增加训练设施，使之覆盖中级和高级军官。[4] 2019 年 9 月 16 日，斯里兰卡和澳大利亚在外交部举行了战略海事对话首轮会议，对话强调了在印度

---

〔1〕 U. S Department of State, "Pacific Reign", https：//www. state. gov/u-s-security-cooperation-in-the-indo-pacific-region/, May 15, 2020.

〔2〕 Barana Waidyatilake, "Sri Lanka and Australia's Strategic Defence Interests", https：//www. lki. lk/blog/sri-lanka-and-australias-strategic-defence-interests/, May 15, 2020.

〔3〕 British News Network, "Sri Lanka and Australia's Strategic Defence Interests", https：//www. britishnewsnetwork. com/news/sri-lanka-australia-hold-discussions-on-strengthening-cooperation-in-key-areas2019092120181800001/, May 15, 2020.

〔4〕 Colombo Page, "Sri Lanka, Australia Hold Discussions on Strengthening Cooperation in Key Areas", http：//www. colombopage. com/archive_ 17A/May26_ 1495811724CH. php, May 15, 2020.

洋海上安全和安保问题上共同努力以及就与蓝色经济有关的倡议进行合作的重要性。次日，斯里兰卡与澳大利亚第三轮高官会谈（Third Round of Senior Officials' Talks）在科伦坡外交部举行，两国就加强在跨国有组织犯罪、国防、和解与人权、发展伙伴关系、外交部合作以及地区和多边问题等多领域的合作进行了讨论。[1]

在海上联合军演方面，除在 2020 年共同参与的东南亚合作与训练演习外，澳大利亚于 2019 年 3 月参加了在斯里兰卡举行的"印太奋进-19"（Indo-Pacific Endeavour-19）多边防务合作演习。澳大利亚派出了皇家海军旗舰、2 艘护卫舰、1 艘补给油船和近 1000 名澳大利亚国防军（ADF）组成的联合特遣部队参加演练，将两国在印度洋海域的安全利益合作上升到了一个新的水平。人道主义援助、灾难救助以及海上监视是澳大利亚国防军在此次军演期间与斯里兰卡海军合作的关键领域。[2] 两国均表示，作为印度洋—太平洋国家，澳大利亚和斯里兰卡正在共同努力，建立以规则为基础的区域秩序，以维护印度洋的自由、开放和包容。[3] 2020 年 3 月，澳大利亚皇家海军护卫舰"帕拉马塔"号（HMAS Parramatta）抵达科伦坡港，进行为期 5 天的友好访问，旨在进一步深化澳大利亚和斯里兰卡之间的海上安全合作。在该护卫舰停留期间，190 名澳大利亚海军官兵和斯里兰卡海军在一系列问题上展开合作演练，包括舰载直升机操作、舰艇登陆、海上搜索、船舶工程、海上监视以及两国军舰航行训练中的协同能力等多个环节，以促使两国海军共享技术知识并强化专业沟通。[4]

（3）与日本的合作

自 1952 年以来，日本和斯里兰卡一直保持着友好关系。日本视斯里兰卡为印度洋上近海航道的关键要冲，是极具潜力的海洋国家，有利于确保海上贸易的自由、开放及不受干扰，由此对日本的经济前景极为重要。日本在社

〔1〕 News. LK, "Sri Lanka, Australia conclude First Maritime Dialogue", https：//news. lk/news/political-current-affairs/item/27349-sri-lanka-australia-conclude-first-maritime-dialogue, May 15, 2020.

〔2〕 Sunday Times, "Australia-Sri Lanka in Military Exercise to Strengthen Defence Ties", http：//www. sundaytimes. lk/190317/news/australia-sri-lanka-in-military-exercise-to-strengthen-defence-ties-340992. html, May 15, 2020.

〔3〕 Ashanthi Ratnasingham, "Australia and Sri Lanka Deepen Cooperation on Indian Ocean Maritime Security", https：//www. lankabusinessonline. com/australia-and-sri-lanka-deepen-cooperation-on-indian-ocean-maritime-security/, May 15, 2020.

〔4〕 Colombo Page, "Royal Australian Navy Ship Parramatta Arrives at Sri Lanka's Port of Colombo", http：//www. colombopage. com/archive_ 20A/Mar07_ 1583565301CH. php, May 15, 2020.

会经济及基础设施等多方面持续为斯里兰卡提供人力资源发展援助和技术支持。两国于2015年发表全面伙伴关系联合声明，围绕五大支柱领域进一步加强双边关系，包括：促进双边投资贸易，在斯里兰卡国家发展规划中的合作，民族和解与和平建设，政治磋商与海上合作，人力资源开发与人员交流，在国际舞台上的支持与合作。[1]

2008年至2017年，共有65艘日本海上自卫队舰艇抵达以科伦坡港为代表的斯里兰卡各港口。日本首相曾力邀斯里兰卡加入美印日三国举办的"马拉巴尔"海军演习，但斯里兰卡尚未对此作出正式回应。2017年年初，在日本提供的贷款项目的支持之下，科伦坡造船厂（Colombo Dockyard Ltd.）为斯里兰卡海岸警卫队建造了两艘85米长的近海巡逻艇（Offshore Patrol Vessels），以增强其海域监视能力。[2]

2018年8月，日本防卫大臣在斯里兰卡进行了为期两天的访问，这是日本防卫大臣首次访问斯里兰卡。两国代表在会晤期间发表谅解声明，同意进一步加强在印度洋的安全合作，日本也承诺将进一步援助斯里兰卡发展海上安全相关能力。同时，日本海上自卫队雷级护卫舰（Ikazuchi）抵达斯里兰卡亭可马里港，对斯里兰卡进行为期三天的正式访问。访问期间，日舰海军指挥官前往斯里兰卡东部海军司令部拜访东部海军地区司令。[3]

2019年7月，日本防卫大臣再次访问斯里兰卡。斯里兰卡总统重申扩大与日本间防务合作的热切愿望，提出应进一步加强两国海军之间的合作，以确保国际海上航线以及国际水域的安全。日本防卫大臣也对近年来日本与斯里兰卡的国防和经济合作进展表示肯定，称两国海军的合作已涵盖海军联合作战训练和后勤保障的多个环节。[4] 两国重申斯里兰卡和日本之间海上合作

---

〔1〕 See MOFA, "Joint Declaration on Comprehensive Partnership between Japan and Sri Lanka", https://www.mofa.go.jp/files/000103273.pdf, May 15, 2020; Daily Mirror, "Sri Lanka's Geostrategic Location Important to Japan", http://www.dailymirror.lk/article/Sri-Lanka-s-geostrategic-location-important-to-Japan-147115.html, May 15, 2020.

〔2〕 Daily FT, "Sri Lanka May become South Asia's Strategic Maritime Communication Centre", http://www.ft.lk/article/610356/Sri-Lanka-may-become-South-Asia-s-strategic-maritime-communication-centre, May 15, 2020.

〔3〕 Sputnik International, "Japan, Sri Lanka Agree to Boost Maritime Security Cooperation", https://sputniknews.com/asia/201808211067363757-japan-srilanka-maritime-cooperation/, May 15, 2020.

〔4〕 News.LK, "Sri Lanka Keen to Expand Defence Cooperation with Japan - President", https://news.lk/news/political-current-affairs/item/26497-sri-lanka-keen-to-expand-defence-cooperation-with-japan-president, May 15, 2020.

的重要性，并签署了关于国防合作的谅解备忘录。[1]

2020 年 5 月，日本防务大臣再度率团与斯里兰卡代表团举行防务会议并签署谅解备忘录。该谅解备忘录的签署，意在加强日本和斯里兰卡在海上安全、海军合作、信息和知识共享、能力建设、对话机制、人员培训、军事教育与研究、多边交流等领域的了解与合作。依据该备忘录相关规定，日本将协助强化斯里兰卡的海防能力，并通过促进两国在相关方面的合作不断提高包括斯里兰卡在内的印太地区国家维护海上安全的能力。[2]

（4）与中国的合作

中斯友好交往历史悠久。斯里兰卡于 1950 年承认新中国，并于 1957 年 2 月与中国建交。1994 年至 2015 年，斯里兰卡不断加强与亚洲国家的合作，中斯关系尤其在 2005 年后得到快速发展。2015 年以来，斯里兰卡新政府坚持奉行独立和不结盟的外交政策，支持和平共处五项原则，与中国保持良好合作。两国在许多重大国际和地区问题上拥有广泛共识，双边关系稳定发展。[3]

2014 年 9 月，斯里兰卡与中国签署《中华人民共和国和斯里兰卡民主社会主义共和国关于深化战略合作伙伴关系的行动计划》（以下简称《中斯行动计划》）以及经贸、基础设施建设、海洋科研、文化、教育等多个领域的合作协议。依据《中斯行动计划》，双方将继续加强防务合作，斯里兰卡欢迎并支持中国提出的构建"21 世纪海上丝绸之路"的倡议，愿积极参与相关合作；双方"同意进一步加入对马加普拉/汉班托塔港项目的投资"，双方同意"进一步加强海洋领域合作，推进科伦坡港口城的建设，签署马加普拉/汉班托塔港二期经营权有关协议"；宣布建立海岸带和海洋合作联委会，探讨在海洋观测、生态保护、海洋资源管理、郑和沉船遗迹水下联合考古、海上安保、打击海盗、海上搜救、航行安全等领域的合作。[4]

---

〔1〕　Colombo Gazette, "Japan Notes Rapid Progress in Defence Cooperation with Sri Lanka", https://colombogazette.com/2019/07/26/japan-notes-rapid-progress-in-defence-cooperation-with-sri-lanka/, May 15, 2020.

〔2〕　Daily FT, "Japan and Sri Lanka Enter into MoU on Defense Cooperation and Exchange", http://www.ft.lk/news/Japan-and-Sri-Lanka-enter-into-MoU-on-Defense-Cooperation-and-Exchange/56-682781, May 15, 2020.

〔3〕　刘耀辉、简天天：《1948 年以来斯里兰卡外交政策的演变》，载《东南亚南亚研究》2018 年第 1 期，第 83—91 页。

〔4〕　梁福龙：《习近平同斯里兰卡总统会谈：港口海上安全合作自贸谈判》，载观察者网，https://www.guancha.cn/indexnews/2014_09_17_267887.shtml，最后访问日期：2020 年 5 月 15 日。

2017 年 3 月，中国国防部长兼国务委员常万全结束了对斯里兰卡的访问。访问中，斯里兰卡总统对"中国在经济、农业、科技、教育、国防等领域对斯里兰卡提供的一贯援助"表示感谢。两国同意促进"以真诚相互支持和长期友好为特征的战略合作伙伴关系"，提出应深化包括国防在内的所有领域的合作。[1]

2018 年 7 月，斯里兰卡和中国在中国大使馆举行的庆祝中国人民解放军成立 91 周年的招待会上，重申加强两国国防联系的积极意愿。斯里兰卡国防部长表示，中国一直是斯里兰卡的宝贵伙伴，两国建交 61 年来，在努力深化务实合作的同时，在地区和国际领域相互支持。中国驻斯里兰卡大使馆武官表示，中国军方高度重视加强与斯里兰卡军方的关系，几年来，两军在人员培训、联合作战和海上安全等领域的沟通与合作不断深化；中国军队倡导共同、全面、合作、可持续的安全观，将继续发展不结盟、不对抗、不针对任何第三方的两军关系。[2]

2019 年 7 月，中国赠予斯里兰卡海军的 P625 护卫舰抵达科伦坡。这艘 2300 吨的军舰于 2015 年在中国海军退役，原为中国人民解放军海军的 053 型护卫舰"铜陵号"。这是中国与位于印度洋战略要地的斯里兰卡深化军事合作的新一轮动作。作为斯里兰卡海军的新成员，P625 护卫舰将主要用于近海巡逻、环境监测和反海盗作战。在正式移交该护卫舰之前，中国海军还在上海对将在此舰服役的 110 多名斯里兰卡海军官兵进行了为期两个月的专业训练。[3]

3. 海上多边防务合作

"加勒对话"是斯里兰卡国防部发起主办的国际海事会议，旨在为各利益攸关方提供加强海洋安全及保障的国际论坛，以通过充分的观点交流促进参与各方的团结合作与伙伴关系。自 2010 年至 2019 年，"加勒对话"已经成功举办 10 届，其年度主题分别为：绘制可持续海上合作路线图；印度洋海洋问题的挑战与战略合作；海上战略合作伙伴关系充满信心、面向未来；印度洋海洋新趋势；海上繁荣的合作与协同；加强海上合作确保海洋安全（相

---

〔1〕 Hindustan Times, "China, Sri Lanka to Deepen Defence Cooperation", https：//www. hindustan-times. com/world-news/china-sri-lanka-to-deepen-defence-cooperation/story-3UmVAjbKp9LNcah5rb n60N. html, May 15, 2020.

〔2〕 Xinhua Net, "China, Sri Lanka Vow to Strengthen Defense Ties", http：//www. xinhuanet. com/ english/2018-07/24/c_ 137345307. htm, May 15, 2020.

〔3〕 Economic Times, "China Gifts Warship to Sri Lanka", https：//economictimes. indiatimes. com/ news/defence/china-gifts-warship-to-sri-lanka/articleshow/70255526. cms, May 15, 2020.

关挑战与前进方向）；促进策略性海事伙伴关系；开阔海洋视野，增强海上安全；协同海事管理；改善心态以应对跨国海洋威胁，回顾"加勒对话"十年。[1]

截至 2019 年，"加勒对话"的与会国家包括：阿富汗、阿根廷、澳大利亚、巴林、孟加拉国、巴西、柬埔寨、加拿大、智利、中国、古巴、埃及、法国、德国、印度、印度尼西亚、伊朗、伊拉克、意大利、日本、肯尼亚、科威特、马来西亚、马尔代夫、缅甸、纳米比亚、荷兰、新西兰、尼日利亚、挪威、阿曼、巴基斯坦、波兰、卡塔尔、罗马尼亚、俄罗斯、沙特阿拉伯、塞内加尔。[2]

由斯里兰卡国防部主持的 2015 年"加勒对话"国际海事会议于 2015 年11 月 24 日闭幕。与会各方承诺支持加强海上安全合作，共同努力加强区域海洋互助协同，制定相关全球战略，应对海洋领域的共同挑战。[3]

在 2016 年的"加勒对话"中，斯里兰卡将印度和中国置于其外交政策的首位，印度海军参谋长及中国人民解放军海军代表的发言均受到特别关注。印度海军代表提出，这一对话平台有利于印度洋各国海军发展本区域海上安全的合作架构。中国海军代表则强调，中国积极倡导和实践以共同安全、综合安全、合作安全、可持续安全为核心的海上安全，重申中国在海盗猖獗的亚丁湾为船舶护航所发挥的作用，愿意在海上安保、海上救援、灾后重建等方面作出贡献。[4]

2017 年的"加勒对话"于当年 10 月 10 日闭幕，共有 51 个国家以及国际组织的代表出席了本次论坛。斯里兰卡国防国务部长在开幕式上表示，海洋的利益攸关方必须有更为广阔的海洋视野，方能促进和加强与友好国家的海上安全合作。美国、中国及印度等国代表分别阐述了本国对于促进海上合作的观点与立场。与会者们发出一致呼声：随着来自海上的安

〔1〕 Galledialogue, "Synergizing for Collaborative Maritime Management", http：//galledialogue. lk/in-dex. php? id =17#, May 15, 2020.

〔2〕 Galledialogue, "Synergizing for Collaborative Maritime Management", http：//galledialogue. lk/in-dex. php? id =14, May 15, 2020.

〔3〕 Navy of Sri Lanka, "'Galle Dialogue 2015' Concludes Pledging Support for Greater Maritime Coop-eration for Secure Seas", https：//news. navy. lk/eventnews/2015/11/25/201511251630/, May 15, 2020.

〔4〕 Asian Mirror, "What Happened At Sri Lanka's Maritime Security Conference This Year?", http：//asianmirror. lk/news/item/21137-what-happened-at-sri-lanka-s-maritime-security-conference-this-year, May 15, 2020.

全威胁与挑战不断增加，各国应该携起手来，承担起维护海洋安全的共同责任。[1]

2018年10月，第9届"加勒对话"在科伦坡开幕。斯里兰卡海军司令重提斯里兰卡在印度洋的关键地位，表达对本国在地理优势外亦面临挑战的担忧，迫切希望与各国共议海上安全问题，分享有益经验。中国海军代表在发言中提出，中国愿意在尊重印度洋各国核心利益和重大关切的基础上，与域内外国家一起，共商海上安全议题，贡献海洋安全治理智慧，交流反海盗行动经验，分担海上维稳职责，提供海上安保支持，共担海上安全责任。[2]

2019年10月，第10届"加勒对话"在"回顾十年"的历程中，提出应"改善心态以应对跨国海洋威胁"。共有55名国家代表、12名国际机构负责人和3名国防工业代表出席了本次论坛。在科伦坡复活节恐怖袭击事件发生6个月后，这一国际海事论坛成功举办，体现出印度洋国家捍卫区域海洋安全的坚定决心，也反映了国际社会对斯里兰卡及其周边安全局势的乐观与信心。[3]

（二）海洋油气资源合作

斯里兰卡于20世纪60年代末着手推进本国的石油勘探事业。在斯里兰卡海上石油的前期勘探中，西方国家各大石油公司的地位举足轻重，并一直在其海上油气资源合作中保持活跃态势。直至2000年，以印度为代表的亚洲周边国家才逐步加入到斯里兰卡海上油气开发的进程中来。

1. 与美国的合作

1975年，锡兰石油公司聘请美国佩克西明太平洋公司（Pexamin Pacific）为顾问，以推动本国对高韦里盆地（Cauvery Basin）区域斯里兰卡所占部分的勘探。1976年，美国西方地球物理公司（Western Geophysical）采集记录了马纳尔岛（Mannar Island）1947公里的二维地震数据以及保克海峡和马纳尔湾2829公里的地震数据。不久后，锡兰石油公司与佩克西明太平洋公司签订了海上区块勘探合同。

---

〔1〕 唐璐、朱瑞卿：《2017年"加勒对话"国际海事会议探讨强化海上安全合作》，载新华网，ht-tp：//www.xinhuanet.com/2017-10/10/c_1121782166.htm，最后访问日期：2021年3月20日。
〔2〕 唐璐、朱瑞卿：《"加勒对话"国际海事会议探讨合作共管海洋》，载新华网，http：//www.xinhuanet.com/2018-10/22/c_1123596999.htm，最后访问日期：2021年3月20日。
〔3〕 ADA Derana, "Galle Dialogue 2019 on 'Refining Mindset to Address Transnational Maritime Threats' Concludes", http：//www.adaderana.lk/news/58520/galle-dialogue-2019-on-refining-mindset-to-address-transnational-maritime-threats-concludes, May 15, 2020.

1976 年，美国马拉松石油公司（Marathon Petroleum）在高韦里盆地尝试开凿了两口钻井，分别为"保克湾 1 号"（Palk Bay-1）和"代尔夫特 1 号"（Delft-1）。遗憾的是，这两口井在钻探中并未发现任何碳氢化合物，马拉松石油公司随即在 1977 年放弃了对该两口钻井的继续勘探。

1981 年，美国城市服务公司（Cities Services Company）收购了高韦里盆地和马纳尔盆地（Mannar Basin）的开发权，并采集了该区域共 1556 公里的地震数据。此外，该公司还在马纳尔湾及保克湾分别采集了 1289 公里及 267 公里的地震数据。同年，城市服务公司在马纳尔湾东北部大陆架开凿了"珍珠 1 号"（Pearl-1）钻井。该钻井位于火山岩床底部，深度为 3050 米，是斯里兰卡当时在马纳尔盆地的唯一钻井。尽管城市服务公司未能在该钻井中发现石油和天然气，但是该钻井穿透了厚度达 850 米的晚白垩世基底砂岩单元（Late Cretaceous basal sandstone unit），从而揭示了马纳尔盆地中重要储集层的存在。与此同时，印度石油天然气公司在高韦里盆地的本国一侧（斯里兰卡与印度海上边界以北约 30 公里处）的油气发现极大地激励了美国城市服务公司的后续投入。该公司在斯里兰卡水域最北端再次开凿了"佩德罗 1 号"（Pedro-1）钻井，钻井深度达 1437 米，却仍未发现任何碳氢化合物。[1]

2018 年 5 月 30 日，斯里兰卡政府与美国斯伦贝谢（Schlumberger）的全资子公司东部生态燃油公司（Eastern Eco DMCC）签订采集数据协议。该协议约定的项目于 2018 年 9 月 3 日起在斯里兰卡的东部海域开启，向西　直至斯里兰卡西部海岸。这一项目意在为斯里兰卡收集更多的地质地震数据，以吸引更多的投资者前往当地开发油气资源。[2]

2020 年，美国贝尔地球空间公司（Bell Geospace）与斯里兰卡石油资源开发秘书处（PRDS）签署服务协议，对斯里兰卡马纳尔盆地和高韦里盆地的海上地震数据进行测试，以推动对斯里兰卡 2019 年油气开采招标项目中的"C1"、"M1"和"M2"区块的勘探。贝尔地球空间公司提供的数据将有助于重新审视现有的地震数据，从而对马纳尔盆地、高韦里盆地及其基底结构有新的认识，并为未来地震勘探的规划提供宝贵的参考数据。[3]

〔1〕 Petroleum Resources Development Secretariat, "Exploration History", http：//www. prds-srilan-ka. com/exploration/origins. faces，May 15，2020.

〔2〕 Ministry of Energy, "Annual Reports", https：//www. petroleummin. gov. lk/web/images/pdf/an-nual_ reports/Performance% 20Report% 202018% 20-% 20English. pdf，May 15，2020.

〔3〕 Petroleum Resources Development Secretariat, "Exploration History", http：//www. prds-srilan-ka. com/exploration/origins. faces，May 15，2020.

2. 与法国的合作

早在 1967 年至 1968 年，法国地球物理总公司（Compaigne General de Geophysicque）便代表当时的锡兰石油公司收集了大约 420 公里陆上地震和 75 公里海上地震的数据。

2016 年 2 月，斯里兰卡政府与法国道达尔勘探与生产有限公司（Total Exploration & Production）签署联合勘探协议，旨在通过对斯里兰卡东海岸的地质调查与分析，评估是否存在具有商业开采价值的石油和天然气，分析斯里兰卡东海岸 JS－5 和 JS－6 两个海上区块的油气前景。[1] 然而，这一勘探活动尚未取得明确进展。2019 年 8 月，道达尔勘探与生产有限公司联合挪威国家石油与天然气公司（Equinor ASA）再度与斯里兰卡政府签订为期两年的海上勘探合同，约定三者为联合研究合作伙伴，继续推进对 JS－5 和 JS－6 区块的勘探，对在斯里兰卡东部海域的成果仍保持乐观预期。[2]

3. 与加拿大的合作

1984 年，加拿大菲尼克斯石油公司（Phoenix Canada Oil Company）、加拿大石油公司（Petro-Canada）和锡兰石油公司签订了三方协议，约定由加拿大石油公司采集马纳尔盆地 980 公里的二维地震数据。这也是在马纳尔盆地进行的第一个综合地震勘探项目。但一如斯里兰卡早期石油勘探的惯常状态，该项目没有任何进展。1984 年，斯里兰卡海上石油勘探开发工作一度陷入停滞，直至 2001 年都基本处于休止状态。[3]

2013 年，斯里兰卡石油资源开发秘书处启动了第二次国际招标，就高韦里盆地和马纳尔盆地的 13 个区块的海上勘探许可权对外招标。[4] 作为本次招标结果，斯里兰卡批准有条件地将高韦里盆地的 "C2" "C3" 区块的勘探许可权授予加拿大博纳维斯塔能源公司（Bonavista Energy），计划在 8 年的合同期内开凿 5 口钻井进行勘探。[5]

---

〔1〕 Ministry of Energy, "Progress Report 2016 and Action Plan 2017", https：//www. petroleummin. gov. lk/web/images/pdf/4-ProgressReport-2016andActionPlan-2017-English. pdf，May 15，2020.

〔2〕 Petroleum Resources Development Secretariat, "Exploration History", http：//www. prds-srilanka. com/exploration/origins. faces，May 15，2020.

〔3〕 Petroleum Resources Development Secretariat, "Exploration History", http：//www. prds-srilanka. com/exploration/origins. faces，May 15，2020.

〔4〕 Ken White, "Southern Hemisphere Offers Prospective and Challenging Opportunities", https：//www. geoexpro. com/articles/2014/02/southern-hemisphere-offers-prospective-and-challenging-opportunities，May 15，2020.

〔5〕 Ministry of Energy, "Progress Report 2016 and Action Plan 2017", https：//www. petroleummin. gov. lk/web/images/pdf/4-ProgressReport-2016andActionPlan-2017-English. pdf，May 15，2020.

4. 与印度的合作

印度石油天然气公司的子公司维迪什油气公司（Oil and Natural Gas Corporation Videsh Ltd.）于 2007 年宣布已从挪威油气公司获得相关地质资料，将开发位于印度南端和斯里兰卡西海岸之间的马纳尔湾地区的油气资源。斯里兰卡政府表示，基于与印度的友好关系，将不通过招标的形式，直接授予印度对马纳尔湾区域相关区块的优先开发权。[1]

2007 年 9 月，斯里兰卡石油资源开发秘书处启动了马纳尔盆地区块勘探权的招标工作，得到了各国公司的积极响应。包括印度凯恩能源有限公司（Cairn India Limited）、塞浦路斯尼克能源有限公司［Niko Resources（Cyprus）Limited］和印度石油天然气有限公司（Oil and Natural Gas Company of India）在内的 3 家公司对第 001 号区块投递了申请书。经斯里兰卡政府的评估，印度凯恩能源有限公司最终中标。2008 年 7 月，斯里兰卡政府与印度凯恩能源有限公司签订石油资源协议，授予印度凯恩能源有限公司在马纳尔盆地的勘探开发权。2011 年，印度凯恩能源有限公司在其中标区块分别开凿了"剑鱼"（Dorado）、"梭鱼"（Barracuda）和"剑鱼北"（Dorado North）三口钻井以展开勘探工作。其中，"剑鱼"钻井位于距斯里兰卡海岸 30 公里处，勘探过程中探测到含气砂岩；"梭鱼"钻井击中了三个产气层，且有液态烃呈现；"剑鱼北"钻井则被证实是一口干井，随后被废弃。2013 年，印度凯恩能源有限公司再次在该区块开凿"叉尾鲶"（Wallago）钻井，但因钻井船故障，该钻井的勘探行动被提前中止。[2] 2015 年，印度凯恩能源有限公司在斯里兰卡海域已经开展了 7 年的勘探工作，但遭油价暴跌影响，该公司被迫放弃了其对斯里兰卡马纳尔盆地区块的勘探权。[3]

5. 与其他国家的合作

20 世纪 70 年代，苏联曾在南亚地区展开油气勘探。1972 年至 1975 年，苏联基于与斯里兰卡政府签订的协议，就斯里兰卡 4837 公里的海上地震数据以及部分陆上地震数据进行了采集和记录，以评估保克湾区域的资源储量。1974 年，苏联在马纳尔岛上开凿"佩萨莱 1 号"（Pesalai 1）钻井，并得到蕴藏天然气的勘探结果，这极大地鼓舞了苏联继续钻探的信心。随后，苏联又

〔1〕《印度即将开发斯马纳尔湾油气资源》，载中华人民共和国商务部网站，http：//lk. mofcom. gov. cn/article/jmxw/200701/20070104244450. shtml，最后访问日期：2020 年 5 月 15 日。

〔2〕 Petroleum Resources Development Secretariat，"Exploration History"，http：//www. prds-srilanka. com/exploration/origins. faces，May 15，2020.

〔3〕 Ministry of Energy，"Progress Report 2015"，https：//www. petroleummin. gov. lk/web/images/pdf/2015-english. pdf，May 15，2020.

陆续在"佩萨莱 1 号"井附近完成了"佩萨莱 2 号"井（Pesalai 2）、"佩萨莱 3 号"井（Pesalai 3）的钻探。但由于后续开凿的两口钻井并未探得显示油气资源的关键储集岩或圈闭结构，苏联最终放弃了该区域，不再做进一步的勘探。

2001 年，挪威诺欧派克地球物理公司（TGS-NOPEC Geophysical Company）与锡兰石油公司洽谈，承接马纳尔盆地地震数据测试项目，采集了马纳尔盆地 1100 公里的二维地震数据。2005 年，诺欧派克地球物理公司进一步在该盆地采集了 4600 公里的地震数据。该公司两次数据收集为其他能源公司的后续勘探提供了马纳尔盆地区域先进且高质量的二维地震数据。但斯里兰卡政府与诺欧派克地球物理公司的合作与宣传，未能成功吸引更多外国公司前来勘探、开采油气资源。2007 年，斯里兰卡政府决定购买诺欧派克地球物理公司在斯里兰卡海域所收集的地震数据的专有权。斯里兰卡根据这些数据将马纳尔盆地划分为 9 个勘探区块，并于 2007 年及 2013 年成功开展了对该盆地多个区块勘探许可权的招标。[1]

2012 年 10 月 11 日，斯里兰卡和马来西亚签署了首个油气勘采谅解备忘录，为两国在油气领域的商业与投资合作提供了良好机遇，也为两国在相关领域更广泛的投资合作铺平道路。这项协议由斯里兰卡石油资源开发秘书处与马来西亚总理府下属马来西亚石油资源公司签署。马来西亚方面认为，斯里兰卡油气工业发展潜力巨大，其经济在 2009 年结束 30 年内战后得到迅速增长，使得斯里兰卡成为外国投资者进入南亚地区市场的重要平台。[2]

（三）海洋渔业合作

作为岛国，斯里兰卡共拥有 21500 平方公里的领海，517000 平方公里的专属经济区。该国的渔业和水产资源业对国内生产总值的贡献约为 1.4%，为约 575000 人（占该国劳动力的 3.7%）提供直接和间接就业。

尽管四面环海，斯里兰卡却一直是以农业及种植经济为主的国家。尽管坐拥丰富的海洋生物资源，且渔业捕捞量逐年上升，但斯里兰卡的渔业捕捞能力仍明显不足。据斯里兰卡渔业和水产资源部所公布的数据，斯里兰卡本国的渔业生产仅能满足国内消费所需鱼类产品总量的约 65%，其余部分则依

---

〔1〕 Petroleum Resources Development Secretariat, "Exploration History", http://www.prds-srilanka.com/exploration/origins.faces, May 15, 2020.

〔2〕 刁倩:《斯里兰卡与马来西亚签首个油气勘探合作备忘录》, 载新华财经网, http://world.xinhua08.com/a/20121011/1037148.shtml, 最后访问日期: 2020 年 5 月 15 日。

靠进口。无论是基于海洋经济发展、渔业资源开发，还是立足国内市场需求及就业机会扩展，斯里兰卡的渔业发展都尚有较大空间。

1. 与印度的合作

斯里兰卡和印度的渔业争端由来已久。这一争端与 1974 年和 1976 年斯里兰卡和印度之间的海上划界协定密切相关。一如前述，该系列协定虽划定了两国海上边界，也保留了两国的特定重叠海域，却未能为两国渔民建立起有效的共享合作机制。[1] 直到 2008 年 10 月斯里兰卡与印度《有关捕鱼安排的联合声明》（Joint Statement on Fishing Arrangements）的达成，两国间因渔业冲突而引发的暴力事件终于得以控制并大幅减少。

2011 年 7 月，印度—斯里兰卡渔业联合工作组第三次会议（The 3rd Meeting of the India-Sri Lanka Joint Working Group on Fisheries）在印度新德里举行。斯里兰卡强调两国渔民在进行捕捞作业时须尊重经协定的海上边界线，两国有必要坚持 2008 年签署的《有关捕鱼安排的联合声明》，并一致认为在任何情况下都不能对对方国家渔民使用暴力，必须高度重视渔民的安全和生计问题。为了两国渔业的可持续发展，制定共同监管措施，斯里兰卡与印度围绕《有关渔业领域发展与合作的谅解备忘录草案》（The Draft Memorandum of Understanding on Development and Cooperation in The Field of Fisheries）进行了交流与讨论。印度方面表示，乐见会议成果的落实，愿意继续向斯里兰卡渔业部门提供资金援助。[2]

2012 年 1 月，斯里兰卡和印度同意就保克湾和马纳尔湾的捕鱼问题达成一个更为全面的谅解备忘录，以解决渔民安全问题、渔业资源的可持续利用问题、海洋生态环境的保护问题以及渔民的生计问题。两国均表示，在维护两国传统捕鱼权利的基础上，将为达成合作而进行真诚的接触和讨论。[3]

2014 年 8 月，印度—斯里兰卡渔业相关问题联合委员会第一次会议（The First Meeting of India-Sri Lanka Joint Committee on Fisheries Related Issues）在印度新德里举行。两国探讨了双边渔业合作的途径，包括建立渔业合作的长效机制、加强两国在渔业能力研究和建设方面的合作等。两国同意继续通

---

〔1〕　See London School of Economics and Political Science，"Exploring Regional Solutions to Fishermen Disputes in South Asia"，https：//blogs. lse. ac. uk/southasia/2017/07/18/exploring-regional-solutions-to-fishermen-disputes-in-south-asia/，May 15，2020.

〔2〕　Sri Lanka Foreign Ministry，"Joint Press Statement 3rd Meeting of the India-Sri Lanka Joint Working Group on Fisheries"，https：//www. mfa. gov. lk/joint-press-statement-3rd-meeting-of-the-india-sri-lanka-joint-working-group-on-fisheries-2/，May 15，2020.

〔3〕　Indian Express， "India，Lanka Mull MoU on Fishing"，https：//www. newindianexpress. com/world/2012/jan/17/india-lanka-mull-mou-on-fishing-330707. html，May 15，2020.

过对话方式解决两国之间的渔业问题。[1]

2016 年 4 月，斯里兰卡和印度签订了新的谅解备忘录。根据此谅解备忘录，经与斯里兰卡渔业和水产资源部协商，印度将向斯里兰卡穆莱蒂武（Mullaitivu）地区的渔民赠送 150 艘渔船和其他捕鱼设备，总价值约为 1 亿卢比。[2]

2016 年 9 月，斯里兰卡和印度再度签订一项谅解备忘录。根据该谅解备忘录，经与斯里兰卡渔业和水产资源部协商，印度将向斯里兰卡南部的汉班托塔（Hambantota）地区提供价值 200 万美元的设备以支持当地渔民和农民的生计。[3]

2. 与越南的合作

2013 年 5 月，越南在斯里兰卡科伦坡启动了"斯里兰卡渔业行业发展技术协助项目"（Technical Assistance Project for Developing Fisheries Sector），计划通过该项目帮助斯里兰卡制定渔业发展的总体规划。斯里兰卡表示，越南拥有先进的水产养殖技术，而斯里兰卡的水产养殖业具有巨大潜力，两国应长期开展务实合作。越南也回应称，其愿意与斯里兰卡分享经验，帮助斯里兰卡发展水产养殖业，为当地渔民提供就业机会，并协力提高斯里兰卡水产出口总额。为此，两国均有意促成两国水产合资企业的建立。[4]

2019 年 10 月，斯里兰卡和越南贸易问题第二次小组委员会会议（Second Sub-Committee Meeting on Trade between Sri Lanka and Viet Nam）于越南河内举行。经讨论，两国决定延长实施 2020—2022 年农业领域合作计划，并着手落实 2020—2022 年双边渔业合作谅解备忘录。[5] 同年 10 月 31 日，斯里

---

〔1〕 Ministry of External Affairs Government of India, "Joint Press Statement on India-Sri Lanka Joint Committee Meeting on Fisheries Related Issues", https：//mea. gov. in/press-releases. htm？dtl/23957/joint + press + statement + on + indiasri + lanka + joint + committee + meeting + on + fisheries + related + issues, May 15, 2020.

〔2〕 Big News Network, "India, Lanka Sign MoU to Supply 150 Boats to Mullaitivu Fishermen", https：//www. bignewsnetwork. com/news/242732243/india-lanka-sign-mou-to-supply-150-boats-to-mullaitivu-fishermen, May 15, 2020.

〔3〕 Financial Express, "India Inks MoU with Sri Lanka to Support Fishermen, Farmers", https：//www. president. gov. lk/parliament/, May 15, 2020.

〔4〕 Ministry of Agriculture and Rural Development of Vietnam, "Viet Nam to Help Sri Lanka Develop Fisheries Sector", https：//www. mard. gov. vn/en/Pages/vietnam-to-help-sri-lanka-develop-fisheries-sector-947. aspx#, May 15, 2020.

〔5〕 Sri Lanka Foreign Ministry, "Second Sub-Committee Meeting on Trade between Sri Lanka and Viet Nam", https：//www. mfa. gov. lk/second-sub-committee-meeting-on-trade-between-sri-lanka-and-viet-nam/, May 15, 2020.

兰卡驻越南大使会见了越南河内人民委员会主席（Chairman of the People's Committee of Ha Noi）。双方多次强调双边合作的重要性，同意应增强两国间包括渔业合作在内的全面合作。斯里兰卡大使提出，两国应充分执行在"斯里兰卡和越南贸易问题第二次小组委员会会议"上达成的协议，斯里兰卡需要在渔业、水产养殖、高科技农业等领域向越南学习。[1]

3. 与泰国的合作

为促进本国远洋渔业发展并为本国捕捞公司寻找新的市场，泰国于 2006 年与斯里兰卡展开贸易谈判。作为谈判成果，斯里兰卡允许泰国渔船在斯里兰卡水域内作业，但以泰国对斯里兰卡鱼类加工厂进行投资为条件。[2]

2016 年 5 月，泰国罐装企业巨头阿努奥集团（Anuorn Group）投资 750 万美元在斯里兰卡建立罐装加工厂和干冰制造厂。为此，阿努奥集团与 600 名渔船主合作，为他们提供现代设备、科技装置和渔业培训，并与他们签署协议购买其渔获产品。随着这一计划的展开，阿努奥集团为斯里兰卡当地渔民提供了先进的技术培训和多方面渔业技能训练，在其生产制造活动覆盖范围内增加了当地渔民的就业机会，提高了其劳动收入。[3]

2018 年 2 月，第四次斯里兰卡—泰国双边政治磋商会议（The Fourth Meeting of the Sri Lanka-Thailand Bilateral Political Consultations）于斯里兰卡科伦坡举行，斯里兰卡和泰国表示将进一步巩固、推进两国双边政治合作和经济合作，并审查、讨论了渔业、旅游等领域的合作事项。[4] 同年 7 月，在两国又一次双边会晤中，斯里兰卡回顾了与泰国农业专家的合作，并对泰国协助斯里兰卡发展和完善农业部门表示感谢。同时，两国决定建立联合工作组，为下一步促进两国渔业合作作出共同努力。[5]

---

〔1〕 Sri Lanka Foreign Ministry, "Ambassador of Sri Lanka to Viet Nam Meets with Chairman of Ha Noi People's Committee Dr. Nguyen Duc Chung", https：//www. mfa. gov. lk/ambassador-of-sri-lanka-to-viet-nam-meets-with-chairman-of-ha-noi-peoples-committee-dr-nguyen-duc-chung/, May 15, 2020.

〔2〕 《泰国将投资远洋渔业》，载中国水产科学研究院网站，https：//www. cafs. ac. cn/info/1053/7990. htm，最后访问日期：2020 年 5 月 15 日。

〔3〕 《泰国罐装加工企业在斯里兰卡投资设厂》，载腾氏水产网，http://www. tensfish. com/news-detailed--20940. html，最后访问日期：2020 年 5 月 15 日。

〔4〕 Sri Lanka Foreign Ministry, "4th Meeting of The Sri Lanka – Thailand Bilateral Political Consultations：27-28 February 2018", https：//www. mfa. gov. lk/4th-meeting-of-the-sri-lanka-thailand-bilateral-political-consultations-27-28-Februaryruary-2018/, May 15, 2020.

〔5〕 Sri Lanka Foreign Ministry, "Joint Press Statement on the Official Visit of His Excellency General Prayut Chan-o-cha, Prime Minister of the Kingdom of Thailand to the Democratic Socialist Republic of Sri Lanka, 12-13 July 2018", https：//www. mfa. gov. lk/sl-thai-jps-eng/, May 15, 2020.

4. 与挪威的合作

挪威对斯里兰卡的经济援助开始于 1965 年。1965 年到 2017 年，挪威向斯里兰卡提供了超过 50 亿挪威克朗的发展援助；仅 2017 年，挪威对斯里兰卡的发展援助就约达 1.7 亿挪威克朗。同时，挪威也积极向斯里兰卡渔业和水产资源部提供技术援助，促进斯里兰卡水产养殖的商业化以及进行渔业合作。[1]

2016 年 12 月，应斯里兰卡政府的请求，挪威向斯里兰卡提供技术援助，以协助其制定一项国家渔业和水产养殖政策。该政策的目标为：第一，引导斯里兰卡渔业适应当前国际新兴市场的需求；第二，培养渔业和水产养殖的相关人才；第三，促进各界对渔业和水产养殖业进行投资。挪威承诺为该政策的制定及执行提供资金。[2]

2017 年 3 月，斯里兰卡和挪威签订了两项价值 150 万美元的协定。其一，同意由挪威协助斯里兰卡制定渔业政策；其二，约定由挪威协助斯里兰卡绘制鱼类资源分布图。此外，挪威还向斯里兰卡捐赠 100 万美元用于支持斯里兰卡北部地区的渔业发展。[3]

2017 年 8 月，挪威研究船"弗里德约夫·南森"号（RV-Dr Fridtjof Nansen）计划于 2018 年驶入斯里兰卡水域，调查包括鱼类资源在内的海洋资源，着重调查大陆架和大陆坡上未开发或者未充分开发的渔业资源，同时将评估该区域海洋生态系统的状态。挪威拟基于该研究船的调查向斯里兰卡提供以下援助：第一，协助斯里兰卡发展可持续的鱼类捕捞作业方式；第二，协助斯里兰卡完善海洋管理制度；第三，邀请斯里兰卡的科学家参与研究过程，帮助斯里兰卡发展现代海洋研究技术。[4]

2018 年 6 月，挪威发展合作国务秘书（State Secretary for Development Co-operation）对斯里兰卡进行了国事访问。两国在访问期间召开了蓝色经济商

---

〔1〕 Royal Norwegian Embassy in Colombo, "Norway-Sri Lanka Relations", https：//www. norway. no/en/sri-lanka/norway-sri-lanka/norway-sri-lanka-relations/, May 15, 2020.

〔2〕 Daliy FT, "Norway Assists Sri Lanka Fisheries Ministry to Formulate National Fisheries and Aquaculture Policy", http：//www. ft. lk/article/588129/Norway-assists-Sri-Lanka-Fisheries-Ministry-to-formulate-national-fisheries-and-aquaculture-policy, May 15, 2020.

〔3〕 Norwegian Embassy in Colombo, "Norway Supports the Sri Lankan Fishery Sector with 2, 5 Million USD", https：//www. facebook. com/norwayinsrilanka/posts/norway-supports-the-sri-lankan-fishery-sector-with-25-million-usdtoday-sri-lanka/596380357227983/, May 15, 2020.

〔4〕 The Sunday Times, "Norwegian Vessel to Dig Up Fish Life, Marine Eco System Data in Sri Lanka", https：//stopillegalfishing. com/press-links/norwegian-vessel-dig-fish-life-marine-eco-system-data-sri-lanka/, May 15, 2020.

务会议（Business Conference on Blue Economy），以促进两国在渔业、水产养殖业等领域的合作，并就渔业领域的持续合作、海洋资源的可持续利用、海洋垃圾管理、海洋空间规划等议题展开详细讨论。此次访问恰逢挪威研究船"弗里德约夫·南森"号抵达斯里兰卡海域正式开始研究计划。该研究船的项目规划及研究航程被视为两国渔业领域合作的重要体现，其在调查鱼类资源、绘制海洋资源图等方面的协作成果及其他技术援助成效等都受到两国的关注与期待。[1]

5. 与韩国的合作

2015年12月，斯里兰卡渔业和水产资源部部长同韩国驻斯里兰卡大使举行会谈。韩国表示愿意尽全力支持斯里兰卡的渔业发展，向斯里兰卡提供渔业相关的教学培训以及专业的技术设备。韩国计划优先在斯里兰卡建立一个渔业学院，为斯里兰卡培养渔业部门的专业人才。[2]

2016年6月，韩国代表团访问斯里兰卡。韩国向斯里兰卡捐赠128000美元用于启动斯里兰卡渔业住房项目的第一阶段工作，并选派部分渔业住房项目受益者前往韩国学习先进的渔业技术。在参观了斯里兰卡南部的渔业村落及社区之后，韩国代表团再度表示，将推动在斯里兰卡有关渔业技术学院、渔船制造厂以及鱼产品加工厂的建立。[3]

2017年3月，经斯里兰卡渔业和水产资源部部长与韩国海洋渔业部部长会商，韩国决定向斯里兰卡国家水产养殖发展管理局提供250万美元，用于发展斯里兰卡的水产养殖业。[4] 同年11月，为纪念两国建交40周年，斯里兰卡总统应韩国总统邀请对韩国进行了国事访问。两国首脑在会晤中同意扩大在农业领域的互利合作。其中，为了扩大渔业领域的合作，两国同意根据2016年两国签订的备忘录，推进斯里兰卡多用途渔港项目的建设。[5]

---

〔1〕 Sri Lanka Foreign Ministry, "Norwegian State Secretary for Development Cooperation visits Sri Lanka", https://www.mfa.gov.lk/stsec-norw/, May 15, 2020.

〔2〕 Daily FT, "Korea Willing to Assist Sri Lanka to Develop Fishing Industry", http://www.ft.lk/business/korea-willing-to-assist-sri-lanka-to-develop-fishing-industry/34-512543, May 15, 2020.

〔3〕 Daily FT, "Korean Assistance to Construct Houses for Sri Lankan Fishing Families", http://www.ft.lk/article/549476/Korean-assistance-to-construct-houses-for-Sri-Lankan-fishing-families, May 15, 2020.

〔4〕《韩国向斯里兰卡注资250万美元发展该国水产养殖业》，载水产养殖网，http://www.fishfirst.cn/forum.php?mod=viewthread&tid=73419&highlight=%CB%B9%C0%EF%C0%BC%BF%A8，最后访问日期：2020年5月15日。

〔5〕 Sri Lanka Foreign Ministry, "The Joint Press Statement between the Republic of Korea and the Democratic Socialist Republic of Sri Lanka", https://www.mfa.gov.lk/joint-press-statement-between-the-republic-of-korea-and-the-democratic-socialist-republic-of-sri-lanka/, May 15, 2020.

2018 年 8 月，斯里兰卡渔业和水产资源部部长同韩国驻斯里兰卡大使举行新一轮会议。双方对在斯里兰卡建立多用途渔港的可行性进行了研究，并最终决定在斯里兰卡建立 4 个多用途渔港。第一个多用途渔港于 2019 年年初在代尔夫特岛（Delft Island）开始建造，将有望促进当地渔业、旅游业、商业的强劲发展。韩国为该建设工程提供了低利率贷款的资金支持，相应贷款将用建成港口的收入来偿还。[1]

6. 与中国的合作

斯里兰卡和中国的交往历史悠久，早在 2000 多年前就有了贸易往来；两国建交之前著名的"米胶协定"[2]，更成为两国近现代贸易的里程碑。自 1957 年建交以来，两国之间的关系一直朝着互助友好的方向发展。2014 年 5 月，两国发展成为战略合作伙伴关系，两国间关系进一步深化，彼此友谊更为巩固，成为历史上大小国家间友好相处的典范。[3]

2013 年 8 月，中国—斯里兰卡海洋领域合作联委会第一次会议在北京举行。两国回顾了在海洋领域合作中取得的成果，并表示斯里兰卡和中国都是海洋国家，海洋在两国的可持续发展中具有举足轻重的地位。因此，加强双方海洋管理部门和科研机构之间的交往，分享双方在海洋与海岸带空间规划、沿海城市发展与海洋环境保护、海岸带灾害预报与应急、海洋科学研究、海上执法以及能力建设与培训等领域的经验与成果，符合两国的共同利益。

中国代表就两国在海洋领域的合作与交流提出了五点建议：第一，与斯里兰卡共建海洋与海岸带联合研究中心，并以该中心为合作平台，邀请双方涉海部门共同参与，逐步拓宽合作领域；第二，积极开展与斯里兰卡渔业和水产资源部、国家水产资源研究开发局及高校的合作；第三，两国制订《中斯海洋领域合作规划》，明确重点合作领域和优先项目；第四，定期召开由

---

〔1〕 Colombo Page, "Construction of Four Multipurpose Fishery Harbors with Korean Assistance to Begin Next Year", http：//www. colombopage. com/archive_ 18B/Aug29_ 1535525584CH. php, May 15, 2020.

〔2〕 1952 年 12 月，中国与斯里兰卡签订为期 5 年的《中国与斯里兰卡关于橡胶和大米的五年贸易协定》，史称"米胶协定"。这一政府贸易协定，不仅开创了新中国与尚未建交、又是不同社会制度国家签订政府贸易协定的先河，而且建立了新中国与斯里兰卡间的贸易关系，见证了两国在患难中的友谊。参见李征：《〈米胶协定〉签订的前前后后——纪念〈米胶协定〉签订 51 周年》，载《中国经贸》2004 年第 2 期，第 24—25 页；张晓东：《米胶协定——新中国首次与非建交国家的贸易实践》，载《档案春秋》2020 第 3 期，第 4—9 页。

〔3〕《中国同斯里兰卡的关系》，载中华人民共和国外交部网站，http：//history. mofcom. gov. cn/？bandr = sllkyzgdjmgx，最后访问日期：2020 年 5 月 15 日。

两国专家参与的中斯海洋科学研讨会；第五，支持斯里兰卡青年科学家申请中国政府海洋奖学金并提供协助。

斯里兰卡代表表示，斯中友好关系源远流长，双方在海洋等多个领域进行了合作，取得了大量成就。斯里兰卡是个岛国，有较长的海岸线，海洋开发在促进生产总值增长的同时，也对环境造成很大压力。中国国家海洋局拥有多个海洋研究所，在海洋领域具有丰富的经验，希望双方可以分享在海洋管理、海洋资源开发利用、海洋环境保护等方面的宝贵经验。[1]

2014 年 7 月，斯里兰卡渔业和水产资源部部长表示，印度洋金枪鱼委员会已授权斯里兰卡与中国在斯里兰卡周边公海开展渔业合作。按照斯里兰卡和中国签订的协议，进行过相关注册登记的中国渔船可以在斯里兰卡周边公海进行捕鱼作业，但需要将捕捞收成的 10% 作为税款交给斯里兰卡政府，斯里兰卡政府则会在本国港口为中国渔船装卸渔获提供便利条件。[2]

2015 年 10 月，应联合国粮食及农业组织的邀请，中国水产科学研究院派研究员赴斯里兰卡执行联合国粮食及农业组织能力建设项目的顾问任务。中国研究员对斯里兰卡 40 余人进行了培训和指导，就水产遗传育种技术、水产遗传改良项目设计和执行、鱼类人工繁殖技术、苗种生产及良种亲本管理等内容举办了专题培训。斯中两国的研究人员还围绕在斯里兰卡实施遗传改良项目以培育优良品系、如何进行亲本管理以提高苗种生产的质量和数量等关键问题进行了探讨，并提出了若干建议。[3]

2015 年 12 月，斯里兰卡渔业和水产资源部部长至黄海水产研究所进行访问交流。黄海水产研究所所长简要介绍了该研究所在机构设置、学科方向、科研成果、研究设施和国际合作等方面的基本情况。斯里兰卡渔业和水产资源部部长则详细介绍了斯里兰卡渔业的发展情况，重点说明了斯里兰卡在渔业产业、基础设施建设和税收等方面的相关政策，并表达了与黄海水产研究所在水产养殖与遗传育种领域进行合作的诉求。斯里兰卡渔业和水产资源部部长提出，斯里兰卡是中国"海上丝绸之路"的重要沿线国家，斯中两国在渔业科技领域的合作前景广阔，斯里兰卡愿意同黄海水产研究所分享在渔业科技等领域取得的经验与成果，希望双方尽快开展渔业科技与产业的实

---

〔1〕 赵宁、高悦：《中斯海洋领域合作联委会一次会议召开》，载《中国海洋报》2013 年 8 月 27 日，第 A1 版。

〔2〕 《斯里兰卡渔业部长表示斯中将在斯周边公海开展渔业合作》，载中国水产科学研究院网站，https：//www.cafs.ac.cn/info/1053/3599.htm，最后访问日期：2020 年 5 月 15 日。

〔3〕 《淡水中心派出专家赴斯里兰卡执行 FAO 顾问任务》，载中国水产科学研究院网站，https：//www.cafs.ac.cn/info/1051/11198.htm，最后访问日期：2020 年 5 月 15 日。

质性合作。双方随后初步确定了未来合作的重点与方向。[1]

2016 年 3 月，斯里兰卡渔业科学大会在首都科伦坡举行。两国与会代表均表示，斯里兰卡和中国在渔业方面有着很多共同点，渔业在两国国民经济中都占有重要地位，两国水环境和海洋资源都相对丰富但也都面临种种限制和挑战，应鼓励两国在渔业科学和渔业经济方面展开充分合作。中国驻斯里兰卡大使在主旨演讲中也指出，两国同为印度洋金枪鱼委员会成员国，在渔业合作上有很大空间；希望两国渔业主管部门能加强沟通，进行定期交流，建立起健全的沟通渠道和机制，积极签订相关协议，促进两国在渔业基础设施投资、渔产品进出口以及水产养殖等方面展开更为广泛的合作。[2]

2019 年 7 月，斯里兰卡渔业和水产资源部常务秘书在访问中国时再度表示，斯里兰卡希望与中国中科院等全球知名科研机构在海洋、生物医药等领域积极开展合作，从而提高斯里兰卡的科技创新能力，提升斯里兰卡及南亚地区的渔业资源保护和可持续开发能力，提高海洋食品安全保障能力和海产品出口水平。斯里兰卡对中国在青年人才培养方面为斯里兰卡提供的支持表示感谢，并邀请中国学者和专家访问斯里兰卡，进一步推动相关渔业合作。[3]

（四）海洋研究合作

斯里兰卡前总统马欣达·拉贾帕克萨（Mahinda Rajapaksa）曾明言，斯里兰卡的未来在于海洋，其国家发展从绿色经济向蓝色海洋经济转变的大幕由此拉开。[4] 作为蓝色海洋经济的重要驱动力，斯里兰卡极为重视其海洋科研的发展，并积极与中国开展了一系列海洋科研合作。

斯里兰卡地处印度洋东西航线要冲，位于国际货运和石油运输的重要战略航道上，被称为印度洋的"十字路口"，其周边海域更是印度洋水汽进入东亚地区的主要通道。作为中国"一带一路"建设的重要沿线国，斯里兰卡具备与中国进行海洋科研合作的天然优势和迫切需求。斯里兰卡政府也是第

---

〔1〕 《斯里兰卡渔业与水生资源开发部部长 Mahinda Amaraweera 一行访问黄海所》，载中国水产科学研究院黄海水产研究所网站，http：//www. ysfri. ac. cn/info/1108/23670. htm，最后访问日期：2020 年 5 月 15 日。

〔2〕 杨梅菊：《中斯将进一步加强渔业合作》，载亚太日报网站，https：//cn. apdnews. com/srilanka/emb/dashizaixian/369347. html，最后访问日期：2020 年 5 月 15 日。

〔3〕 任霄鹏：《张亚平会见斯里兰卡渔业与水生资源部常秘》，载中国科学院网站，http：//www. cas. cn/sygz/201907/t20190709_ 4698910. shtml，最后访问日期：2020 年 5 月 15 日。

〔4〕 Sundayobserver，"Ocean University to Make Lanka A Global Leader in Marine Science"，http：//archives. sundayobserver. lk/2014/08/31/fea07. asp，May 15, 2020.

一个以官方声明形式支持中国"21 世纪海上丝绸之路"倡议的国家。[1]

2013 年 8 月，斯里兰卡和中国海洋领域合作联合委员会第一次会议在北京举行，双方代表团就建立斯里兰卡和中国海岸带与海洋研究发展中心进行了深入交流。斯里兰卡表示，其大力开发海洋资源在促进生产总值增长的同时，也对海洋环境造成了重大影响，希望能与拥有众多海洋研究所的中国进行海洋管理、海洋资源开发利用、海洋环境保护、海洋科研等方面的合作，并同意了定期召开有双方专家参与的斯中海洋科学研讨会的建议。[2] 同年 9 月，在斯里兰卡卢胡纳大学（University of Ruhuna）校长和中国科学院副院长张亚平的共同见证下，卢胡纳大学与中国科学院南海海洋研究所"热带海洋环境联合观测与应用中心"正式成立。该中心的建立使卢胡纳大学在斯里兰卡海洋研究领域占据重要地位。[3]

2014 年 9 月，斯里兰卡国防与城市发展部常务秘书和中国国家海洋局局长正式签署了《中国国家海洋局与斯里兰卡国防与城市发展部关于建立中斯联合海岸带与海洋研究与开发中心的谅解备忘录》，该备忘录的签署以及海岸带与海洋研究与开发中心的建立将为深化两国在海洋科技与海洋研究领域的合作提供重要的平台。[4]

2015 年 8 月，斯里兰卡卢胡纳大学再度与中国科学院南海海洋研究所携手成立中国—斯里兰卡联合科教中心（China-Sri Lanka Joint Centre for Education and Research, CSL-CER，以下简称中斯中心）。中斯中心在南亚季风爆发核心区域设置了海洋大气相关实地检测系统和近岸海洋观测仪器，并承担着年一度的印度洋科学考察航次任务。中斯中心也是斯里兰卡与他国合办的第一个海洋科学研究中心。该中心在 2015 年、2016 年相继举办两届中国—斯里兰卡联合季风气候和海洋环境研讨会，促进了两国在海洋和大气研究方面的交流。2016 年 4 月，由印度洋海洋事务合作组织秘书处主办，斯里兰卡环境部、中国国家海洋局、中国驻斯里兰卡大使馆协办的斯里兰卡与中国海洋经济与管理合作论坛顺利召开。时任中国驻斯里兰卡大使易先良在论坛开幕式上表示，加强海洋合作符合斯里兰卡和中国的根本利益。该论坛为期 3

〔1〕 邱华盛等：《建设"中斯科教合作中心"推进"一带一路"战略》，载《中国科学院院刊》2015 年第 3 期，第 421—425 页。

〔2〕 赵宁、高悦：《中斯海洋领域合作联委会一次会议召开》，载《中国海洋报》2013 年 8 月 27 日，第 A1 版。

〔3〕 "China Invests in New Center in Sri Lanka to Strengthen Collaboration on Marine Sciences", http://www. xinhuanet. com/english/2018-09/29/c_ 137501493. htm, May 16, 2020.

〔4〕 曾瑞鑫：《建立中斯联合海岸带与海洋研究与开发中心》，载中国海洋网，http://www. china. com. cn/haiyang/2014-09/20/content_ 33565664. htm，最后访问日期：2021 年 3 月 20 日。

天，主要围绕海洋环境保护、海洋科学研究、海洋管理等议题展开讨论，为两国进一步加强海洋科研合作奠定了基础。[1]

2016 年 7 月，中斯中心主要合作伙伴斯里兰卡卢胡纳大学和斯里兰卡渔业与海洋学院代表访问中国科学院南海海洋研究所，围绕南海海洋研究所的科研成果及科学愿景展开了交流，对两国间有关海洋科学硕士班的人才培养模式表示肯定和认同。[2] 同年 5 月和 12 月，斯里兰卡与中国共同举办了第一届与第二届斯里兰卡—中国海洋科技合作研讨会，意在介绍斯里兰卡沿岸海域科学研究、斯里兰卡远洋科学研究以及中国海洋研究所的卫星海洋遥感、南海北部海流观测等科研现状，并对今后的合作重点进行详细规划，就开展海洋地质、海洋生态学研究、卫星遥感、海岸带管理等领域的合作达成了共识。双方确定，在未来的 3—4 年内，将以海洋生物地球化学观测及风暴潮预报研究为主要的研发突破口，合作申请研究经费，以开展联合科考的实践活动。[3]

2018 年 9 月，斯里兰卡卢胡纳大学与中国科学院、中斯中心在斯里兰卡南部城市马特勒（Matara）联合建立海洋科技综合实验观测平台。作为斯里兰卡和中国共同设立的首个海洋常规研究与科教融合办公场所，双方致力于将这一平台打造成印度洋地区科教国际合作的标志性成果，继续推进斯里兰卡与中国在印度洋海域的全面科教合作。新启用的平台也将为斯里兰卡日后的海洋环境监测提供支持。[4]

2020 年 1 月，斯里兰卡与中国启动了斯里兰卡—中国海洋与生态国际合作科考航次。该科考航次于 1 月 5 日至 17 日在斯里兰卡南部和东部的专属经济区内进行考察。两国的多位科学家受邀参与这一科考航次，按计划共同对该区域内 33 个站的水文、生物、化学、气象和水深进行综合调查，所获数据和样本由斯里兰卡和中国共同享有。以此次科考获得的样本和数据为契机，两国将进一步深化海洋科技合作，进一步加强在海洋观测、气候变化、海洋

〔1〕 赵妍：《中国驻斯里兰卡大使：加强海洋合作符合中斯两国根本利益》，载国际在线网，http：//news. cri. cn/20160421/ea7e6a2c-e76b-cf2f-1fdc-1188c134412a. html，最后访问日期：2021 年 3 月 20 日。

〔2〕 陈丹：《斯里兰卡卢胡纳大学代表团访问南海海洋所》，载中国科学院网站，http：//www. cas. cn/yx/201608/t20160802_ 4570439. shtml，最后访问日期：2021 年 3 月 20 日。

〔3〕 冉梨华：《第二届中国—斯里兰卡海洋科技合作研讨会在我所召开》，载自然资源部第二海洋研究所网站，http：//www. sio. org. cn/redir. php？ catalog_ id = 84&object_ id = 72896，最后访问日期：2021 年 3 月 20 日。

〔4〕 朱瑞卿：《中科院首个境外海洋观测平台在斯里兰卡启用》，载中国科学院网站，http：//www. cas. cn/cm/201809/t20180929_ 4664984. shtml，最后访问日期：2021 年 3 月 20 日。

生态保护等领域的交流与协同。[1]

（五）区域性国际合作

1. 南亚区域合作联盟

南亚区域合作联盟（以下简称"南盟"）的宗旨在于，促进本区域内国家经济、社会、文化、技术和科学等领域的积极合作，从而保障南亚各国人民的福利、改善人民的生活水平，共同推动南亚地区的全方位发展。同印度、巴基斯坦及孟加拉国一样，斯里兰卡也是 1985 年成立的南盟的八大成员国之一，其在南盟框架下的合作主要集中在海上安全保障和海洋渔业发展领域。

2017 年 7 月，南盟在斯里兰卡首都科伦坡举行了南盟第八次内政部长会议，该次会议由斯里兰卡法律、秩序和南部发展部（Sri Lankan Ministry of Law, Order and Southern Development）与斯里兰卡内务部、文化事务部等共同承办。会议主要审议了南盟警务合作、南盟恐怖主义犯罪、毒品犯罪及海盗犯罪相关海上安全等问题，旨在强调在信息技术高速发展的背景下，确保南亚地区免受恐怖主义侵袭，从而保障海上航运安全。各成员国在此次会议上都作出郑重承诺，愿意加强双边和区域合作，控制严重危害人类的各项罪行。[2]

2019 年 4 月，斯里兰卡参加了由南盟农业中心在尼泊尔博卡拉举行的"在水塘、湖泊、河流和海水中使用网箱和围栏饲养以促进南亚水产养殖多样化的区域磋商会"（Regional Consultation on Fish Culture in Cages and Pens in Reservoirs, Lakes, Rivers and Marine Waters for Aquaculture Diversification in South Asia）。该次会议的主旨在于就应对南亚地区所面临的粮食短缺问题展开讨论，寻求方案以保障有近 20 亿人口的南亚地区的粮食安全。该会议主题的确定与南亚地区的发展息息相关。在南亚地区人口快速增长的大背景下，该区域国家对渔业产品的需求大幅增加，也促使南盟举办该会议为区域内各国分享水产养殖经验提供了宝贵机会。[3] 斯里兰卡作为印度洋中举足轻

---

[1]　王自堃：《我所主持中国与斯里兰卡国际合作海洋科考航次启动》，载自然资源部第二海洋研究所网站，http://www.sio.org.cn/redir.php?catalog_id=84&object_id=310118，最后访问日期：2021 年 3 月 20 日。

[2]　SAARC, "List of Activites", http://saarc-sec.org/assets/responsive_filemanager/source/List_of_Activities/List%20of%20Activities%202017-2018.pdf, May 17, 2020.

[3]　SAARC, "Secretary General", http://saarc-sec.org/news/detail_front/secretary-general-of-saarc-addressed-the-inaugural-session-of-the-regional-consultation-on-fish-culture-in-cages-and-pens-in-reservoirs-lakes-rivers-and-marine-waters-for-aquaculture-diversification-in-south-asia-in-pokhara, May 17, 2020.

重之岛国，具有得天独厚的海洋资源，占据绝佳的航道位置，必然会在今后的发展中与以推动蓝色海洋经济增长为目标的南盟各国建立更多的合作，这既符合该地区的发展大势，也符合斯里兰卡本国的国家利益。

2. 南亚环境合作计划

1980 年 3 月，联合国南亚国家环境规划署（United Nations Environment Programme of the South Asian Countries）在其组织的一次政府间专家小组会议上，一致通过了建立一个致力于保护和管理环境的次区域组织的建议，并达成了推进本地区国家在环境领域互助互惠的共识。这即为南亚环境合作计划（SACEP）的由来。早在 1981 年，斯里兰卡就通过了《科伦坡宣言》（Colombo Declaration），按下了南亚环境合作计划的启动键，成为该计划最早的成员之一。1982 年，南亚环境合作计划由斯里兰卡、印度、巴基斯坦、孟加拉国、不丹、马尔代夫六国正式组建成立，成为南亚地区第一个政府间的环境合作机制。

斯里兰卡在南亚环境合作计划框架下参与实施了多项积极举措以践行该组织宗旨。1984 年，南亚环境合作计划的国家联络点会议在泰国曼谷举行。在该次会议中，区域内的五个海洋国家斯里兰卡、印度、巴基斯坦、孟加拉国和马尔代夫一致同意应当采取实际行动促进南亚海洋地区环境保护事业的发展，并制订了一项保护和管理南亚海洋环境的行动计划。1989 年 11 月至 12 月，南亚环境合作计划在泰国曼谷和联合国环境署、国际海事组织成立了关于南亚海洋污染紧急行动的讲习班（UNEP／IMO Workshop on South Asia Marine Pollution Emergency Action），该讲习班旨在培训有能力应对突发海洋环境事故的人员，并建立相关的应急机制。1991 年 6 月 10 日至 14 日，斯里兰卡作为东道主，在科伦坡和南亚环境合作计划共同举办了南亚地区沿海资源管理规划研讨会（Workshop on Coastal Resources Management Planning in SACEP Region），集中讨论了南亚国家对于沿海资源的有效利用和合理规划相关问题。作为 1991 年研讨会的后续，1993 年 12 月 20 日至 23 日，斯里兰卡在科伦坡与南亚环境合作计划、联合国环境署、联合国亚太经济社会委员会（U. N. Economic and Social Commission for Asia and the Pacific）共同举办关于保护南亚海洋区域沿海和海洋环境的管理策略讲习班，促进了海洋环境领域研究的交流。此后，斯里兰卡和南亚环境合作计划多次在科伦坡举行关于海洋环境、海洋资源以及海洋生物保护的讲习班，加强了对南亚地区海洋发展的保障。

1999 年 12 月至 2000 年，审议南亚区域溢油应急计划草案（Draft South Asian Regional Oil Spill Contingency Plan）的第一次高级官员会议和第二次高级官员会议在斯里兰卡陆续举行。两次会议所审议的草案成为南亚地区处理紧急溢油事件的指导性文件。此后数年，斯里兰卡还承办了南亚环境合作协会规划下的多项培训活动。如2014年，包括南亚沿海和海洋系统养分污染范围研究（Scoping Study of Nutrient Pollution on the Coastal and Marine Systems of South Asia）在内的一系列研究活动相继在斯里兰卡科伦坡举行。这些研究活动的举办确立了斯里兰卡在南亚环境合作协会海洋国家中不可或缺的地位，也有力地带动了其本国海洋研究的发展与进步。[1]

3.《亚洲地区反海盗及武装劫船合作协定》

斯里兰卡是《亚洲地区反海盗及武装劫船合作协定》（以下简称《反海盗合作协定》）的14个亚洲缔约国家之一。该区域合作协定以加强亚洲地区打击海盗与武装抢劫船舶为宗旨，与国际海事组织、国际刑事警察组织（ICPO）、亚洲船东协会（ASA）、波罗的海国际海运理事会（BIMCO）、石油公司国际海事论坛（OCIMF）、世界海事大学（WMU）等多个国际性组织保持积极合作。根据《反海盗合作协定》的愿景，协定缔约方在《反海盗合作协定》框架下建成亚洲打击海盗及持械抢劫船只的资讯中心，以减少此类活动对于亚太区域各航道船只正常航行的威胁。当前，《反海盗合作协定》已通过位于新加坡的信息交流中心（Information Sharing Center），加强了区域内国家的海盗信息共享、打击海盗能力的建设和紧急情况的合作安排。通过加入《反海盗合作协定》，斯里兰卡进一步保障了其位于印度洋东西航线"十字路口"的航运利益，不仅有效抑制了猖獗的海盗活动，更有利于与协定内其他国家进行信息交流，共同保障本地区的海上安全。[2]

4. 环印度洋联盟

环印度洋联盟（IORA）是在南非前领导人纳尔逊·曼德拉（Nelson Mandela）倡议下于1997年建立的区域性政府间合作组织。该组织依托印度洋的地理环境与资源基础，意在促进印度洋区域内各国家经济的持续增长，同时使海洋环境得到平衡保护。当前，环印度洋联盟聚焦于六个优先领域和两个重点领域。六个优先领域分别是：海上安全与安保、贸易和投资便利化、渔业管理、灾害风险管理、旅游文化交流以及学术、科学和技术；两个重点领域分别是：蓝色海洋经济和女性的经济自主。[3]

1997年，斯里兰卡作为参加了环印度洋联盟第一次部长级会议的14个国家之一，成为该组织发展的主要奠基者。2013年，环印度洋联盟在澳大利亚珀斯（Perth）发布了关于《和平、高效和可持续利用印度洋及其资源的原

---

〔1〕　SACEP, "Milestones", http：//sacep. org/milestones, May 17, 2020.
〔2〕　SACEP, "About", http：//www. sacep. org/programmes/south-asian-seas/about, May 17, 2020.
〔3〕　IORA, "About IORA", https：//www. iora. int/en/about/about-iora, May 17, 2020.

则》（Principles For Peaceful Productive And Sustainable Use Of The Indian Ocean And Its Resources）的第一份部长级宣言。2014 年，包括斯里兰卡在内的环印度洋联盟各成员国在澳大利亚珀斯签署了《搜救合作谅解备忘录》（Memorandum of Understanding on Search and Rescue Cooperation），以实现印度洋上各成员国之间搜寻与救援活动的通力合作。2018 年 9 月，环印度洋联盟在斯里兰卡科伦坡举办了海上安全和保安工作组的启动研讨会。该研讨会的举办进一步促进了印度洋沿岸国家有关海上安全信息的必要交流与合作。2019 年，在孟加拉国首都达卡举行的第三届环印度洋联盟蓝色经济部长级会议（BEC-Ⅲ）上，斯里兰卡与环印度洋联盟各成员方达成了积极促进本地区可持续蓝色经济发展的共识，各方都将在充分利用印度洋自然资源和海洋环境的基础之上，履行相应的克制和保护义务。环印度洋联盟还为包括斯里兰卡在内的各成员国进行了一系列符合其组织宗旨的培训，如 2019 年举行的"促进海上互联互通的印度洋港口和航运业可持续性发展培训"（Sustainable Development for Ports and Shipping in the Indian Ocean for Maritime Connectivity）等。这一系列培训有效地促进了本区域海洋合作机制的发展[1]

5. 环孟加拉湾多领域经济技术合作倡议

斯里兰卡与印度、孟加拉国同为环孟加拉湾多领域经济技术合作倡议（BIMSTEC）的发起国之一。作为孟加拉湾区域的团体，该合作倡议成为连接南盟和东盟的桥梁，对于两者之间的合作交流起到了关键的作用。该组织的目的在于，利用区域的固有资源和团体整合优势，基于各成员国在不同领域的目标，经由相互合作来鼓励信息共享、加速经济增长，主要合作领域包括公共卫生、渔业、海洋环境管理等[2]

2019 年 11 月 7 日至 8 日，第一届环孟加拉湾多领域经济技术合作倡议港口会议在印度举行，包括斯里兰卡在内的各成员国参加了会议。该次会议旨在为成员国之间的海事互动提供一个便利的合作平台，使以港口为主导的互联互通倡议成为各成员国之间进行资源共享的最佳实践[3] 2019 年 11 月 20 日至 22 日，斯里兰卡参与了环孟加拉湾多领域经济技术合作倡议在印度古鲁格（Gurugram）的印度洋信息融合中心（Information Fusion Centre-Indian Ocean region）举行的国家沿海安全研讨会。该研讨会旨在提供一个论坛，分享保障沿海安全的专业知识和经验，引导各成员国对于海事领域安全的关

〔1〕 IORA，"Milestones"，https：//www. iora. int/en/about/milestones，May 17，2020.
〔2〕 BIMSTEC，"About BIMSTEC"，https：//bimstec. org/? page_ id＝189，May 17，2020.
〔3〕 BIMSTEC，"BIMSTEC Ports Conclave"，https：//bimstec. org/? event＝bimstec-ports-conclave，May 17，2020.

注，尝试形成有益合力。[1]

（六）全球性国际组织框架下的合作

斯里兰卡于 1972 年加入国际海事组织，努力贯彻其"在干净的海洋上安全、可靠和高效地运输"的宗旨，并积极配合其下设的海上安全委员会、海洋环境保护委员会、法律委员会、技术合作委员会等职能机构的相关工作。

斯里兰卡在国际海事组织框架下批准了 20 余项国际条约。如，《1965 年便利国际海上运输公约》《1974 年国际海上人命安全公约》《1972 年国际海上避碰规则公约》《关于 1973 年国际防止船舶造成污染公约的 1978 年议定书》；等等。

2015 年 11 月 2 日至 6 日，斯里兰卡与国际海事组织、南亚环境合作计划进行了在"加强南亚环境合作计划地区（斯里兰卡、孟加拉国、印度、马尔代夫和巴基斯坦）海洋污染防范和响应的区域合作机制"（Enhancing Regional Cooperatio Mechanisms on Marine Pollution Preparedness and Response in the SACEP Region-Bangladesh, India, Maldives, Pakistan and Sri Lanka）下的区域性演习，以测试该区域应急计划的操作规程，从而确定其在现实情境下效果的可能差距。各参与方在演习后就本次区域演习成果举行了专门研讨会，以促进参演国家间有关各演习环节的收获与信息的交流，增强该区域日后处理类似问题的应变能力。作为国际海事组织的成员国，斯里兰卡在船舶管理、海上航行安全、海洋污染防治等多方面都获得了与组织内其他成员方合作的较顺畅通道，也共同为推进国际海事事务的发展作出贡献。[2]

---

〔1〕　BIMSTEC，"Workshop"，https：//bimstec. org/？ event = coastal-security-workshop-for-bimstec-countries，May 17，2020.

〔2〕　International Maritime Organization，"Status of IMO Treaties"，https：//wwwcdn. imo. org/localre-sources/en/About/Conventions/StatusOfConventions/Status% 20-% 202021. pdf，January　23，2021.

七、对中国海洋法主张的态度

（一）对"南海仲裁案"的态度

2013 年 4 月，为"南海仲裁案"组建仲裁庭之时，国际海洋法法庭时任日籍庭长柳井俊二最初任命斯里兰卡籍资深外交官平托出任庭长。平托因夫人系菲律宾籍而特地征询争端双方的意见，并得到菲方的首肯。但在随后的仲裁程序中，由于平托流露出仲裁庭对本案无管辖权的裁决倾向，美国、日本及菲律宾均表示出严重担忧，菲律宾遂貌似公正地向仲裁庭提出撤换平托的要求。是年 5 月，平托被迫辞职。[1]

2016 年 7 月，中国外交部长王毅在科伦坡与斯里兰卡外长萨马拉维拉（Mangala Samaraweera）举行会谈时，介绍了中国在南海问题上的立场，强调中方坚持通过对话谈判和平解决争议。中国根据国际法所承认的合法权利，不接受、不参与菲律宾单方面提起的所谓"南海仲裁案"，不承认、不执行所谓仲裁裁决。萨马拉维拉则表示，斯里兰卡理解并赞赏中方的有关立场，支持直接当事方根据国际法和国际惯例，通过对话协商解决有关争议，维护南海地区的和平与稳定。[2]

（二）在"一带一路"框架下与中国合作的态度

斯里兰卡是古代海上丝绸之路的重要节点，"一带一路"倡议自提出以来，便得到了斯里兰卡的坚定支持。以科伦坡港口城、汉班托塔港等重大项目建设为龙头，中国企业参与了在斯里兰卡的大批基础设施建设项目，斯中经济合作不断深化。[3]

2014 年 11 月，斯里兰卡外交部下属智库卡迪加马国际关系与战略研究

---

〔1〕《驻马来西亚大使黄惠康在马来西亚〈东方日报〉和〈星报〉发表署名文章〈公道自在人心〉》，载中华人民共和国外交部网站，https：//www. fmprc. gov. cn/web/gjhdq_ 676201/gj_ 676203/yz_ 676205/1206_ 676716/1206x2_ 676736/t1383086. shtml，最后访问日期：2020 年 4 月 12 日。

〔2〕《斯里兰卡理解并支持中方在南海问题上的立场》，载中华人民共和国外交部网站，https：//www. fmprc. gov. cn/web/gjhdq_ 676201/gj_ 676203/yz_ 676205/1206_ 676884/xgxw_ 676890/t1378891. shtml，最后访问日期：2020 年 4 月 12 日。

〔3〕徐惠喜：《"一带一路"释放中国与南亚合作潜力》，载《经济日报》2017 年 6 月 22 日，第 9 版。

院与中国驻斯里兰卡大使馆合作举办"21 世纪海上丝绸之路研讨会"。斯里兰卡中央银行行长，外交部、学术界、商界知名人士等近 150 人参加。斯里兰卡中央银行行长表示，"21 世纪海上丝绸之路"倡议与斯里兰卡打造海运、贸易、能源、航空、知识"五大中心"战略十分契合，斯方愿与中方加强合作，推进"21 世纪海上丝绸之路"建设。[1]

2016 年 7 月，斯里兰卡总理在科伦坡会见中国外交部长王毅时表示，"21 世纪海上丝绸之路"是中方提出的重要倡议，斯里兰卡愿发挥印度洋枢纽的位置优势，同中方共建海上丝绸之路，全面提升两国务实合作水平。王毅表示，斯里兰卡具有突出区位优势，能够连接亚非，辐射南亚次大陆。中方愿同斯方一道，抓住当前重要机遇，沿着共建"21 世纪海上丝绸之路"的方向，进一步发掘中斯两国合作潜力，带动双方各领域务实合作再上新台阶，推动中斯战略合作伙伴关系持续发展。[2]

2017 年 5 月，斯里兰卡积极参加首届"一带一路"国际合作高峰论坛，与中国及多个国家在"一带一路"建设框架下达成五项新的合作，具体包括：第一，中国政府与斯里兰卡政府签署了经贸合作协议；第二，中国政府与斯里兰卡政府签署了关于促进投资与经济合作框架协议；第三，中国商务部与斯里兰卡发展战略与国际贸易部签署了投资与经济技术合作发展中长期规划纲要；第四，中国国家开发银行与斯里兰卡等国的有关机构签署了港口、电力、工业园区等领域基础设施融资合作协议；第五，中国出口信用保险公司同斯里兰卡等国的同业机构签署了合作协议。[3]

2018 年 10 月，由斯里兰卡—中国社会文化合作协会、中国人民对外友好协会联合主办的庆祝"一带一路"五周年友好论坛在斯里兰卡首都科伦坡开幕。斯里兰卡议长作为开幕式主宾在讲话中祝贺"一带一路"倡议迎来五周年。他表示，斯中友好关系历久弥新，斯里兰卡自古就是海上丝绸之路上的枢纽国家。目前，斯中两国在"一带一路"建设中开展多领域合作，希望

---

〔1〕《驻斯里兰卡大使吴江浩出席斯知名智库举办的"21 世纪海上丝绸之路"研讨会》，载中华人民共和国外交部网站，https：//www. fmprc. gov. cn/web/zwbd_ 673032/gzhd_ 673042/t1208897. shtml，最后访问日期：2020 年 4 月 26 日。

〔2〕《斯里兰卡总理希望斯中共建海上丝路》，载中华人民共和国外交部网站，https：//www. fmprc. gov. cn/web/zyxw/t1378903. shtml，最后访问日期：2020 年 4 月 26 日。

〔3〕《"一带一路"国际合作高峰论坛成果清单》，载中国政府网，http：//www. gov. cn/xinwen/2017-05/16/content_ 5194255. htm? gs_ ws＝tsina_ 6363053 23348716746，最后访问日期：2020 年 3 月 1 日。

未来斯中合作能够更好地惠及两国民众。[1]

2019 年 4 月，斯里兰卡出席了第二届"一带一路"国际合作高峰论坛并与中国及多个国家和国际组织等达成六项新的合作协议，具体包括：第一，中国农业农村部与斯里兰卡、巴基斯坦和孟加拉国等国的农业部门共同发布《促进"一带一路"合作 共同推动建立农药产品质量标准的合作意向声明》；第二，中国商务部与联合国开发计划署签署了在斯里兰卡的可再生能源三方合作项目协议；第三，中国与包括斯里兰卡、新加坡等在内的 13 个国家的 33 个来自交通部门、海关部门、重要港口企业、港务管理局和码头运营商的代表共同成立了"海上丝绸之路"港口合作机制并发布了《海丝港口合作宁波倡议》；第四，中国科学院与联合国教科文组织、斯里兰卡佩拉德尼亚大学、比利时皇家海外科学院、巴基斯坦科学院、俄罗斯科学院、欧洲科学与艺术院等 37 家共建"一带一路"国家的科研机构和国际组织发起成立"一带一路"国际科学组织联盟；第五，中国美术馆与包括斯里兰卡、俄罗斯、希腊、孟加拉国、匈牙利、土耳其、波兰等在内的 18 个国家的 21 家美术馆和重点美术机构共同成立了丝绸之路国际美术馆联盟；第六，中国国家开发银行与斯里兰卡人民银行签署了融资合作协议。[2]

2019 年 7 月，中国驻斯里兰卡大使与斯里兰卡总理举行中斯"一带一路"重大项目工作会谈，就科伦坡港口城、汉班托塔港和中部高速公路第一标段等项目最新进展和尚待解决的问题进行了深入的探讨磋商。双方充分肯定斯中"一带一路"重大项目取得的积极进展，积极评价有关项目的经济效益和社会效益，同意携手落实好两国领导人的重要共识，共同努力推动科伦坡港口城、汉班托塔港的立法工作以及中部高速公路的前期准备工作，更好更快地造福两国和两国人民。[3]

2020 年 2 月，斯里兰卡总统、总理等政要出席仪式，庆祝"一带一路"建设项目——斯里兰卡南部高速公路延长线全线通车。在 2020 年 1 月下旬斯里兰卡国内报告首例新冠肺炎确诊病例后，其国内疫情一度给原定于 2020 年

---

[1]《庆祝一带一路五周年友好论坛在斯里兰卡举行》，载中华人民共和国商务部网站，http://fec. mofcom. gov. cn/article/fwydyl/zgzx/201810/2018 1002799319. shtml，最后访问日期：2020 年 4 月 26 日。

[2]《第二届"一带一路"国际合作高峰论坛成果清单》，载中华人民共和国外交部网站，https://www. fmprc. gov. cn/web/ziliao_ 674904/zt_ 674979/dnzt_ 674981/qtzt/ydyl_ 675049/zyxw_ 675051/t1658760. shtml，最后访问日期：2020 年 3 月 1 日。

[3]《程学源大使与斯里兰卡总理维克拉马辛哈举行中斯"一带一路"重大项目工作会谈》，载中华人民共和国商务部网站，http://lk. mofcom. gov. cn/article/jmxw/201907/2019070288603 3. shtml，最后访问日期：2020 年 4 月 26 日。

2 月底前完工的项目收尾工程带来不小挑战。项目方及时邀请公共卫生专员介绍防疫知识，联系医疗机构为员工体检，打消员工疑虑并做好防范。对此，斯里兰卡公路发展局官员表示："中国企业克服了新冠病毒带来的不利影响，展现出强大的动员能力。"[1]

值得注意的是，"中巴经济走廊"和"孟中印缅经济走廊"是"一带一路"在南亚的旗舰项目，作为南亚岛国的斯里兰卡却并非这两大项目的成员国。然而，这丝毫不能否定斯里兰卡大力支持"一带一路"倡议的态度，更没有影响斯里兰卡大力参与"一带一路"建设的热情。可以预见，未来斯中两国在"一带一路"框架下还将进一步开展更为密切的合作。

---

〔1〕　张继业等：《疫情面前，"一带一路"朋友圈这里最暖》，载中华人民共和国商务部对外投资和经济合作司官网，http://fec. mofcom. gov. cn/article/fwydyl/zgzx/202003/20200302945428. shtml，最后访问日期：2020 年 4 月 26 日。

结　语

　　斯里兰卡由海而生、以海为伴。特殊的地理位置不仅使海洋对国家的影响体现在经济、政治和文化的方方面面，也让其海洋法律体系具有鲜明的"岛国"特色。无论是海洋专门机构的设置，还是海洋相关的法律体系充实与规则完善，无论是海洋领域条约体系的参与，抑或是国家间海洋争端的解决，斯里兰卡都表现出不输域内其他海洋国家的热情，甚至在通过协议解决海洋争端的态度与成效等方面表现出更大的诚意与努力。同时，由于"岛国"的地理位置和国内经济建设的需要，斯里兰卡的国际海洋合作也以海洋防务合作和海洋渔业合作为主。基于本国的实力与愿景，斯里兰卡对中国的涉海涉边事务并无过多参与；而基于自身的发展所需，斯里兰卡对"一带一路"倡议又展现出前所未有的投入与期待。可以认为，支持"一带一路"是斯里兰卡基于本国现实国情和利益需要所作出的必然选择，也将成为斯里兰卡国家海洋战略规划的重要内容与方向。

参考文献

一、中文文献

1. 刘兴武编著：《斯里兰卡》，上海辞书出版社 1984 年版。

2. 张汝德主编：《当代孟加拉国》，四川人民出版社 1999 年版。

3. 何道隆主编：《当代斯里兰卡》，四川人民出版社 2000 年版。

4. 厉以宁、王武龙主编：《中国企业投资分析报告》，经济科学出版社 2006 年版。

5. 时光慧、祁艺主编：《中国石油天然气集团公司发展概况》，中华人民共和国年鉴社 2017 年版。

6. 黄素奕、林一歆：《能源与节能技术》（第三版），中国电力出版社 2016 年版。

7. 赵长生：《法律体系的哲学思考》，载《法学》1991 年第 6 卷。

8. 李征：《〈米胶协定〉签订的前前后后——纪念〈米胶协定〉签订 51 周年》，载《中国经贸》2004 年第 2 期。

9. 易传剑：《我国海洋法律体系的重构——以海权为中心》，载《广东海洋大学学报》2010 年第 2 期。

10. 汤喆峰、司玉琢：《论中国海法体系及其建构》，载《中国海商法研究》2013 年第 3 期。

11. 张湘兰、叶泉：《建设海洋强国的法律保障：中国海洋法体系的完善》，载《武大国际法评论》2013 年第 1 期。

12. 初北平、曹兴国：《海法概念的国际认同》，载《中国海商法研究》2015 年第 3 卷。

13. 曹兴国、初北平：《我国涉海法律的体系化完善路径》，载《太平洋学报》2016 年第 9 卷。

14. 贺鉴、王璐：《海上安全：上海合作组织合作的新领域》，载《国际问题研究》2018 年第 3 期。

15. ［孟］基肖尔·库梅尔·班萨克等：《孟加拉国视角下的"一带一路"及孟中印缅经济走廊建设》，载《南亚东南亚研究》2018 年第 3 期。

16. 刘耀辉、简天天：《1948 年以来斯里兰卡外交政策的演变》，载《东南亚南亚研究》2018 年第 1 期。

17. 张晓东：《米胶协定——新中国首次与非建交国家的贸易实践》，载《档案春秋》2020 第 3 期。

18. 邱华盛等：《建设"中斯科教合作中心"推进"一带一路"战略》，载《中国科学院院刊》2015 年第 3 期。

19. 赵宁、高悦：《中斯海洋领域合作联委会一次会议召开》，载《中国海洋报》2013 年 8 月 27 日，第 A1 版。

20. 徐惠喜：《"一带一路"释放中国与南亚合作潜力》，载《经济日报》2017 年 6 月 22 日，第 9 版。

二、外文文献

1. Richard F. Nyrop et al. , *Area Handbook for the Persian Gulf States*, Cabin John, Wildside Press, 2008.

2. Rizwan Hussain, *Pakistan and the Emergence of Islamic Militancy in Afghanistan*, Aldershot, Hampshire：Ashgate, 2005.

3. Syed Farooq Hasnat, *Global Security Watch：Pakistan*, California, ABC-CLIO, 2011.

4. Pirouz Mojtahed-Zadeh and BahadorZarei, "Maritime Boundary Delimitations in the Persian Gulf", *International Studies Journal* 54, 2017.

5. Yoshifumi Tanaka, *Predictability and Flexibility in the Law of Maritime Delimitation*（*Second Edition*）, Oxford, Hart Publishing, 2019.

6. M. Hassan Shetol et al. , "Present Status of Bangladesh Gas Fields and Future Development：A Review", *Journal of Natural Gas Geoscience* 6, 2019.

三、数据库和网站

（一）中文数据库和网站

1. 中华人民共和国条约数据库，http：//treaty. mfa. gov. cn。

2. 中华人民共和国外交部网站，https：//www. fmprc. gov. cn。

3. 中华人民共和国驻塞尔维亚共和国大使馆网站，http：//rs. chineseembassy. org。

4. 中华人民共和国驻孟加拉人民共和国大使馆经济商务处网站，http：//bd. mofcom. gov. cn。

5. 中华人民共和国驻斯里兰卡大使馆经济商务处网站，http：//lk. mofcom. gov. cn。

6. 中华人民共和国商务部网站，http：//www. mofcom. gov. cn。

7. 中华人民共和国商务部对外投资和经济合作司网站，http：//fec. mofcom. gov. cn。

8. 中华人民共和国商务部亚洲司网站，http：//template1. mofcom. gov. cn。

9. 中华人民共和国商务部中国企业境外商务投诉服务中心网站，http：//shangwutousu. mofcom. gov. cn。

10. 中华人民共和国农业农村部渔业渔政管理局网站，http：//www. yyj. moa. gov. cn。

11. 中国政府网，http：//www. gov. cn。

12. 中共中央对外联络部网站，https：//www. idcpc. gov. cn。

13. 中国地质调查局网站，https：//www. cgs. gov. cn/。

14. 中国一带一路网，https：//www. yidaiyilu. gov. cn。

15. 新华网，http：//www. xinhuanet. com/。

16. 新华财经网，http：//world. xinhua08. com/。

17. 人民网时政频道，http：//politics. people. com. cn/。

18. 人民网国际频道，http：//world. people. com. cn/。

19. 环球网国际新闻频道，http：//world. huanqiu. com/。

20. 环球网国内新闻频道，https：//china. huanqiu. com/。

21. 环球网军事频道，https：//mil. huanqiu. com/。

22. 腾讯新闻网，https：//news. qq. com/。

23. 搜狐网，http：//www. sohu. com/。

24. 中国网，http：//www. china. com. cn/。

25. 央广网，http：//www. cnr. cn/。

26. 新浪新闻网，http：//news. sina. com. cn/。

27. 新浪军事网，http：//mil. news. sina. com. cn/。

28. 中国新闻网，http：//www. chinanews. com/。

29. 观察者网，https：//www. guancha. cn/。

30. 中国自然资源部第二海洋研究所网站，http：//www. sio. org. cn/。

31. 中国自然资源部第三海洋研究所网站，http：//www. tio. org. cn/。

32. 中国水产科学研究院网站，http：//www. cafs. ac. cn/。

33. 中国水产科学研究院珠江水产研究所网站，https：//www. prfri. ac. cn/。

34. 中国水产科学研究院黄海水产研究所网站，http：//www. ysfri. ac. cn/。

35. 中国南海研究院网站，http：//www. nanhai. org. cn/。

36. 青岛海洋科学与技术试点国家实验室网站，http：//www. qnlm. ac/。

37. 中国水产养殖网，http：//www. shuichan. cc/。

38. 国际船舶网，http：//www. eworldship. com/。

39. 中国船贸网站，http：//www. csoc. cn/。

40. 上海海事大学网站，https：//immse. shmtu. edu. cn/。

41. 中国科学院网站，http：//www. cas. cn/。

42. 中国法学网，http：//iolaw. cssn. cn/。

43. 中国教育在线网，https：//www. eol. cn/。

44. 新丝路网，http：//www. me360. com/。

45. 国防信息网，http：//www. dsti. net/。

46. 国际在线网，http：//news. cri. cn/。

47. 亚太日报网站，https：//cn. apdnews. com/。

48. 印度世界广播网，http：//airworldservice. org/。

49. 石油圈网，http：//www. oilsns. com/。

50. 海峡风，http：//www. fishexpo. cn/。

51. 腾氏水产网，http：//www. tensfish. com/。

（二）外文数据库和网站

1. Oceans & Law of The Sea（United Nations），https：//www. un. org/Depts/los/index. htm.

2. UN Treaty Collection，https：//treaties. un. org/.

3. International Seabed Authority，https：//www. isa. org. jm/.

4. International Maritime Organization，http：//www. imo. org/.

5. World Bank，https：//databank. worldbank. org/.

6. International Whale Comission，https：//iwc. int/home.

7. Commission for the Conservation of Antarctic Marine Living Resources，https：//www. ccamlr. org/.

8. Global Ocean Data Assimilation Experiment，https：//www. godae. org/.

9. International Collective in Support of Fishworkers，https：//indianlegal. icsf. net/.

10. Indian Ocean Tuna Commission，https：//www. iotc. org/.

11. The Network of Aquaculture Centres in Asia and the Pacific，https：//enaca. org/.

12. ECOLEX，https：//www. ecolex. org/.

13. The Indian Rim Association，https：//www. iora. int/.

14. Bay of Bengal Initiative for Multi-Sectoral Technical and Economic Cooperation，https：//bimstec. org/.

15. ReCAAP, http：//www. recaap. org/.

16. Globe Environment Facility, https：//www. thegef. org/.

17. FAO, http：//www. fao. org/home/en/.

18. United Nations University, http：//archive. unu. edu/.

19. UNESCO, http：//www. unesco. org/.

20. InfoFish, http：//infofish. org/.

21. Asian Infrastructure Investment Bank, https：//www. aiib. org/en/index. html.

22. The Commonwealth, https：//thecommonwealth. org/.

23. International Union for Conservation of Nature, https：//www. iucn. org/.

24. IRAM, https：//iramcenter. org/.

25. SAARC, https：//www. saarc-sec. org/.

26. SACEP, http：//sacep. org/.

27. IEA, https：//www. iea. org/.

28. Permanent Court of Arbitration, https：//pca-cpa. org/.

29. Convention on the Conservation of Migratory Species of Wild Animals, https：//www. cms. int/.

30. Department of Government Information of Sri Lanka, https：// www. dgi. gov. lk/.

31. Permanent Mission of The People's Republic of China to The United Nations Office at Geneva And Other International Organizations in Switzerland, http：//www. china-un. ch/.

32. Bangladesh Ministry of Foreign Affairs, https：//mofa. gov. bd/.

33. Bangladesh China Friendship Center, https：//bangladeshchina. org/.

34. Laws of Bangladesh, http：//bdlaws. minlaw. gov. bd/.

35. Bangladesh Parliament, https：//www. parliament. gov. bd/.

36. Banglapedia, http：//en. banglapedia. org/.

37. Bangladesh Minstry of Fisheries and Livestock, https：//mofl. gov. bd/.

38. Department of Fisheries of Bangladesh, http：//fisheries. gov. bd/.

39. Bangladesh Mistry of Shipping, https：//mos. gov. bd/.

40. Bangladesh Department of Shipping, http：//dos. gov. bd/.

41. Bangladesh Shipping Corporation, http：//bsc. portal. gov. bd/.

42. Bangladesh Marine Academy, http：//macademy. gov. bd/.

43. Bangladesh National Marine Institute, http：//www. nmi. gov. bd/.

44. Directorate of Seamen & Emigration Welfare, https：//dsw. gov. bd/.

45. Bangladesh Code, http：//bdcode. gov. bd/.

46. Bangladesh Minsty of Power, Energy and Mineral Resource, https：//mpemr. gov. bd/.

47. Bangladesh Energy and Mineral Resource Division, https：//emrd. gov. bd/.

48. Banglades Oil Gas and Mineral Corporation, http：//www. petrobangla. org. bd/.

49. The Ministry of Water Resources of Banglades, https：//mowr. gov. bd/.

50. Water Resource Planning Organization of Banglades, http：//www. warpo. gov. bd.

51. Ministry of Civil Aviation and Tourism of Banglades, https：//mocat. gov. bd/.

52. Bangladesh Tourism Board, http：//tourismboard. gov. bd/.

53. Department of Environment of Banglades, http：//www. doe. gov. bd/.

54. Ministry of Defence of Banglades, https：//mod. gov. bd/.

55. Bangladesh Navy, https：//www. navy. mil. bd/.

56. Bangladesh Coast Guard, http：//coastguard. gov. bd/.

57. Durham University, https：//www. dur. ac. uk/.

58. American Society of International Law, https：//www. asil. org/.

59. DhakaTribune, https：//www. dhakatribune. com/.

60. U. S. Embassy in Bangladesh, https：//bd. usembassy. gov/u-s-ambassador-visits-sylhet/.

61. Naval Technology, https：//www. naval-technology. com/.

62. Langkawi-Insight, https：//www. langkawi-insight. com/.

63. CDC Group Plc, https：//www. cdcgroup. com/.

64. World Fish, https：//www. worldfishcenter. org/.

65. Philippines Department of Foreign Affairs, https：//www. dfa. gov. ph/.

66. Government of Sri Lanka, https：//www. gov. lk/.

67. Parliament of Sri Lanka, https：//www. parliament. lk/.

68. President of SriLanka, https：//www. president. gov. lk/.

69. Office of the Cabinet of Ministers of SriLanka, http：//www. cabinetoffice. gov. lk/.

70. Mistry of Fisheries of Sri Lanka, https：//www. fisheries. gov. lk/.

71. Ministry of Power, Energy and Business Development, http：//power-

min. gov. lk/.

72. Judicial Service Commission Secretariat, http：//www. jsc. gov. lk/.

73. Hierarchy Structure, https：//www. hierarchystructure. com/.

74. Ministry of Fisheries and Aquatic Resources, https : //www. fisheries. gov. lk/.

75. Department of Fisheries & Aquatic Resources, https：//www. fisheries-dept. gov. lk/.

76. National Aquatic Resources Research and Development Agency, http：//www. nara. ac. lk/.

77. National Aquaculture Development Authority, http：//www. naqda. gov. lk/about-us/.

78. Ceylon Fisheries Corporation, http：//www. cfc. gov. lk.

79. Lloyds Register, https：//www. lr. org/en/.

80. Cey-Nor Foundation Limited, http：//ceynor. gov. lk/.

81. Sri Lanka Sustainable Energy Authority, http：//www. energy. gov. lk/.

82. Ministry of Petroleum Resources Development, https：//www. petroleum-min. gov. lk/.

83. Petroleum Resources Development Secretariat, http：//www. prds-srilan-ka. com/.

84. Coastal Conservation & Coastal Resources Management Department, http：//www. coastal. gov. lk/.

85. Ministury of Ports &Shipping, http：//portcom. slpa. lk/.

86. Merchant Shipping Secretariat, http：//www. dgshipping. gov. lk/.

87. Ceylon Shipping Corporation Ltd, http：//www. cscl. lk/.

88. Port Authority, https：//www. slpa. lk/.

89. Department of Meteorology, http：//meteo. gov. lk/.

90. Ministry of Cultural and Art Affairs, https：//www. cultural. gov. lk/.

91. Central Cultural Fund, http：//www. ccf. gov. lk/.

92. Foreign Ministry of Sri Lanka, https：//www. mfa. gov. lk/.

93. Sri Lanka Coast Guard, "Overview", http：//www. coastguard. gov. lk/.

94. Sri Lanka Navy, "History", https：//www. navy. lk/.

95. RaknaArakshaka Lanka Limited, http：//rallsecurity. lk/.

96. Lawnet, "Navy", https：//www. lawnet. gov. lk/.

97. Department of Government Printing of Sri Lanka, http：//documents.

gov. lk/.

    98. Colombo Gazette, https：//colombogazette. com/.

    99. Daily FT, http：//www. ft. lk/.

    100. The Lakshman Kadirgamar Institute, https：//lki. lk/.

    101. Colombo Page, http：//www. colombopage. com/.

    102. Ministry of Foreign Affairs of Japan, https：//www. mofa. go. jp/.

    103. Asian Mirror, http：//asianmirror. lk/.

    104. Ministry of Agriculture and Rural Development of Vietnam, https：//www. mard. gov. vn/.

    105. Royal Norwegian Embassy in Colombo, https：//www. norway. no/.

    106. Indian legal. icsf, https：//indianlegal. icsf. net/.

    107. Air World Service, http：//airworldservice. org/.

    108. Sputnik International, https：//sputniknews. com/.

    109. ADA Derana, http：//www. adaderana. lk/.

    110. Arabnews, https：//www. arabnews. com.

    111. Gulfnews, https：//gulfnews. com.

    112. Heinonline, https：//heinonline. org. .

    113. Voice Of Journalists, https：//www. voj. news.

    114. The Express Tribune, https：//tribune. com. pk.

    115. Pakchina News, http：//pakchinanews. pk.

    116. Dawn, https：//www. dawn. com.

    117. The Geopolitics, https：//thegeopolitics. com.

    118. Theindubusinessline, https：//www. thehindubusinessline. com/.

    119. Thefishsite, https：//thefishsite. com/.

    120. Voice of Journalists, https：//www. voj. news/.

    121. Navy Times, https：//www. navytimes. com/.

    122. JODC, https：//www. jodc. go. jp/.

    123. Pakobserver, https：//pakobserver. net/.

附　录

附录 1 孟加拉国《1974 年领水及海洋区域法》[1]

Territorial Waters and Maritime Zones Act, 1974

An act to provide for the declaration of the territorial waters and maritime zones.

Whereas clause (2) of Article 143 of the Constitution provides that Parliament may, from time to time, by law provide for the determination of the territorial waters and the continental shelf of Bangladesh;

And whereas it is necessary to provide for the declaration of the territorial waters, continental shelf and other maritime zones and for matter ancillary thereto;

It is hereby enacted as follows:

Short title

1. This Act may be called the Territorial Waters and Maritime Zones Act, 1974.

Definitions

2. In this Act, unless there is anything repugnant to the subject or context:

(a) "conservation zone" means a conservation zone established under section 6;

(b) "contiguous zone" means the zone of the high seas declared by section 4 to be the contiguous zone of Bangladesh;

(c) "continental shelf" means the continental shelf of Bangladesh referred to in section 7;

(d) "economic zone" means the zone of the high seas declared under section 5 to be the economic zone of Bangladesh;

(e) "territorial waters" means the limits of sea declared under section 3 to be the territorial waters of Bangladesh.

Territorial waters

3. (1) The Government may, by notification in the official Gazette, declare the limits of the sea beyond the land territory and internal waters of Bangladesh which shall be the territorial waters of Bangladesh specifying in the notification the baseline:

(a) from which such limits shall be measured; and

(b) the waters on the landward side of which shall form part of the internal waters of

---

[1] See Laws of Bangladesh, "The Territorial Waters and Maritime Zones Act, 1974", http: //bdlaws. minlaw. gov. bd/act-details-467. html, April 5, 2021.

Bangladesh.

(2) Where a single island, rock or a composite group thereof constituting the part of the territory of Bangladesh is situated seawards from the main coast or baseline, territorial waters shall extend to the limits declared by notification under sub-section (1) measured from the low waterline along the coast of such island, rock or composite group.

(3) The Sovereignty of the Republic extends to the territorial waters as well as to the air space over and the bed and subsoil of, such waters.

(4) No foreign ship shall, unless it enjoys the right of the innocent passage, pass through the territorial waters.

(5) Foreign ship having the right of innocent passage through the territorial waters shall, while exercising such right, observe the laws and rules in force in Bangladesh.

(6) The Government may, by notification in the official Gazette, suspend, in the specified areas of the territorial waters, the innocent passage of any ship if it is of opinion that such suspension is necessary for the security of the Republic.

(7) No foreign warship shall pass through the territorial waters except with the previous permission of the Government.

(8) The Government may take such steps as may be necessary:

(a) to prevent the passage through the territorial waters of any foreign ship having no right of innocent passage;

(b) to prevent and punish the contravention of any law or rule in force in Bangladesh by any foreign ship exercising the right of innocent passage;

(c) to prevent the passage of any foreign warship without previous permission of Government; and

(d) to prevent and punish any activity which is prejudicial to the security or interest of the Republic. Explanation-In this section "warship" includes any surface or sub-surface vessel or craft which is or may be used for the purpose of naval warfare.

Contiguous zone

4. (1) The zone of the high seas contiguous to the territorial waters and extending seawards to a line six nautical miles measured from the outer limits of the territorial waters is hereby declared to be the contiguous zone of Bangladesh.

(2) The Government may exercise such powers and take such measures in or in respect of the contiguous zone as it may consider necessary to prevent and punish the contravention of, and attempt to contravene, any law or regulation in force in Bangladesh relating to:

(a) the security of the Republic;

(b) the immigration and sanitation; and

(c) customs and other fiscal matters.

Economic zone

5. (1) The Government may, by notification in the official Gazette, declare any zone of the high seas adjacent to the territorial waters to be the economic zone of Bangladesh specifying therein the limits of such zone.

(2) All natural resources within the economic zone, both living and non-living, on or under the seabed and sub-soil or on the water surface or within the water column shall vest exclusively in the Republic.

(3) Nothing in sub-section (2) shall be deemed to affect fishing within the economic zone by a citizen of Bangladesh who uses for the purpose vessels which are are not mechanically propelled.

Conservation zone

6. The Government may, with a view to the maintenance of the productivity of the living resources of the sea, by notification in the official Gazette, establish conservation zones in such areas of the sea adjacent to the territorial waters as may be specified in the notification and may take such conservation measures in any zone so established as it may deem appropriate for the purpose including measures to protect the living resources of the sea from indiscriminate exploitation, depletion or destruction.

Continental shelf

7. (1) The continental shelf of Bangladesh comprises:

(a) the seabed and subsoil of the submarine areas adjacent to the coast of Bangladesh but beyond the limits of the territorial waters up to the outer limits of the continental margin bordering on the ocean basin or abyssal floor; and

(b) the seabed and subsoil of the analogous submarine areas adjacent to the coasts of any island, rock or any composite group thereof constituting part of the territory of Bangladesh.

(2) Subject to sub-section (1), the Government may, by notification in the official Gazette, specify the limits thereof.

(3) No person shall, except under and in accordance with the terms of, a licence or permission granted by Government explore or exploit any resources of the continental shelf or carry out any search or excavation or conduct any research within the limits of the continental shelf:

Provided that no such licence or permission shall be necessary for fishing by a citizen of Bangladesh who uses for the purpose vessels which are not mechanically propelled.

Explanation: Resources of the continental shelf include mineral and other non-living resources together with living organisms belonging to sedentary species, that is to say, organisms which at the harvestable stage, either are immobile on or under the seabed or are unable to move except in constant physical contact with the seabed or the subsoil.

(4) The Government may construct, maintain or operate within the continental shelf installations and other devices necessary for the exploration and exploitation of its resources.

Control of pollution

8. The Government may, with a view to preventing and controlling marine pollution and preserving the quality and ecological balance in the marine environment in the high seas adjacent to the territorial waters, take such measures as it may deem appropriate for the purpose.

Power to make rules

9. (1) The Government may makes rules for carrying out the purposes of this Act.

(2) In particular and without prejudice to the generality of the foregoing power, such rules may provide—

(a) for the regulation of the conduct of any person in or upon the territorial waters, contiguous zone, economic zone, conservation zone and continental shelf;

(b) for measures to protect, use and exploit the resources of the economic zone;

(c) for conservation measures to protect the living resources of the sea;

(d) for measures regulating the exploration and exploitation of resources within the continental shelf;

(e) for measures designed to prevent and control of marine pollution of the high seas.

(3) In making any rule under this section the Government may provide that a contravention of the rule shall be punishable with imprisonment which may extend to one year or with fine which may extend to five thousand takas.

附录 2 孟加拉国关于领海基线的《1974 年通告》[1]

Notification No. LT-I/3/74 of the Ministry of Foreign Affairs, Dacca, 13 April 1974

No. LT-I/3/74. In exercise of the powers conferred by sub-section (1) of section 3 of the Territorial Waters and Maritime Zones Act, 1974 (Act No. XXVI of 1974), and in supersession of any previous declaration on the subject, the Government is pleased to declare that the limits of the sea specified in paragraph 2 beyond the land territory and internal waters of Bangladesh shall be the territorial waters of Bangladesh.

2. The limits of the sea referred to in paragraph 1 shall be twelve nautical miles measured seaward and the baselines set out in paragraph 3 so that each point of the outer limit of the sea to the nearest point inward on the baselines is twelve nautical miles.

3. The baselines from which territorial waters shall be measured seaward are the straight lines linking successively the baseline points set out below:

Baseline Point   Geographical Co-ordinates Baseline Point

Baseline Point	Latitude	Longitude
No. 1	21° 12′00″N.	89° 06′45″E.
No. 2	21° 15′00″N.	89° 16′00″E.
No. 3	21° 29′00″N.	89° 36′00″E.
No. 4	21° 21′00″N.	89° 55′00″E.
No. 5	21° 11′00″N.	90° 33′00″E.
No. 6	21° 07′30″N.	91° 06′00″E.
No. 7	21° 10′00″N.	91° 56′00″E.
No. 8	20° 21′45″N.	92° 17′30″E.

...

No. LT-I/3/74. In exercise of the powers conferred by sub-section (1) of section 5 of the Territorial Waters and Maritime Zones Act, 1974 (Act No. XXVI of 1974), the Government is pleased to declare that the Zone of the high seas extending to 200 nautical miles measured from the baselines shall be the economic zone of Bangladesh.

---

[1] See UN Office of Legal Affairs, "Notification No. LT-I/3/74 of the Bangladesh Ministry of Foreign Affairs, Dacca, of 13 April 1974", https://www. un. org/Depts/los/LEGISLATION-ANDTREATIES/PDFFIL ES/BGD_ 1974_ Notification. pdf, March 20, 2021.

附录3 孟加拉国关于领海基线的《2015 年通告》[1]

বাংলাদেশ গেজেট

অতিরিক্ত সংখ্যা

কর্তৃপক্ষ কর্তৃক প্রকাশিত

মঙ্গলবার, নভেম্বর ১০, ২০১৫

Government of the People's Republic of Bangladesh

Ministry of Foreign Affairs

Notification

Date, 04 November, 2015

S.R.O. No. 328-Law/2015/MOFA/UNCLOS/113/2/15—In exercise of the powers conferred by sub-section (1) of section 3 and section 5 of the Territorial Waters and Maritime Zones Act, 1974 (Act No. XXVI of 1974), the Government is pleased to declare the Baseline, Territorial sea, and Exclusive Economic Zone of People's Republic of Bangladesh as follows,——

1. Baseline

(A) The list of geographical points described below shall be the baseline for the people's Republic of Bangladesh.

(B) This baseline consists of straight and normal baselines that join the outermost points of the lowest low water line, islands and reefs along the coast as marked on the large scale charts published or, as the case may be, notified from time to time by the Government of the People's Republic of Bangladesh.

---

[1] See Division for Ocean Affairs and The Law of The Sea Office of Legal Affairs, "S. R. O. No. 328-Law/2015/MOFA/UNCLOS/113/2/15, 4 November 2015", *The Law of the Sea Bulletins*, 90, United Nations, 2017, p. 46.

(C) The baseline from which the breadth of the Territorial Sea, Contiguous Zone, and Exclusive Economic Zone shall be measured seaward are the straight lines linking successively the baseline points 1 to 4 as shown below in the table :

TABLE

Baseline Points	Baseline Point identifier	Latitude in WGS84	Longitude in WGS84	Outer Limit
(1)	(2)	(3)	(4)	(5)
1.	Land Boundary Terminus (LBT)	21-38-40.2N	89-09-20.0E	TS, CZ
2.	Putney Island	21-36-39.2N	89-22-14.0E	TS, CZ, EEZ
3.	Dakhin Bhasan Char	21-38-16.0N	90-47-16.5E	TS, CZ
4.	Cox's Bazar	21-25-51.0N	91-57-42.0E	TS, CZ
From baseline point 4 the base line shall follow the low water line up to Teknaf point and St. Martin's Island				
5.	Southern end of St. Martin's Island	Low water line		TS, CZ, EEZ

Explanation : Internal Waters

The water comprised within the baselines established in this notification are part of the internal waters of the people's Republic of Bangladesh.

2. Territorial Sea

The limits of the Territorial Sea shall be twelve (12) nautical miles measured seaward from the baselines set out in this document so that each point of the outer limit of the sea to the nearest point inward on the baselines is twelve nautical miles.

3. Exclusive Economic Zone (Economic Zone)

The outer limit of the Exclusive Economic Zone of Bangladesh is traced in such a manner that every point of the mentioned outer limit is at a distance of two hundred nautical miles from the nearest baseline point.

Explanation:

a. Geodetic Framework: In this notification points defined by geographic coordinates are determined by reference to the World Geodetic System 1984 (WGS 84). Points are connected by geodesic lines realised in the WGS 84.

b. Illustrative Chart: The chart in Annex I attached herewith, provides a general illustration of the baseline and territorial sea limit of the People's Republic of Bangladesh.

4. (1) The notification no. LT-I/3/74 dated 13 April 1974 issued by the Ministry of Foreign Affairs is hereby repealed;

(2) Notwithstanding such repeal, anything done or any action taken under the notification mentioned in clause (1), shall be deemed to have been done or taken shall remain valid.

5. This notification shall be deemed to have come into effect on 08th August 2015.

By the order of the President,

REAR ADMIRAL (RETD.) MD. KHURSHED ALAM
Secretary, Maritime Affairs Unit
Ministry of Foreign Affairs.

附录4 《2018 年孟加拉国海洋区域法 （草案）》[1]
第一至第七部分

The Bangladesh Maritime Zones Act, 2018（Draft）
PART Ⅰ ~ PART Ⅶ

An act to provide for the declaration and determination of the maritime zones for the purpose of exploring and exploiting living and non-living resources and to provide for the suppression of piracy, armed robbery, theft and to make provisions for punishment and for matters connected therewith;

WHEREAS clause（2）of Article 143 under PART XI of the Constitution provides that Parliament may from time to time by law provide for the determination of the boundaries of the territory of Bangladesh and of the territorial seas and the continental shelf of Bangladesh;

AND WHEREAS it is necessary to determine maritime boundaries of territorial sea, internal waters, continental shelf, contiguous zone and Exclusive Economic Zone between Bangladesh and its neighbouring coastal States in the territorial sea in accordance with the 14 March 2012 Judgment of the International Tribunal for the Law of the Sea in the Dispute concerning delimitation of the maritime boundary between Bangladesh and Myanmar in the Bay of Bengal（Bangladesh/Myanmar）and the 7 July 2014 Award of the Arbitral Tribunal in the Bay of Bengal Maritime Boundary Arbitration between Bangladesh and India;

AND WHEREAS it is necessary to suppress maritime terrorism and unlawful acts against the safety of maritime navigation and to provide for matters connected therewith or incidental thereto;

AND WHEREAS it is necessary to guide on international law applicable to armed conflicts at sea and to give conscious effect of the intrinsic, ecological, social, economic, scientific, educational, values of ocean governance, armed conflicts at sea and its components and protection of marine environment;

AND WHEREAS it is expedient and necessary to amend the Act "The Territorial Waters and Maritime Zones Act, 1974（Act XXVI of 1974）" to fulfill the objectives.

It is hereby enacted as follows:

---

[1] See Ministry of Foreign Affairs, "The Bangladesh Maritime Zones Act, 2018", https: //mofa. portal. gov. bd/sites/default/files/files/mofa. portal. gov. bd/page/6aac40c8_ cdc3 _ 4418 _ 8755 _ db68 f0ec9d5a/Bangladesh% 20Maritime% 20Zone% 20Act% 202018% 20% 28Draft% 29% 2023% 20Dec% 2018. pdf, April 12, 2020.

PART I

Short Title and Commencement

1. (1) This Act may be cited as "The Bangladesh Maritime Zones Act, 2018".

(2) It shall come into force on such date as the Government may, by notification in the Official Gazette, specify.

Interpretation

2. In this Act—

(1) "Aircraft" means a machine that is able to fly by gaining support from the air with countering the force of gravity by using dynamic lift of an airfoil, not against the earth surface and also includes free or tethered balloon, air ship, kite, drone, glider and flying machines;

(2) "Artificial Island" means a man-made extension of the seabed where or not such extension breaks the surface of the superjacent waters during high tide;

(3) "Authority" means the International Seabed Authority;

(4) "Autonomous Underwater Vehicle (AUV)" means a robot that travels underwater without requiring input from an operator;

(5) "Baseline" means the low-water line or where applicable the system of straight lines as notified from time to time in the official gazette of Bangladesh from which the breadth of the territorial sea is measured;

(6) "Chart datum" means the tidal level to which depths on a nautical chart are referred to constitute a vertical datum;

(7) "Continental margin" comprises the submerged prolongation of the land mass of Bangladesh, and consists of the seabed and subsoil of the shelf, the slope and the rise. It does not include the deep ocean floor with its oceanic ridges or the subsoil thereof;

(8) "Continental Slope" is that part of the continental margin that lies between the shelf and rise;

(9) "Convention" means the United Nations Convention on the Law of the Sea (UNCLOS), 1982;

(10) "Due publicity" means the notification of a given action for general information through appropriate authority within a reasonable amount of time in a suitable manner;

(11) "Geodesic" is a curve that defines the shortest distance between two points on a given surface;

(12) "Geodetic datum" positions and orients a geodetic reference system in relation to the geoid and astronomical reference system;

(13) "Government" means the Government of the People's Republic of Bangladesh;

（14）"Harbour works" means the permanent manmade structures built along the coast which form an integral part of the harbour system such as jetties, moles, quays or other port facilities, coastal terminals, wharves, breakwaters, sea walls, etc;

（15）"Historic waters" means the internal waters landwards of the baseline that have been historically recognized as forming an integral part of Bangladesh;

（16）"Installations" include a permanently moored vessel, a communication cable, an oil pipeline, a military surveillance installation, a pipeline which is used for the transfer of any substance to or from a vessel, a research, exploration or production platform around the coast of Bangladesh, an exploration or production platform including oil rig used in the prospecting for or mining of any substance, an exploration or production vessels used in the prospecting for or mining of any substance, a telecommunication apparatus as defined in section 1 of the Bangladesh Telecommunications Act 2001, a vessel or equipment used for the exploration or exploitation of the seabed, any other structure whether permanent or temporary within the maritime zones, which is being or intended to be used for or in connection with the exploration and exploitation and conservation and management of the natural resources;

（17）"Island" means a naturally formed area of land, surrounded by water, which is above water at high tide;

（18）"Low water line" is defined as "intersection of the plane of low water" with the shore; the line along a coast or beach, to which the sea recedes at low water as marked on the large scale chart officially recognized by the Government. The actual level of water taken as low water for charting purposes is known as the level of Chart Datum;

（19）"Maritime zones" means the internal waters, the territorial sea, the contiguous zone, the exclusive economic zone, the continental shelf, the high seas and the Area;

（20）"Master" includes every person lawfully having for the time being, in command or charge of a vessel not being a vessel of war;

（21）"Marine Pollution" means the introduction by man, directly or indirectly, of substances or energy into the marine environment of Bangladesh, including estuaries, which results or is likely to result in such deleterious effects as harm to living resources and marine life, hazards to human health, hindrance to marine activities, including fishing and other legitimate uses of the sea, impairment of quality for use of sea water and reduction of amenities;

（22）"Mouth of river" is the place of discharge of a river into the ocean;

（23）"Nautical Miles (NM)" is a unit used in measuring distances at sea, equal to 1852 meters;

（24）"Remotely Operated Underwater Vehicle (ROV)" means non-autonomous remotely operated sub-aquatic vehicle, which is controlled and powered from the surface by an operator/pilot via an umbilical or using a remote control;

(25) "Seabed" means the top of the surface layer of the sand, rock, mud or other material lying at the bottom of the sea and immediately above the subsoil;

(26) "Sedimentary rock" means the rock formed by the consolidation of sediment that has accumulated in layers;

(27) "Safety zone" means zones established by Bangladesh around artificial islands, installations and structures in which appropriate measures to ensure the safety both of navigation and of the artificial islands, installations and structures are taken. Such zones shall not exceed a distance of 500 metres around them, except as authorized by generally accepted international standards or as recommended by the competent international organization;

(28) "Straight line" shall mean in this Act as a geodesic joining two points on the earth's surface;

(29) "Submarine" includes any underwater vehicle however propelled;

(30) "Submarine cable" is an insulated, waterproof wire or bundle of wires or fibre optics for carrying an electric current or a message under water;

(31) "Subsoil" means all naturally occurring matter lying beneath the seabed or deep ocean floor;

(32) "Superjacent waters" means the waters overlying the seabed or deep ocean floor;

(33) "Thalweg" means the line of maximum depth along a river channel. It may also refer to the line of maximum depth along a river valley or in a lake;

(34) "Tide" means the periodic rise and fall of a surface of the oceans and other large bodies of water due principally to the gravitational attraction of the moon and the sun on a rotating earth;

(35) "Unmanned Underwater Vehicles (UUVs)" means any underwater vehicles that are able to operate without a human occupant and may include Remotely Operated underwater Vehicles (ROVs), and Autonomous Underwater Vehicles (AUVs);

(36) "Vessel" includes ship, boat or any other mode of water transport employed in navigation for transporting passengers, goods etc. but does not include a warship;

(37) "Waste" includes any matter prescribed to be waste and any matter, whether liquid, solid, gaseous or radioactive, which is discharged, emitted or deposited in the environment in such volume, composition or manner as to cause an adverse effect;

(38) "Warship" means a ship belonging to the armed forces of a State bearing the external marks distinguishing such ships of its nationality, under the command of an officer duly commissioned by the government of the State and whose name appears in the appropriate service list or its equivalent, and manned by a crew which is under regular armed forces discipline;

(39) "Water column" is a vertical continuum of water from sea surface to seabed.

Act to override other laws

3. Notwithstanding anything contained in any other law for the time being in force, the provisions of this Act shall have the effect.

PART Ⅱ Territorial Sea Baseline

4. (1) For the purposes of this Act "Bangladesh" means all the territory of the People's Republic of Bangladesh including inland waters and water column superjacent to the seabed, of the seabed and its sub-soil thereof the internal waters, historic waters, the territorial sea, to the extent that the area called Contiguous Zone, Exclusive Economic Zone, Continental Shelf in accordance with international law has been or may hereafter be designated under Bangladesh law as area within which Bangladesh exercise sovereignty and sovereign rights with respect to the exploration and exploitation of the natural resources of the water column, seabed and its sub-soil.

(2) The Territorial Sea Baseline (TSB) of Bangladesh, from which the breadth of the Territorial Sea is measured seaward, enclosing those waters, which as a result of their close inter-relationship with the land, have the character of internal water shall consist of series of geodesics joining the base points at—

(a) Land Boundary Terminus (LBT) (21°38′40. 2″N, 89°09′-20. 0″E);

(b) Putney Island (21°-36′-39. 2″N, 89°-22′-14. 0″E);

(c) The appropriate base point located along the furthest seaward extend of the low water line at Dakshin Bhasan Char (21°-38′-16. 0″N, 90°-47′-16. 5″E); and

(d) finally ending at base point at Cox's Bazar (21°-25′-51. 0″N, 91°-57′-42. 0″E);

(e) The TSB South of Cox's Bazar from base point (d) 21°-25′-51. 0″N, 91°-57′-42. 0″E) shall be normal baseline i. e. the low water line along the coast up to Teknaf point and Southern end of St. Martin's Island as marked on the large scale chart officially recognized by Bangladesh.

(3) The government may amend the above baseline by official gazette from which the Territorial Sea of Bangladesh shall be measured.

PART Ⅲ Internal Waters

5. "Internal waters" of Bangladesh means the areas of the sea that are on the landward side of the TSB from where the breadth of the territorial sea is measured; up to the mouths of all rivers, historic waters, outer limits of the ports, and harbours; Historic wa-

ters mean the body of waters over which Bangladesh has exercised its open, effective, long term and continuous authority.

Closing Line

6. Closing line is a dividing line between the inland waters enclosing river mouths and the internal waters, historic waters and normal baseline.

Rights over the Internal Waters

7. (1) The sovereignty of Bangladesh extends beyond its land territory to the water column, the seabed and its subsoil, and the air space over the internal water.

(2) Bangladesh, in exercising its sovereignty, has exclusive rights and jurisdiction over the internal waters;

8. Bangladesh can exercise its right to suspend the movement of any vessel and warship in the internal waters.

PART Ⅳ   The Territorial Sea

9. The territorial sea comprises areas of the sea having defined not exceeding 12 NM from the nearest base points of the TSB and normal baselines, measured seaward from the TSB.

Limits of the Territorial Sea

10. (1) "Territorial Sea" of Bangladesh shall be measured 12 NM from the TSB;

(2) For the purpose of delimiting the territorial sea, the outermost permanent harbor works which form an integral part of the existing harbour system of Bangladesh like Chattogram and Mongla Port and their assigned outer anchorages, Matarbari port, Payra Port and Saint Martin's anchorage etc. ; all be treated as forming part of the coast.

Rights over the Territorial Sea

11. (1) The sovereignty of Bangladesh extends beyond its land territory to the water column, seabed, subsoil and the airspace over the territorial sea;

(2) Bangladesh, in the exercise of its sovereignty, has exclusive jurisdiction over the territorial sea, subject to the Convention and other international laws;

Rights of Innocent Passage in the Territorial Sea

12. (1) For the purposes of this section, "innocent passage" means navigation through the territorial sea for the purpose of traversing that sea without entering the internal waters or proceeding to or from internal waters to call at port facilities of Bangladesh;

(2) Innocent passage shall be continuous and expeditious and not prejudicial to the peace, good order or security of Bangladesh and shall include stopping and anchoring, but only in so far as they are incidental to ordinary navigation or are rendered necessary by force

majeure or distress or for the propose of rendering assistance to persons, vessels or aircraft in danger or distress.

(3) In exercising the right of innocent passage, a foreign vessel shall comply with the laws of Bangladesh, any order, direction, license or any other authority relating to the exercise of innocent passage through the territorial sea.

(4) Any determination of non-innocent passage by a ship must be made on the basis of acts it commits while in the Territorial Sea and not on the basis of cargo, means of propulsion, flag sate and destination on purpose. For the purpose of resource conservation, environmental protection and navigational safety, Government may establish certain restrictions on the right of innocent passage of foreign vessels and may adopt with due publicity laws and regulations relating to innocent passage through the territorial sea in respect of all or any of the following areas:

(a) safety of navigation and the regulation of maritime traffic;

(b) protection of navigation aids and other facilities and installations;

(c) protection of cables and pipelines;

(d) conservation of the living resources of the sea;

(e) prevention of the infringement of fisheries regulations;

(f) preservation of the environment and the prevention, reduction and control of pollution thereof;

(g) prevention of infringement of customs, fiscal, immigration or sanitary regulations;

Regulating Innocent Passage

13. (1) A foreign warship, including a submarine and any other underwater vessel of war, may enter or pass through the territorial sea after giving prior notice to the Government.

(2) A submarine or any other underwater vehicle like ROV, AUV, and UUV etc, whether or not a vessel of war, exercising the right of innocent passage through the territorial sea shall navigate on the surface and show its flag while passing through the territorial sea.

(3) The Government may, in the interest of safety of navigation and by order designate sea lanes and prescribe traffic separation schemes for the regulation of the passage of vessels through the internal waters and territorial sea.

(4) A master of a submarine, not of a vessel of war, including ROV, AUV, and UUV, if contravenes sub-section (2) and thus commits an offence, shall be punishable with imprisonment for a term which may extend to five years or with fine which may extend to taka four hundred million or with both. In addition, the Maritime Zones Tribunal may order the forfeiture of the submarine and any such vehicle.

14. (1) The passage of a foreign vessel is prejudicial to the peace, good order and security of Bangladesh and the passage is not innocent if, while in the territorial sea, the

vessel engages in—

(a) any threat or use of force against the sovereignty, territorial integrity or political independence of Bangladesh or any other act which violates the principles of international law embodied in the Charter of the United Nations;

(b) any exercise or practice with weapons of any kind;

(c) any act aimed at collecting information, which would be prejudicial to the defence or security of Bangladesh;

(d) any act of propaganda circulated to affect the defence or security of Bangladesh;

(e) launching of, landing on any aircraft;

(f) launching of, landing on board of any military device;

(g) loading or unloading of any commodity, currency or person contrary to the customs, excise, immigration or sanitation laws or regulations of Bangladesh;

(h) any act of willful pollution in contravention of the Convention;

(i) any fishing activities;

(j) carrying out of research or surveying activities;

(k) any act designed to interfere with any system of communication or any other facility or installation in Bangladesh; or

(l) any other activity not directly related to its passage.

(2) The master of a foreign vessel or submarine, not of a vessel of war, who takes part in or caused the vessel or submarine to be engaged in, and any other person on board who takes part in, any activity specified in subsection (1) —

(a) commits an offence and shall be punishable with imprisonment for a term which may extent to five years or with fine which may extent to taka four hundred million or with both; and

(b) where the offence is continued after conviction, the master and the other person who were convicted, each commits a further offence and is liable on conviction to a fine of taka twenty four million for each day on which the offence is continued, and in addition any designated court may order the forfeiture of the vessel or submarine.

Security Measures

15. (1) The Government may make orders and exercise powers and take measures in relation to the territorial sea as considered necessary in the interest of the peace, good order or security of Bangladesh, including the suspension, whether absolutely or subject to any exceptions and qualifications as the Government considers appropriate, of the right of innocent passage of all or any class of foreign vessels through any area of the territorial sea.

(2) In the event the Government exercises power under subsection (1), such suspension shall take effect only after having been duly published.

（3）There is no right of innocent passage for all types of aircraft through the territorial sea and cannot pass without the prior expressed consent of the Government.

（4）Advanced notification or authorization for innocent passage of warships and naval auxiliaries, ships owned or operated by a State and used only on non-government, non-commercial service and of nuclear powered warship or warships and naval auxiliaries carrying nuclear weapons or specific cargos, through the Territorial Sea will be required.

（5）Ship to ship transfer of fuel and goods in the territorial sea or internal water must be done through advanced notification.

Foreign Vessels Carrying Nuclear or Other Hazardous Wastes

16. （1）A master of a foreign vessel shall not store, transport or permit to store or transport any nuclear or other inherently dangerous or noxious substances, harmful substances and hazardous wastes in the internal waters and territorial sea except with the prior permission of the Government.

（2）Where any foreign nuclear-powered vessel or foreign vessel carries nuclear or other inherently dangerous or noxious substances while exercising the right of innocent passage through the territorial sea, the master of the vessel shall, in relation to the vessel and substances, carry the necessary documents and shall observe the precautionary measures that are established for those vessels by the International Atomic Energy Agency (IAEA) applicable to the carrying of those substances for the time being in force.

（3）A vessel carrying radioactive materials shall not pass through any part of the internal waters or territorial sea, unless prior notification of intended passage and the route to be taken by the vessel through those waters or the sea has been intimated in accordance with regulations.

（4）A vessel to which subsections above refer may be required to confine its passage to sea lanes as may be prescribed.

（5）A master of a vessel who contravenes this section commits an offence shall be punishable with imprisonment for a term which may extend to seven years or with fine which may extent to taka twelve hundred million or with both but shall not be less than taka eight hundred million.

（6）The Government may make additional regulations for the passage of vessels carrying nuclear and radioactive substances and hazardous waste through all or any part of the internal waters and territorial sea.

（7）Regulations made under this section shall provide for the action that may be taken, including stopping and boarding vessels to ensure compliance with the regulations.

Discharge of Harmful Substances and Hazardous Wastes

17. （1）A master of a foreign vessel shall not discharge or permit to discharge any

nuclear or other inherently dangerous or noxious substances, harmful substances and hazardous wastes in the internal waters and territorial sea except with the prior written permission of the Government.

(2) A master of a vessel who contravenes this section commits an offence and shall be punishable with imprisonment for a term which may extend to ten years or with fine which may extend to taka four thousand million but shall not be less than taka two thousand million.

Criminal Jurisdiction on Board a Foreign Ship

18. (1) The criminal jurisdiction of Bangladesh should only be exercised on board a foreign ship passing through the territorial sea to arrest any person or to conduct any investigation in connection with any crime committed on board the ship during its passage in the following cases:

(a) if the consequences of the crime extend to Bangladesh;

(b) if the crime is of a kind to disturb the peace of Bangladesh or the good order of its territorial sea;

(c) if the assistance of the local authorities has been requested by the master of the ship or by a diplomatic agent or consular officer of the flag State; or

(d) if such measures are necessary for the suppression of illicit trafficking in narcotic drugs or psychotropic substances.

(2) The above provisions may not affect the right of Bangladesh to take any steps authorized by its laws for the purpose of an arrest or investigation on board a foreign ship within the internal waters or passing through the territorial sea after leaving internal waters.

Civil Jurisdiction in Relation to Foreign Ships

19. (1) The Government should not stop or divert a foreign ship passing through the territorial sea for the purpose of exercising civil jurisdiction in relation to a person on board the ship.

(2) The Government may not levy execution against or arrest the ship for the purpose of any civil proceedings, save only in respect of obligations or liabilities assumed or incurred by the ship itself in the course or for the purpose of its voyage through the territorial sea of Bangladesh.

(3) Sub-sections above are without prejudice to the right of Bangladesh, in accordance with its laws, to levy execution against or to arrest, for the purpose of any civil proceedings, a foreign ship lying within the internal waters or in the territorial sea, or passing through the territorial sea after leaving internal waters.

Sea Lanes and Traffic Separation Schemes

20. (1) Bangladesh may, with regard to the safety of navigation where necessary,

require foreign ships exercising the right of innocent passage through its territorial sea to use sea lanes and traffic separation schemes as it may designate or prescribe for the regulation of the passage of ships; and in particular, tankers, nuclear-powered ships and ships carrying nuclear or other inherently dangerous or noxious substances or materials may be required to confine their passage to such sea lanes.

(2) The Government shall clearly indicate sea lanes and traffic separation schemes on charts to which due publicity shall be given by Directorate General of Shipping.

Rights of Laying Submarine Cables and Pipelines

21. The Government has the right under general international law to lay and maintain submarine cables in waters under their sovereignty, including internal waters, and territorial sea.

PART V   The Contiguous Zone

22. The Contiguous Zone refers to an area seaward of the territorial sea in which Bangladesh may exercise the control necessary to prevent or punish infringement of its customs, fiscal, immigration and sanitary laws and regulations that occur within its territory or territorial sea.

Limits of the Contiguous Zone

23. "Contiguous zone" of Bangladesh may not extend beyond 24 NM from the territorial sea baselines.

Grounds for Denial of Entry

24. Where the Government has reasonable grounds to believe that in the contiguous zone a vessel has committed or likely to commit (as per the information of last port of call or any other) an offence in relation to the customs, fiscal, immigration or sanitary laws or regulations of Bangladesh, the Government may, subject to international obligations, deny that vessel's entry into Bangladesh, including the territorial sea.

Commission of Offences in the Contiguous Zone

25. (1) The Government may exercise such powers and take such measures in or in respect of the contiguous zone as it may consider necessary to prevent and punish the contravention of, and attempt to contravene the customs, fiscal, immigration or sanitary laws and regulations in the contiguous zone which are in practice in Bangladesh.

(2) The Government may make regulations that permit, in the contiguous zone, the exercise of controls necessary to—

(a) prevent infringement of any customs, fiscal, immigration or sanitary laws or regulations within Bangladesh, its internal waters and territorial sea; and

(b) punish the infringement of those laws or regulations committed within Bangladesh, including its internal waters and territorial sea.

(3) Subject to subsection above, where there is reasonable ground to believe that a vessel has committed an offence in the contiguous zone in respect of any customs, fiscal, immigration or sanitary laws or regulations of Bangladesh, every power of arrest, entry, search or seizure or other power that could be exercised in Bangladesh in respect of that offence may also be exercised in the contiguous zone.

(4) A power of arrest shall not be exercised without the consent of the Government in the contiguous zone on board any vessel registered outside Bangladesh.

(5) Without limiting subsections above, the Government may exercise other powers and take measures in or in relation to the contiguous zone if the Government considers it necessary for the security of Bangladesh.

(6) Any person who commits an offence in the contiguous zone or enters Bangladesh having committed an offence in the contiguous zone shall be punishable with imprisonment for a term, which may extend to seven years or with fine which may extend to taka three hundred and fifty million or with both.

PART VI　The Exclusive Economic Zone

26. "Exclusive Economic Zone (EEZ)" of Bangladesh comprises an area of the sea beyond and adjacent to the territorial sea extending to a line every point of which is at a distance of 200 NM from the nearest points of the territorial sea baselines/normal baseline of the nearest coastline.

Limits of the Exclusive Economic Zone

27. The Exclusive Economic Zone of Bangladesh comprises area of sea extending to a line every point of which is at a distance of 200 NM, from the nearest point of the territorial sea baseline with geographical coordinates of 18°15′54. 12″N, 89°21′47. 56″E (along the Bangladesh-India Maritime Boundary line) and 17°52′34. 06″N, 90°15′4. 66″E (along the Bangladesh-Myanmar Maritime Boundary line) respectively.

Rights and Duties in the Exclusive Economic Zone

28. (1) In accordance with international law and in particular Article 56 of the Convention, Bangladesh, in the EEZ has—

(a) Sovereign rights for the purpose of exploration, exploitation, conservation and management of the natural resources, both living and non-living as well as for producing energy from tides, currents and winds;

(b) Exclusive rights and jurisdiction for the construction, maintenance or operation of artificial island, offshore terminals, installations and other structures and devices necessary for the exploration and exploitation of the resources of the zone or for the convenience of shipping or for any other purposes.

(c) Jurisdiction to authorize, regulate and control marine scientific research;

(d) Jurisdiction to preserve and protect the marine environment and to prevent and control marine pollution;

(e) Jurisdiction with regard to customs, fiscal, health, security and immigration laws over artificial islands, installations and structures;

(f) Any other rights that are recognized by international law;

(2) In the EEZ, other States enjoy freedom of navigation and over-flight and other internationally lawful uses of the sea related to those except military exercise.

29. The rights specified in this section with respect to the seabed and subsoil shall be exercised in accordance with applicable international law.

Submarine Cables and Pipelines

30. Submarine cables refer to communication cables that include telegraph, telephone, and high-voltage power cables, telecommunications cables, particularly the new fiber-optic cables, which are essential to modern internet communications. Pipelines include those, which deliver water, oil and natural gas, and other commodities.

Exercise of Jurisdiction in Laying Cables and Pipelines

31. According to this Act, no States shall be allowed to lay any submarine cables and pipelines in its EEZ or continental shelf except with the consent of the Government. With respect to the course of the cables/pipelines and in all areas, States shall take into account existing infrastructure, the interests of other marine users, and environmental impacts.

Submarine Cables and Pipelines in the EEZ and on the Continental Shelf

32. Other States/entities may lay and operate submarine cables and pipelines in Bangladesh's EEZ and continental shelf subject to these limitations:

(a) The government may not impede the laying (of new cables) or maintenance of (new and existing) cables, subject to Bangladesh's right to take reasonable measures to explore its continental shelf and to exploit the natural resources of its shelf, and the reduction and control of pollution from pipelines (but not cables).

(b) Exercise of Bangladesh's rights over the continental shelf must not infringe or result in any unjustifiable interference with others' right to lay and maintain cables on its shelf.

(c) Delineation of the course for laying pipelines (but not cables) on the continental shelf is subject to the consent of the Government.

(d) The government has the right to establish conditions for cables or pipelines entering into its territory or territorial sea, and its jurisdiction over cables and pipelines constructed or used in connection with exploration or exploitation of its natural resources, or the operation of artificial islands, installations and structures under its jurisdiction.

(e) Existing cables are protected from being interfered with in the laying of new cables; all States are required to have "due regard to cables already in position". Particular care is to be taken to ensure that the possibility of repairing existing cables is not prejudiced. In the case of a continental shelf extending more than 200 miles, incidents and activities involving cables and pipelines on the extended shelf are covered by the continental shelf provisions.

Protections for Submarine Cables and Pipelines

33. This Act addresses the breaking or injury to a submarine cable or pipeline, and provide for indemnity for loss incurred by a ship in its efforts to avoid injuring a cable or pipeline. In this respect they apply to incidents of navigation and activities involving cables and pipelines in all maritime areas beyond the outer limits of the territorial sea.

34. Bangladesh shall consider the act of breaking or injuring a submarine cable beneath the high seas, willfully or by culpable negligence, in such a manner as to liable to interrupt or obstruct telegraphic or telephonic communications, and similarly the breaking of a submarine pipeline or high-voltage power cable, and to conduct calculated or likely to result in such breaking or injury a punishable offence. It does not apply to any break or injury caused by persons who acted merely with the legitimate object of saving lives or their ship, after having taken all necessary precautions to avoid doing so.

35. Bangladesh shall adopt the laws and regulations necessary to provide that, if persons/entities subject to its jurisdiction who are owners of a submarine cable or pipeline beneath the high seas, in laying or repairing that cable or pipeline, causes a break in or injury to another cable or pipeline, they shall bear the cost of the repairs.

36. If any owners of any ships that have sacrificed an anchor or fishing gear in order to avoid injury to a submarine cable, shall enjoy indemnity.

37. The Convention on the International Regulations for Preventing Collisions at Sea (COLREGs), 1972 contains some protections for cable laying ships. Nevertheless, these cables form part of the critical infrastructure of the Bangladesh's economy.

Authority to Explore or Exploit the Exclusive Economic Zone

38. (1) No person, including a foreign government and an international organization, may—

(a) explore or exploit any natural resources whether living or non-living;

(b) carry out any search or excavation, or conduct any research; or

(c) drill or construct, maintain or operate any artificial island, off shore terminal, installation or other structure or device for any purpose in the exclusive economic zone, except under and in accordance with the terms of a license or letter of authority granted by the Government.

(2) Nothing in this section shall apply to fishing by a citizen of Bangladesh.

(3) (a) Any person who contravenes subsection (1) commits an offence and shall be punishable with fine which may extend to taka four hundred million. Inaddition, the Maritime Zones Tribunal before which the person is convicted may order the forfeiture of any vessel and equipment used in the commission of the offence.

(b) The provisions of subsection 3 (a) shall not apply to the violations of the fisheries laws or regulations of Bangladesh. Such violations shall be governed by the relevant provisions of the laws of Bangladesh.

Declaration of Designated Areas in the Exclusive Economic Zone

39. (1) The Government may make regulations to—

(a) provide for the authorization of persons or organizations to explore natural resources, or to recover or attempt to recover any such resources, in accordance with such terms and conditions as may be determined by the Government.

(b) declare any area to be a Marine Protected Area as a measure to conserve rare marine species including fishes, and marine mammals from extinct.

(c) regulate the laying of pipelines or cables;

(d) provide for the authorization and regulation of any drilling; and

(e) regulate the construction, operation and use of artificial islands and installations and structures for the purposes in accordance with the Article 56 of the Convention; and

(f) protect the marine environment of the designated area.

Extension of Norms, Regulations and Measures to the Exclusive Economic Zone

40. The norms, regulations and measures for the prevention, reduction and control of pollution from vessels, aircraft, artificial islands, scientific research stations, installations and structures which are in effect within the limits of the internal waters and territorial sea shall extend to the exclusive economic zone, taking into account international rules and standards, international treaties and conventions to which Bangladesh is a party.

Conservation of the Living Resources

41. (1) The Government shall determine the allowable catch of the living resources in the EEZ and shall intimate from time to time through gazette notifications. Bangladesh, taking into account the best scientific evidence available to it, shall ensure through proper conservation and management measures that the maintenance of the living resources in the EEZ is not endangered by over-exploitation. As appropriate, other coastal States and competent international organizations, whether sub-regional or global, may cooperate to

that end.

(2) Foreign vessels shall not fish within the territorial seas and EEZ of Bangladesh.

Utilization of the Living Resources

42. (1) Bangladesh will promote the objective of optimum utilization of the living resources in the EEZ without prejudice to Article 61 of the Convention. The Government will determine its capacity to harvest the living resources of the EEZ.

(2) Bangladesh shall exercise its sovereign rights to explore, exploit, conserve, and manage the living resources in the EEZ and take such legal measures as appropriate for ensuring compliance with the laws and regulations adopted by Bangladesh in the EEZ. Bangladesh may also comply with the relevant UNCLOS provisions to notify the flag State when such measures will be taken.

Stocks Occurring within the EEZ of Two or More Coastal States or both Within the EEZ and in an Area Beyond and Adjacent to it

43. Where the same stock or stocks of associated species occur both within the EEZ and in an area beyond and adjacent to the zone, Bangladesh and the States fishing for such stocks in the adjacent area shall seek, either directly or through appropriate sub-regional or regional organizations, to agree upon the measures necessary for the conservation of these stocks in the adjacent area.

Highly Migratory Species and Marine Mammals

44. (1) Bangladesh and other States, whose nationals fish highly migratory species in the region, shall cooperate directly or through appropriate international organizations with a view to ensuring conservation and promoting the objective of optimum utilization of such species throughout the region, both within and beyond the EEZ. The regions for which no appropriate international organization exists, Bangladesh and other States, whose nationals harvest these species in the region, shall cooperate to establish such an organization and participate in its work.

(2) The Government shall enjoy the right to prohibit, limit or regulate the exploitation of marine mammals. Other States are also expected to cooperate with a view to the conservation of marine mammals and in the case of cetaceans shall in particular work through the appropriate international organizations for their conservation, management and study.

Navigation in the Exclusive Economic Zone

45. Other States may not conduct military activities such as anchoring, exercises, etc. within the EEZ but may only do so with the obligations to have due regard to Bangladesh's resource and other rights as well as the rights of other States as set forth in the convention. All vessels over 100 Gross Registered Tonnages (GRT) to declare and report

any hazardous cargo carried on board at least 24 hours before entering Bangladesh's EEZ. Following Bangladesh's jurisdiction in its Exclusive Economic Zone with regard to protection, preservation of marine environment and its obligations to prevent, reduce and control pollution of the marine environment, these obligations must be carried out in consistent with international laws.

Enforcement of Laws and Regulations

46. (1) The Government may exercise its sovereign rights to explore, exploit, conserve and manage the living resources in the exclusive economic zone, take such measures, including boarding, inspection, arrest and judicial proceedings, as may be necessary to ensure compliance with the laws and regulations adopted by it in conformity with the Convention.

(2) The Government shall promptly, in cases of arrest or detention of a foreign fishing vessel, notify the action taken to the flag State through appropriate diplomatic channels. Arrested vessels and their crews shall be promptly released upon the posting of reasonable bond or other security by the flag State.

(3) Penalties for violations of fisheries laws and regulations in the exclusive economic zone will be in accordance with the laws and regulations enunciated by the Government.

(4) With regard to environmental protection, The Government shall use existing mechanism which could enable it to effectively monitor, regulate or prevent incidents related to Ship to Ship (STS) transfers occurring in Exclusive Economic Zone and which does not require any changes to following regulations of existing International Convention for the Prevention of Pollution from Ships (MARPOL):

i. Oil Pollution Preparedness, Response and Cooperation (OPRS);

ii. Long Range Identification and Tracking (LRIT);

iii. Automatic Identification System (AIS);

iv. Conditions of port entry for STS transfer;

v. Regulation of STS Service providers that operate from Bangladesh;

vi. Voluntary measures and bilateral agreement between coastal and flag States.

Illegal, Unreported and Unregulated Fishing (IUU)

47. (1) To prevent, deter and eliminate illegal, unreported and unregulated fishing, Government in any of her ports, may notify fishing vessels to inform the port about detail of its fishing operations while requesting permission to dock or enter at a port, and permission to dock can be denied if there are good reason to believe that the vessel was engaged in IUU fishing. Any port authorities of Bangladesh as a part of other measures may carry out inspections of equipment, paperwork, catches, and ship's records.

(2) Bangladesh may ensure that they continue to exercise control over vessels flying

their flags in areas beyond their national jurisdiction, and may ensure that IUU-catch products are not entering national and international market.

(3) If required, to prevent, deter and eliminate illegal, unreported and unregulated fishing, Bangladesh may act in accordance with the Port State Measures Agreement (PSMA) of Food and Agriculture Organization (FAO).

Penalty for Illegal, Unreported and Unregulated Fishing

48. If any person involves in or helps any person to involve in illegal, unreported and unregulated fishing and destructive fishing practices, shall be punishable with imprisonment for a term which may extend to one year or with fine which may extend up to taka eight million, or with both.

PART VII The Continental Shelf

49. The Continental Shelf of Bangladesh comprises the seabed and subsoil of the submarine areas that extend beyond the territorial sea throughout the natural prolongation of its land territory to the outer edge of the continental margin.

Limits of the Extended Continental Shelf

50. (1) Since the outer edge of the continental margin of Bangladesh extends beyond 200 NM from the base line, the Government may, by regulation, establish the outer limits of the continental shelf based on the principles and methods of delineation of the continental shelf beyond that point specified in Article 76 of the Convention; and especially to:

(a) the outermost fixed points at each of which the thickness of sedimentary rocksis at least 1 percent of the shortest distance from such point to the foot of the continental slope; or

(b) the outer limits of the continental shelf on the seabed, drawn in accordance withsub-section above, shall not exceed 100 nautical miles from the 2,500 metre isobaths;

(c) the foot of the continental slope as referred in sub-section (a) above, shall be determined as the point of maximum change in the gradient at its base, and the outer limits of its continental shelf, by straight lines not exceeding 60 nautical miles in length, connecting fixed points, defined by coordinates of latitude and longitude.

(2) For the purposes of sub-section above, the continental margin comprises the submerged prolongation to the land mass of Bangladesh consisting of the seabed and its subsoil, the slope and the rise of the continental shelf, but does not include the deep ocean floor with its oceanic ridges or its subsoil.

(3) In accordance with international law and in particular Article 77 of the Convention, Bangladesh shall exercise sovereign rights over the continental shelf to explore itand exploit its natural resources.

51. Subject to Article 84 of the Convention, the Government may, by notification in the Official Gazette, specify the outer limits of the Continental Shelf.

52. No person or organization shall, except under and in accordance with the terms of a license or permission granted by the Government, explore or exploit any resources of the continental shelf or carry out any search on the continental shelf. No such license or permission shall be necessary for fishing by a citizen of Bangladesh who uses vessels which are not mechanically propelled.

Rights and Jurisdictions in the Continental Shelf

53. (1) In the continental shelf Bangladesh shall have exclusive sovereign rights and jurisdiction for the purposes of—

(a) exploring and exploiting its natural resources;

(b) authorizing and regulating the construction, operation, maintenance and use of artificial islands, off-shore terminals, installations and other structures and devices, including designated safety zones, necessary for the exploration and exploitation of the resources of the continental shelf or for the convenience of shipping or for any other economic purpose;

(c) authorizing and regulating drilling for any purposes;

(d) authorizing, regulating and controlling marine scientific research;

(e) preserving and protecting the marine environment, and preventing and controlling marine pollution; and

(f) constructing artificial lands, installations and structures, including jurisdiction with regard to customs, fiscal, health, safety and immigration laws and regulations.

(2) The natural resources, to which subsection (1) (a) refers, consist of mineral and other non-living resources of the seabed and subsoil together with living organisms belonging to sedentary species, that is to say, organisms which, at the harvestable stage, either are immobile on or under the seabed or are unable to move except inconstant physical contact with the seabed or subsoil.

License or Authority to Explore or Exploit Resources

54. (1) No person, including a foreign government and an international organization, may—

(a) explore or exploit any resources;

(b) carry out any search or excavation, or conduct any research; or

(c) drill or construct installations or other structure or devices for any purpose inthe continental shelf, except under and in accordance with the terms of alicense or a letter of authority granted by the Government.

(2) Any person or organization who contravenes sub-section (1) commits an offence

andshall be punishable with imprisonment for a term which may extend to three yearsor with fine which may extend to Taka two hundred and forty million or with both. In addition, the Maritime Zones Tribunal before which the person was convicted may order the forfeiture of any vessel and equipment used in the commission of the offence.

Declaration of Designated Area

55. The Government may, by order:

(1) declare any area of the continental shelf to be a designated area for any purpose; and

(2) make any provision considers necessary with respect to—

(a) exploration, exploitation and protection of the resources of the continental shelf within the designated area;

(b) preservation and protection of the marine environment of the designated area;

(c) conducting of marine scientific research in the designated area;

(d) safety and protection of artificial islands, off-shore terminals, installations, and other structures and devices in the designated area;

(e) customs and other fiscal matters in relation to the designated area; and

(f) the entry into and passage through the designated area by foreign vessels by the establishment of fairways, sea lanes, traffic separation schemes or any other mode of navigation which is not prejudicial to the interests of Bangladesh.

Exercise of Jurisdiction in the Continental Shelf

56. (1) Bangladesh has the jurisdiction to exercise laws and regulations with regard to customs, fiscal, health, security and immigration in relation to the artificial islands, installations and structures, including safety zones, on the continental shelf.

(2) (a) The laws and regulations of Bangladesh shall be extended to the continental shelf to the extent permitted by international law.

(b) In particular, the laws of Bangladesh shall apply to artificial islands, installations and structures, including safety zones, on the continental shelf as if they were located in the territorial sea.

(3) Rights in the continental shelf that are not stipulated in this Act, shall be exercised in accordance with the Convention, international law and any other laws of Bangladesh.

(4) The Government shall not impede the laying or maintenance of any submarine cables or pipelines on the continental shelf by other States provided that the express consent of the Government shall be necessary for the delineation of the course for the laying of the cables or pipelines.

(5) In exercising its rights and performing its duties in the continental shelf, Bangla-

desh shall have due regard to the rights and duties of other States and shall act in a manner compatible with international law.

Grey Area

57. (1) Grey areas of Bangladesh are two separate areas beyond 200 nm of the EEZ and situated separately within the 200 nm EEZs of Myanmar and India, as determined by the judgment of the ITLOS (Bangladesh-Myanmar maritime boundary case, 2012) and Arbitral Tribunal award (Bangladesh-India maritime boundary case, 2014) respectively.

(2) The water column on each segment of the Grey Area shall belong to Myanmar and India respectively, and the water column on their common overlapping grey area shall be owned by both the countries.

(3) In grey areas, Bangladesh shall have sovereign and exclusive rights for the purpose of exploring and exploiting the natural resources of the seabed and sub-soil together with the living organisms belonging to sedentary species.

(4) Bangladeshi fishermen according to international law may not exploit living resources in the grey area belonging to other States.

…

附录 5 2019 年缅甸致联合国秘书长照会[1]

RECEIVED

FEB 1 5 2019

PERMANENT MISSION OF THE REPUBLIC OF THE UNION OF MYANMAR
TO THE UNITED NATIONS, NEW YORK

DIVISION FOR OCEAN AFFAIRS
AND THE LAW OF THE SEA

TEL (212) 744-1271 · FAX (212) 744-1290
EMAIL myanmar.mission@verizon.net

10 EAST 77th STREET
NEW YORK, NY 10075

No. 57 / 03 09 45

The Permanent Mission of the Republic of the Union of Myanmar to the United Nations presents its compliments to the Secretary-General of the United Nations and has the honour to refer to the Communication No. M.Z.N.118.2016. LOS (Maritime Zone Notification) dated 7th April 2016, regarding the deposit of a list of geographical coordinates of points by the People's Republic of Bangladesh to measure the breadth of its territorial sea, pursuant to Article-16, Paragraph-2 of the United Nations Convention on the Law of the Sea (UNCLOS).

The Republic of the Union of Myanmar and the People's Republic of Bangladesh both as States Parties to the United Nations Convention on the Law of the Sea (UNCLOS) enjoy the rights afforded by the UNCLOS and thus have legal obligations to respect the duty to abide by and respect and strictly follow the principles enshrined in rights and duties of Member States as provided in the Article 33 Annex VI of the 1982 United Nations Convention on the Law of the Sea (UNCLOS) and other relevant legal instruments including customary international law of the sea.

Most importantly, the Government of the Republic of the Union of Myanmar notes that Bangladesh's 10 fathom baseline amendment (i.e. new baseline points) is not in line with the ITLOS's judgment since new baseline points particularly the new points number 2 (21° 36' 39.2" N; 89° 22' 14.0'' E) and 5 (Southern end of the St. Martin's Island-Coordinate not identified) caused seaward shift of Bangladesh's Exclusive Economic Zone and encroaches into the Myanmar's Exclusive Economic Zone and minimizes the Grey Area recognized by the ITLOS. Such initiative by the Government of the People's Republic of

---

[1] See UN Office of Legal Affairs, "Communication from The Permanent Mission of Myanmar Dated 15 February 2019 with Respect to The Deposit by Bangladesh (M. Z. N. 118. 2016. LOS of 7 April 2016) of A List of Geographical Coordinates", https：//www. un. org/Depts/los/LEGISLATION-ANDTREATIES/PDFFILES/NV57-030945% 28corrected% 29. pdf, March 20, 2021.

Bangladesh is in violation of the judgment of the ITLOS and the provisions of the UNCLOS.

In this connection, the Government of the Republic of the Union of Myanmar would like to recall paragraph 3 and 4 of the jurisdiction of the ITLOS and draws the attention of the Secretary-General of the United Nations to the non-observance of Bangladesh to fully comply with the verdict given by the International Tribunal for the Law of the Sea (ITLOS) with regard to the "Dispute Concerning Delimitation of the Maritime Boundary between the two countries in the Bay of Bengal".

The Government of the Republic of the Union of Myanmar, therefore, objects the new baseline points used by Bangladesh to determine its straight baselines and the resultant seaward shift of Bangladesh's Exclusive Economic Zone which undermine Myanmar's sovereign rights and encroachment into Myanmar's Exclusive Economic Zone in the Grey Area as there is compelling evidence to show alternation and violation of the judgment of the ITLOS.

The Permanent Mission of the Republic of the Union of Myanmar to the United Nations in New York avails itself of this opportunity to renew to the Secretary-General of the United Nations the assurances of its highest consideration.

New York, 15 February 2019

The Secretary-General of the United Nations

(Atten: Division for Ocean Affairs and the Law of the Sea)

附录6　孟加拉国缔结和加入的国际海洋法条约

（一）联合国海洋法公约及其相关条约

序号	条约名称	签署日期 （年/月/日）	批准日期 （年/月/日）
1	《联合国海洋法公约》 United Nations Convention on the Law of the Sea	1982/12/10	2000/7/21
2	《关于执行 1982 年 12 月 10 日〈联合国海洋法公约〉第十一部分的协定》 Agreement Relating to the Implementation of Part XI of the United Nations Conventions on the Law of the Sea, 10 December 1982	1994/11/16	2001/7/27
3	《执行 1982 年 12 月 10 日〈联合国海洋法公约〉有关养护和管理跨界鱼类种群和高度洄游鱼类种群的规定的协定》 Agreement for the Implementation of the Provisions of the United Nations Convention on the Law of the Sea of 10 December 1982 relating to the Conservation and Management of Straddling Fish Stocks and Highly Migratory Fish Stocks	1995/12/4	2012/12/5

（二）缔结与加入的其他海洋海事条约

类别	条约名称	签署/批准/ 加入/接受日期 （年/月/日）	对孟加拉国 生效日期 （年/月/日）
与海上安全相关的条约	《1972 年国际海上避碰规则公约》 Convention on the International Regulations for Preventing Collisions at Sea, 1972	1978/5/10	1978/5/10
	《1971 年特种业务客船协定》 Special Trade Passenger Ships Agreement, 1971	1978/8/10	1978/11/10
	《1971 年特种业务客船协定 1973 年议定书》 Protocol on Space Requirements for Special Trade Passenger Ships, 1973	1978/11/10	1979/2/10
	《1974 年国际海上人命安全公约》 International Convention for the Safety of Life at Sea, 1974	1981/11/6	1982/2/6
	《1974 年国际海上人命安全公约 1988 年议定书》 Protocol of 1988 relating to the International Convention for the Safety of Life at Sea, 1974, as amended	2002/12/18	2003/3/18

续表

类别	条约名称	签署/批准/加入/接受日期（年/月/日）	对孟加拉国生效日期（年/月/日）
与海上安全相关的条约	《国际移动卫星组织公约》 Convention on the International Mobile Satellite Organization, 1976	1993/9/17	1993/9/17
	《1965年便利国际海上运输公约》 Convention on Facilitation of International Maritime Traffic, 1965	2000/9/21	2000/11/20
	《1979年国际海上搜寻救助公约》 International Convention on Maritime Search and Rescue, 1979	2011/8/8	2011/9/7
	《制止危及海上航行安全非法行为公约》 Convention for the Suppression of Unlawful Acts against the Safety of Maritime Navigation, 1988	2005/6/9	2005/9/7
	《制止危及大陆架固定平台安全非法行为议定书》 Protocol for the Suppression of Unlawful Acts against the Safety of Fixed Platforms Located on the Continental Shelf, 1988	2005/6/9	2005/9/7
与船员相关的条约	《1978年海员培训、发证和值班标准国际公约》 International Convention on Standards of Training, Certification and Watchkeeping for Seafarers, 1978	1981/11/6	1984/4/28
与海洋环境保护相关的条约	《控制船舶有害防污底系统国际公约》 International Convention on the Control of Harmful Anti-Fouling Systems On Ships, 2001	2018/7/7	2018/9/7
	《1969年国际干预公海油污事故公约》 International Convention Relating to Intervention on the High Seas in Cases of Oil Pollution Casualties, 1969	1981/11/6	1982/2/4
	《1990年国际油污防备、反应和合作公约》 International Convention on Oil Pollution Preparedness, Response and Co-operation, 1990	20014/7/23	2004/10/23
	《关于1973年国际防止船舶造成污染公约的1978年议定书》 Protocol of 1978 Relating to the International Convention for the Prevention of Pollution from Ships, 1973	2002/12/18	2003/3/18
	《1973年国际防止船舶造成污染公约1978年议定书附则三、附则四、附则五》 International Convention for the Prevention of Pollution from Ships, 1973 as modified by the Protocol of 1978 relating thereto, Annex III, IV, V	2002/12/18	2003/3/18

续表

类别	条约名称	签署/批准/加入/接受日期（年/月/日）	对孟加拉国生效日期（年/月/日）
与海洋环境保护相关的条约	《经1978年议定书修订的1973年国际防止船舶造成污染公约的1997年议定书》 Protocol of 1997 to amend the International Convention for the Prevention of Pollution from Ships, 1973, as modified by the Protocol of 1978 relating thereto	2002/12/18	2005/5/19

附录 7 斯里兰卡《1976 年第 22 号海洋区域法》[1]

Maritime Zones Law No. 22 of 1 September 1976

Section 1

1. This Law may be cited as the Maritime Zones Law, No. 22 of 1976.

Section 2

2. (1) The President of the Republic of Sri Lanka may, by Proclamation published in the Gazette, declare the limits of the sea beyond the land territory and internal waters of Sri Lanka which shall be the territorial sea of Sri Lanka, specifying in such Proclamation the baselines from which such limits shall be measured. The waters on the landward side of such baselines shall form part of the internal waters of Sri Lanka.

(2) Where an island or rock, or a group of islands and rocks, or a group of islands or a group of rocks, constituting part of the territory of Sri Lanka is situated seaward from the main coast or baseline, the territorial sea shall extend to the limits declared by the Proclamation under subsection (1) measured from the low-water mark of ordinary spring tides along the seaward edge of such island or rock, or group of islands and rocks, or group of islands or group of rocks.

(3) The sovereignty of the Republic extends to the territorial sea and to the airspace over the territorial sea as well as to its bed and subsoil.

Section 3

3. (1) Ships of all States shall enjoy the right of innocent passage through the territorial sea. Passage is innocent only so long as such passage is not prejudicial to the peace, good order or security of the Republic;

Provided that no foreign warship shall enter or pass through the territorial sea except with the prior consent of, and subject to such conditions as may be specified by, the Minister.

(2) No foreign aircraft shall enter or pass through the airspace above the territorial sea, except in accordance with the written laws in force in Sri Lanka;

Provided that no foreign military aircraft shall enter or pass through the airspace above the territorial sea except with the prior consent of, and subject to such conditions as may be

---

[1] See UN Office of Legal Affairs, "Maritime Zones Law No. 22 of 1 September 1976", https://www.un.org/Depts/los/LEGISLATIONANDTREATIES/PDFFILES/LKA_1976_Law.pdf, March 20, 2021.

specified by, the Minister.

(3) A foreign ship or foreign aircraft which acts in contravention of the provisions of this section is liable to confiscation.

(4) The Minister may, by Order published in the Gazette, suspend, in a specified area or areas of the territorial sea the right of innocent passage of any ship, if, in his opinion, such suspension is necessary in order to safeguard the peace, good order or security of the Republic.

Section 4

4. (1) The President may, by Proclamation published in the Gazette, declare the limits of a zone contiguous to the territorial sea and extending seaward from the outer limits of the territorial sea which shall be the contiguous zone of Sri Lanka.

(2) Where there is a reasonable apprehension of the contravention of any written laws of Sri Lanka in relation to:

(a) The security of the Republic;

(b) Immigration, health and sanitation;

(c) Customs and other revenue matters, the relevant Minister shall take such measures as may be necessary in respect of the contiguous zone in order to secure the enforcement of, or to prevent the contravention of, such laws.

Section 5

5. (1) The President may, by Proclamation published in the Gazette, declare any zone of the sea adjacent to the territorial sea, as well as the seabed and subsoil thereof, to be the exclusive economic zone of Sri Lanka. The limits of such zone shall be specified in the Proclamation.

(2) All the natural resources, both living and non-living, within the exclusive economic zone, on and under the seabed and in the subsoil and on the water surface and within the water column shall vest in the Republic.

(3) In the exclusive economic zone the Republic has—

(a) sovereign rights for the purpose of exploration, exploitation, conservation and management of the natural resources, both living and non-living, as well as for the production of energy from tides, winds and currents, and for other economic uses;

(b) exclusive rights and jurisdiction to authorize, regulate and control scientific research;

(c) exclusive rights and jurisdiction for the construction, maintenance or operation of artificial islands, off-shore terminals, installations and other structures and devices necessary for the exploration and exploitation of the resources of the zone, for the convenience of shipping or for any other purpose; and

(d) other rights recognized by international law.

Section 6

6. (1) The continental shelf of Sri Lanka shall comprise:

(a) the sea-bed and sub-soil of the submarine areas that extend beyond the territorial sea of Sri Lanka throughout the natural prolongation of the land territory of Sri Lanka to the outer edge of the continental margin or to a distance of two hundred nautical miles from the base-line from which the territorial sea is measured where the outer edge of the continental margin does not extend up to that distance; and

(b) the sea-bed and sub-soil of the analogous submarine areas adjacent to the coast of any island or rock, or group of islands and rocks, or group of islands or group of rocks, constituting part of the territory of Sri Lanka.

(2) All the natural resources, both living and non-living, on and under the sea-bed and in the sub-soil of the continental shelf shall vest in the Republic.

(3) In respect of the continental shelf the Republic has:

(a) sovereign rights for the purpose of exploration, exploitation, conservation and management of the natural resources, both living and non-living;

(b) exclusive rights and jurisdiction to authorize, regulate and control scientific research;

(c) exclusive rights and jurisdiction for the construction, maintenance or operation of artificial islands, off-shore terminals, installations and other structures and devices necessary for the exploration and exploitation of the resources of the continental shelf, for the convenience of shipping or for any other purpose; and

(d) other rights recognized by international law.

Section 7

7. (1) The President may, by Proclamation published in the Gazette, declare any zone of the sea adjacent to the territorial sea, and of the seabed and subsoil thereof, to be the pollution prevention zone of Sri Lanka. The limits of such zone shall be specified in the Proclamation.

(2) The relevant Minister shall take such steps as may be necessary to control and prevent the pollution of, and to preserve the ecological balance within, such zone.

Section 8

8. Notwithstanding the provisions of this Law or any other written law:

(a) the boundary between Sri Lanka and India in the waters from Palk Strait to Adam's Bridge shall be the arcs of Great Circles between the following positions in the sequence given hereunder defined by latitude and longitude:

Position 1: 10°05′North, 80° 03′East

Position 2: 09° 57′North, 79° 35′East

Position 3: 09° 40. 15′North, 79° 22. 60′East

Position 4: 09° 21. 80′North, 79° 30. 70′East

Position 5: 09° 13′North, 79° 32′East

Position 6: 09° 06′North, 79° 32′East;

(b) the boundary between Sri Lanka and India in the Gulf of Mannar shall be the arcs of the Great Circles between the following positions in the sequence given hereunder defined by latitude and longitude:

Position 1m: 09° 06. 0′North, 79° 32. 0′East

Position 2m: 09° 00. 0′North, 79° 31. 3′East

Position 3m: 08° 53. 8′North, 79° 29. 3′East

Position 4m: 08° 40. 0′North, 79° 18. 2′East

Position 5m: 08° 37. 2′North, 79° 13. 0′East

Position 6m: 08° 31. 2′North, 79° 04. 7′East

Position 7m: 08° 22. 2′North, 78° 55. 4′East

Position 8m: 08° 12. 2′North, 78° 53. 7′East

Position 9m: 07° 35. 3′North, 78° 45. 7′East

Position 10m: 07° 21. 0′North, 78° 38. 8′East

Position 11m: 06° 30. 8′North, 78° 12. 2′East

Position 12m: 05° 53. 9′North, 77° 50. 7′East

Position 13m: 05° 00. 0′North, 77° 10. 6′East;

(c) the boundary between Sri Lanka and India in the Bay of Bengal shall be the arcs of Great Circles between the following positions in the sequence given hereunder defined by latitude and longitude:

Position 1 b: 10° 05. 0′North, 80° 03. 0′East

Position 1 ba: 10° 05. 8′North, 80° 05. 0′East

Position 1 bb: 10° 08. 4′North, 80° 09. 5′East

Position 2 b: 10° 33. 0′North, 80° 46. 0′East

Position 3 b: 10° 41. 7′North, 81° 02. 5′East

Position 4 b: 11° 02. 7′North, 81° 56. 0′East

Position 5 b: 11° 16. 0′North, 82° 24. 4′East

Position 6 b: 11° 26. 6′North, 83° 22. 0′East.

Section 9

9. (1) The President may by Proclamation published in the Gazette declare the limits of the historic waters of Sri Lanka.

(2) The Republic of Sri Lanka shall exercise sovereignty, exclusive jurisdiction and

control in and over the historic waters, as well as in and over the islands and the continental shelf and the seabed and subsoil thereof within such historic waters.

Section 10

10. As soon as may be convenient after the coming into operation of this Law, and thereafter whenever necessary, the Minister may require the Surveyor-General to publish or cause to be published a map indicating the low-water mark of ordinary spring tides, the baselines for measurement of the territorial sea, and the outer limits of the territorial sea and other maritime zones and jurisdiction of Sri Lanka declared in accordance with the provisions of this Law.

Section 11

11. Notwithstanding anything to the contrary in any other written law, every reference in any written law to the expressions "territorial waters", "territorial sea", "coastal waters", "contiguous zone", "exclusive economic zone", "continental shelf" or "pollution prevention zone" shall be read and construed subject to and in accordance with the provisions of this Law.

Section 12

12. In order to give effect to the principles and provisions of this Law, all written laws in force in Sri Lanka shall be read and construed as though the applicability of such laws, wherever relevant, extends to the limits of the contiguous zone, the exclusive economic zone, the continental shelf, or the pollution prevention zone, as the case may be.

Section 13

13. (1) The Minister may make regulations for the purpose of giving effect to the provisions of this Law.

(2) Every regulation made by the Minister shall be published in the Gazette and shall come into operation on the date of such publication or upon such later date as may be specified in the regulation.

(3) Every regulation made by the Minister shall, as soon as convenient after its publication in the Gazette, be brought before the National State Assembly for approval. Every regulation which is not so approved shall be deemed to be rescinded as from the date of such disapproval, but without prejudice to anything previously done thereunder.

Section 14

14. In any proceedings before any court in Sri Lanka, if a question arises as to whether any act or omission has been done or omitted to be done within or without the territorial sea of Sri Lanka, or in any other zone or jurisdiction declared under this Law, a certificate of the Minister signed by him shall be prima facie proof of the place where such act or omission was done or omitted to be done.

Section 15

15. In this Law, unless the context otherwise requires:

"foreign aircraft" shall have the same meaning as in the Air Navigation Act;

"military aircraft" means an aircraft which, by reason of the equipment contained therein, could be used for any warlike purpose;

"ship" means any description of ship or vessel or boat, or any other description of vessel used in navigation on or below the waters and not exclusively propelled by oars, paddles or poles, and includes all equipment, apparel and appurtenances (excluding supplies for maintenance) which are necessary for the navigation and conduct of the business of the ship; and

"warship" means a ship which, by reason of the equipment contained therein, could be used for any warlike purpose.

附录 8　斯里兰卡《基于〈1976 年第 22 号海洋区域法〉的 1977 年总统公告》[1]

Presidential Proclamation of 15 January 1977 in pursuance of Maritime Zones Law No. 22 of 1 September 1976

WHEREAS the national State Assembly has enacted the Maritime Zones Law, No. 22 of 1976, which provides for the declaration of the territorial sea and other maritime zones of Sri Lanka and all other matters connected therewith or incidental thereto;

AND WHEREAS it has become necessary to declare in accordance with the provisions of the said Maritime Zones Law the extends respectively, of the territorial sea, the contiguous zone, the exclusive economic zone, the pollution prevention zone and the historic waters;

NOW THEREFORE, I, William Gopallawa, President of the Republic of Sri Lanka, do by this Proclamation declare, in pursuance of the powers vested in me by section 2, 4, 5, 7 and 9 respectively of the Maritime Zones Law, No. 22 of 1976:

(1) That the territorial sea of Sri Lanka shall, notwithstanding anything in any prior proclamation declaring the territorial sea of Sri Lanka, and except as provided in paragraph 7 (iii) hereof, extend to the sea to a distance of 12 nautical miles measured from the baselines described in paragraph (2);

(2) that the breadth of the territorial sea shall be measured from the low-water mark of ordinary spring tides along the coast of the mainland and along the seaward edge of islands:

Provided that for the purpose of determining the baselines for delimiting the territorial sea:

(i) a low-tide elevation which lies wholly or partly within the breadth of sea which would be territorial sea if all low-tide elevations were disregarded for the purpose of the measurement of the breadth thereof shall be treated as islands,

(ii) permanent installations further out to sea which form an integral part of a port system shall be considered as part of the coast of the mainland,

(iii) the method of straight baselines may be employed in drawing the baselines where there are deep bays and inlets in the coast or where there is a fringe of islands immediately

---

[1]　See UN Office of Legal Affairs, "Presidential Proclamation of 15 January 1977 in pursuance of Maritime Zones Law No. 22 of 1 September 1976", https://www. un. org/Depts/los/LEGISLATIONANDTREATIES/PDFFILES/LKA_ 1977_ Proclamation. pdf, March 20, 2021.

adjacent to the coast, provided that such baselines shall not depart appreciably from the general direction of the coast and the areas of the sea lying landward from these lines shall be sufficiently closely linked to the land domain to be subject to the régime of internal waters;

Provided further that the baseline from which the breadth of the territorial sea shall be measured in the sea north of Point Pedro shall be the arc of Great Circle between the following positions defined by latitude and longitude in the Palk Strait:

(i) 09° 49′8″ North, 80° 15′2″ East,

(ii) 10° 05′0″ North, 80° 03′0″ East;

(3) That the contiguous zone of Sri Lanka shall extend 24 nautical miles seaward from the baselines from which the territorial sea is measured;

(4) that the exclusive economic zone of Sri Lanka shall extend to the sea to a distance of 200 nautical miles from the baselines from which the territorial sea is measured;

(5) that the pollution prevention zone shall extend to the sea to a distance of 200 nautical miles from the baselines from which the territorial sea is measured;

(6) that notwithstanding anything in paragraphs (4) and (5), the exclusive economic zone and the pollution prevention zone of Sri Lanka in the Gulf of Manner and the Bay of Bengal shall extend to the sea up to the maritime boundary between Sri Lanka and India as defined in section 8 of the Maritime Zones Law No. 22 of 1976.

(7) that the historic waters of Sri Lanka shall comprise the areas of sea in the Palk Strait, Palk Bay and the Gulf of Mannar bounded by:

(a) the coast of the mainland of Sri Lanka;

(b) the maritime boundary between Sri Lanka and India as defined in Section 8 of the Maritime Zones Law, No. 22 of 1976;

(c) the arc of Great Circle between the following positions defined by latitude and longitude in the Gulf of Mannar:

(i) 08° 15′0″ North, 79° 44′0″East,

(ii) 08° 22′2″ North, 78° 55′4″East; and

(d) the arc of Great Circle between the following positions defined by latitude and longitude in the Palk Strait:

(i) 09° 49′8″ North, 80° 15′2″East,

(ii) 10° 05′0″ North, 80° 03′0″East;

(iii) the historic waters in the Palk Bay and Palk Strait shall form part of the internal waters of Sri Lanka;

(iii) the historic waters in the Gulf of Mannar shall form part of the territorial sea of Sri Lanka.

附录 9 斯里兰卡《2000 年制止危及海上航行安全非法行为法》[1]

Suppression of Unlawful Acts against The Safety of Maritime Navigation Act，No. 42 of 2000

An Act to Give Effect to the Convention for the Suppression of Unlawful Acts against the Safety of Maritime Navigation；and to Provide for Matters Connected therewith or Incidental thereto.

Preamble

WHEREAS the Convention for the Suppression of Unlawful Acts against the Safety of Maritime Navigation was adopted in Rome on the Tenth day of March One Thousand Nine Hundred and Eighty Eight：

AND WHEREAS Sri Lanka intends to accede to the aforesaid Convention：

AND WHEREAS it is necessary to make legal provision to give effect to Sri Lanka's obligations under the aforesaid Convention：

NOW THEREFORE，be it enacted by the Parliament of the Democratic Socialist Republic of Sri Lanka as follows；

[9th August，2000]

1. This Act may be cited as the Suppression of Unlawful Acts against the Safety of Maritime Navigation Act，No. 42 of 2000 and shall come into operation on such date as the Minister，by Order published in the Gazette，certifies as the date on which the Convention for the Suppression of Unlawful Acts against the Safety of Maritime Navigation adopted in Rome on March 10，1988，（hereinafter referred to as "the Convention"）enters into force in respect of Sri Lanka.

2. The Minster may，from time to time，by Order published in the Gazette，certify the Stales which are parties to the Convention. A State in respect of which an Order is made under this section is hereinafter referred to as "a Convention State".

3. （1）Any person who，unlawfully and intentionally—

（a）seizes，or exercises control over，a ship，by force or threat of force or by any

---

[1] Lawnet，"Suppression of Unlawful Acts against The Safety of Maritime Navigation"，https：//www. lawnet. gov. lk/suppression-of-unlawful-acts-against-the-safety-of-maritime-navigation-3/，March 20, 2021.

other form of intimidation ;

(b) commits an act of violence against a person on board a ship, which act is likely to endanger the safe navigation of such ship;

(c) destroys, or causes damage to, a ship or its cargo so as to endanger, or to be likely to endanger, the safe navigation of such ship;

(d) places or causes to be placed, in any manner whatsoever, a device or substance which is likely to destroy or cause damage to a ship or its cargo and so as to endanger, or to be likely to endanger, the safe navigation of such ship;

(e) destroys, or seriously damages, maritime navigational facilities or seriously interferes with their operation, so as to endanger, or to be likely to endanger, the safe navigation of a ship;

(f) communicates information which he knows to be false, thereby endangering the safe navigation of a ship; or

(g) injures or kills any person, in connection with the commission or the attempted commission of any of the offences set out in paragraphs (a) to (f) of this subsection, shall be guilty of an offence under this Act.

(2) Any person who—

(a) attempts to commit;

(b) aids or abets the commission of;

(c) threatens to commit,

an offence under subsection (1) shall be guilty of an offence under this Act.

In this subsection, "abet" has the same meaning as in sections 100 and 101 of the Penal Code.

(3) A person guilty of an offence under subsection (1) or subsection (2) of this section, shall on conviction after trial on indictment, by the High Court be punished with imprisonment for a term not exceeding twenty years.

(4) (a) Where the master of a ship, whether registered in Sri Lanka or not, has reasonable grounds to suspect that any person on board that ship has committed an offence under subsection (1) or subsection (2) he may deliver such person to an appropriate officer in Sri Lanka or in a Convention State.

(b) Where the master of a ship intends to deliver any person in Sri Lanka or any other Convention State in accordance with the provisions of paragraph (a), he shall give notice thereof to an appropriate officer in Sri Lanka or the Convention Slate, as the case may be" —

(i) of his intention to deliver that person to an appropriate officer in Sri Lanka or the Convention State, as the case may be ; and

(ⅱ) of his reasons for doing so.

(c) Any notice under paragraph (b) by a master of a ship shall be given, wherever practicable, before that ship has entered the territorial sea of Sri Lanka or that Convention State, as the case may be.

(d) Where the master of a ship delivers any person to an appropriate officer in Sri Lanka or a Convention State, as the case may be, he shall

(ⅰ) make to an appropriate officer in Sri Lanka or the Convention State, as the case may be, such oral or written statements relating to the alleged offence as that officer may reasonably require ; and

(ⅱ) deliver to that appropriate officer, such other evidence relating to the alleged offence as is in the master's possession.

(e) The master of a ship who fails, without reasonable cause, to comply with the provisions of paragraph (b) or paragraph (d) shall be guilty of an offence under this Act, and shall on conviction be punished with a fine not exceeding fifty thousand rupees.

(f) In this subsection—

"appropriate officer" means—

(ⅰ) in relation to Sri Lanka, a police officer or an officer of the Immigration and Emigration Department; and

(ⅱ) in relation to any other Convention State, an officer discharging functions corresponding to the functions discharged by the officers referred to in subparagraph (ⅰ);

"Master" in relation to a ship, has the same meaning as in the Merchant Shipping Act, No. 52 of 1971.

4. (1) The High Court of Sri Lanka holden in Colombo or the High Court established by Article 154P of the Constitution for the Western Province shall, notwithstanding anything in any other law, have exclusive jurisdiction to try offences under this Act.

(2) Where an act constituting an offence under this Act is committed outside Sri Lanka, the High Court referred to in subsection (1) shall have jurisdiction to try such offence as if it were committed within Sri Lanka if—

(a) the offence is committed against, or on board, a ship registered in Sri Lanka at the time the offence is committed;

(b) the person who committed the act is present in Sri Lanka;

(c) such act is committed by a citizen of Sri Lanka or by stateless person who has his habitual residence in Sri Lanka;

(d) during the commission of such act, a citizen of Sri Lanka is seized, threatened, injured or killed;

(e) such act is committed in order to compel the Government of Sri Lanka to do, or abstain from doing, any act.

5. Where a person who is not a citizen of Sri Lanka is arrested for an offence under this Act, such person shall be entitled—

(a) to communicate without delay, with the nearest appropriate representative of the State of which he is a national or which is otherwise entitled to protect his rights, or if he is a stateless person, with the nearest appropriate representative of the State in the territory of which he was habitually resident; and

(b) to be visited by a representative of that State.

6. The Extradition Law, No. 8 of 1977 is hereby amended by the addition, immediately before Part B of the Schedule to that Law, of the following item:

" (45) An offence covered by the Convention for the Suppression of Unlawful Acts against the Safety of Maritime Navigation, signed at Rome on March 10, 1988. "

7. Where there is an extradition arrangement made by the Government of Sri Lanka with any Convention State in force on the date on which this Act comes into operation, such arrangement shall be deemed, for the purposes of the Extradition Law. No. 8 of 1977, to include provision for extradition in respect of the offences specified in the Schedule to this Act.

8. Where there is no extradition arrangement made by the Government of Sri Lanka with any Convention State, the Minister may, by Order published in the Gazette, treat the Convention, for the purposes of the Extradition Law. No. 8 of 1977, as an extradition arrangement made, by the Government of Sri Lanka with that Convention State providing for extradition in respect of the offences specified in the Schedule to this Act.

9. The Government of Sri Lanka shall afford all such assistance to, and may through the Minister request all such assistance from, a convention State as may be necessary for the investigation and prosecution of an offence under section 3 or of an offence specified in the Schedule to this Act including, assistance relating to the taking of evidence and statements and the serving of process.

10. In the event of any inconsistency between the Sinhala and Tamil texts of this Act, the Sinhala text shall prevail.

11. In this Act "ship" means a vessel of any type whatsoever not permanently attached to the seabed and includes dynamically supported craft, submersible and other floating craft but does not include a warship, a ship owned or operated by a Slate or used as a naval auxiliary or for customs or police purposes or a vessel which has been withdrawn from navigation or is laid up.

附录 10　斯里兰卡《1981 年海岸保护法》（部分）[1]

Coast Conservation Act, No. 57 of 1981

An Actto Make Provision for A Survey of the Coastal Zone and the Preparation of A Coastal Zone Management Plan; to Regulate and Control Development Activities within the Coastal Zone; to Make Provision for the Formulation and Execution of Schemes of Work for Coast Conservation within the Coastal Zone; to Make Consequential Amendments to Certain Written Laws; and to Provide for Matters Connected therewith or Incidental Thereto.

Be it enacted by the Parliament of the Democratic Socialist Republic of Sri Lanka as follows:

[9th September , 1981]

1. This Act may be cited as the Coast Conservation Act, No. 57 of 1981, and shall come into operation on such date as the Minister may appoint by Order published in the Gazette (hereinafter referred to as the "appointed date") .

PART I　ADMINISTRATION

2. The administration, control, custody and management of the Coastal Zone are hereby vested in the Republic.

3. For the purposes of this Act

(a) there shall be appointed a Director of Coast conservation (hereinafter referred to as "the Director ") ;

(b) there may be appointed

(i) such number of Deputy Directors and Assistant Directors ; and

(ii) such other officers.

as may be necessary to assist the Director in the administration and implementation of the provisions of this Act.

4. The Director shall be responsible

(a) for the administration and implementation of the provisions of this Act;

(b) for the formulation and execution of schemes of work for coast conservation within

---

[1]　Lawnet, "Coast Conservation", https: //www. lawnet. gov. lk/coast-conservation-3/, March 20, 2021.

the Coastal Zone ; and

(c) for the conduct of research, in collaboration with other departments, agencies and institutions for the purpose of coast conservation.

5. The Government Agent of any administrative district within which any part of the Coastal Zone is situated may, upon an authorization in writing by the Director and subject to the general direction and control of the Director, exercise, perform and discharge within that administrative district, all or any of the powers, duties and functions conferred or imposed on, or assigned to, the Director by Part Ⅲ of this Act.

6. There shall be established a Coast Conservation Advisory Council (hereinafter referred to as "the Council") consisting of the following members :

(a) the person for the time being holding the office of the Secretary to the Ministry of the Minister in charge of the subject of Coast Conservation, who shall be the Chairman of the Council;

(b) a senior officer of the Ministry of the Minister in charge of the subject of Tourism nominated by such Minister;

(c) a senior officer of the Ministry of the Minister in charge of the subject of Shipping nominated by such Minister;

(d) a senior officer of the Ministry of the Minister in charge of the subject of Local Government nominated by such Minister;

(e) a senior officer of the Ministry of the Minister in charge of the subject of Home Affairs nominated by such Minister;

(f) a senior officer of the Ministry of the Minister in charge of the subject of Industries nominated by such Minister;

(g) the person for the time being holding the office of the Director, who shall act as Secretary to the Council;

(h) the Director of the body or other person responsible for aquatic resources, research and development;

(i) the person for the time being holding the office of the Land Commissioner or his representative;

(j) the person for the time being holding the office of the General Manager of the Urban Development Authority established by the Urban Development Authority Law, No. 41 of 1978, or his representative;

(k) the person for the time being holding the office of the Director of Irrigation or his representative;

(l) three other members appointed by the Minister, one of whom shall be a member of the academic staff of one of the Universities in Sri Lanka, one of whom shall be representative of the voluntary organizations concerned with the coastal environment and one of whom shall be representative of the fishing industry,

A member appointed under this paragraph is hereinafter referred to as an "appointed member".

7. The functions of the Council shall be to

(a) advise the Minister on all development activities proposed to be commenced in the Coastal Zone;

(b) review the Coastal Zone Management Plan prepared in accordance with the provisions of Part II of this Act and furnish recommendations, if any, thereon to the Director;

(c) review the environmental impact assessments furnished to the Director in connection with applications for permits under section 14, and make comments if any, thereon to the Director;

(d) inform the Director of the need for schemes of work within the Coastal Zone, whenever such need arises; and

(e) advise the Minister or the Director, as the case may be on any other matter relating to coast conservation that may be referred to the Council by the Minister or the Director, as the case may be.

8. (1) Every appointed member of the Council shall hold office for a period of three years, unless he earlier vacates office by death , resignation or removal.

(2) The Minister may, if he considers it expedient to do so, by Order published in the Gazette, remove from office any appointed member of the Council without assigning any reason therefor and such removal shall not be called in question in any court.

(3) An appointed member may at any time resign his office by letter to that effect addressed to the Minister.

(4) If an appointed member of the Council dies or resigns or is removed from office, the Minister may, having regard to the provisions of paragraph (1) of section 6, appoint any other person to be a member in place of the member who dies, resigns or is removed from office.

(5) A member who has been appointed under subsection (4) shall, unless he earlier vacates his office by death, resignation or removal, hold office for the unexpired period of the term of office of his predecessor.

(6) Where an appointed member of the Council is by reason of illness, infirmity or absence from Sri Lanka for a period of not less than three months, temporarily unable to perform the duties of his office, it shall be the duty of such member to so inform the Minister in writing. The Minister may, having regard to the provisions of para graph (1) of section 6, appoint another person to act in the place of such member.

(7) Any appointed member of the Council who vacates office other than by removal shall be eligible for reappointment.

9. No act or proceeding of the Council shall be invalid by reason only of the existence of any vacancy in the Council or any defect in the appointment of a member of the Council.

10. (1) A meeting of the Council shall be held at least once in every two months.

(2) The Chairman or in his absence, the Director or in the case of the absence of both, a member elected by the members present, shall preside at meetings of the Council.

(3) All questions for decision at any meeting of the Council shall be decided by the vote of a majority of the members present. In the case of an equality of votes, the member presiding shall have a casting vote.

(4) The quorum for any meeting of the Council shall be seven members and subject to the provisions of this section, the Council may regulate its own procedure.

PART II   COASTAL ZONE MANAGEMENT

11. (1) As soon as practicable after the appointed date, the Director shall cause a survey to be made of the Coastal Zone and shall prepare a report based on the results of such survey. The report shall include

(a) an inventory of ail structures, roads, excavations, harbours, outfalls, dumping sites and other works located in the Coastal Zone;

(b) an inventory of all coral reefs found within the Coastal Zone;

(c) an inventory of all commercially exploitable mineral deposits, both proven and suspected, located within the Coastal Zone;

(d) an inventory of all areas within the Coastal Zone or religious significance or of unique scenic value or of value for recreational purposes, including those areas most suitable for recreational bathing;

(e) an inventory of all estuarine or wetland areas within the Coastal Zone with an indication of their significance as fisheries or wildlife habitat;

(f) an inventory of all areas within the Coastal Zone of special value for research regarding coastal phenomena, including fisheries and shell fisheries, sea erosion, littoral movements and related subjects;

(g) an inventory of all areas within the Coastal Zone from which coral, sand, sea shells or other substances are regularly removed for commercial or industrial purposes;

(h) an assessment of the impact of sea erosion on the Coastal Zone including a quantified indication, by geographical location, of the amount of land lost thereby, an estimate of the economic cost of such loss and the extent to which human activity has contributed to such loss;

(i) an estimate of the quantities of sand, coral, sea shells and other substances being removed from the Coastal Zone, together with an estimate of the extent to which such quantities can be supplied from other sources or other materials and an analysis of the economic practicability of doing so; and

(j) a census, classified by geographical areas, and by activity, of all workers currently engaged on a regular basis in the removal of coral, sand, sea shells or other substances from the Coastal Zone and a census of the dependants of such workers and estimate of the per capita income obtained from these activities.

(2) In preparing the report under subsection (i), the Director shall have regard to relevant data and information collected or compiled by Government departments, institutions and other agencies, and it shall be the duty of the heads of such departments, institutions and agencies to furnish any such data or information as may be reasonably required by the Director for the purpose of preparing such report.

12. (1) The Director shall, not later than three years after the appointment date a comprehensive Coastal Zone Management Plan (hereinafter referred to as "the Plan"), based on the results of the survey made in pursuance of section 11. The Plan shall include

(a) the guidelines to be used in determining the suitability of particular development activities in the Coastal Zone;

(b) proposals which deal with the following subjects:

(i) land use;

(ii) transport facilities;

(iii) preservation and management of the scenic and other natural resources;

(iv) recreation and tourism;

(v) public works and facilities, including waste disposal facilities, harbours and power plants;

(vi) mineral extraction;

(vii) living resources;

(viii) human settlements;

(ix) agriculture; and

(x) industry,

within the Coastal Zone;

(c) proposals for the reservation of land or water in the Coastal Zone for certain uses, or for the prohibition of certain activities in certain areas of the Coastal Zone;

(d) a comprehensive programme for the utilization of manpower displaced as a direct result of more effective Coastal Zone regulation ; and

(e) recommendations for strengthening Governmental policies and powers and the conduct of research for the purposes of coast conservation.

(2) The Council shall, within sixty days of the Plan being submitted to it by the Director, make modifications, if any to the Plan and submit the Plan to the Minister for provisional approval.

(3) Upon the submission of the Plan to the Minister under subsection (1), he shall make it available for public inspection. Any person may, within sixty days of the date on which the Plan is made available for public inspection , submit any comments thereon to the Minister in writing.

(4) At the end of the period of sixty days referred to in subsection (3), the Minister may provisionally approve the Plan subject to such modifications, if any, as he may consider necessary having regard to any comments submitted to him under that subsection and shall submit the Plan to the Cabinet of Ministers for final approval. Upon the approval of the Plan by the Cabinet of Ministers, the Minister shall cause the Plan to be published in the Gazette. The Plan shall come into operation on the date of such publication or on such later date as may be specified therein.

(5) The Plan shall be revised during the period of four years commencing from the date of coming in to operator of the Plan and within a period of four years from the date of every revision of the Plan and the provisions of subsections (2), (3) and (4) shall, mutatis mutandis, apply in respect of every such revision.

(6) The Minister may, on the recommendation of the Council, make such regulations as may be necessary to give effect to any of the provisions of the Plan including regulations regulating the use of the foreshore by members of the public, or any development activity within the Coastal Zone.

(7) The Minister may make such regulations as may be necessary to give effect to any of the provisions of the Plan including regulations restricting and controlling the use of the foreshore by members of the public or prohibiting or controlling any development activity within the Costal Zone.

13. The Minister may, having regard to the long term stability, productivity and environmental quality of the Coastal Zone, prescribe the criteria to be used in determining whether a permit should be issued under section 14 upon an application made in the behalf to the Director after the appointed date and prior to the date of coming into operation of the Plan.

PART Ⅲ   PERMIT PROCEDURE

14. (1) Notwithstanding the provisions of any other law, no person shall engage in

any development activity other than a prescribed development activity within the Coastal Zone except under the authority of a permit issued in that behalf by the Director.

(2) The Minister may, having regard to the effect of those development activities on the long term stability, productivity and environmental quality of the Coastal Zone, prescribe the categories of development activity which may be engaged in within the Coastal Zone without a permit issued under subsection (1).

(3) An application for a permit to engage in any development activity within the Coastal Zone shall be made to the Director in the prescribed manner. Every such application shall be in the prescribed form, shall contain the prescribed particulars and be accompanied by the prescribed fee.

15. No permit shall be issued by the Director under this Part unless the proposed development activity

(a) is consistent with the Coastal Zone Management Plan and any regulations made to give effect to such Plan, or if the application is received prior to the date of coming into operation of such Plan, satisfies the criteria prescribed under section 13, and

(b) will not otherwise have any adverse effect on the stability, productivity and environmental quality of the Costal Zone.

16. (1) Upon receipt of an application for a permit to engage in a development activity within the Coastal Zone, the Director may require the applicant to furnish an environmental impact assessment relating to such development activity and it shall be the duty of the applicant to comply with such requirement. Every environmental impact assessment furnished under this section shall contain such particulars as may be prescribed.

(2) The Director shall, on receipt of an environmental impact assessment furnished to him by an applicant in compliance with any requirement imposed on such applicant under subsection (1)

(a) submit a copy of such assessment to the Council for its comments, if any ; and

(b) by notice published in the Gazette, notify the place and times at which such assessment will be available for inspection by the public, and invite the public to make its comments, if any, thereon.

(3) (a) The Council shall, within sixty days of an environmental impact assessment being submitted to it under subsection (1), make its comments, if any, thereon to the Director.

(b) Any member of the public may within thirty days of the date on which a notice under paragraph (b) of subsection (2) relating to such assessment is published in the Gazette make his comments, if any, thereon to the Director.

(4) In deciding whether to issue a permit under section 14 authorizing a person to en-

gage in a development activity within the Coastal Zone, the Director shall have regard to any comments made under subsection (3) on the environmental impact assessment, if any, relating to such activity and any development projects commenced by the Urban Development Authority in any area declared to be an urban development area under the provisions of the Urban Development Authority Law, No. 41 of 1878.

(5) The Director shall, within sixty days of the receipt by him of any comments made under subsection (3) make the decision referred to in subsection (4).

17. The Director may attach to any permit issued under this Part, such conditions as he may consider necessary for the proper management of the Coastal Zone, having regard to the Coastal Zone Management Plan, or to any scheme of work for coast conservation.

18. (1) A permit issued under section 14 shall remain in force for such period as the Director may specify there in.

(2) The holder of a permit may, not less than one month prior to the date of expiration of such permit, apply for a renewal of such permit. An application for renewal of a permit shall be in the prescribed form and shall be accompanied by the prescribed fee.

(3) Where the holder of a permit desires to transfer the permit to another person, such holder may apply to the Director for permission to effect such transfer, and the Director may by order permit such transfer subject to the payment of the prescribed fee.

19. The Director may make an order varying the conditions attached to any permit issued under section 14 or revoking such permit if he is satisfied that

(a) the permit-holder has contravened any of the conditions attached to such permit; or

(b) such variation or revocation is necessary as expedient for the proper management of the Coastal Zone.

An order of the Director varying the conditions attached to a permit issued under section 14 or revoking such permit shall state the grounds therefor, and the Director shall cause a copy of such order to be served on the permit-holder.

20. (1) Where any condition attached to a permit issued under section 14 requires the execution by the permit-holder, of a scheme of work and where the permit-holder fails to execute such scheme, the Director may, by notice in writing, require the permit-holder to execute within such period as may be specified in such notice, such scheme.

(2) Where a person on whom a notice is issued under subsection (1) fails to execute the scheme of work referred to in such notice within the period specified therein, the Director may, after offering that person an opportunity to show cause, execute such scheme and shall be entitled to recover the costs thereof from such person.

21. Any person aggrieved by an order of the Director refusing to issue a permit under

section 14, or an order under subsection (3) of section 18 refusing to permit the transfer of any such permit or an order tinder section 19 varying the conditions attached to any such permit or revoking any such permit or requirement imposed by the Director under subsection (1) of section 20 may, within thirty days of the date of the notice imposing such requirement or such order, at the case may be, appeal therefrom to the Secretary to the Ministry of the Minister in charge of the subject of Coast Conservation. The decision of the Secretary on any such appeal shall be final.

22. Nothing in this Part of this Act shall be read and construed as requiring a person to obtain a permit under the main section 14 for the maintenance or dredging of existing navigation channels if the dredged spoils are deposited in disposal areas approved by the Director.

PART Ⅳ　GENERAL

23. (1) Notwithstanding anything in section 14, where any person who was engaged, on the day immediately preceding the appointed date, in any development activity within the Coastal Zone, being an activity which was lawful according to the law in force on that date makes, within twenty days of the appointed date, an application for a permit under section 14 in respect of that activity, it shall be lawful for such person to engage in that activity until the determination of that application.

(2) Where an application made by a person referred to in subsection (1) for a permit under section 14 is refused by the Director and such person is compelled, in consequence of such refusal, to abandon any equipment or fixtures used for, or in connection with, the development activity in respect of which that application was made, such person shall be entitled to reasonable compensation for the equipment or fixtures so abandoned.

24. (1) The Director or any officer authorized by him in writing, may issue permits subject to such conditions as he the fore may impose having regard to the Plan, for the occupation, for any period not exceeding three years, of any part of the foreshore or bed of the sea lying within the Coastal Zone.

(2) The Director may, after such inquiry as he may deem necessary, cancel any permit if he is satisfied that the permit-holder has contravened any of the conditions attached to such permit,

(3) Any person aggrieved by an order of the Director or of any officer authorized in writing by the Director refusing to issue a permit under subsection (1) or cancelling a permit under subsection (2) may appeal therefrom to the Secretary to the Ministry of the Minister in charge of the subject of Coast Conservation. The decision of the Secretary on any

such appeal shall be final.

25. (1) Where the Director finds that the quality of the water in the Coastal Zone or the stability of the Coastal Zone is being adversely affected by the intrusion of any waste or foreign matter or by physical activity, he shall

(a) if the source of such waste or foreign matter is within the Coastal Zone or if such activity lies within the Coastal Zone, require, by a notice in writing, the person responsible therefor to take such corrective measures as are specified in such notice or to desist from such activity ; and

(b) if the source of such waste or foreign matter, or if such activity, is not within the Coastal Zone, request the appropriate local authority or agency to take such measures as may be necessary to prevent such intrusion or activity.

(2) A local authority or agency to which a request is made by the Director under paragraph (b) of subsection (1) shall take all steps within its power to comply with such request. If a local authority is unable to comply with any such request, it may notify the Director accordingly and upon such notification the Director shall take such measures as may be necessary to prevent such intrusion or activity.

26. It shall be lawful for the Director or any officer generally or specially authorized by him in writing, at any reasonable time to enter upon any land within the Coastal Zone and then do such acts as may be reasonably necessary for the purpose of executing any scheme of work or of ascertaining whether the conditions attached to any permit issued under this Act are being or have been complied with or of making any survey, examination or investigation, preliminary or incidental to the exercise of any power or the discharge of any function under this Act, or any regulations made thereunder.

27. The Director may, by a notice in writing, require any person engaged in any development activity within the Coastal Zone under the authority of a permit issued under this Act, to furnish him with such returns and information as may be prescribed and it shall be the duty of such person to comply with the requirements of such notice.

28. (1) Any person who acts in contravention of the provisions of section 14 shall be guilty of an offence under this Act and shall on conviction, after summary trial before a Magistrate, be liable in the case of a first offence, to a fine not less than five hundred rupees and not exceeding twenty-five thousand rupees or to imprisonment of either description to a term not exceeding one year or to both such fine and imprisonment, and in the case of a second or subsequent offence, a fine of not less than one thousand rupees and not exceeding fifty thousand rupees or to imprisonment of either description for a term not exceeding two years or to both such fine and imprisonment,

(2) Upon the conviction of any person of an offence under subsection (1), the Mag-

istrate may make order declaring that any vessel, craft, boat, vehicle, equipment or machinery used in, or in connection with, the commission of that offence together with any article or substance found on board such vessel, craft, boat or vehicle shall be forfeited. Upon such order, the property referred to in the order shall vest absolutely in the State. Such vesting shall take effect

(a) after the expiration of the period within which an appeal may be preferred to the Court of Appeal against the order of forfeiture; or

(b) where an appeal has been prefered to the Court of Appeal against the order of forfeiture, upon the determination of the appeal confirming or upholding the order of forfeiture:

Provided, however, that the Court may make order releasing any vessel, craft, boat, vehicle, equipment, machinery, article or substance if it is proved that such vessel, craft, boat, vehicle, equipment, machinery, article or substance belongs to a person other than the person convicted of the offence and that other person satisfies the court that he had no knowledge that it would be used in, or in connection with, the commission of the offence.

29. (1) Any person who

(a) fails to comply with the requirements of a notice sent by the Director under paragraph (a) of subsection (1) of section 25;

(b) resists or obstructs, the Director or any officer in the exercise of any power conferred on the Director or such officer;

(c) fails to comply with the requirements of a notice issued under section 27;

(d) makes any statement, which to his knowledge is, false or incorrect, in any return or information furnished by him in compliance with a notice issued by the Director under section 27, shall be guilty of an offence under this Act and shall on conviction, after summary trial before a Magistrate, be liable to a fine of not less, than one thousand five hundred rupees and not exceeding twenty-five thousand rupees or to imprisonment of either description for a term not exceeding six months or to both such fine and imprisonment.

30. (1) Every person who is guilty of an offence under this Act shall, in addition to the fines prescribed under Ejections 28 and 29, be liable to a fine not exceeding five hundred rupees for each day on which the offence is continued after conviction.

(2) This Act shall be deemed to be an enactment enumerated in the Schedule to the Informers Reward Ordinance.

31. (1) No person shall, with effect from the appointed date, erect or construct any unauthorized structure, house, hut, shed or other building on any part of the Coastal Zone.

(2) The Director may, by giving notice to the owner or occupier, as the case may be, by affixing a notice to some conspicuous part of such structure, house, hut, shed or other building, direct such owner or occupier to take down and remove such unauthorized structure, house, hut, shed or other building within such time as the Director may specify in the notice.

(3) Any person aggrieved by any direction of the Director made under subsection (2) may, within three days from the affixing of the notice, appeal therefrom to the Secretary of the Ministry of the Minister in charge of the subject of Coast Conservation. The decision of the Secretary on any such appeal shall be final.

(4) Where any such structure, house, hut, shed or other building is not taken down and removed within the time specified in the notice or within such time as may be specified by the Secretary when rejecting the appeal, the Director shall cause the structure, house, hut, shed or other building to be taken down and removed, and the expenses incurred by the Director in doing so, shall be recovered from the owner or the occupier as a debt due to the State.

32. (1) The Minister may make regulations in respect of any matter for which regulations are authorized to be made, or required to be prescribed, under this Act.

(2) Every regulation made by the Minister shall be published in the Gazette and shall come into operation on the date of such publication or on such later date as may be specified in the regulation.

(3) Every regulation made by the Minister shall, as soon as convenient after its publication in the Gazette, be brought before Parliament for approval. Any regulation which is not so approved shall be deemed to be rescinded as from the date of disapproval, but without prejudice to anything previously done thereunder. Notification of the date on which any regulation is so deemed to be rescinded shall be published in the Gazette.

33. (1) Every permit issued by a Government Agent or prescribed officer under section 62 of the Crown Lands Ordinance shall be deemed to be a permit issued under subsection (1) of section 24 of this Act.

(2) Every regulation made under section 59 of the Crown Lands Ordinance shall be deemed to be a regulation made under section 32 of this Act.

(3) Every licence granted under section 63 of the Crown Lands Ordinance shall be deemed to be a permit issued under section 14 of this Act.

34. Nothing in this Act shall be read and construed as derogating from the powers or rights of the Republic, in or over, the Coastal Zone or soil of the Coastal Zone or the area of sea declared, under the Maritime Zones Law, No. 22 of 1976, to be the territorial sea of Sri Lanka.

35. No suit, prosecution or other legal proceeding shall be instituted against the Director, a Deputy Director, any Assistant Director or any other officer for any act which in good faith is done or purported to be done by such Director, Deputy Director, Assistant Director or other officer under this Act or any regulations made thereunder.

PART V
AMENDMENT AND MODIFICATION OF CERTAIN WRITTEN LAWS

...

附录 11 《1974 年斯里兰卡与印度两国间关于历史性水域边界及相关事项的协定》[1]

Agreement between Sri Lanka and India on the Boundary in
Historic Waters between the two Countries and Related Matters
26 and 28 June 1974

The Government of the Republic of Sri Lanka and the Government of the Republic of India,

Desiring to determine the boundary line in the historic waters between Sri Lankaand India and to settle the related matters in a manner which is fair and equitable to both sides,

Having examined the entire question from all angles and taken into account the historical and other evidence and legal aspects thereof,

Have agreed as follows:

Article 1

The boundary between Sri Lanka and India in the waters from Palk Strait to Adam's Bridge shall be arcs of Great Circles between the following positions, in the sequence given below, defined by latitude and longitude:

Position 1: 10° 05′North, 80° 03′East

Position 2: 09° 57′North, 79° 35′East

Position 3: 09° 40. 15′North, 79° 22. 60′East

Position 4: 09° 21. 80′North, 79° 30. 70′East

Position 5: 09° 13′North, 79° 32′East

Position 6: 09° 06′North, 79° 32′East

Article 2

The co-ordinates of the positions specified in Article 1 are geographical co-ordinates and the straight lines connecting them are indicated in the chart annexed hereto which has been signed by the surveyors authorized by the two Governments, respectively.

Article 3

The actual location of the aforementioned positions at sea and on the sea-bed shall be

---

[1] See UN Office of Legal Affairs, "Agreement between Sri Lanka and India on the Boundary in Historic Waters between the two Countries and Related Matters 26 and 28 June 1974", https://www. un. org/Depts/los/LEGISLATIONANDTREATIES/PDFFILES/TREATIES/LKA-IND1974BW. PDF, March 20, 2021.

determined by a method to be mutually agreed upon by the surveyors authorized for the purpose by the two Governments, respectively.

Article 4

Each country shall have sovereignty and exclusive jurisdiction and control over the waters, the islands, the continental shelf and the subsoil thereof, falling on its own side of the aforesaid boundary.

Article 5

Subject to the foregoing, Indian fishermen and pilgrims will enjoy access to visit Kachchativu as hitherto, and will not be required by Sri Lanka to obtain travel documents or visas for these purposes.

Article 6

The vessels of Sri Lanka and India will enjoy in each other's waters such rights as they have traditionally enjoyed therein.

Article 7

If any single geological petroleum or natural gas structure or field, or any single geological structure or field of any other mineral deposit, including sand or gravel, extends across the boundary referred to in Article 1 and the part of such structure or field which is situated on one side of the boundary is exploited, in whole or in part, from the other side of the boundary, the two countries shall seek to reach agreement as to the manner in which the structure or field shall be most effectively exploited and the manner in which the proceeds deriving therefrom shall be apportioned.

Article 8

This Agreement shall be subject to ratification. It shall enter into force on the date of exchange of the instruments of ratification which will take place as soon as possible.

Colombo, 26 June, 1974.
New Delhi, 28 June, 1974.

附录 12 《1976 年斯里兰卡与印度两国间在马纳尔湾和孟加拉湾的海上边界及相关事项的协定》[1]

Agreement between Sri Lanka and India on the Maritime Boundary between the two Countries in the Gulf of Mannar and the Bay of Bengal and Related Matters

23 March 1976

The Government of the Republic of Sri Lanka and the Government of the Republic of India,

Recalling that the boundary in the Palk Strait has been settled by the Agreement between the Republic of Sri Lanka and the Republic of India on the Boundary in Historic Waters between the Two Countries and Related Matters, signed on 26/28 June, 1974,

And desiring to extend that boundary by determining the maritime boundary between the two countries in the Gulf of Mannar and the Bay of Bengal,

Have agreed as follows:

Article 1

The maritime bondary between Sri Lanka and India in the Gulf of Mannar shall be arcs of great circles between the following positions, in the sequence given below, defined by latitude and longitude:

Position 1 m: 09° 06'.0 N　79° 32'.0 E

Position 2 m: 09° 00'.0 N　79° 31'.3 E

Position 3 m: 08° 53'.8 N　79° 29'.3 E

Position 4 m: 08° 40'.0 N　79° 18'.2 N

Position 5 m: 08° 37'.2 N　79° 13'.0 E

Position 6 m: 08° 31'.2 N　79° 04'.7 E

Position 7 m: 08° 22'.2 N　78° 55'.4 E

Position 8 m: 08° 12'.2 N　78° 53'.7 E

Position 9 m: 07° 35'.3 N　78° 45'.7 E

Position 10 m: 07° 21'.0 N　78° 38'.8 E

Position 11 m: 06° 30'.8 N　78° 12'.2 E

---

[1] See UN Office of Legal Affairs, "Agreement between Sri Lanka and India on the Maritime Boundary between the two Countries in the Gulf of Mannar and the Bay of Bengal and Related Matters 23 March 1976", https://www.un.org/Depts/los/LEGISLATIONANDTREATIES/PDFFILES/TREATIES/LKA-IND1976MB.PDF, March 20, 2021.

Position 12 m: 05° 53'. 9 N   77° 50'. 7 E

Position 13 m: 05° 00'. 0 N   77° 10'. 6 E

The extension of the boundary beyond position 13 m will be done subsequently.

Article 2

The maritime bondary between Sri Lanka and India in the Bay of Bengal shall be arcs of great circles between the following positions, in the sequence given below, defined by latitude and longitude:

Position 1 b: 10° 05'. 0 N   80° 03'. 0 E

Position 1 ba: 10° 05'. 8 N   80° 05'. 0 E

Position 1 bb: 10° 08'. 4 N   80° 09'. 5 E

Position 2 b: 10° 33'0 N   80° 46'. 0 E

Position 3 b: 10° 41'. 7 N   81° 02'. 5 E

Position 4 b: 11° 02'. 7 N   81° 56'. 0 E

Position 5 b: 11° 16'. 0 N   82° 24'. 4 E

Position 6 b: 11° 26'. 6 N   83° 22'. 0 E

Article 3

The coordinates of the positions specified in Articles I and II are geographical coordinates and the straight lines connecting them are indicated in the chart annexed hereto, which has been signed by the surveyors duly authorised by the two Governments respectively.

Article 4

The actual location at sea and on the sea-bed of the positions specified in Articles I and II shall be determined by a method to be mutually agreed upon by the surveyors authorised for the purpose by the two Governments, respectively.

Article 5

(1) Each Party shall have sovereignty over the historic waters and territorial sea, as well as over the islands, falling on its side of the aforesaid boundary.

(2) Each Party shall have sovereign rights and exclusive jurisdiction over the continental shelf and the exclusive economic zone as well as over their resources, whether living or non-living, falling on its side of the aforesaid boundary.

(3) Each Party shall respect rights of navigation through its territorial sea and exclusive economic zone in accordance with its laws and regulations and the rules of international law.

Article 6

If any single geological petroleum or natural gas structure or field, or any single geological structure or field of any mineral deposit, including sand or gravel, extends across the boundary referred to in Articles I and II and the part of such structure or field which is situated on one side of the boundary is exploited, in whole or in part, from the other side of the boundary, the two countries shall seek to reach agreement as to the manner in which the structure or field shall be most effectively exploited and the manner in which the proceeds deriving therefrom shall be apportioned.

Article 7

The Agreement shall be subject to ratification. It shall enter into force on the date of exchange of instruments of ratification, which shall take place as soon as possible.

New Delhi, 23 March 1976.

附录 13 《1976 年斯里兰卡、印度和马尔代夫间关于确定在马纳尔湾的三国交界点的协定》[1]

Agreement between Sri Lanka, India and Maldives concerning the Determination of the Trijunction Point between the three Countries in the Gulf of Mannar 23, 24 and 31 July 1976

The Government of the Republic of Sri Lanka, the Government of the Republic of India and the Government of the Republic of Maldives,

Recalling the Agreement between Sri Lanka and India on the Maritime Boundary between the two countries in the Gulf of Mannar, etc. , signed in March 1976,

Noting the negotiations which are being conducted between India and Maldives concerning the maritime boundary between their two countries in the Arabian Sea,

And desiring to determine the location of the trijunction point between Sri Lanka, India and Maldives in the sea beyond the Gulf of Mannar,

Have agreed as follows:

Article 1

The trijunction point between Sri Lanka, India and Maldives in the sea beyond the Gulf of Mannar, which is equidistant from the nearest points on the coasts of Sri Lanka, India and Maldives respectively, shall be the point, which has been agreed to be called point T, defined by latitude and longitude as follows:

Point T: 04° 47. 04" N (latitude) 77° 01. 40" E (longitude)

Article 2

The trijunction point (point T), whose geographical coordinates have been mentioned in Article I, has been indicated in the chart annexed hereto, which has been signed by the persons duly authorised for the purpose by the three Governments, respectively.

Article 3

The actual location at sea and on the sea-bed of the trijunction point shall be determined by a method to be mutually agreed upon by the persons authorised for the purpose by the three Governments, respectively.

---

[1] See UN Office of Legal Affairs, "Agreement between Sri Lanka, India and Maldives concerning the Determination of the Trijunction Point between the three Countries in the Gulf of Mannar 23, 24 and 31 July 1976", https://www. un. org/Depts/los/LEGISLATIONANDTREATIES/PDFFILES/TREATIES/LKA-IND-MDV1976TP. PDF, March 20, 2021.

Article 4

This Agreement shall come into force upon signature. If the Agreement is signed on different dates, it shall enter into force on the date of last signature.

Colombo: 23 July, 1976

Colombo: 24 July, 1976

Male: 31 July, 1976

附录 14　斯里兰卡缔结和加入的国际海洋法条约

（一）联合国海洋法公约及其相关条约

序号	公约名称	签署日期（年/月/日）	批准日期（年/月/日）
1	《联合国海洋法公约》 United Nations Convention on The Law of the Sea	1982/12/10	1994/7/19
2	《关于执行 1982 年 12 月 10 日〈联合国海洋法公约〉第十一部分的协定》 Agreement Relating to the Implementation of Part XI of the United Nations Conventions on the Law of the Sea, 10 December 1982	1994/7/29	1995/7/28
3	《执行 1982 年 12 月 10 日〈联合国海洋法公约〉有关养护和管理跨界鱼类种群和高度洄游鱼类种群的规定的协定》 Agreement for the Implementation of the Provisions of the United Nations Convention on the Law of the Sea of 10 December 1982 relating to the Conservation and Management of Straddling Fish Stocks and Highly Migratory Fish Stocks	1996/10/9	1996/10/24
4	《关于国际海洋法法庭特权和豁免的协定》 Agreement on the Privileges and Immunities of the International Tribunal for the Law of the Sea	1999/6/30	未批准
5	《关于强制解决争端之任择签字议定书》 Optional Protocol of Signature concerning the Compulsory Settlement of Disputes	无	1958/10/30

（二）缔结与加入的其他海洋海事条约及其他条约

类别	条约名称	签署/批准/加入/接受日期（年/月/日）	对斯里兰卡生效日期（年/月/日）
与海上航行安全相关的条约	《1972 年国际海上避碰规则公约》 Convention on the International Regulations for Preventing Collisions at Sea, 1972	1978/1/4	1978/1/4
	《1974 年国际海上人命安全公约》 International Convention for the Safety of Life at Sea, 1974	1983/8/30	1983/11/30

类别	条约名称	签署/批准/加入/接受日期（年/月/日）	对斯里兰卡生效日期（年/月/日）
与海上航行安全相关的条约	《制止危及海上航行安全非法行为公约》 Convention for the Suppression of Unlawful Acts against the Safety of Maritime Navigation, 1988	2000/9/4	2000/11/3
	《国际移动卫星组织公约》 Convention on the International Mobile Satellite Organization, 1976	1981/12/15	1981/12/15
	《国际移动卫星组织业务协定》 Operating Agreement on the International Mobile Satellite Organization, 1976	1976/9/3	1986/6/10（1985 年修正案） 2000/2/4（1998 年修正案）
	《国际防止海上油污公约》 International Convention for the Prevention of Pollution of the Sea by Oil	1983/8/30	1983/11/30（1997/9/24 退出）
	《1969 年国际油污损害民事责任公约》 International Convention on Civil Liability for Oil Pollution Damage, 1969	1983/4/12	1983/7/11（2000/1/22 退出）
	《1971 年设立国际油污损害赔偿基金国际公约》 International Convention on the Establishment of an International Fund for Compensation for Oil Pollution Damage, 1971	1983/4/12	1983/7/11（2000/1/22 退出）
	《关于 1973 年国际防止船舶造成污染公约的 1978 年议定书》 Protocol of 1978 Relating to the International Convention for the Prevention of Pollution from Ships, 1973	1997/6/24	1997/9/24
	《1973 年国际防止船舶造成污染公约 1978 年议定书附则三、附则四、附则五》 International Convention for the Prevention of Pollution from Ships, 1973 as modified by the Protocol of 1978 relating thereto, Annex Ⅲ, Ⅳ, Ⅴ	1997/6/24	1997/9/24（附件Ⅲ、附件Ⅴ） 2003/9/27（附件Ⅳ）
	《1969 年国际干预公海油污事故公约》 International Convention relating to Intervention on the High Seas in Cases of Oil Pollution Casualties, 1969	1983/4/12	1983/7/11
	《修正〈1969 年国际油污损害民事责任公约〉的 1992 年议定书》 Protocol of 1992 to amend the International Convention on Civil Liability for Oil Pollution Damage, 1969	1999/1/22	2000/1/22
	《修正〈1971 年设立国际油污损害赔偿基金国际公约〉的 1992 年议定书》 Protocol of 1992 to Amend the International Convention on the Establishment of an International Fund for Compensation for Oil Pollution Damage, 1971	1999/1/22	2000/1/22

类别	条约名称	签署/批准/加入/接受日期（年/月/日）	对斯里兰卡生效日期（年/月/日）
与船舶管理相关的条约	《1966年国际船舶载重线公约》 International Convention on Load Lines, 1966	1974/5/10	1974/8/10
	《联合国班轮公会行动守则公约》 Convention on a Code of Conduct for Liner Conference	1975/6/30	1983/10/6
	《1971年特种业务客船协定》 Special Trade Passenger Ships Agreement, 1971	1981/11/10	1982/3/10
	《1973年特种业务客船舱室要求议定书》 Protocol on Space Requirements for Special Trade Passenger Ships, 1973	1982/3/10	1982/6/10
	《1969年国际船舶吨位丈量公约》 International Convention on Tonnage Measurement of Ships, 1969	1992/3/11	1992/6/11
	《1965年便利国际海上运输公约》 Convention on Facilitation of International Maritime Traffic, 1965	1998/3/6	1998/5/5
	《1978年海员培训、发证和值班标准国际公约》 International Convention on Standards of Training, Certification and Watchkeeping for Seafarers, 1978	1987/1/22	1987/4/22
与渔业管理相关的条约	《关于设立印度洋—太平洋渔业理事会的协定》 Agreement for the Establishment of the Indo-Pacific Fisheries Council	1949/2/21	1949/2/21
	《建立印度洋金枪鱼委员会协定》 The Agreement for the Establishment of the Indian Ocean Tuna Commission	1994/6/13	1996/3/27
	《亚洲—太平洋水产养殖中心网协议》 Agreement for the Establishment of the Network of Aquaculture Centres in Asia and the Pacific	1989/1/15	1990/1/11
	《养护和管理印度洋和东南亚海龟及其栖息地的谅解备忘录》 Memorandum of Understanding concerning Conservation and Management of Marine Turtles and their Habitats of the Indian Ocean and South East Asia	2001/6/23	2001/9/1
	《关于港口国预防、制止和消除非法、不报告、不管制捕鱼的措施协定》 Agreement on Port State Measures to Prevent, Deter and Eliminate Illegal, Unreported and Unregulated Fishing	2011/1/20	2016/2/5